INDOMITABLE

The Life of BARBARA GRIER

by

Joanne Passet

BELLA
BOOKS

2016

Bella Books, Inc.
P.O. Box 10543
Tallahassee, FL 32302

First Edition 2016

Cover Designer: Judith Fellows
Cover Photo: Barbara Grier, NWSA Conference, 1978.
              Photo by Joan E. Biren

ISBN: 978-1-59493-471-1

TABLE OF CONTENTS

INDOMITABLE

The Life of BARBARA GRIER

by

Joanne Passet

BELLA
BOOKS

2016

PROLOGUE

❧

Because of her promotion of the written word, Barbara Grier was one of the most important lesbians of the twentieth century. Those who worked closely with her viewed Barbara as an indomitable force: driven and focused. Yet she was not the woman some people in the LGBT movement wanted or expected her to be. Born in 1933, Barbara grew up in a world where lesbians and gays were virtually invisible, either discussed in coded language or dismissed as deviant and destructive. As a young lesbian, she discovered books held the power to alleviate her isolation and feed her dreams. As a result, lesbian literature became the axis around which her world revolved—its detection, acquisition, writing, editing, publishing and, most important of all, its promotion. Confident books held the key to changing "the ways in which young women grow up and see themselves," she set out with single-minded determination to ensure lesbians like her teenaged self could find positive portrayals of themselves in print. In the process, she helped preserve lesbian literary and intellectual heritage.[1]

A mistress of communication, whether by pen, typewriter, telephone or computer, Barbara led a life marked by three distinct phases, each of which remained grounded in her core mission: books. During the first phase of her coming out and active involvement with the homophile movement of the 1950s, Barbara's participation can be described as a *virtual* life. She possessed an instinctive ability to create a sense of intimacy on paper, one that invited highly personal confidences from hundreds of correspondents, many of them deeply closeted. Next, with life partner Donna J. McBride as her catalyst, Barbara embarked on the lesbian-feminist *movement* phase of her career in the 1970s. Though she shared movement goals of acceptance and equality, she found it difficult to comprehend fully feminist politics and its approach to life. By the mid-1980s, Barbara found herself "in the awkward position of belonging to a movement whose goals may match ours but whose methods and restrictions do not at all..."[2] Transforming herself yet again, she, along with Donna, fully embraced the *entrepreneurial* phase of her life. Through Naiad Press, Barbara played a major role in "the expansion of the small press...and for making it clear that bookstores can carry gay and lesbian fiction successfully," according to publisher Sasha Alyson (of Alyson Publications). When critics charged Naiad's success had shaped public perceptions of lesbian literature and "scaled down the reach," Barbara remained unfazed: "Yeah, I publish for the sixteen-year-old reader." Familiar with controversy, she won more battles than she lost and kept moving forward, fueled by her immeasurable sense of mission.[3]

A lesbian Facebook in a pre-Facebook era, Barbara was a compulsive correspondent who interacted with many leading gays and lesbians during the second half of the twentieth century; therefore, her story offers a unique window into the history of that critical era, shedding light on its personalities, organizations, and issues. With a prescient sense of its historical value, she systematically archived her personal and business correspondence, and comprehensively collected books, magazines and newspapers documenting gay and lesbian stories. Correspondents included well-known activists, publishers and writers, among them Nancy Bereano, Marion Zimmer Bradley, Rita Mae Brown, Barbara Gittings, Karla Jay, Franklin "Frank" Kameny, Del Martin, Jane Rule and May Sarton. Barbara also preserved the voices of hundreds of lesser-known lesbians and gays.

Emboldened by a sense of mission, Barbara placed her faith in texts rather than in organizations. Standing on the shoulders of pioneering lesbian bibliographer Jeannette Howard Foster, she patiently and doggedly identified and recorded lesbian and gay characters in all kinds of novels, her results published in three editions of *The Lesbian in Literature*. After rising from contributor to editor and publisher of *The Ladder*, a monthly publication of the Daughters of Bilitis, Barbara later co-founded Naiad as a lesbian publishing company. Bold and willing to take risks, she refused to let lack of resources, staff and skills stay progress, and instead forged ahead with sheer force of will, learning as she went. With arrogance, confidence and conviction steeped in pragmatism and an old-fashioned work ethic, Barbara never wavered from her goal of increasing lesbian visibility on the printed page.

Several women played significant roles in the life and education of Barbara Grier. During a twenty-year relationship with an intensely private Helen Bennett, Barbara gained an appreciation for discipline, control and order. In a second, nearly forty-year personal relationship with Donna McBride, Barbara learned the importance of adventure, play and spontaneity, and their complementary business partnership ensured Naiad books found their way around the world. By a twist of fate, Jeannette Howard Foster moved from Indiana to Kansas City (where Barbara then lived) after leaving her position as librarian for noted sex researcher Alfred C. Kinsey. In Barbara, Foster found an eager protégé who shared her passion for lesbian literature and history. Novelist Jane Rule, whose correspondence with Barbara spanned three decades, brought color to Barbara's black and white worldview by challenging her assumptions and beliefs and introducing her to other writers and poets. Rule also served as a vital sounding board as Barbara grew into her roles as editor and publisher.

As Rule discovered, Barbara was prone to action, not introspection. A complex individual, Barbara knew many people but had only a few close friends. During five decades of activism she wrote thousands of words, but most were constructed with a goal in mind, whether it was validating an isolated lesbian's existence or persuading someone to do her a favor. Barbara's correspondence with Rule offers the most intimate glimpses of her daily life, aspirations and perspective on topics ranging from books to politics to relationships. Read in sequence, their letters reveal two obsessive compulsive correspondents: Rule a worldly author, and Barbara a romantic who experienced the wider world vicariously and lacked a grounded understanding of its complexity. Despite their differences, Rule appreciated Barbara's "flamboyant delight in the marketplace," and recognized that when it came to the promotion of lesbian books, Barbara had no peers.[4]

Barbara Grier was a conundrum. She wanted others to view her as a devil (hence her favorite pseudonym, Gene Damon, or Gene the devil), yet she devoted herself to affirming the lives of dozens of isolated correspondents. Upon meeting them, however, she often appeared rude and insensitive. Despite this lack of interpersonal skills, she developed into a consummate networker with contacts around the globe. She shared younger feminists' goal of equality, but eschewed their politics and considered their cooperative approach to publishing inefficient. Speaking frankly, Barbara could at once be perceived by others as "brusque and gracious, brutally honest and generous, biting and good-hearted."[5] A pragmatist and an opportunist, she hungered for the power and influence she regarded as necessary to accomplish lasting change. As she was fond of saying, "You can't change the world and everyone in it if you don't have power...and the people who control the press control the world."[6]

Barbara never doubted books held the key to improving the lives of lesbians and gays. Because of her vast correspondence during the 1950s and 1960s with readers of *The Ladder*, she recognized the need to promote books to people beyond the reach of the lesbian and gay movement and its bookstores. Buoyed by her fanaticism, Barbara's commitment to preserving and nurturing lesbian writing prevailed, and with the books she left in her wake, lesbian invisibility became impossible.

A firm believer in the American Dream, and the embodiment of a Horatio Alger rags-to-riches narrative, Barbara discovered a formula for success in lesbian publishing, and along with partner Donna McBride transformed Naiad into the largest lesbian publishing company in the world. Success, and its accompanying power, made it difficult for Barbara to maintain relationships with Naiad co-founders and with employers, authors and women in the lesbian-feminist movement. Yet, whether individuals liked her or not, Barbara achieved her goal of ensuring that "[e]very sixteen-year-old in the world, when she comes out, should be able to walk into a store and find a book saying yes, you're a lesbian, and you're wonderful!" When asked how she would like to be remembered, Barbara paused before replying "[I]f my name is known one hundred years from now, then what I've done [too] will be, and that's what I've done it for."[7]

CHAPTER ONE

༷

Growing Up Gay with the Help of Literature

"I've always considered myself a garden variety lesbian, resistant to blight and guaranteed to grow."

–Barbara Grier, 1982[1]

When readers opened the July 1958 issue of *The Ladder*, they found an essay titled "My Daughter Is a Lesbian," by one Mrs. Dorothy Lyles. Allegedly written by Barbara Grier's mother, Dorothy Grier, the essay portrayed a highly perceptive woman who recognized her precocious and strong-willed girl was "a little different from the average child." After learning of her daughter's lesbianism, Mrs. Lyles wisely responded with "love, appreciation and understanding…not censure, shame or withdrawal."[2] Whether apocryphal or authentic, this is the experience Barbara wished for every young lesbian. When she came of age in the late 1940s and early 1950s, being a lesbian entailed fear, doubt and even danger. At a time when an increasingly pervasive popular culture reinforced images of lesbians as deviant and self-destructive, few women possessed courage to admit their lesbianism to parents, husbands, teachers or employers. The repercussions were too risky: one might be committed to a mental hospital, expelled from school or evicted from an apartment. Government agencies fired suspected homosexuals and teachers lost their jobs. Mothers faced the prospect of losing custody of their children in cases of divorce.

Dorothy Grier's matter-of-fact acceptance of lesbianism, unusual in 1940s America, was one of the greatest gifts she could have given her daughter. She also endowed her with several important life skills, including a positive self-image, a flair for the dramatic and techniques for coping with adversity. Years later Barbara tended to romanticize her childhood, omitting her father Philip Grier's philandering nature, episodes of poverty and the teenage angst that had contributed to her drive to succeed. Recasting reality into a more acceptable narrative, she emphasized her mother's love and the stable relationship she had with lover Helen Bennett for two decades. If pressed for additional details, Barbara mentioned having a physician father (untrue) and lesbian sister, but generally gave the impression that her childhood had been quite unremarkable. Nothing was further from the truth.

Somewhat ironically, Barbara's happiest memories of childhood date to the Great Depression of the 1930s. Born in Cincinnati, Ohio, on November 4, 1933, she spent much of her first decade in Detroit, a city ravaged by industrial unemployment and labor unrest. On the surface, her father, Philip Strang Grier, appeared sophisticated, well-educated and successful. A short man with an ego as big as Napoleon's, he earned a bachelor's degree in pharmacy from Ferris Institute (today Ferris State University) in 1924 and had risen to a management position at the Detroit-based Shapiro's Drug Store by the time he married Dorothy Vernon Black in the early 1930s.[3]

Raised by a single mother, Dorothy grew up in a female-centered household headed by her grandmother, Barbaretta Niven Brown. Known as Retta, she emigrated from Canada to Hornellsville, New York, after the Civil War, married briefly, and gave birth to a daughter, Mabel, in 1878.[4] In the late 1890s, the extended Niven family moved to New York City so Retta's sisters, Della and Anabel, could pursue acting careers. In addition to appearances in Broadway musicals, they spent the summers as part of a traveling theatrical troupe. Accompanied by their niece Mabel, they billed themselves as The Niven Sisters and toured throughout the Midwest and South.[5] While on the road, Mabel reportedly married William Lyles Black long enough to become pregnant with Dorothy, born in 1902. Coming of age in the extended Niven family, Dorothy acquired a love of popular show tunes, a bawdy sense of humor and an openness to the homosexuals she encountered in the theatrical world. Her love of New York City endured long after the family moved to Detroit in the mid-1910s.

With the growth of the auto industry and the meteoric rise of Christian Science in the first quarter of the twentieth century, Detroit was an ideal location for the enterprising Retta Niven Brown, by then a widow, to flourish. Embracing one of the few respectable occupations open to an uneducated woman, she opened a boardinghouse and established herself as a Christian Science practitioner. The large house at 47 Smith Avenue accommodated her extended family, which included her sisters Della and Annabel, daughter Mabel and granddaughter Dorothy.[6]

Strong-willed like her mother, Mabel Brown Black governed her daughter's every move, leaving Dorothy unprepared to think independently. In the 1920s, the pleasingly plump Dorothy became a stenographer in one of the city's many steel plants, and by her late twenties had concluded that marriage was not in her future. One day, however, a girlfriend introduced her to a divorced pharmaceutical salesman named Philip Grier. The sheltered young woman impulsively said yes when her smooth-talking suitor proposed after a short courtship.

Once the initial excitement of their marriage faded, Dorothy knew she had made a foolish mistake. Philip was more of a confidence man than a family man. In fact, his personality and behavior bore an uncanny resemblance to that of his great-grandfather, James Jesse Strang, founder of the Strangite faction of the Church of Jesus Christ of Latter-day Saints. Born in upstate New York in 1813, Strang moved to Nauvoo, Illinois, in the early 1840s to join Joseph Smith and his followers. After Smith's assassination in 1844, Strang claimed to be his chosen successor. When the majority of believers chose to follow Brigham Young, Strang led a breakaway group north to Wisconsin, where he claimed to have a divine vision sealing his fate as their leader. In 1850, Strang and more than two hundred Strangites moved to Beaver Island, the largest island in Lake Michigan. As the self-proclaimed "King of the Kingdom of God on Earth," Strang published a newspaper, books and pamphlets advocating his beliefs. His suppression of the local liquor trade, embrace of polygamy and requirement that women wear bloomers fed local opposition to Strang's dictatorial ways.[7]

Arrested for violating several federal laws, Strang successfully defended himself in court and upon his release launched a successful campaign for a seat, as a Democrat, in the Michigan House of Representatives. By 1856, however, the original inhabitants of Beaver Island had tired of his controlling ways, and in June an assassin shot him in the back. He died several weeks later. Strang's five wives and nearly one dozen children quickly dispersed. Three months pregnant, his first polygamous wife, Elvira Eliza Field, placed James, the son born after his father's death, with the David Grier family near Charlotte, Michigan. Thinking it wise to sever all ties to his notorious father, the family changed his name to Charles J. Grier.[8]

Charlie Grier, as he became known, grew up to become an attorney and practiced law in St. Paul, Minnesota. By the 1920s, he and his wife, Glycine Tower, had returned to the family farm in Michigan with their two sons, Philip and Paul. The older boy, Philip (Barbara's father), apparently inherited some of his illustrious and egocentric ancestor's hunger for power and women. While a student at Ferris Institute, he married Iva Schneckenberger in 1922, earned a B.S. degree in pharmacy two years later and passed the Michigan State Board exam for pharmacists. By the time Iva filed for divorce eight years later on the grounds of cruelty, Philip had fathered two sons, William and Brewster, but felt no obligation to provide for them after he married Dorothy Black. Upon learning that his sons had resorted to shooting crows to keep food on the table, Dorothy secretly slipped their mother small amounts of money and food.[9]

It did not take Dorothy long to realize Philip was a pathological liar who liked to impress women by passing himself off as a physician during his travels as a pharmaceutical company salesman. He had a penchant for women in uniform, especially nurses and waitresses. Determined to avoid the short-lived relationships of her mother and grandmother, the hopelessly romantic Dorothy forgave his womanizing and kept her marriage together by keeping her temper and "not digging too deeply in the barrel."[10] The couple moved frequently to accommodate Philip's perpetual quest for advancement. In the fall of 1933 they were living in Cincinnati, Ohio, when Dorothy gave birth to the first of their three children, named Barbara Glycine after her maternal great-grandmother Barbaretta and paternal grandmother Glycine.[11]

Oblivious to her father's philandering and scheming, Barbara relished being an only child for the first six years of her life. She delighted in the times when Philip took "Daddy's girl" to museums or taught her to ride a bicycle. The loss of her two front teeth during a childhood accident left her with a permanent partial plate and a reluctance to smile for the camera, but did not dampen her sense of adventure. She listened for hours as her father told colorful stories about their family, and she later chose many of her pen names from both sides of her family tree. Unfortunately, her chain-smoking, heavy-drinking, womanizing father preferred dressing well and driving nice cars to taking responsibility for his wife and daughters. When they moved from one town to the next, as they frequently did, he routinely left unpaid rent, store accounts and utility bills.[12]

After Dorothy gave birth to a second daughter, Diane, in 1939, Philip became an intermittent presence in the home. Determined to keep the girls close to their father and to pressure him into providing for them, Dorothy followed him from Detroit to Chicago to several small communities in Colorado. Philip returned home just often enough to get her pregnant a third time, but by the time she gave birth to Barbara's youngest sister, Penelope (Penni), in October 1943, Philip had abandoned his family for good. After witnessing her father's treatment of her mother, Barbara reflected years later that he could "charm anyone into anything—any sex, any age, and then literally skin them inside and out. I don't think my father noticed anyone at all except himself. He wasn't cruel, but he suffered from a permanent erection."[13]

Disillusioned and disappointed with her father, Barbara struggled to navigate the emotional chaos wrought by her parents' failed relationship. Their experience did not match what she had seen in movies or read about in novels. In her anger, she lashed out at her mother: "You let my father make you into a mewling puking idiot. I can understand why you had me, but why did you have the other two mistakes?" Unable to rely on her father, disappointed by her mother's behavior and separated by nearly six years from her next youngest sister, Barbara sought refuge in books. Her favorites quickly became stories about unrequited love, noble heroines and unattainable women.[14]

In the years to come, the Grier family's failure to put down roots in any one community affected all of the girls by positioning them as perpetual outsiders. It was especially difficult for the adolescent Barbara. In addition to being the product of a broken home, she was precocious, and other children resented her eagerness to answer her teacher's questions. They taunted her by twisting her middle name, Glycine (the botanical name for wisteria), into glycerin and Lysol.[15] One of the short stories she wrote later in life was set in the Colorado of her pre-teenage years and recounted how seventh-graders stoned an unpopular girl as she walked home from school. Whether the stones were real or fictional, Barbara's lack of social skills had their origins in childhood.

Dorothy Grier struggled to cope in wartime Colorado Springs. Philip, true to form, could not be relied upon to provide financial support. Meanwhile, economic opportunities for women had shrunk as veterans returned home from World War II to reclaim their jobs. By 1946, the now-divorced Dorothy had become so overwhelmed by the difficulty of feeding, clothing and housing her daughters that she returned home to Detroit after placing eight-year-old Diane and three-year-old Penni in a Catholic orphanage in Oklahoma City. Separated because of their age difference, they could not even console one another about the abrupt change in their lives or the abandonment they felt. Barbara, who balked at the prospect of life in an orphanage, remained briefly with her father, who had remarried, but made herself so intentionally disagreeable that he soon consented to let her join her mother.[16]

For the next year, Dorothy and Barbara lived with nonjudgmental, outgoing and positive Aunt Anabel (Nana), who provided a supportive atmosphere while Dorothy re-composed her life. Barbara flourished in the artistic, female-centered house at 50 Webb Avenue, where her mother and aunt would spontaneously break into songs from operas and Broadway musicals. Barbara remembered her mother singing "every opera, every operetta number" to the point that her childhood became a series of musical numbers. She also absorbed valuable lessons passed down from her great-grandmother, the Christian Science practitioner Retta Brown. From Retta's legacy, Barbara learned "that I was the master of my body…I also learned that you don't have to feel pain if you don't want to and the way you surmount difficulty was to work twice as hard."[17] A quick study, Barbara learned to deal with difficulties by experiencing them and then moving on, seemingly without regret. She may have fretted about upcoming events, but she refused to linger on past flaws or missteps. While this trait led some to regard Barbara as insensitive, it was a survival tactic that served her well throughout her life.

Barbara made the earth-shattering discovery of her lesbianism shortly before her thirteenth birthday. In retrospect, she remembered developing crushes on slightly older girls beginning in her eighth year, when she fell "madly in love with my babysitter."[18] She also routinely fell in love with "lady gym teachers" and was devastated when her family's frequent moves forced her to leave them behind. Childhood, she reflected, was "wrapped in a memory of sitting silently in the right hand [sic] corner of the back seat of cars travelling away from this city or that, weeping."[19] In 1946, at age thirteen, Barbara informed her friend, Barbara Shier, that she was crazy about her. Aware such feelings ran counter to most societal practice, they decided to research the subject. After taking the Woodward Avenue streetcar to the Detroit Public Library, Barbara marched up to the reference librarian with Shier in tow and requested books about homosexuals, a term she had discovered in her father's medical dictionary. Returning home after a day of research, Barbara matter-of-factly informed her mother: "I am a homosexual."[20]

Unlike many parents of the era, Dorothy Grier was remarkably nonjudgmental about her daughter's sexuality. As a young woman she had encountered gays and lesbians in the New York City theatre scene, and she was untroubled by religious condemnations of homosexuality, in part because she grew away from her mother's faith and became an agnostic. Thus, when there were momentary upsets during Barbara's teen years because of her lesbianism, her mother never acted "as if there was anything shameful or degrading." Upon hearing her daughter's news, Dorothy matter-of-factly informed Barbara that the correct term for female homosexuals was "lesbian" and explained that her feelings for girls could be a phase, but either way, she should just "play as honest a game always as possible." Her mother further explained that some people would disapprove but most would judge her as a person, not a type. She also planted the seed for Barbara's later interest in biography by naming several "fine people in history" who were homosexuals yet "still honored and successful."[21]

Since the Griers were a reading family, Dorothy knew her daughter would want titles of books about lesbians. She recommended two: Radclyffe Hall's *The Well of Loneliness* (1928), which she had read while Barbara was still in the womb, and a novel about an operatic diva. Her ability to recall plot but not title provided Barbara with her first opportunity for lesbian literary detection, and in time she identified the second book as Marcia Davenport's *Of Lena Geyer* (1936). Through reading and further conversation with her understanding mother, Barbara accepted the feelings she had for babysitters, classmates, family friends and even relatives as something positive.

Barbara's self-esteem flourished because of her mother's sensitive treatment of her sexuality, and also because her teachers recognized her academic potential and encouraged her intellectual curiosity. During Barbara's freshman year in high school she was chosen, along with other gifted students, to take a battery of tests at the University of Michigan. At their conclusion she learned she was eligible for a four-year scholarship to the university. Since this achievement coincided with her coming out as a lesbian, Barbara concluded lesbians must be superior individuals. Her aspirations thus fueled, she dreamed of studying psychiatric medicine and becoming a physician.[22]

By mid-1948 Dorothy had recovered enough to resume her responsibilities as a mother to three daughters. While it might have been easier for Dorothy to remain with her family in Detroit, an environment she loved second only to the New York City of her childhood, she chose to live in close proximity to Philip Grier, the womanizer she hopelessly continued to love. Accompanied by Barbara, Dorothy retrieved Diane and Penni from the orphanage and rented a home in Colorado Springs, less than three hours' drive from Leadville, Colorado, where Philip was living with his third wife, a nurse named Marie Upp.

As the lesbian daughter of an agnostic, Barbara certainly did not conform to *Saturday Evening Post* images of post-World War II era teenagers. Classmates in Colorado Springs viewed her as a city slicker and know-it-all because she never hesitated to respond when teachers asked questions. Dorothy, preoccupied with providing food and shelter for her daughters, was not a disciplinarian. As a result, Barbara "was already doing pretty much what I pleased." She later recalled: "I was as wild as the law allows from thirteen on. I fell in love in every town and tried to go to bed with each of them."[23] Her pattern was to choose women who were just beyond her reach because of their age or social class, and on occasion they returned just enough attention to encourage her advances.

Unabashedly proud of her lesbian identity, Barbara found it difficult to comprehend why some members of the community regarded her as a threat. During the social and political upheavals following the Great Depression and World War II, however, Americans became increasingly concerned about what they deemed aberrant sexual behavior. The much publicized release of Alfred Kinsey's *Sexual Behavior in the Human Male* (1948) heightened general awareness of homosexuality. Selling more than 200,000 copies, the book revealed that a significant percentage of people had at least one same-sex experience, and that ten percent of males in Kinsey's sample were "predominantly homosexual between the ages of 16 and 55." At the same time, politicians like senators Kenneth Wherry (R-Nebraska) and Joseph McCarthy (R-Wisconsin) incorporated fear of sexual perversion into their attacks on Communists and liberals. Magazine articles warned readers of the inherent danger of gender inversion, urging citizens to be on their guard against effeminate men and lesbian wives. In this context, police, psychologists, school counselors and others who worked with teenagers sought to curb the homosexual behaviors they associated with delinquency.[24]

Barbara's open interest in women greatly distressed her Colorado Springs high school counselor, who wrung his hands and lamented, "Whatever are we going to do with you?" Once, the parents of a young woman Barbara wanted to bed objected to her walking their daughter back and forth to practice at the Broadmoor Hotel's ice-skating arena. Another time, Barbara was called to the counselor's office and confronted by two police officers who took her to the station and grilled and badgered her for several hours because she had spoken to a woman at a bus stop. Before releasing Barbara, they issued a strict injunction that she should never again use the bus stop or go near this woman's workplace. Unfortunately, it was the Peak Theatre, one of Barbara's favorite places to while away the hours. The encounter merely strengthened her resolve, and as her counselor observed, Barbara was not afraid of people and it was virtually impossible to intimidate her.[25]

The public library often provided Barbara with a safe haven during the chaos of her teen years, and books became her steadfast friends. As long as she had the printed word, there was nothing from which she could not escape, mentally or otherwise. "Books are things to read, to hold to the light, to put on shelves sometimes so that the sun strikes them with amber tones, to hold to your chest for comfort."[26] Alienated from mainstream peers and emotionally detached from her younger sisters, Barbara followed a path similar to many other pre-Stonewall era gays and lesbians who searched books to find validation of their identity and a sense of connectedness to the gay and lesbian past. Books with gay and lesbian content, however minimal it might be, validated their existence by offering assurance that they were not aberrations, and provided the language needed for discussing their sexuality.

Barbara's book-collecting habit began at sixteen when she stole her local library's only copy of *The Well of Loneliness*. Her desire to own lesbian books intensified in 1950 when a deeply closeted older woman named "Peggy" furtively shared several treasured items she kept hidden in the trunk of her car: *Diana* by Diana Fredericks, *Loveliest of Friends* by G. Sheila Donisthorpe, and *We Too Are Drifting* by Gale Wilhelm. Inspired, Barbara searched the shelves of Cramer's bookstore in Kansas City, Missouri, for a used copy of the Wilhelm book, and by the end of the year had discovered nearly a dozen lesbian titles that became the foundation of her collection. Over the years, as her library grew into the thousands, the cheap, stained 1938 reprint of *We Too Are Drifting* occupied a special place in her heart. "I shared it," she explained, "indeed, took good advantage of it during the courtship of my first serious lover."[27]

In addition to novels, Barbara developed a love for poetry and an obsession with the poets who created it. Because of her conviction that many of the world's creative and powerful women were lesbians, she spent many hours trying to confirm that her favorite poets were lesbians. In her teens she was "madly in love" with American lyric poet Sara Teasdale, read all of her works, and sensed that Teasdale's emotional connections were with women, not men. She put Teasdale aside after laying out her evidence to lesbian bibliographer Jeannette Howard Foster, who told her the poet was not "pertinent." Years later, in the 1970s, when feminist literary scholars explored the poet's intense female friendships, Barbara felt vindicated because her earlier suspicion had been confirmed.[28]

Barbara's coming of age as a lesbian coincided with the proliferation of fiction with gay and lesbian characters in the late 1940s. According to literary historian Ray Lewis White, World War II led Americans "to write seriously and to read understandingly" about homosexual life, in part because the military prompted recruits to define their sexuality. In the postwar years authors became increasingly frank in their discussion of gay and lesbian themes and characters. Gore Vidal's *The City and the Pillar* (1948), a gay coming-of-age story, is significant as one of the first novels to challenge stereotypes by featuring an athletic and masculine gay protagonist. More typically, novelists portrayed gay characters in a negative light. Richard Brooks's *The Brick Foxhole* (1945), for instance, recounted the murder of a gay interior decorator who picked up soldiers. In another instance, Mary B. Miller, who wrote *The Christmas Tree* (1949) under the pseudonym Isabel Bolton, told the story of a gay man who killed his lover by pushing him over a balcony to illustrate "part of the monstrous, wholesale and unspeakable melodrama that was afflicting the world today." In contrast, fictional lesbians of the 1940s appeared less dangerous than their male counterparts. In Dorothy Cowlin's *Winter Solstice* (1943), a same-sex romantic attachment cured a woman after eight years of invalidism, but the relationship was brief and ended when both women married. Meanwhile, most of the devoted readers who devoured *Ladies' Home Journal* columnist Gladys Taber's charming tales of two women's life together at Stillmeadow Farm remained unaware of its mild-mannered presentation of lesbian companionship.[29]

Readers who sought franker portrayals of homosexuality had to look elsewhere, and beginning in the 1950s they found it in the emerging paperback book market readily available at newsstands. The publication of *Women's Barracks* (1950), by Tereska Torrès, opened the floodgates with its tale of the passionate attachments formed between experienced older women and young innocents living and working together in an urban military barracks. In order to be published, such books had to conform to societal proscriptions requiring authors to depict lesbians as depraved and self-destructive. As the 1950s progressed, readers could select from many books written by male authors, as well as novels by Ann Bannon, Valerie Taylor, and Marijane Meaker, whose pseudonyms included Ann Aldrich and Vin Packer. In addition to popularizing the word "lesbian," argues historian Yvonne Keller, pulp novels ensured that images of lesbian life, no matter how tawdry, reached a mass audience.[30] Many pulps also presented lesbians as normal working-class or low-level professional women, a significant departure from earlier literary works portraying lesbians as wealthy women.

Initially, Barbara felt satisfied just to find gays and lesbians portrayed in novels, but the more she read, the more she became aware of the disconnect between her mother's calm acceptance of lesbianism and the negative stigma permeating printed portrayals of lesbians in the 1940s and 1950s. She lacked the vocabulary to articulate her feelings, but instinctively knew that the pulp fiction market and the small handful of lesbian titles in the press played a major role in shaping how lesbians viewed themselves. As much as Barbara loved dramatic stories about tortured souls, she yearned for the existence of positive lesbian fiction, even if she had to create it herself.

During that time, Barbara took refuge in darkened movie theaters, where she watched Bette Davis in *Dark Victory* (1939), and Humphrey Bogart and Lauren Bacall in *To Have and Have Not* (1944) and *Key Largo* (1948). She especially admired Davis and Katharine Hepburn for their "wonderful figures" and the boyish roles they so often played. When movie theaters closed for the night, Barbara lounged in hotel lobbies reading newsstand magazines or walked in local parks, all the while dreaming of a time when films featured heroines falling in love with one another.[31]

Growing up without close adult supervision, Barbara had no one to discourage her association with local "toughs." After the Griers settled in Kansas City, Kansas, during her senior year in high school, she hung out with a young man named Zedick Braden, who taught her lessons about street smarts and survival skills that informed her behavior later in life. When he took her cruising in his car, he had a wooden plate attached to the bumper and used it to push aside cars that got in his way. Years later, when Barbara found herself in difficult situations, she jokingly wished it were possible to summon him and his car to the rescue.[32]

Barbara attended three high schools during her senior year: one in Colorado Springs; another in Dodge City, Kansas; and the third in Kansas City, Kansas. According to Barbara, the move from Dodge City to Kansas City occurred because she was caught making out with another girl in the teachers' lounge. When Barbara graduated from Wyandotte High School in Kansas City, in the spring of 1951, she knew there was no money for college, so she searched for and found the first of many clerical-level jobs she would hold in her lifetime.

Once in Kansas City, Dorothy Grier had settled into a stable secretarial position and at long last was able to provide Diane and Penni, then thirteen and nine, with the stability that had eluded Barbara's childhood. Dorothy made household chores enjoyable by telling funny stories and singing show tunes. Diane and Penni recall other children flocking to their home because Dorothy was "every child's friend," someone "who had nothing to offer but understanding, kindness and friendship." On Friday afternoons, the two girls took the bus downtown to meet their mother at the end of the work week. After rushing to the bank to deposit her pay so checks written earlier in the week would not bounce, Dorothy treated the girls to a restaurant meal and a movie, her six hours of heaven each week.[33]

Meanwhile, Barbara spent so little time at home that her younger sisters regarded her as a stranger. Once, when she came home ill, they took great delight in tormenting the relative stranger lying in the bedroom. In a tearful moment years later, Penni (ten years younger than her oldest sister) confessed that she had no memories of times spent with Barbara, not even holidays or birthdays. Barbara, on the other hand, had fond memories of taking Penni to the movies. "I had, I thought, been very close to her. It was something of a shock to discover years later that I had deserted her."[34]

* * *

By her early twenties, Barbara Grier had rough edges in need of smoothing. The lack of parental nurturing, the hand-to-mouth existence after her tenth year, and exposure to the wild side of life whether real or vicarious, imbued her with a "cur instinct" that was never far from the surface. Economic realities killed Barbara's dream of a college education, but also fueled her determination to succeed. Later in life, she described herself as a "garden variety lesbian, resistant to blight and guaranteed to grow." Steeped in the Horatio Alger novels she had read as a young girl, Barbara emerged from childhood convinced that anyone who tried could rise from rags to riches with hard work and determination.[35] Setting out to find the stability and material comfort that had eluded her as a young girl, Barbara found both in a part-time job at the Kansas City Public Library in Missouri, where she met a woman who would change her life.

CHAPTER TWO

৵৬

Becoming Gene Damon

"I may not be your most ardent fan but I bet I don't miss by much."
—Gene Damon (Barbara Grier) 1962[1]

As a teenager, Barbara Grier liked to make librarians and bookstore clerks squirm by asking for books about homosexuality. Whenever she saw someone who looked sweet, pleasant and innocent, Barbara amused herself by harassing her. One day in the fall of 1951, she approached the petite, dark-haired woman on duty in the literature and popular reading section of the Kansas City Public Library and requested *The Well of Loneliness*. Much to her surprise, the librarian replied that yes, the library owned it as well as several other titles Barbara might want to read. Her interest piqued—in the librarian as well as the books she recommended—Barbara found herself drawn to Helen Bennett.[2]

Sixteen years Barbara's senior, Helen had grown up in rural Iowa. Years later, Helen attributed her reclusive tendencies to her fishbowl childhood. As the daughter of a minister, she was expected to be absolutely circumspect in personal and professional life, and to conform in dress, speech and mannerisms. After graduating from college in the 1930s, Helen taught school in Washita Township, Oklahoma, before consenting to marry "Shorty" Bennett. She did not love him, but felt pressure to conform to societal expectations. Like many lesbians of her generation, she searched books for information about homosexuality but found little that was helpful. By the time Helen met Barbara, she had given a great deal of thought to the subject, not only because of herself but also because of her brother. A revival preacher, Harold Burkhart was attracted to men and liked to visit gay bars. His involvement as a material witness in a murder allegedly involving a gay man reinforced Helen's fear of the homosexual world.[3]

Confident and brash, eighteen-year-old Barbara set out to seduce thirty-four-year-old Helen. Having completed her senior year at Wyandotte High School the previous spring, Barbara took a part-time job shelving books at the public library, and initiated conversations with Helen whenever time permitted. Their friendship blossomed, and soon they were going for lunches at a nearby café. Outwardly, Barbara displayed a devil-may-care attitude, but in reality she felt on the verge of self-destruction. "I was tired and scared," she later reflected, "and needed so much permanence."[4] As much as Barbara loved her mother, she longed for the security that came with Helen Bennett's orderly life.

The two women became lovers in late February 1952, when Helen invited Barbara to her home. The cautious married librarian's willingness to enter a relationship with the precocious teen foreshadowed the powers of persuasion Barbara would employ throughout her life. Helen insisted they be very circumspect, a requirement that appealed to Barbara's cloak-and-dagger sense of adventure. One afternoon, Helen's husband arrived home unexpectedly and Barbara hid behind a door. Alarmed by the incident, Helen knew something had to change.[5]

Exploring her options carefully, Helen requested a leave of absence from the library to enroll in a master's degree program at the University of Denver School of Librarianship. Separating from her husband, she thought it wise to avoid mentioning Barbara would join her in Denver. Barbara's mother Dorothy was complicit in the two women's plans to "run away" together. On the evening of September 17, 1952, Helen said goodbye to her family in Kansas City and boarded the train for Denver. Meanwhile, Dorothy drove Barbara to Topeka. When Helen's train stopped in Topeka, Barbara joined her, as planned, and the two embarked upon their new life as a lesbian couple.[6]

For the next two years, Helen and Barbara constructed a "cocoon-wrapped world" in Denver, one consisting of daily and weekly routines and intense privacy. Like many lesbian couples of the era, they kept the nature of their relationship secret, passing as roommates and taking great care always to refer to each other as "my friend." Barbara easily adapted to her new life and "really didn't mind being just with Helen, and never seeing anyone." During leisure hours, the couple took long walks, went to movies and concerts, and celebrated special occasions by giving each other books. While Helen was at school, Barbara worked in a clerical capacity at *The Denver Post* and wrote short stories for fun. One sad note marred their sojourn when Helen learned in October that her brother had been killed in a car-train accident.[7]

Helen and Barbara were happy in Denver, and upon earning her master's degree in the spring of 1953, Helen accepted a professional position there. The following year, however, the tug of Helen's family and her sense of filial responsibility proved too powerful to resist. The couple returned home and settled into a quiet "married" existence.[8]

Kansas City had made significant strides in its cultural and economic development since its days as a cattle town. The presidencies of Harry S. Truman and Dwight D. Eisenhower brought national attention to the region. The prominence of Hallmark Cards, headquartered there since the early twentieth century, and the leadership of Roy A. Roberts at *The Kansas City Star* also contributed to the city's vibrancy.

Like their counterparts in many other Midwestern communities, Kansas City's gays and lesbians led closeted lives. Homophobia flourished in the wake of Joseph McCarthy's linkage of homosexuality to communism, and was further reinforced by the medical-psychological establishment's classification of homosexuality as a disease. Fearing arrest, confinement to mental hospitals, loss of jobs and being pronounced unfit parents, gays and lesbians retreated deeper into their closets. There was one well-known gay bar in the city, but Helen and Barbara never dreamed of going there because to do so would expose them to potential scandal. Moreover, a white-collar middle-class woman like Helen would have had little in common with its clientele, other than her sexual orientation.[9]

Once back in Kansas City, Helen's reclusive tendencies escalated. As someone who viewed the outside world as a threat, she futilely attempted to control outsiders' access to their home by limiting Barbara's interactions with others. Even Barbara's mother and sisters felt unwelcome on the one or two occasions they visited the apartment. To teenaged sisters Diane and Penelope, Helen appeared unbending, unfriendly and unbearably quiet. They didn't understand why Barbara would want to be with such an unhappy person.[10] In chameleon-like fashion, Barbara adapted to Helen's requirements and became increasingly reclusive, learning to prefer the company of cats to people.

Life with Helen came with limitations, but it also filled Barbara's deep-seated need for order and stability. Helen's income as a librarian ensured Barbara never lacked the basic supplies that had been so scarce during her childhood, and she could begin collecting gay and lesbian books in earnest. Moreover, Helen helped Barbara develop key traits that contributed to her success later in life: discipline, hard work and organization. Structure provided a reassuring comfort, and Barbara was eager to please, even when Helen's insistence upon regimentation became excessive. Each week Helen neatly folded their cloth napkins and arranged them by color in the drawer, and on Sunday evenings she assembled a week's worth of sack lunches, lining them up in the refrigerator like soldiers standing at attention.[11]

Though Barbara readily adapted to Helen's need for order and routine, she found it more difficult to suppress the pride she took in her lesbian identity. Drawing upon information gleaned from books and movies, Barbara adopted what she believed to be lesbian dress and behavior. The uniform, according to her younger sister, consisted of a replica of men's dark, laced-up wingtip shoes and a solid-colored men's suit jacket worn over a plain, long-sleeved white or beige shirt tucked into un-tapered black slacks. Barbara wore her wavy brown hair cut short and never donned makeup or jewelry. Occasionally, she wore a black skirt that came down to her black or brown cotton socks. Barbara also adopted what she perceived as a lesbian demeanor, speaking to others in a terse manner with exasperated sighs. Inevitably, she carried an armload of books.[12]

Even though Helen and Barbara lived a "don't ask, don't tell" existence, Barbara believed most people, even Helen's parents, understood they were a lesbian couple. "With the ever increasing awareness of H[omosexuality] in general," she explained to Daughters of Bilitis co-founder Del Martin in 1962, "we are so thoroughly accepted as a couple even by the unconscious people that the other day in a group of married & single women (technically) I was included in a general statement as one of the married ones."[13]

While Helen pursued her library career, Barbara worked in a series of clerical positions. Her work ethic and ability to self-promote ensured she had no difficulty securing positions. She boasted that she could read the classified ads in the morning paper and find work by day's end. A job changer, Barbara moved with ease into positions at public libraries, life insurance companies, department stores, banks and retail businesses. She always worked hard for her employers, but she never missed an opportunity to advance her real love, the pursuit of anything related to lesbian literature. While working as an assistant in the catalog department of the Kansas City (Missouri) Public Library, she found spare minutes to search reference sources for short stories and books containing lesbian themes and characters. Clerical positions with Pyramid Life Insurance Company, Dictaphone, and Draughon's Business College provided her with access to typewriters, stationery and postage. Often, she spent lunch hours typing letters or using the telephone. When working in the credit department of Macy's Department Store, she honed her powers of persuasion by speaking with customers who had fallen behind on their payments and she was able to use the company WATS (Wide Area Telephone Service) line to make free (to her) phone calls to used book dealers and her gay and lesbian correspondents.[14]

The Autodidact and Book Collector

Hungry for knowledge, Barbara compensated for her lack of post-secondary education by doggedly reading "all the things I would read if I had gone to college and majored in literature."[15] Her self-designed course of study sometimes lacked depth, but the breadth of exposure gave her the confidence to discuss almost any topic. In a typical week during the mid-1950s, she skimmed through fifteen to twenty books. Initially, when she fell in love with a particular author, she obsessively devoured everything—books, short stories and essays by her or him, as well as biographical material and literary criticism, because she wanted to know the personality responsible for creating the body of work. After reading an author's complete body of work, she turned to literary criticism, and in time she absorbed a broad, if unschooled, understanding of the American, British and Canadian authors she read.

Barbara's systematic search for lesbian literature dates to this time. A quick study, she benefited from Helen's knowledge of library resources, and by the mid-1950s was spending "hours and hours reading reviews and checking the fine print listings in countless periodicals," always on the alert for clues to homosexual content. Carefully noting each title on a three-by-five-inch slip of paper, Barbara amassed shoe-boxes full of bibliographic citations and personal commentary about each book's gay or lesbian content. Her obsession with lesbian biography also dates from this era.[16] Stealing spare minutes from her staff position in the Kansas City Public Library's cataloging department, Barbara religiously scanned *Kirkus Reviews*, the *New York Times Book Review*, *Booklist*, *Library Journal*, *Publishers Weekly*, and many other sources for hints of homosexuality. When she found an author, poet or artist who addressed gay themes, she systematically examined everything that person had created in the hope of finding more. The most expedient and affordable way to access the works was through interlibrary loan, earning her the reputation of being the woman who requested "that" literature.

Barbara's obsession with identifying literature with gay and lesbian content manifested itself in book collecting, and later book reviewing. After identifying titles of books she wished to purchase, she scoured used bookstores and book catalogs until she located an affordable copy. Accustomed to begging, bartering and, on occasion, stealing, Barbara set out to build a comprehensive collection of gay and lesbian books. When she began collecting, the number of books published in English each year seemed manageable, in part because so much of it consisted of inexpensive pulp fiction flooding the newsstands. Later, as the publication of hardcover books expanded, Barbara started requesting complimentary review copies to keep the cost of her pursuit manageable. As more and more books lined the walls of their apartment, Helen Bennett good-naturedly joked that Barbara would sell their furniture to make more room for bookcases.[17]

Jeannette Howard Foster

Due to an amazing coincidence of space and time, Barbara was able to supplement her individual course of study with the equivalent of a private tutorial with arguably the world's leading scholar of lesbian literature at the time. One day in the fall of 1956, Barbara was looking for something in the *Cumulative Book Index* and spotted a pre-publication announcement for a bibliography titled *Sex Variant Women in Literature*. After all the effort she had expended to locate lesbian books, she was shocked to discover another person had the same goal. When she went to the Cokesbury Bookstore to order a copy, Barbara "nearly fainted with shock" to discover the author, Jeannette Howard Foster, worked nearby at the University of Kansas City (now University of Missouri at Kansas City). Wasting no time, Barbara phoned the university library and asked to speak with Miss Foster. Informed that "Dr. Foster" was out of the office, she phoned her home number and requested a meeting.[18]

A grandmotherly figure who wore locally manufactured shirtdresses and sensible shoes, Foster was comfortable with her lesbianism. In her previous position as librarian of Alfred C. Kinsey's Institute for Sex Research in the late 1940s and early 1950s, she was not easily shocked by coarse language, nudity or discussions of sexuality. Strong-willed, Foster had left Kinsey's employ because she thought he might attempt to claim ownership of the research she had done for *Sex Variant Women in Literature*. When she and her life partner, Hazel Toliver, searched for work, the University of Missouri-Kansas City was the only institution where both could find employment.[19]

From their first meeting, Barbara found much to admire and emulate in Foster, especially her frank speech, self-acceptance and broad knowledge of homosexuality and literature. One day when the two women stopped at a bookstore, Foster purchased a stack of lesbian pulp novels. When the clerk started putting them in a paper bag, the older woman declared that as a librarian, she was not ashamed to be seen with books. Clutching the garish paperbacks to her chest, she marched out the door. From Foster's example, Barbara learned to pursue lesbian research and book collecting without hesitation or embarrassment, as though it were a completely normal activity.[20]

Barbara respected Foster's courage in the wake of McCarthyism. When mainstream and university presses refused to publish her painstakingly researched book about lesbian literature, Foster resorted to Vantage, a vanity press that necessitated the use of her life savings to subsidize the cost of publication. Much to her disappointment, *Sex Variant Women in Literature* received virtually no reviews in mainstream periodicals. A *Kansas City Star* book critic did review the work, finding it compellingly written and objective, with value to psychiatrists, doctors, ministers, students of literature, and laymen. Foster, however, was dismayed by the review's title: "Women Sex Deviates in Books." Despite the paucity of reviews, librarians acquired the book for their collections, and when gay and lesbian readers found it on the shelves, they immediately recognized its value. Barbara, who had begun work on a similar compilation, appreciated the years of meticulous and time-consuming research that had gone into the book. Foster responded to her praise, and in February 1957 presented Barbara with a copy inscribed "To this volume's first fan."[21]

As Foster's protégée, Barbara eagerly absorbed instructions on how to decode reviews of books with gay and lesbian content. On her own, she had discovered that checking school and college novels as well as southern gothics often yielded lesbian content. Reviewers typically offered unsympathetic treatments of homosexuality in literature, so Barbara had learned to look for such phrases as "for discriminating readers," or key words like "sinister," "frank," "daring," "distasteful," "neurotic," "precocious," and "unconventional." Under Foster's tutelage, Barbara honed her skills of detection by spending a summer reading and discussing thousands of reviews published in *Book Review Digest* from its beginning in 1902 through 1956. That assignment taught her that, at best, "the reviews are just the beginning, and you have to read a long time to learn to interpret the reviewers. Even then, you must read many books which just might be pertinent, to find those that are." Foster was thrilled to find someone who cared about books as much as she did, and in the years to come, Barbara built on Foster's foundation.[22]

As the first published scholar of lesbian literature, Foster had attempted to examine every title she identified. Because of the difficulty in gaining access to gay and lesbian titles in the first half of the twentieth century, she purchased them whenever possible. Inspired by the librarian-bibliographer's example, and aided by the discipline instilled in her by Helen Bennett, Barbara dedicated herself to carrying Foster's important work forward. Barbara was by nature a comprehensive collector, but her friendship with Foster reinforced her desire to amass the largest private library of gay and lesbian literature in the United States.[23]

In her early sixties, Jeannette Howard Foster was thirty-eight years and one day older than her young admirer. Barbara had a history of falling in love with older women, and Foster had experienced a series of less-than-satisfying relationships until she met Toliver in the late 1940s. By the time Barbara and Foster met, Toliver had moved to St. Charles, Missouri for a position at Lindenwood College while Foster remained behind in Kansas City. Drawn together by a shared passion for lesbian literature, the mentor and her protégé often spent Sunday afternoons together while Helen visited her parents and, as long as Foster remained in Kansas City, they phoned each other nearly every day.[24] After Foster's move to St. Charles, Missouri, in 1960, and to Pocahontas, Arkansas, in 1974, Barbara relied on correspondence and occasional visits to sustain her friendship with Foster. Helen tolerated the relationship because of her respect for Foster's scholarship and because she believed the scholar was a good influence on Barbara.

Foster's impact on Barbara was profound. She validated the younger woman's intense interest in lesbian literature and provided her with tools to carry the work forward. Foster also extended Barbara's education. As someone who had grown up in a privileged family with the benefit of art lessons, European travel and doctoral study, she raised her protégée's awareness of and appreciation for art, classical music and poetry. An avid letter writer, Foster had no qualms about sending fan letters to authors whose work she admired and suspected of having homosexual tendencies. Tactfully worded, they often elicited replies. Empowered by her status as a scholar and librarian, she contacted the novelist Mary Challans (who wrote as Mary Renault) and the poet May Sarton, among others. In her enthusiasm, Foster shared this correspondence with Barbara, along with letters she received from others in her vast network of authors, book collectors, educators and librarians.

Expanding Relationships

Like Foster, Barbara cultivated relationships with used-book dealers, among them Julia Newman of the Tenth Muse Bookshop.[25] Barbara discovered Newman one day when Helen brought home a secondhand fiction and literature catalog from Tenth Muse. Careful examination revealed the catalog contained a number of titles Barbara had been chasing, and her friendship with the Greenwich Village book dealer grew from that first order. Newman, who enjoyed the hunt for elusive titles and Barbara's "unbounded enthusiasm," responded patiently to her many questions about books and took pity on Barbara's limited budget, charging only a one-dollar markup. In October 1960, while Newman visited used bookstores in New Orleans, she found a copy of French writer Colette's *The Pure and the Impure*. Aware of what the 1932 novel would mean to Barbara, she had a fake newspaper made bearing the headline "Colette Found in New Orleans Bookshop" and sent both items to her collector friend.[26]

In a pen relationship that spanned a decade, Barbara and Julia grew close as they exchanged personal stories. Julia had lived for a time in the basement of Chip's Bookshop and, according to Barbara, struggled with drugs and was a white woman who had a black baby. Barbara liked to call herself Julia's "needle friend" because she sensed Newman was gay and was "not above telling her so now and again." Newman's accounts of life in New York City, her Jewish heritage, and her claim to be bisexual tested some of Barbara's preconceived ideas about class, ethnicity and sexuality. They quarreled good-naturedly about Barbara's labeling of bisexuality as immoral because she believed it implied promiscuity. When Julia passed through Kansas City in late 1966, she visited Barbara's workplace to deliver a birthday bouquet of yellow roses. The following Sunday they spent several hours talking privately under the Wyandotte High School bleachers, taking refuge there to escape Helen's detection. After Newman relocated to San Francisco, their friendship waned because Julia's new girlfriend did not approve of her close friendship with Barbara.[27] Not wanting to leave her friend without a reliable bookseller, Newman recommended Howard Frisch, of Village Books and Press.

As Barbara's correspondence expanded and her book collecting developed into an obsession, Helen grew concerned about the growing amount of "weird" mail arriving in their mailbox. Given obscenity prosecutions in the news, her fears were not unfounded. What if an envelope or package tore open and exposed lurid contents to the mailman or an inquisitive neighbor? Moreover, since dealers in gay and lesbian literature often were unknown entities, there was a possibility of police entrapment, as well as potential for unsolicited pornography or unsavory characters arriving on their doorstep. Barbara's solution was to adopt a pseudonym and to have mail directed to General Delivery rather than the home she shared with Helen. When contemplating names she might choose, she remembered her childhood wish to change her middle name from Glycine to Gene. The androgynous name possessed strength, simplicity, safety and flexibility to a young woman embarking on correspondence with dealers in adult books. Barbara, who liked the idea of being "Gene, the Devil," paired Gene with Damon, the German word for demon (minus the umlaut).[28]

Gays and lesbians laid the foundation for social movement much earlier on the West Coast than in the nation's heartland. The women and men who gravitated to Los Angeles and San Francisco following World War II often met in bars, one of the few places that tolerated their presence. With the rise of homophobia in the 1950s, bars became increasingly vulnerable to police raids and corruption, and individuals who eschewed the bar scene created alternatives by forming social organizations and creating publications.[29] Despite repressive postal laws that linked homosexual publications to obscenity, print offered a powerful alternative to gays and lesbians and soon became a key tool in building the community that would subsequently mobilize to fight for its civil rights.

In September 1955, a San Francisco-based lesbian named Rose Bamberger spoke with Phyllis Lyon and Del Martin about organizing a secret society for lesbians. Little did they realize that this social club would evolve into the first national organization for lesbians. Its name, Daughters of Bilitis (ch), paralleled the Daughters of the American Revolution but came from Pierre Louÿs's erotic poems of lesbian love, *the Songs of Bilitis*, first published in Paris in 1894. DOB members met in one another's homes and initially were so fearful of public exposure that they hesitated to exchange last names and phone numbers. In time, the DOB's monthly gatherings evolved into a series of public forums featuring religious and medical authorities brave enough to speak publicly about homosexuality. Lesbians attempting to cope with immense bigotry and the threat of job loss, imprisonment, shock treatment, and even mutilation considered the DOB "a haven of sanity."[30] Membership included many wounded souls, spurned by their families and bruised by a culture that labeled them sick and deviant. Meeting attendance fluctuated, with women dropping in and out of the organization as their life situations changed.

While some lesbians who lived in or passed through San Francisco took part in DOB picnics, parties, business meetings and lectures, those who lived in middle America initially remained beyond its reach. In October 1956, DOB co-founders Phyllis Lyon and Del Martin created a monthly newsletter titled *The Ladder*. Starting with just seventeen paid subscribers, its readership grew faster than DOB membership as women living in social and geographic isolation subscribed. Just one year later, the DOB claimed 55 members while *The Ladder*'s mailing list had grown to four hundred names.[31]

As eager as some women were for the kind of information they could find in *The Ladder*, it took courage to subscribe in the chilly post-McCarthy climate. Those in government positions or teaching in public schools knew they would lose their jobs if employers suspected them of being homosexual. They worried that issues of the magazine might be intercepted by a husband, parent or nosy neighbor. Renters feared losing apartments if landlords accidentally discovered the nature of the publication that arrived in the plain brown wrapper. One woman, who either received an unsolicited copy or changed her mind about subscribing, protested: "I cannot possibly imagine why I should receive this trash in my mail." To ensure that the DOB removed her name from its list, she threatened to notify the postal authorities.[32]

Jeannette Howard Foster had no reservations about receiving gay and lesbian materials through the mail. As a scholar of gay and lesbian print culture, she read widely. Her contacts at Alfred C. Kinsey's Institute for Sex Research kept her informed as gay and lesbian periodicals began publication. She subscribed to *ONE*, the monthly magazine published by ONE, Inc., and *Mattachine Review*, first issued in January 1955. Foster discovered *The Ladder* a few months after its inception, and enjoyed seeing it publish a review of her book the following May by fantasy writer Marion Zimmer Bradley.

Falling in Love with The Ladder

Upon learning about *The Ladder* from Foster, Barbara sent for copies, took one look "and fell in love." One reason for *The Ladder*'s spectacular growth was that the publication, unlike a public meeting, offered a place where even those deeply ensconced in their closets could find community. For the next fifteen years, Barbara became the magazine's most dedicated reader and contributor. The first of her many letters to *The Ladder* appeared in August 1957. Writing as "G.D. [Gene Damon]," she exclaimed: "I have now received and thoroughly read (and reread) five issues of THE LADDER, and I feel I must write and congratulate you on your magnificent work for all of us."[33]

Zealous in her promotion of *The Ladder*, Barbara discovered many were willing to borrow her copies, but few were bold enough to subscribe. Undeterred by her lack of money, Barbara bought gift subscriptions for her mother, sister Diane and others she thought would benefit from its message. In missives to editor Del Martin, many of which were published in the "Readers Respond" column, Barbara admonished others: "[W]e are all Lesbians and we ought to stand together…We have a common need, we need acceptance."[34]

After spending the previous five years exhaustively researching gay and lesbian literature, Barbara wanted to share her results with others. "I shall undoubtedly bombard you," she informed Martin, "with or without reply." Eager to help as the magazine transitioned from a house organ to a multi-faceted publication, Barbara flooded the editor with stories, articles and news items. Her published pieces escalated from one item in 1957, the year she discovered the magazine, to nineteen the following year. When Barbara began submitting pieces, Martin encouraged her to use varied names because it gave the appearance of multiple people writing for *The Ladder*. During the next decade, *The Ladder* published Barbara's work 211 times. Readers knew her best as Gene Damon, but she also concocted names from her family tree, including Vern Niven and Lennox Strang (sometimes appearing as "Strong" due to typographical errors). Other pseudonyms included Marilyn Barrow, Irene Fiske, Dorothy Lyle, Malvina Creet and Gladys Casey. Barbara's contributions to the "Readers Respond" column were so prolific that she also employed numerous initials, including "B.G.," "G.D.," and "V.N.," which she kept track of in a little brown notebook. When writing for such publications as *ONE* and *Mattachine Review*, she branched out, using the pseudonym Larry Marvin.[35] Of all the names Barbara used, she favored Gene Damon and set out to build her alter ego's reputation as an unsurpassed authority on lesbian literature.

Barbara's penchant for publicity surfaced often during her early interactions with Martin. Barbara boasted she was a "born promoter" and enjoyed increasing people's awareness of books with gay and lesbian content because she wanted homosexuals to know they had a history. "We have an enormous, rich heritage," she explained to freelance editor and critic Lyndall Cowan, one of her many pen friends, but "what we do not have is enough publicity."[36] One of the ways she helped remedy this problem was by proactively approaching book publishers to request permission to reprint covers and author photos in *The Ladder*. Upon learning Bantam Books planned to issue a paperback reprint of *The Price of Salt*, which Patricia Highsmith originally had published under the pseudonym Claire Morgan, Barbara sought and obtained permission from the publisher to reproduce the book's cover in *The Ladder*. Only then did she inform the editor of what she had done.

Barbara could not understand why other women seemingly did not feel as passionately about *The Ladder* as she did. When Martin complained about lack of help to prepare monthly mailings, Barbara lamented living so many miles away. In a letter published in the "Readers Respond" column, she told subscribers they could show support by reading "every copy on arrival" and commenting "vociferously by mail," sending monetary contributions, submitting items for publication, and recruiting new subscribers. Following her own advice, Barbara devoured each issue the day she received it, discussed it with Helen and anyone else who would listen, and then prepared detailed critiques for the editor. If *The Ladder* arrived late, as it often did, she inundated the DOB office with frantic inquiries about its whereabouts. Despite her limited income, she enclosed small donations of cash in many of her letters. She also felt strongly about women purchasing their own copies of magazines and books rather than relying on borrowed copies. How else, she demanded, would the publications they treasured remain in business?[37]

Barbara loved *The Ladder* in its entirety, but her favorite part was its fiction and poetry. "Most or at least half of us," she confided to Martin, "are just not interested in the intellectual study of Lesbianism." Even though the heterosexual clergymen, physicians and psychologists who wrote articles for *The Ladder* had good intentions, she believed they could never comprehend gay or lesbian realities. Since lesbians felt maligned and mistreated by society, she argued, they needed the emotional release and reassurance found in fiction. Steeped in the romantic and melodramatic novels and movies of the 1930s and 1940s, Barbara argued readers of *The Ladder* wanted to "be fed" through their hearts.[38]

Aware of Barbara's deepening desire to become a writer, Helen Bennett suggested she quit her clerical work and write full-time. Barbara felt rewarded and encouraged to see her first short story, "Chance," published in the November 1957 issue of *The Ladder* under the pseudonym Gene Damon. It, like other stories she wrote in the 1950s, captured a day in the life of ordinary lesbians—girls living across the hall and working in offices—who were anything but deviants. Often on journeys to self-discovery, characters had chance encounters and made meaningful eye contact, but nothing more. Barbara made a brief foray into writing poetry with "Iniquity," inspired by her admiration for author Gale Wilhelm. She also wrote short semiautobiographical pieces like "When I Was 17," describing her encounter with a lesbian classmate whose self-hatred vanished when she found a loving partner.[39]

Barbara had much to share about other topics as well. From an early age, she had understood that the abolition of self-hatred was a crucial first step in the fight for gay and lesbian rights, and throughout her life she urged others to come out of their closets. In the November 1957 issue she began the public process of coming out. Accepting herself and all that resulted from her sexual identity, "B.G." declared, "I am a Lesbian.

In that simple statement I mean to express the most outstanding single part of my whole existence." While acknowledging homosexuals suffered from mistreatment and persecution, the defiant young woman refused to be cowed: "So I can't take my little piece of chalk and write my beloved's name on the nearest sidewalk...Don't run away angry!...Stand up and accept yourself."[40]

Barbara lived within Helen's constraints, yet she desperately wanted readers of *The Ladder* to view Gene Damon and her partner as the living embodiment of an ideal lesbian couple. In "Lesbian Marriage," published in August 1958, she presented their lesbian partnership as comparable to a heterosexual marriage. No matter what the relationship, people faced obstacles on the path to happiness. In Barbara's case, these included a sixteen-year age difference and her partner's reluctance to come out to her parents as a lesbian. Countering individuals who claimed lesbians could not manage financially in a world dominated by men, Barbara boasted that she and her partner not only lived together in a lovely apartment, but also owned a car and were accepted as "an inseparable pair" at work.[41] Despite her optimistic portrayal, she and Helen had never lived as openly as she suggested, but were instead still living a "don't ask, don't tell" existence.

Barbara did not hesitate to express her views on such topics as unfair taxation and gay civil rights. Since it was going to take years "for real and absolute integration to take place between homosexual and heterosexual people," she thought the first step must be obtaining such social and legal privileges as "joint income tax returns for lesbian couples, marriage ceremonies and the legal recognition of these ceremonies, and equal insurance rates for homosexual couples." Others took note. "I like B.G.'s contributions of late," wrote a reader from Pasadena. "I share her self-acceptance but not her self-confidence, although I admire both."[42]

In contrast with Barbara, Helen remained reluctant to write for *The Ladder* but did assist Barbara with research for her articles. Helen's training as a librarian enabled her to locate much elusive information, leading Barbara to compare her to "a truffle hound after clues."[43] A grammarian, Helen also edited Barbara's work, which was filled with deficits in grammar and spelling due to the gaps and interruptions in her schooling. Eventually Helen succumbed to Barbara's insistence that they research and write articles together. In addition to writing stories, one of Barbara's favorite activities was ferreting out historical examples of lesbians. As a librarian, Helen possessed research skills that aided in this quest, and soon the two were co-authoring (with Helen writing as Lee Stuart) biographical profiles for *The Ladder* featuring such strong-minded figures as the French novelist Colette, Queen Christina of Sweden, and the sculptor Rosa Bonheur.[44]

As a collector and aspiring bibliographer, Barbara was thrilled to discover "Lesbiana," a numbered annotated bibliography that first appeared in the March 1957 issue of *The Ladder*. Initially, editor Del Martin compiled the column from citations and short reviews submitted by readers. Barbara's first review, *Warped Women*, appeared as entry #25 the following September. "I know," she explained in a letter to the editor, "the years of frustration and work involved in collecting a library of gay literature." Boasting a personal library of "some 300 works of fiction, poetry and drama [by gay men and lesbians], with perhaps 200 devoted to women," Barbara increased her contributions to the column until she wrote virtually every entry.[45]

Starting with the November 1966 issue, Barbara, writing as Gene Damon, assumed sole responsibility for "Lesbiana," and transformed it from an annotated bibliography into a narrative review format. Adopting an engaging, entertaining and frank tone, Gene Damon provided readers with social commentary, humorous quips, summaries of authors' careers, and advice on life. She lavished praise on favorite titles, like Maureen Duffy's *The Microcosm* (1966), describing it as "the first novel to treat Lesbianism objectively," while informing readers that *I Am Mary Dunne*, by Brian Moore, was "well worth reading even though the heroine is a distressing dunce." Barbara had a soft spot for mysteries like Ruth Rendell's *From Doon with Death*, which she pronounced "a very romantic Lesbian mystery—with tremendous appeal for all reader levels." Subscribers could rely on her to inform them about the release of such important reprints as *The Price of Salt*, which Barbara considered "one of the two or three all time [*sic*] best in the field."[46]

Unable to limit her commentary to fiction, Barbara reviewed films, like the one adapted from Violette Leduc's *Thérèse and Isabelle*, calling it "worse than the book…see it if you must, but you have been warned." She gave purchase information for a pamphlet of use for "any among you who are having problems involving your parents accepting your Lesbianism." Barbara also periodically acknowledged the dozens of women, by location if not always by name, who sent her "notes and notices, clippings and reviews, clues to the multitudes of titles uncovered, discovered and re-discovered in the endless lifelong pursuit of yet another title that belongs in the story of Lesbiana."[47] For those who joined Barbara's army by helping amass the information, and for many who devoured the column, "Lesbiana" became a lifeline.

Marion Zimmer Bradley

In the January 1958 issue of *The Ladder*, Barbara read that science fiction writer Marion Zimmer Bradley planned to publish a mimeographed list of lesbian books that had appeared since the publication of *Sex Variant Women in Literature*, plus a few titles Jeannette Howard Foster had missed. Barbara responded immediately to the announcement and offered to assist with the identification of titles.[48]

Born in 1930, Bradley developed a passion for books as a child. After marriage to Robert A. Bradley in 1949, and motherhood the following year, she began grappling with her attraction to women. Unable to share these feelings with family and friends, the Rochester, Texas, woman sought answers in books. She also began writing fiction. After her agent, Forrest J. Ackerman, recognized the hint of same-sex eroticism in her work, he suggested she join the Daughters of Bilitis and read *The Ladder.* A collector of gay and lesbian books, Bradley announced to readers of *The Ladder* in March 1958 that she planned to publish a checklist of lesbian books and would mail it to anyone who reimbursed her for postage. Barbara devoured the twelve-page publication with the ambiguous title, *Astra's Tower, Special Leaflet #2*, and then offered to assist Bradley in compiling a new edition.[49]

In the next few years, Barbara's pen friendship with Bradley waxed and waned as they exchanged book news. Determined to improve the quantity and quality of the first checklist's coverage, Barbara sent numerous titles and annotations for future updates. In fact, she mailed so many entries that when *Astra's Tower, Special Leaflet #3*, appeared in March 1959 it had skyrocketed to forty-three pages, but Bradley failed to name Gene Damon as a contributor. The following year when she issued a cumulative checklist, Bradley corrected the omission by acknowledging Gene Damon as "my collaborator and co-editor." Thrilled to contribute to both publications, Barbara nonetheless resented Bradley's lack of attention to detail, and hand-corrected her copies, while also adding such sarcastic comments as "Nuts" and "She's crazy, see Foster" in the margins.[50]

The Supreme Court decision in *Smith v. California* (1959), a case involving possession of "obscene" books, upheld the freedom of the press and, according to Bradley, contributed to a "flood of trash and borderline erotica" on the market. Referring to herself and Gene Damon as "completists," she assured readers of their 1960 checklist that they had waded through "all this newsstand slush…because experience has taught us that even the worst peddlers of commercialized sex-trash sometimes come up with exceptionally well-written, honest and sincere work." Still, they took care to warn readers of trash by labeling books with little or no redeeming value as "SCV" ("Short Course in Voyeurism").[51]

In the late 1950s and early 1960s, Bradley's original paperback novels began appearing under a variety of pseudonyms, and she devoted less time to bibliographic research. Hints of marital strain in Bradley's correspondence, evident as early as 1961, heightened Barbara's concern about the checklist's future. Because of this and because she believed Bradley vacillated "between accepting and rejecting the homosexual element in her personality," Barbara considered her co-editor unreliable. "I never know from one week to the next whether she is willing to continue the lists or not," she fretted to Martin in early 1962. Convinced the bibliography must continue because it filled such an important void, Barbara knew Helen would never permit her to take over the responsibility from Bradley because it meant too much contact with the outside world. If Bradley could not continue, Barbara noted, "I will try to interest Howard Frisch…in the project." The two had exchanged book news for several years, and she thought he could be persuaded to carry the project forward. As anticipated, Bradley published her last checklist in 1961, divorced her husband in 1964, and moved to Berkeley to pursue graduate study and a writing career. Barbara and Bradley continued to correspond about the possibility of another checklist as late as May 1964, but it never materialized.[52] Instead, Bradley found great success as an author in the fantasy genre.

* * *

In the 1950s and early 1960s, women who wanted to know more about lesbian sexuality, lesbian literature and lesbian lives had few constructive options. If they went to the library they could not find "lesbian" or "lesbian fiction" in the card catalog, only "homosexuality." Moreover, subject headings generally were not assigned to works of fiction until the 1980s. If the library owned books on sexual behavior, librarians often shelved them in a separate location due to the risk of theft and vandalism and sometimes to limit access to adult readers. Women might happen upon a lesbian pulp novel at the local newsstand or discover occasional articles about the medical treatment of homosexuality, but otherwise the topic proved elusive.

It was in this context that *The Ladder* gained national visibility. Readers, unable to find information anywhere else, started mailing their questions to its editorial offices. Del Martin and Phyllis Lyon attempted to respond, but theirs was a more direct form of activism, one that emphasized crusading for social recognition of the homosexual. In contrast, Barbara Grier believed in the power of literature to transform individual lives. Literature not only proved lesbians had always existed, but also that they had a rich and valuable history. Ultimately, Barbara's dedication to preserving and promoting this history carried her influence into a world far beyond Kansas City. In the fight for gay and lesbian civil rights, books became her activism and weapon of choice.

CHAPTER THREE

❧

The View from Kansas City

"Left alone with Helen and a very few friends (all by mail), I can give my entire energy to all Lesbians..."

–Barbara Grier, 1964[1]

As curious as Barbara Grier was about the gay and lesbian movement emerging in San Francisco, she declined Del Martin's 1961 invitation to visit Daughters of Bilitis headquarters because of her conviction that actual contact with lesbians would distract from her focus on lesbian literature. "I cannot pass an obvious girl on the street," she explained, "without being reduced to a blood pounding state of curiosity." As intrigued as she was by the personalities who engaged in DOB politics, Barbara concluded that it was best for her to remain in the relative isolation of Kansas City, where she could focus on her research and satisfy her curiosity about activities in the wider world through correspondence with a growing network of women and men.[2]

After Barbara left her paid work at day's end, she channeled her boundless energy and intense curiosity into literary and biographical research, all of it focused on ferreting out secrets from the lesbian past. Eager to share her discoveries with others, she decided to write a series of biographical essays to give readers of *The Ladder* a history they could point to with pride. Once Barbara chose a subject, she read every book and article available on the woman's life in order to compile evidence of her lesbianism, bisexuality or transvestitism. Helen Bennett encouraged Barbara's study of famous women because she considered library research safe.

When Barbara expressed an interest in consulting others for assistance with her research, Helen urged caution. Explaining that they needed to safeguard their privacy, she advised Barbara to limit her correspondence to just a few individuals: the current editor of *The Ladder*, selected book dealers, and Marion Zimmer Bradley. She justified reading all of Barbara's incoming and outgoing mail by stating they should have no secrets. Helen offered to let Barbara do likewise, but had such limited correspondence that there was virtually nothing to read. Barbara gave the appearance of complying with her partner's request, but had, in fact, discovered a way to send and receive letters without Helen's knowledge. Like traveling salesmen who lacked permanent addresses, she instructed correspondents to direct letters to her (or any of her pseudonyms) in care of General Delivery, Kansas City, Kansas. Since Helen did not monitor Barbara's visits to the post office, it was possible to retrieve and respond to them undetected.[3]

Barbara Gittings and the DOB

One day in the fall of 1958, Del Martin forwarded a Gene Damon fan letter to Barbara's home address. An East Coast DOB member named Barbara Gittings wanted to correspond with Gene Damon about lesbian books, and Martin vouched for her credibility. Keenly aware that Helen barely tolerated her current level of contact with the outside world, Barbara replied immediately to Martin, saying she was too busy to undertake any new correspondence. As soon as she arrived at work the next morning, however, she wrote Gittings, explained the situation and said they could write if Gittings used General Delivery. Unfazed by the request, Gittings struck up a correspondence with Barbara in care of the "birdcage," as she liked to call it. After an initial flurry, the pen friendship faded because Gittings realized her new correspondent was "a mad mad bookworm" with little interest in discussing other topics.[4]

A year older than Barbara, Gittings had begun exploring her sexuality during her freshman year at Northwestern University in the early 1950s. Like many others of her generation, she went to the library "to find out what it meant to be a homosexual," and she spent so much time researching the topic that she flunked out of college. She did not recognize herself in the tomes on sexual deviance she consulted, and after returning to her family in Delaware, the inquisitive young woman began reading novels known to have lesbian characters or themes. One day Gittings's father discovered *The Well of Loneliness* in her room, denounced it as immoral, and insisted she burn it. Instead, she took greater care in hiding the book, acquired additional titles and decided to move to Philadelphia.[5]

Gittings often took the train to New York City, where she attempted to use books as vehicles for connecting with other lesbians. When combing through Manhattan's used bookstores, Gittings found Donald Webster Cory's *The Homosexual in America* and was delighted to learn that the author, whose real name was Edward Sagarin, lived in New York City. When they met, Sagarin told her about two homosexual organizations on the West Coast: ONE, Inc., and the Mattachine Society. Eager to learn more, Gittings traveled west in the summer of 1956, attended their meetings, and learned about the recently established Daughters of Bilitis. Her visit to San Francisco coincided with a DOB meeting, where she met DOB president Del Martin. Impressed with Gittings's enthusiasm and initiative, Martin encouraged her to organize a DOB chapter on the East Coast.[6] Fewer than a dozen women attended the first meeting of the New York chapter of the DOB in September 1958. Energetic and zealous, Gittings became the New York DOB's founding president and first editor of a newsletter she produced each month by using her employer's equipment and supplies after hours and without permission.[7]

As a chapter of the national organization, the New York DOB was expected to embrace the DOB's four purposes, which appeared on the inside front cover of each issue of *The Ladder* and never mentioned the word "lesbian." They included: 1) "Education of the variant," 2) "Education of the public," 3) "Participation in research projects," and 4) "Investigation of the penal code as it pertains to the homosexual…" In the pre-feminist 1950s and early 1960s, many members accepted the DOB's admonition that the lesbian needed to assimilate even if it meant adopting "a mode of behavior and dress acceptable to society." Some within the New York chapter disagreed, however, and business meetings often became bogged down in "rambunctious discussion of the butch-femme angle of Lesbianism."[8]

Separated from DOB headquarters by several thousand miles, Gittings and members of the New York chapter found themselves increasingly at odds with the national leadership's priorities. Gittings boldly challenged the national's adherence to an agenda forged in the mid-1950s and charged that a disproportionate amount of chapter dues funded San Francisco-based initiatives. Pointing to the emergence of chapters in New York, Los Angeles and Chicago, she argued that it was time for national leaders to develop "an atmosphere in which members and chapters outside the city of origin [San Francisco] could creatively work for the *goals* [emphasis added] of the organization," not the maintenance of a remote national office.[9]

DOB Politics

The DOB became increasingly visible in the early 1960s. When officers convened the first national assembly in San Francisco in 1960, most attendees came from the surrounding area. Two years later when Gittings traveled to Hollywood, California, for the DOB's second national meeting, approximately one hundred participants listened attentively as legal, medical, religious and mental health experts explored the conference theme, "Potentials: The Lesbian in Society." Members also discussed mass media portrayals of lesbians, and watched with pride when "Terry," the president-elect of the Los Angeles chapter, was interviewed by Paul V. Coates for his nationally syndicated tabloid-style television program, *Confidential File*.[10]

To outsiders, the organization appeared successful and flourishing, yet those who attended the business meeting realized that DOB faced several serious challenges. Jaye Bell, who had succeeded Martin as DOB president in 1960, informed participants that membership fees and donations failed to generate enough income to keep the organization from operating in the red. Part of the problem stemmed from *The Ladder*. Many lesbians who lived beyond the reach of a DOB chapter subscribed to the magazine but did not join the organization. With subscriptions far outpacing DOB membership, the society struggled to cover the costs of paper, printing, and postage. Additionally, most of the volunteers who typed, proofread and mailed the monthly publication were members of the San Francisco chapter. Over time, some had grown weary of the responsibility and drifted away, leaving the remaining volunteers overworked.[11]

After she stepped down as DOB president in 1960, Martin assumed the role of *Ladder* editor, though it had never been her top priority. Taking a laissez-faire approach to the position while looking for someone to succeed her, she assembled whatever material readers contributed along with items she wanted to insert. "I was just biding my time," she explained, "until we found another one."[12] By the national meeting's end, no one had stepped forward to take Martin's place. Frustrated, yet unwilling to let the magazine die, she agreed to continue with the aid of two assistant editors, known by the pseudonyms Marty Elliott and Agatha Mathys. As fall yielded to winter, Martin grew impatient with continuing lack of interest in the position. "Has the magazine lost its importance to the organization?" she pondered. "Is the voice of the homophile press to be left entirely to the masculine-oriented publications?" Responding to Martin's plea, Barbara Gittings became editor in March 1963. For the next three-and-one-half years she worked diligently to transform *The Ladder* into a professional publication that would attract "thinking people" to the DOB.[13]

From her home in Kansas City, Barbara Grier sensed some of the tensions developing within the DOB, but she remained intently focused on her quest to discover and collect gay and lesbian literature. Using the persona of Gene Damon for virtually all her correspondence, she focused on constructing her reputation as a literary expert by writing monthly "Lesbiana" columns, occasional stand-alone reviews and an annual review of lesbian literature for *The Ladder*. Barbara did not limit herself to lesbian literature, but also read and critiqued gay male novels. Her essays and reviews began appearing in *Mattachine Review* in 1962, and in 1963 she had a regular column titled "Literary Scene." Given that magazine's predominantly male readership, the column offered readers an informal overview of fiction and nonfiction books "on themes of sex variation." She knew the magazine's editor, Harold "Hal" Call, from his years of working for *The Kansas City Star*.[14]

When Barbara Gittings became editor of *The Ladder* in early 1963, Martin assured her she would have no problem finding enough material to fill its pages because Gene Damon had volunteered "to do research work on any article you may wish to assign." Shifting allegiance from Martin to Gittings, Barbara informed the new editor that her predecessor had been "overly casual." Elaborating, she explained: "Really that is the 'flaw' of the whole organization—no organization—no one willing or able to perform efficiently or keep records." Barbara enthusiastically approved of Gittings's plan to develop *The Ladder* into a high-quality magazine as long as she preserved "its appeal and importance to the lonely subscriber in Mudville!"[15]

Barbara began to have second thoughts after Gittings began implementing her plans. During the first six months of the new editor's reign, Gittings published virtually none of Barbara's contributions and returned a large number of the unused stories and articles. Seeking to improve quality as well as appearance, Gittings explained to Martin that she planned to run "a tight ship." More formally educated than Barbara, Gittings was a perfectionist in grammar, spelling, word usage, construction and coherence. Such details, she insisted, were "absolutely essential to the reputation and the intellectual level of the magazine."[16] Barbara, notorious for grammatical errors and misspellings, resented the implication that her work lacked quality, yet she also wanted to see *The Ladder* grow stronger.

Gittings's attitude toward Barbara softened after she and partner Kay Tobin Lahusen, who also worked diligently on *The Ladder*, stopped in Kansas City on their way to DOB headquarters in San Francisco in the summer of 1963. After talking with Barbara face-to-face and seeing her private library, Gittings left town with a much deeper appreciation for her commitment to the cause and her vast network of connections. From that point forward, Gittings cultivated Barbara as an ally, seeking advice and confiding in her. She further ingratiated herself by suggesting that *The Ladder* feature a picture of Gene Damon on the cover of an upcoming issue. Quickly discouraging the plan, Barbara explained: "I'm a ham & would love to get part of me on the cover of THE LADDER but Helen would have 30 kittens." It was one thing for Gene Damon to contribute to the publication, but it would never do for Kansas City residents to see Barbara Grier's picture featured on the cover of a lesbian magazine at their local newsstand. To placate Gittings, Barbara sent two hand-drawn images of women's heads and expressed pleasure and surprise when one of them appeared on the November cover credited to Cricket. Barbara playfully signed her next letter "Chirp Chirp to you and Kay from the largest domestic cricket in the U.S."[17]

Encouraged by Gittings's publication of several of her pieces in the October and November issues, Barbara resumed flooding *The Ladder*'s editor with articles and reviews. Gittings gave her three full pages for "Lesbiana" in the November issue, but it failed to make a dent in Gene Damon's backlog of unpublished reviews. When Barbara's other unpublished work once again accumulated, she matter-of-factly asked Gittings to return everything for which she had no use because she wanted to place it elsewhere. "I'll bug the hell out of you until you do—remember that for me everything is NOW not later."[18]

In her determination to formalize and systematize the production of *The Ladder*, Gittings soon found herself in conflict with DOB president Jaye Bell and other officers. Three thousand miles removed from her production staff, Gittings sent frequent, minutely detailed instructions and admonishments. According to the editor, the San Francisco volunteers failed to forward reader mail and manuscripts submitted for publication. Other flaws included poor typing and proofreading, and monthly issues often mailed late. To resolve the problem, Gittings proposed they develop a schedule and conduct their business in writing rather than by phone calls so there would be a written record of transactions. Tensions between the San Francisco and New York locales escalated, and Bell, distressed by the "personal disputes causing disruption within the organization," resigned in November 1963. By year's end, Cleo Bonner (who used the pseudonym Cleo Glenn in *The Ladder*) became the DOB's first African-American president. A dedicated worker, she also retained her responsibilities as circulation manager and unofficially managed the national office. Barbara, impressed with the new president's work ethic, pronounced Cleo Glenn a "fireball."[19]

Content Clashes

After assuming the editorship in 1963, Gittings repeatedly tested the limits of DOB's authority by challenging the organization's stand on issues related to *The Ladder*. From its beginning, the word *lesbian* had not appeared on the magazine's cover, and the only clue to its content was contained in small print: "For Sale to Adults Only." In a quietly subversive act, Gittings initiated the practice of listing a feature story's title on the cover, one that included the word lesbian. She began with the September 1963 issue, which asked "Why Is a Lesbian?" and continued until March of the following year, when she changed the magazine's name to *The Ladder: A Lesbian Review*. Reader letters, at least the ones Gittings chose to publish, pronounced the cover "superb, elite, refined," and applauded the subtitle as a "forthright addition."[20] While DOB officers acquiesced to the change, they blocked Gittings's plans to remove "For Sale to Adults Only" by citing California law. When Gittings omitted it from the October and December 1963 issues, Glenn bought a rubber stamp with those words and added it to all copies mailed to readers in her state. Gittings also clashed with the national office on the inclusion of the DOB statement of purpose in each issue, which, since *The Ladder*'s inception in 1956, had consumed a full page. In April 1964, Gittings prompted further irritation when she boldly condensed the statement from twenty-four to thirteen lines.

Tempers continued to flare as DOB members discussed the Baker Memorial Scholarship. In 1962, Del Martin had been instrumental in establishing a scholarship in memory of Blanche M. Baker, a San Francisco psychologist and advocate for gay and lesbian mental health. In August 1963, Gittings attacked Martin's plan by publishing a letter from Gene Damon in which she argued that creating a few small scholarships was an example of "creating a way to fly before we learn to walk." The DOB, she continued, would have a greater impact if it invested money in "making *The Ladder* a stronger and progressively more powerful propaganda tool." In addition to reaching women from all walks of life, she continued, attorneys, educators, and physicians could use the magazine to influence public opinion. The following December, Barbara exploded when she opened her copy of *The Ladder* and discovered that a full page of her "Lesbiana" column had been removed to make space for a Baker Memorial Scholarship fund appeal. Unaware that Martin had made the cut when the San Francisco chapter pasted up the issue, Barbara accused Gittings of cutting her review and demanded to know if it was "divine retribution for my criticism?"[21]

After pondering the situation, Gittings decided she could use Barbara's anger to her advantage. Informing Barbara that she and Kay had "a sweet, dirty little scheme up our sleeves," she proposed that "Contentious Grier will ride again—and we have the very vehicle!"[22] When Gittings and Lahusen briefed Barbara by phone, they told her they wanted to change the DOB's name and to challenge several pet projects, among them the scholarship fund and the DOB Book Service, founded in 1960 as a mail-order book service to serve the needs of women who lacked convenient and affordable access to lesbian books. From Gittings's vantage point, it appeared Del Martin was using her influence to have friends' books selected for distribution by the book service and then arranging positive reviews in *The Ladder*. Jess Stearn's latest book, *The Grapevine*, was a prime example.[23]

In 1964 many Americans were talking about *The Grapevine*, a best-selling journalistic exposé of the lesbian's secret life. Stearn's book, which allegedly explained why women gravitated to a "world of unnatural lust," resonated with homophobic Cold War-era readers. Lesbian critics of the book objected to its portrayal of them as an invisible threat to American society, but Martin was pleased that the author had included some discussion of *The Ladder* and the Daughters of Bilitis. Appalled by Martin's endorsement of the book, Gittings fumed: "That review was an absolute fraud, a prostitution of our position for the sake of selling the book thru the book service…Her standards are simply different and actually we disagree with her almost across the board on political matters as well."[24]

Barbara concurred, pronouncing *The Grapevine* "a crass journalistic paste-up" in her annual review of lesbian literature. When Gittings urged her to attend the upcoming DOB convention to voice objections to Martin's actions, however, the reclusive Barbara refused. "It looks like you are looking for a 'Patsy,' a role I do not feel like playing." Elaborating, she reminded Gittings of her preference for solitude. "If a DOB convention took place in my backyard I'd leave town…I'm an orator but only back here behind my pen." Aware that her social reclusiveness was an alien concept to some, Barbara continued: "I don't know how to explain this to you without sounding nutty. My love—my work and books all stem from isolation…Left alone with Helen and a very few friends (all by mail), I can give my entire energy to all Lesbians—Added to a group…you'd destroy me inside & you'd lose what I can & do give."[25]

Undaunted, Gittings found other ways to engage Barbara in the work of the DOB. As editor of *The Ladder*, she had become overwhelmed by letters from readers. Who better to respond to book queries, she implored, than Gene Damon? Barbara proved to be such a good correspondent that Gittings proposed she become the DOB's corresponding secretary. "You are one of the few people, if not the only person, we'd trust with the job. Who else can write?" Not surprisingly, Barbara declined, citing her full-time job, the research and writing she already did for the checklists she co-edited with Marion Zimmer Bradley, and the hours needed to prepare her monthly *Mattachine Review* column. She also wanted to avoid the "internecine warfare." "I loathe disorganization," she explained. "DOB should have its name changed from Daughters of Bilitis to Sisters of Bedlam." Perhaps most important, Helen was "horribly upset" by the prospect. "I wait for the day she sets me and the cat & the books out on the porch," Barbara lamented. "She doesn't approve—you know—of any of this and barely tolerates the parts I do, i.e., the books."[26]

Gittings continued her quest to professionalize *The Ladder* while relying heavily on Barbara's contributions to fill its pages. Lest the quantity of items published go to Barbara's head (eleven items appeared in the first three issues of the year), Gittings ruthlessly exercised her editorial pen. In addition to correcting typos and grammar, she edited reviews for content and, on some occasions, removed passages that altered Barbara's intent. Tension escalated when Gittings and Lahusen questioned the validity of some titles Barbara included in her annual review of lesbian literature, calling them trash. The editor was especially incensed by "the favorable squib" Barbara had given W. D. Sprague's *The Lesbian in Our Society* in her January 1964 "Lesbiana" column. The book, available to DOB members through the DOB Book Service, and published by Midwood Tower, featured a naked woman on the cover and described "the third sex" as "a problem that must be faced!" Barbara had been reviewing Midwood Tower books for some time, but Gittings's awareness of the company increased after Cleo Glenn sold them a full-page ad in *The Ladder* for just twenty-one dollars. Arguing that it should have cost more than a hundred twenty-five dollars, Gittings exploded: "THE LADDER is already providing Midwood Tower with tremendous free advertising, especially through the LESBIANA column." One way to strike back—at DOB and at Midwood—was to ask Barbara to remove the trash. "She'll squawk right back," Gittings explained to Florence "Conrad" Jaffy, DOB's research director. "*She's* not intimidated by my aura of intellect or class or whatever it is and so we often disagree yet work together well."[27]

As predicted, Barbara went on the defensive and threatened to take her work elsewhere. Everything she wrote for *The Ladder*, she explained, bored her to death except the reviews and biographical or historical pieces. "I do it because I care about DOB & the magazine. If you choke off the yearly list (my lollipop) I'll throw my ball & jacks at you." The editor could, she allowed, "cut the hell out of anything but leave my yearly list alone—please, please, please."[28] What Gittings failed to appreciate was Barbara's dedication to validating every book with lesbian content. She recognized readers came from all walks of life and read for many different reasons: self-improvement, self-understanding, escape. Without fully recognizing the significance of her actions, Barbara was contesting the power of mainstream literary critics. As she knew from personal experience and from the many women who wrote to her, any book that helped a lesbian recognize herself in print was worthy of recognition and preservation.

Undaunted by Barbara's bluster, Gittings pushed for more change. She insisted Barbara replace the trash books in her annual review of lesbian literature with reviews of quality nonfiction. When Barbara explained she barely had enough time to read the fiction, let alone tackle the nonfiction, Gittings suggested Florence Jaffy could become her co-compiler. Jaffy, however, had no interest in taking on the assignment. Turning from reviews to Barbara's biographical essays, Gittings challenged Barbara's identification of several literary and historical figures as closeted lesbians, arguing there were loopholes in the proof. Angered to have her scholarship impugned, Barbara proclaimed: "I am a self-appointed expert, but if you know of any university giving PhDs in Lesbian Literature and History, bet I'll earn the first one."[29]

Barbara, Gittings and Lahusen shared a mutual desire to see *The Ladder* grow and evolve into a high-quality publication, and their shared frustration with the San Francisco production office united them despite differences in style, priorities and methods. Gittings's arguments with the DOB officers in San Francisco reinforced Barbara's conviction that she wanted nothing to do with organizational politics. After someone erroneously mislabeled her "Lesbiana" column, Barbara wanted nothing more than to "write a bitch letter to S[an] F[rancisco]," but restrained herself because she thought Gittings could use her "best and most effectively as a silent partner."[30]

The 1964 DOB Meeting, New York City

As the New York chapter moved forward with plans to host the annual convention in June 1964, Gittings remained confrontational. Meanwhile DOB president Cleo Glenn, along with Joan Oliver, *The Ladder*'s production manager, remained silent to "avoid the verbal battle" they knew would ensue. Working in a vacuum, Gittings responded with more efforts to micromanage. By May, she informed Barbara, she fully expected to "be under some real fire," and possibly even dismissed as editor of *The Ladder*. She seemingly had forgotten how difficult it had been to find an editor when Del Martin stepped down from that position.[31]

Barbara had no interest in attending the national meeting in New York, instead experiencing it vicariously through Jeannette Howard Foster's colorful descriptive summaries of leading figures in attendance. Though Barbara knew them only through correspondence, she sensed the "power & fire" of Del Martin and the "charm & light" of Phyllis Lyon. Based on Foster's impressions, Barbara advised Gittings to stop fighting Martin and her San Francisco acolytes because the "'power and the glory' is still in her paws as far as that Goddamned mickey mouse [*sic*] called politics is concerned." Above all, she urged, Gittings should avoid dividing and destroying the DOB because it would kill the magazine that served as the lifeblood for Barbara and thousands of lesbians throughout the country.[32]

Upon learning of Foster's impressions, Gittings informed Barbara that the elderly woman had seen the convention "through romantic haze." If Barbara exchanged places with her and was "forced to deal with these prejudiced and frumpy thinkers," she would think differently. The vote on condensing the DOB's statement of purpose, Gittings elaborated, confirmed her belief that the majority of members were satisfied with the status quo. Thirty-six voted in support of Gittings's decision to condense the statement while thirty-seven wanted to retain the original document in its entirety. Contending that DOB co-founder Martin had created an atmosphere that stifled the magazine and the organization, Gittings argued Martin was "still geared to thinking largely in terms of the poor little bar-fly who's going to learn to wear a skirt and climb the ladder and be forever grateful to Den Mother Del."[33] Yet times had changed, and unless the DOB developed new leadership and modernized, Gittings predicted it would have nothing to offer the next generation.

In her eagerness to preserve *The Ladder*, Barbara urged Gittings to stay out of the politics and focus on the magazine. "My God—you've really improved it worlds, isn't that enough?" Going a step further, Barbara likened professional lesbians to dictators: "A good 75% of the bright Lesbians are didactic power hungry anti-social dictators crossed with a mild touch of sadism…the other 25% are passive hostiles." Consequently, it was silly for Gittings to waste her energy on politics when she could serve countless others who depended upon *The Ladder*'s message, indeed its very existence. "We can't sweat too much blood over smoke-filled tables," Barbara urged, "and have energy for the rest, and the rest is the most."[34]

Determined to pursue her goal of producing a more sophisticated, high-quality magazine for lesbians, Gittings remained a strident critic of DOB leaders. Until her editorship, she contended, *The Ladder* had never reached more than a small audience because its editors were distracted by their pursuit of multiple activities. Gittings felt compelled to micromanage many aspects of the magazine's publication because geographic distance from the site of production and dependence on volunteers contributed to numerous miscommunications. DOB president Glenn, along with Martin and Lyon, viewed Gittings's failure to meet deadlines as an opportunity to oust the contentious editor.[35]

The 1966 National Planning Conference, Kansas City

Barbara's personal and activist worlds began to collide when the National Planning Conference of Homophile Organizations scheduled an organizational meeting in Kansas City for February 19-20, 1966. California activist Harold "Hal" Call, who knew Gene Damon was in reality Barbara Grier, assumed she would handle local arrangements and listed her real name and address on a mimeographed flyer sent to potential attendees. They included representatives from fifteen homophile organizations across the United States. When gay men began writing her home address with requests for hotel reservations, Barbara flew into a panic. She knew if Helen found out, "I would be put out PDQ—because after all this is her address too." In keeping with her goal of remaining low-profile, Barbara entertained Gittings and Lahusen at her apartment while Helen was at work, and attended the conference just long enough on Saturday morning to meet individuals she had only known through correspondence, among them Del Martin, Phyllis Lyon, Harold Call, Don Slater (founder of *ONE* magazine), and gay rights activist Frank Kameny. Years later, Martin recalled the encounter as her first attempt to "pawn" the editorship of *The Ladder* off on Barbara.[36]

As much as Barbara admired Kameny, who had been dismissed from the U.S. Army Map Service in 1957 because of his homosexuality, she abhorred his advocacy of picketing. A Midwestern Republican in the 1950s and 1960s, Barbara had been unnerved by the anti-war protests and race riots rocking the nation in the late 1960s. Picketing, she argued, lacked dignity, lowered the image of the homosexual in the public eye, and "went a hell of a long way toward destroying the image I have carefully built." Also influenced by Helen's conservatism, her preferred strategy for gaining gay rights was to live a life beyond reproach, and to show that gays and lesbians were superior individuals. When Kameny defended his method, Barbara conceded "it will no doubt get you the law reform you want" but warned that doing this "will set back the social progress of the homosexuals another 100 years."[37]

Barbara's negative view of picketing did not waver, whether the protestors contested the war in Vietnam or fought for civil rights. "I fear them because of the mob instinct that rules them," she told Kameny. "Dictators have used them…They get out of hand and defeat themselves…but sometimes they defeat everyone." Gittings attributed Barbara's objections to class differences, convinced that she and other white-collar reformers objected to picketing because they were middle-class and associated perceived picketing as a tool employed by less privileged members of society.[38]

As meeting minutes confirm, National Planning Conference attendees modeled themselves on the East Coast Homophile Organizations, which had formed in 1963 to link the activism of homophiles in New York City, Philadelphia, and Washington, D.C. Bringing gay men and lesbians together from approximately fourteen groups, the NPC strived to determine "our movement's basic goals, to agree on our ideology, and to plan the strategies for achieving our aims." From the outset, leaders such as Martin and Lyon questioned the organization's ability to address the needs of lesbians. More fundamentally, Barbara questioned the value of amalgamation. "When we have amalgamated and absorbed and homogenized and pasteurized ourselves thoroughly, we can become one of the shapeless, formless, meaningless 'walk alike, talk alike, think alike' things which now live in this country—and then who will write our poetry, our novels of INTENSITY, who will burn at futile fires, howl at moons aimlessly??"[39]

The North American Conference of Homophile Organizations emerged from the Kansas City planning meeting and scheduled its first official meeting in the summer of 1966. Concerned women's issues would be buried, newly elected DOB president Shirley Willer made a feminist-tinged plea urging delegates to recognize that "the problems of the male homosexual and the female homosexual differ considerably." Women, she argued, seldom faced police harassment and arrest for "solicitation, wash-room sex or transsexual attire." The most significant issue, she declared, was that "the Lesbian is discriminated against not only because she is a Lesbian, but because she is a woman." In contrast, Gittings strenuously objected to such rhetoric. As someone who had thrown her full support to Frank Kameny and NACHO, she thought it "stupid for Shirley Willer to imply that job problems, family problems and such are problems peculiar to the lesbian which the male homosexual doesn't have."[40] While Barbara cared about these issues, her brief participation in the NACHO meeting had affirmed what she knew all along: her forte lay in print activism, not organizational politics.

Extending the Reach

As Gittings, Willer and others became more and more embroiled in DOB politics, Barbara focused on building Gene Damon's reputation and extending her influence. When readers picked up issues of DOB chapter newsletters, *Drum*, the *Janus Society Newsletter*, *Mattachine Review* and *The Ladder*, they found reviews and letters written by Gene Damon. In late 1963, Barbara learned about the establishment of the Minorities Research Group, the first organization in the United Kingdom openly devoted to the interests of lesbians. With its emphasis on research and dissemination of information, MRG announced its intent to publish that nation's first lesbian magazine, *Arena Three*. Upon learning the news, Barbara sent an enthusiastic airmail letter to *Arena Three* editor Esme Langley expressing her delight. She also was thrilled to learn the inaugural issue would include an article about Irish-born Iris Murdock, a writer Barbara had sensed was lesbian. In return correspondence, Langley expressed eagerness to have an American contributor to the magazine and suggested Barbara write something for an upcoming issue.[41]

In her capacity as editor of *The Ladder*, Gittings exchanged ideas with Langley even as she closely scrutinized her counterpart's publication. "THE LADDER is no longer the only Lesbian magazine in the English-speaking world," she informed DOB's Glenn. "We're going to be up against some bright competition."[42] Gittings wanted Barbara to write for *Arena Three* instead of reviewing gay male books for the *Janus Society Newsletter*. Urging her to stop "feeding the enemy," Gittings argued *Arena Three* "deserves you *more*. Look, you have no idea what it takes to start a magazine…Esme is working hard on a dozen fronts at least." In short order, Barbara struck up a correspondence with Langley as well as with *Arena Three*'s literary editor, Clare Barringer.[43]

"Barringer" was in reality Pamela Rust, a magazine copy editor for the British edition of *Readers Digest*. She cautiously expressed willingness to exchange book news with the American, but nothing on the scale Barbara envisioned. "I cannot get too deeply involved in this operation. It fascinates me, but I will not take on what I cannot properly do." Her measured response provided all the encouragement Barbara needed, and she set out to cultivate her new contact by mailing complimentary copies of the checklists. Gene Damon's first review appeared in *Arena*

Three in June 1964, and by September she had become known as "Our American contributor." Her work appeared there off and on throughout the next four years, enhancing her reputation as a lesbian literary critic and expanding her network of contacts in the English-speaking world.[44]

CHAPTER FOUR

Paper Romances and Pen Friendships

"...the pen is a devilish weapon. Intellectual seduction is far more insidious than any other kind."

–Barbara Grier, 1977[1]

"If I look too closely at the past 6 years of my life," Barbara Grier wrote in June 1965, "I can see the minutes or days when I moved away from the path I set for myself." When she first went away to Denver with Helen Bennett in the fall of 1952, Barbara "did not balk at all at the ways in which the relationship was firmed up." Indeed, by decade's end, she was touting her lesbian relationship to readers of *The Ladder* as equal to any heterosexual marriage, a monogamous lifetime commitment. Thus, any deviation from her ideal constituted more than personal failure. Locked into this stereotyped view of relationships, she dedicated herself to serving as living propaganda for lesbianism. By the mid-1960s, however, she admitted to herself that something was missing. She still loved Helen and enjoyed being with her, but knew "it is possible to have 101 reasons to be happy and contented and only tiny ones not to be and suddenly have them blow up into enormous mushrooms of discontent."[2]

Years of living with an intensely private and controlling woman left Barbara hungry for contact with other lesbians. Threatened by her partner's desire to have other friends, Helen could only find one possible interpretation for it, and that was infidelity. Barbara, who admitted there was "a sexual basis" behind her craving, revealed a polarized view of lesbians as respectable or wild when she acknowledged she "would have been a veritable hell on wheels, dyke type" had it not been for Helen.[3] Their regimen of strict routines, constant work and self-imposed rules had curbed, but not eliminated, Barbara's impulses. Involvement with *The Ladder* expanded her awareness of the world outside Kansas City, soon whetting her appetite to make other friends, even if they existed only on paper.

Each year dozens of women wrote to Gene Damon because she was one of the most visible and responsive lesbians writing for *The Ladder*. Their letters touched a chord in Barbara, who remembered the years she had spent feeling alienated and lonely. "In a world of atomic blasts, and a shake-up in enemy land," their yearning for validation reminded her of "the gasp of a million waterless fish." Barbara could not let a form letter suffice as her response. Patiently and thoroughly, she answered their questions and encouraged them to share their dreams and fears. Touched by their confidence, Barbara wished she had the ability to "send one 'instant girl' to every one of them" because she believed "loneliness kills, and so many of them die inside without love." Though Barbara believed herself "quite immune to the dangers of pity," she began questioning her ability to remain neutral when one of her lonely correspondents "got into a real pickle."[4]

Barbara's frankness and her tendency toward flirtatiousness sometimes yielded unintended consequences. The frequency of her letters and the thoroughness with which she responded led some correspondents to think she cared about them romantically when, in fact, she merely wanted to alleviate loneliness and promote self-acceptance. At ease when discussing sexual topics and having read widely on the subject, she offered clinical details about orgasms while urging women to view sexual expression as healthy, something to celebrate and enjoy. "[I]t really bugs me," she informed one correspondent, "to think of any woman who is not freely sexually happy...it never bothers me to realize that lots of straight women aren't happy, how in hell could they be...but Lesbians...no, that is a no no." Succumbing to the freedom of the typed page, Barbara occasionally suggested she would help a woman discover her sexual potential, if only the two lived in closer proximity. A few women took her declaration seriously and traveled to Kansas City for an encounter. Ill-equipped to handle anyone who became overly dependent on her for their emotional health, Barbara responded with silence and rudeness. "I feel guilty," she explained to *Ladder* editor Barbara Gittings, "but I cannot carry the weight of all of them on my all too vulnerable back."[5]

Evelyn Mancini

In August 1961, a Florida woman who recently had come out to herself as a lesbian wrote to the Daughters of Bilitis for information. Confiding that "I feel a little like the prodigal child who has come home at last after years of desertion," Evelyn M. fretted that others in the "Twilight World" might consider her a pariah since she was married and had several children. After fourteen months and one hundred twenty hours in counseling at a family guidance clinic, her counselor threw up his hands and gave her *The Ladder*'s address. Del Martin responded to her initial letter but forwarded a subsequent inquiry to Barbara, who responded in the guise of Gene Damon.[6]

Like many lesbians of her generation, Evelyn M. felt isolated and lonely. Responding to Gene Damon's concern and questions, she relaxed and poured out her life story. "She is a very nice person," Barbara informed Martin, "and I feel very sorry for her."[7] Evelyn M. had acknowledged her lesbianism during her youth, but conformed to societal expectations by suppressing that aspect of her identity and marrying. Years later she summoned the courage to subscribe to *The Ladder*, but burned every issue after reading it because she could not risk her children discovering the magazine and telling their father.

Barbara proved to be an ideal correspondent for Evelyn M., who finally revealed that her surname was Mancini. Compulsively checking her post office box daily, she responded to the married woman's letters immediately upon receipt. The frequency and empathy with which she wrote encouraged further sharing of hopes and dreams, and heightened the two women's sense of connection. When Barbara learned Mancini yearned to become a writer, she offered to read and critique her stories. Pronouncing "A Sunday Kind of Love" "terrific," Barbara encouraged her to submit it to *The Ladder* for publication. The semiautobiographical story, which appeared in the May 1963 issue, featured a woman struggling to choose between her male suitor and a female friend. At the end, she confidently declares: "I know what I am now! I know what I want! Don't make me wait any longer!"[8]

In Barbara's mind, paper romances could not be equated to physical infidelity. Even as she flirted with Mancini on paper, she editorialized in *The Ladder* about "this business of near infidelity" that seemed to characterize lesbian relationships. The public had such a "hideous stereotype" of lesbians because of their reputation for "the short marriage, quick divorce, quick re-marriage syndrome." Viewing the world in black and white with no shades of gray, Barbara pronounced such behavior "simply not right, not moral, not even sensible" because it implied "a lack of self-discipline." Lesbians, she declared to Del Martin, needed to accept adult responsibilities and restrictions. "What they all too blithely ignore," she elaborated, "is that this 'big excitement' this, to put it bluntly, 'itching clitoris,' is just what happens in between those dark moments of blubbering despair."[9]

Encouraged by the warm and caring tone in her pen friend's letters, Mancini eventually summoned the courage to leave her husband and start a new life. Stunned by the news, Barbara blamed herself for playing a role in the breakup. She cared about Mancini, but had no intention of leaving Helen because of a paper flirtation. Her only recourse, it seemed, was to let the correspondence cease. Several years later Barbara learned Mancini had become a teacher and had a book accepted for publication. "She says," Barbara explained with relief to her new pen friend, Jane Rule, that "I was the catalyst."[10]

Jane Rule

When Barbara read a review of Jane Rule's *Desert of the Heart* in the spring of 1964, she knew immediately that the Canadian novelist was "a true blue queer" and sent her a fan letter. Writing as Gene Damon, she praised Rule for her courage in writing openly about lesbianism, for her "return to the 'romantic' era," and for writing "perhaps the only serious fictional study of Lesbianism" since Patricia Highsmith's *The Price of Salt* (1952).[11]

Based on their initial correspondence, Barbara concluded Rule failed to comprehend the significance of her book because she lacked knowledge of the history of lesbian literature. Determined to provide her new pen friend with a crash course in lesbian literature, she mailed Rule a copy of Foster's *Sex Variant Women in Literature* and the checklists compiled with Marion Zimmer Bradley. Rule responded with admiration for her new correspondent's knowledge of the subject, but confessed she lacked the patience or motivation "to read as you do through miles of junk so that I can find several books which are worth reading."[12]

Rule's subsequent response inaugurated an almost weekly correspondence between the two obsessive letter writers as they discussed favorite books and authors. Barbara's insatiable curiosity compelled her to learn all she could about her new pen friend. Certain most novelists based their fiction on life experience, she tracked down every short story Rule had ever published and read them carefully for details. Discouraging Barbara's tendency to view her writing as autobiographical, Rule declared, "I am neither Ann nor Evelyn. I am not Silver, though I share her height. I invent them all for my purposes, let readers use them for theirs."[13]

When the Canadian mentioned the possibility of meeting later in the summer when she was in the States attending to some family matters, Barbara went into a tailspin. It would be impossible to entertain Rule and her traveling companion, Helen Sonthoff, at home because she could not allow her two worlds to collide. "[F]or some years," Barbara informed Rule, "my roommate has taken the position that 'outside contact' is dangerous, regardless of the individual, and for this reason we see no one socially with so little exception that it is hardly worth remarking."[14] Unwilling to forgo an encounter with the author, Barbara provided careful instructions about days and times they could meet, along with phone numbers where Rule could leave messages. Intrigued by the cloak-and-dagger nature of Barbara's response, Rule and Sonthoff made arrangements to meet her at the Cock and Bull Steakhouse in Kansas City, Missouri.

On the evening of August 20, 1964, an awestruck Barbara met the woman who was to become a trusted friend and advisor. Approximately six feet tall, Rule held herself with confidence and exuded charisma. In stark contrast to Barbara, the New Jersey native grew up in a privileged family, attended private schools and the all-female Mills College, and toured Europe. She met Sonthoff, who became her life partner, while teaching in Massachusetts at the Concord Academy. Disturbed by the political climate of the 1950s, and especially by McCarthyism, the two women immigrated to Vancouver, Canada, where both found teaching positions at the University of British Columbia.[15]

Barbara seldom drank more than a beer or two, but on that August evening she spent five alcohol-soaked hours savoring Rule's company and her cosmopolitan worldview. Rule and Sonthoff dropped an inebriated Barbara off near her apartment, but only after she had concocted an elaborate excuse for Helen. At the time, Rule wondered why Barbara felt the need to be so secretive and wished that she felt comfortable enough in her relationship with Helen to express her need to socialize with other people.[16]

The rapport Barbara and Rule established over dinner became the foundation for a deeply intimate and at times brutally honest friendship that challenged Barbara's provincial views, expanded her horizons and served as a touchstone in the years to come. Struggling with the uncertainty rooted in her chaotic childhood and uneven education, Barbara initially spent hours researching, drafting and rewriting each letter. In October 1964, she finally conceded: "I am incapable of apostolic prose and cannot compete with your mind." Fortunately, Rule refused to be placed on a pedestal. "I am not superior, either in fact or in attitude," she clarified, "and I refuse to let the fact that I have written a book you care about turn me into someone who must be particularly challenged or isolated." As an unapologetically polyamorous woman, Rule wrote freely about sexuality and relationships. Her frankness encouraged Barbara to articulate long-suppressed thoughts and dreams. In fact, she became so eager to share that she sometimes wrote to Rule more than once a day. "There is no way for me to follow the rules in this," she apologized. "I…must simply write to you when and if I feel like it."[17]

Pamela Rust

At the same time Barbara mailed her first letter to Rule, she began corresponding with Pamela Rust, who as Clare Barringer provided book reviews for the British lesbian publication *Arena Three*. Rust proved to be nearly as compulsive about letter writing as Barbara, and their letters flew back and forth across the Atlantic. Barbara learned about Rust's service in the Women's Auxiliary Air Force during World War II and her work as a secretary to the managing director at *Vogue* before joining the staff of *Reader's Digest*. Like Barbara, she harbored dreams of becoming a novelist and was well read.[18]

Rust initially wrote to Barbara's home address, but Helen grew disturbed by the frequency of their communication and its increasingly personal tone. Taking precautions, Barbara shifted Rust's correspondence to her post office box, and in the privacy it afforded, the intercontinental friends spent five weeks in late summer and early autumn 1964 exploring the possibility of a future together. Barbara contemplated leaving Helen and moving to England, while Rust explored the possibility of transferring to her company's headquarters in Pleasantville, New York. In retrospect, Rust realized it was not boldness that led her to consider joining Barbara in the States, but rather "being at a low ebb and clutching at straws." When Rust mentioned she would be in the States at the invitation of the parent company of *Reader's Digest* in late October, Barbara grew alarmed by the prospect of her two worlds colliding. She abruptly terminated their communication by informing Rust that Helen might be dying of cancer, a claim that had no basis in truth. "All I had to do was contemplate leaving [Helen]," Barbara explained to Rule, "to become overcome with the illness which created the cruel letter to Pamela."[19]

Unknown to Barbara, Rust had begun corresponding with Rule after reviewing *Desert of the Heart* for *Arena Three*. In time, she told Rule about the situation with Barbara, and Rule decided to intervene. When Barbara learned Rule knew about her flirtation with Rust, she confessed: "I would have [told you] long ago had I been able to break my own pride down to that extent. So many years of feeling invulnerable and superior to the rest of the unhappy many have left me ill-prepared to face loving her (there, I got that down on paper) without much hope of having her in any capacity." Confessing that her feelings had not changed despite what she had written in her final letter to Rust, Barbara dramatically declared: "I do love her much, much more than I thought was even possible for me."[20]

Impatient with Barbara's weakness for paper romances, Rule dismissed the situation as "idiotic" and an infatuation. "What on earth can you mean by love," she demanded, "if you can talk so about someone you've never laid eyes on, much less spent time enough with?" Blunt of necessity, Rule concluded that Barbara was either self-indulgent or desperate. The "Kansas City Kid," she sarcastically chided, is "riding airmail stamps into the never-never land of RD [*Reader's Digest*] romance" and "taking a correspondence course in love long enough to get an A before dropping the course." Rule also rejected Barbara's tendency to blame Helen's controlling ways for the situation. "It takes two people to create the isolation you describe," she argued when making a case for Barbara's complicity. "If it hadn't appealed to you somehow, you wouldn't have put up with it." Going a step further, Rule suggested Barbara enjoyed playing the role of a proud, secretive criminal. "Right now you're a devil needing to get reinstated," Rule observed perceptively, "and martyrdom is one way."[21]

In Rule's opinion, Barbara had two choices, but both required her to "be honest with herself." She could leave Helen because she needed to, without "love letters crowding the issue," and then explore the possibility of a relationship with Rust or someone else. Or she could stay with Helen and make changes that would prevent her from being "driven to this kind of mess." Based on their brief acquaintance, Rule concluded that Barbara lacked the capacity for more complex personal relationships. As proof, she pointed to her compulsive categorization of people (and also characters in books) as either saints or devils. Reflecting on their dinner at the Cock and Bull Restaurant, Rule speculated that Barbara had classified her as a "heller" because of the flirtatious banter she exchanged with their waitress. "[F]or me," Rule explained, "taking random pleasure in the world of people is a natural and undangerous delight," far better than Barbara's tendency to restrain desires until they became unbearable, even destructive.[22]

Attempting to restore herself in Rule's good graces, Barbara denied anything was wrong with the relationship she had with Helen, and suggested that the situation with Rust had been greatly exaggerated. "Without making an even more colossal ass of myself," she explained, "I must find some way to make you pour a little salt on everything I say…I never see wrecks, I see cataclysmic events—my summer storms are gully washers." Her response angered Rule, who argued that it was unreasonable to expect friends and correspondents to sort out truth from fiction. "I suggest that you're old enough now to get over admiring your own ability to exaggerate and misrepresent." She also had tired of Barbara's portrayal of herself as living an ideal life and she considered her references to helping the less fortunate "smug, misguided and brutal."[23] Concluding they disagreed on so many topics, Rule declared that there was no point in further correspondence.

Rule let three months pass without writing to Barbara. Then, troubled by the way their pen friendship had ended on a note of anger, she reconnected so they could close that chapter of their lives on a more civil note. In a newsy update, Rule mentioned plans to visit England for three weeks in May. Other than opening with, "I am really very glad that you wrote," Barbara's cordial reply gave no hint that she harbored any ill feelings toward Rule. She commented on book reviews, family matters and her work on the checklist, closing with wishes for a good trip and an admission that she missed receiving Rule's letters.[24]

Because of the hiatus in their correspondence, Rule did not know that Rust had stunned Barbara by phoning her at work two days before Christmas. Unable to resist the tug of unrequited love, a sentimental Barbara agreed to resume correspondence with one stipulation: that they confine their conversation to books and authors. That resolve proved impossible and Barbara's innate flirtatiousness once again found expression. Giving her romantic impulses free rein, she made inquiries about the process for obtaining a work visa in England and resumed dreaming of their future together.[25]

While Rule was in England that spring, she visited Rust and initiated a brief affair. It caused some amusement one day when five of Barbara's airmail letters dropped through Rust's mail slot onto the floor while Rule was in her apartment. Upon her return to Vancouver, Rule's attempt to inform Barbara about the time she had spent with Rust prompted emotions ranging from anger to despair. Certain that Rule had no intention of ending her long-term relationship with Sonthoff, Barbara melodramatically declared herself ready to leave Helen "now that I know her health permits a decision I had no moral right to make before" [referring to the earlier claim that Helen had cancer]. Announcing her intention to bring the woman she loved to the States, Barbara beseeched Rule to leave Rust alone so she could get the stardust out of her eyes. "I could forgive you for taking the one person I love away from me—but not if you don't even want her."[26]

Rule countered Barbara's emotional indignation within hours of receiving her letter. "[M]orality is a tough word and you sling it around as if you'd invented it." Barbara had cited morals as the reason she could not leave Helen the previous fall, and now she claimed a moral right to keep Helen uninformed about the relationship with Rust in case it did not materialize into something more concrete. If she adhered to the moral code she preached, Rule contended, Barbara would instead tell Helen about the affair and stop making Rust "play the role of the scarlet woman in the post office box." Accusing Barbara of attempting to ride "for months with a foot in each boat," Rule defended her actions on the grounds that she had never misled Rust, a rational, intelligent woman fully capable of making her own choices.[27]

Assuring Barbara she was not her enemy, Rule proceeded to confuse her friend by relaying some of what she had shared with Rust. "I've told her I think a good part of you is juvenile delinquent...And I've told her I think you're badly misled in some of your notions about 'the cause.'" In Rule's opinion, Barbara's approach to the homophile movement resembled that of a new convert to a cause. In order to be a spokeswoman for it, she thought it necessary to maintain an ideal relationship. Now that she had "fallen," Barbara's only recourse was to idealize the fall, thus rendering Helen a villain and herself noble because she had sacrificed great love to the ideal. Aware her assessment was blunt, Rule hastened to assure Barbara that she did not intend "to destroy any world you may be able to make, rather to bless it and be glad of it if it is possible."[28]

After calling for a truce in mid-June 1965, Rule continued to challenge Barbara's conception of morality. If Barbara pursued a relationship with Rust, she predicted, it would be "devilishly hard not to hold Pamela at least partially responsible for your failure with Helen," while Rust would find it difficult to trust Barbara. Insistent that Barbara needed to strive for a relationship based on freedom rather than fear or paranoia, Rule urged her to tell Helen about the situation. If their relationship was dead, she advised, both would be better off without it. Despite Rule's recommendations, Barbara justified keeping Helen in the dark. "I have not and never would be able to have with Helen the kind of relationship you two have apparently managed," she explained. Yet the machinations Barbara resorted to in order to connect with others had led her to develop a skewed version of truth. She readily admitted having "trouble telling what is 'the truth' from day to day, because for god's [sic] sake it changes every day." She also found the necessity of maintaining the post office box distasteful, but given the nature of her relationship, privacy trumped honesty.[29]

As Barbara and Rule worked to resolve their differences, Rust stopped responding to Barbara's missives. Barbara initially attributed the silence to a "romantic and miserable mist" that descended upon Rust after Rule's visit, but she had no way to anticipate how Rust would feel toward her once it had dissipated. Unable to concentrate on her lesbian literary research, Barbara unleashed her emotions in a series of letters, taking a different approach each time. When it became evident Rust would not respond, Barbara resigned herself to the situation. A year later when Rust surprised her with another letter, she responded with "vague politeness" and let their pen friendship fade into nothing.[30]

May Sarton

Barbara filled the void left by the end of her correspondence with Rust by submerging herself in work. While scanning *Kirkus* one day in 1965, she spotted a review of May Sarton's *Mrs. Stevens Hears the Mermaids Singing*, a novel containing hints of lesbian content. Unable to contain her excitement, Barbara sent a praise-filled fan letter to the author that included one subtle sentence indicating the significance of Sarton's work to lesbians. "After A SHOWER OF SUMMER DAYS sent me to reading your books," Barbara explained, "I hoped for another, better treatment, which THE SMALL ROOM filled."[31]

Sarton, whose family had fled from Belgium to Boston in 1915 when she was just three years old, felt "rather nervous" about the publication of *Mrs. Stevens Hears the Mermaids Singing* in September 1965. Since her first volumes of poetry and fiction appeared in the 1930s, she had worked hard to build her reputation as a writer. Upon receiving Barbara's letter, Sarton pronounced her "perceptive" to recognize her treatment of "the theme" in her two earlier works as well as her intent in the new novel. "You have guessed right, of course...I have waited a long time to do it (I am 53!) but I felt that the time had come for someone to treat this subject in imaginative rather than sexual terms—to talk openly about homosexuality not mixed up with crime and-or drug-taking."[32] She felt proud of the book, but knew that with its disclosure of her own sexuality, she risked losing readers.

Barbara relished the idea of Sarton's revelation, and wanted to see the book widely reviewed. In an attempt to impress the author, she noted she would be reviewing it for "two little magazines." Eager to generate more exposure for Sarton, Barbara contacted her publisher, W. W. Norton & Company, to request permission to feature the author's photo on the cover of *The Ladder*. Sarton, who had refused to allow her photo to appear on the dust jacket, was horrified. "I have very strong feelings *against* a photograph of me appearing on the cover of this kind of magazine," she admonished, explaining that photos encouraged too much unwanted fan mail. "I should have believed that you had more sense," she chided Barbara after the matter had been resolved.[33]

Undeterred, Barbara believed the ultimate goal of lesbian visibility trumped an author's need for personal privacy. "I am not really a rat fink, but I do feel the LADDER has to be pushed," Barbara explained to editor Gittings. Consultation with an attorney convinced her that the publisher, not Sarton, had the final say in the photograph's use. Only fear of Helen's disapproval dampened Barbara's enthusiasm. "If Helen ever found out," she confided to Gittings, "she would be furious, I mean really furious" because of her strong feelings about respecting personal privacy.[34] Consequently, Barbara decided to leave the ultimate decision up to *The Ladder*'s editor.

Obsessed with Sarton, Barbara devoured the author's entire body of work in preparation for writing a comprehensive review. Gittings was an exacting editor and had seen enough of Barbara's reviews in *The Ladder* to doubt her ability to tackle such an important and complex project. One solution, she suggested, was for Barbara to collaborate with Jeannette Howard Foster or *Arena Three* reviewer Clare Barringer because both possessed broad knowledge of literary criticism. If Barbara needed a fuller explanation, Gittings concluded, she would comply but warned "it will mean going into specifics about your limitations as a writer!"[35]

Insulted by Gittings's stipulation, Barbara informed her editor, "I have not seriously objected to your continued use of words such as vapid, cliché, pedestrian, limp, inaccurate, tiresome—and dozens of others—which you have consistently used in your 'requests' for re-writes—but has it ever dawned on you that I've written for half-a-dozen other editors—some with actual credentials in the field…" Protesting that she would "go to hell for T.L. [*The Ladder*] any day—and for any good editor—*yourself included*," she demanded to know why Gittings had treated her "worse in some ways than the coast [DOB] treats you." Under the circumstances, Barbara requested that the editor return all her articles, stories and reviews unless she planned to use them within the next two years. As far as the Sarton review was concerned, Barbara suggested Gittings could read it in *ONE*. Familiar with Barbara's flare-ups, the editor teasingly addressed her next letter "Dear Tail that Would Wag the Dog," and resumed discussing *Ladder* and Daughters of Bilitis business as though nothing had changed.[36]

Contrary to Gittings's assessment, Barbara considered herself well qualified to review Sarton's work. Besides their personal correspondence,

Barbara had gained additional insights from Jeannette Howard Foster, who had shared a fourplex apartment building with Sarton the previous year when she served as a poet-in-residence at Lindenwood College in St. Charles, Missouri. Growing close over drinks and numerous dinners, Sarton explained how her love for Wellesley College president Margaret Clapp had resulted in her non-reappointment to the faculty. Aware of Foster's love of poetry, Sarton even shared copies of the love poems she had written to Clapp. Unable to resist sharing the poems, Foster typed copies and mailed them to Barbara.[37]

After *Mrs. Stevens Hears the Mermaids Singing* appeared in the fall of 1965, Barbara resumed corresponding with the author, cultivating her friendship by sending gifts of books, clippings of reviews and a copy of the review she had written. As their connection deepened, Sarton offered praise as well as constructive criticism of Barbara's writing. She noted "a lot of good solid perception" in Barbara's review essay, but challenged her to ask more of herself as a writer. Claiming to write Barbara out of affection and respect, Sarton encouraged her to shed her secretive ways and begin reviewing for mainstream journals, where her "perspicacity and sensitivity would reach all the people. not just one little segment." An advocate of the universality of experience, Sarton reasoned that Barbara could achieve more "by writing understandingly for and about *all* women and using your own name."[38]

Emboldened by her prior correspondence with Rule, Barbara felt comfortable sharing her ideas with Sarton. The poet and novelist did not hesitate to let Barbara know if her ideas seemed absurd. Upon learning Barbara viewed lesbians as superior beings, Sarton noted that she had seen "too many homosexual women romanticize their 'difference' into a kind of genius." As the two sparred back and forth, it became evident Sarton thought homosexuals should use their talents openly instead of remaining in "a cozy little secret society where they can feel safe and even superior to the rest of the world." Despite their disagreements, Sarton found it a "great comfort to be in communication with someone who believes all I once believed, and who thus restores my courage and my sense of myself."[39]

Barbara's sympathetic letters provided temporary relief for the woman who had been on a nonstop emotional roller coaster because of her unrequited love for Margaret Clapp. As their correspondence extended into 1966, Sarton grew comfortable enough with Barbara to mail her copies of the love poems "to see what you think." Exercising wisdom, Barbara did not reveal she already had seen them. Instead, she lavished encouragement and praise on the poet, who found it "very heartening to know that you believe I am not a total failure." After Sarton called her "the best friend an elderly, depressed writer ever had," Barbara thought the moment had come when she could pose more personal questions.[40]

While preparing the Sarton review essay, Barbara compiled detailed notes on every character in *Mrs. Stevens Hears the Mermaids Singing*. She believed they were based on real people, and she was eager to know their identities. In her relentless quest to document lesbian history, Barbara took advantage of their budding friendship and pressed for confirmation of her theories. Within a few weeks, however, Sarton grew wary of the ceaseless inquiries and bitterly regretted sharing the poems. "I have grown fond of you…But the truth is that I am not really interested in lesbian gossip, and that, I fear is your stock in trade." Barbara's eagerness to uncover lesbian affairs in real life as well as in literature had pushed Sarton to her limit, especially when the inquiries were about the author's close friends. "If you really do have respect for me, as you say you do, please stop trying to find out who Dorothy is or was." Going on the attack, Sarton called Barbara a hypocrite because she pushed for others to expose themselves while hiding behind fake names. Even more troubling, she continued, was Barbara's shallowness and smugness, "which makes for a rather slick and evasive approach to life *and* art." Indeed, Sarton doubted anything had ever moved Barbara very deeply, and therefore she was "cut off from poetry which can only speak to those who are or have been."[41] With that, she terminated their correspondence. Barbara was disappointed, but in characteristic fashion she blamed Sarton's personality for the breakdown in their communication and shifted her attention to other correspondents.

Maureen Duffy

Undeterred by the outcome of her correspondence with Sarton, Barbara moved forward with her pursuit of all things lesbian. Just days after receiving the poet's parting shot, she happened upon an announcement of a book called *The Microcosm* and fired off a fan letter to its author, British novelist Maureen Duffy. Barbara pronounced the book "the first definitive Lesbian novel," and promised Duffy she would do everything in her power to promote it in the United States. Unlike Sarton, Duffy did not object to her image being used to publicize the book. Because of Barbara's efforts, the November 1966 issue of *The Ladder* featured Duffy's picture on its cover as well as Barbara's positive review within.[42]

Barbara's brief yet meaningful correspondence with Duffy and her multiple readings of *The Microcosm* expanded and complicated her understanding of homosexuality. Through the eyes of the novel's central character, a bar-room philosopher named Matt, the reader encounters a diverse array of lesbians, all of them living on the social margins because of their sexual orientation. In a stream-of-consciousness narrative, Matt struggles to reconcile her yearnings for others with the realities of her secure relationship with Rae, even as she offers advice to the physical education teacher who fears being discovered by a pupil, and the married woman who is unable to admit her sexuality. Ultimately, Matt realizes the lesbian world is no microcosm, as she initially believed. Instead, she announces, lesbians are "part of society, part of the world whether we or society like it or not."[43]

In the 1950s and 1960s, Barbara's limited exposure to the gay and lesbian communities left her with a class-based understanding of butch and femme. Until she read *The Microcosm* she had considered herself "a particularly noisy opponent of what I term the 'butch-femme dichotomy,'" equating middle-class professional women with femmes and butches with working-class bar culture. Duffy's treatment of Matt opened her eyes to another explanation. "I don't think I realized that it was ever an inside thing," she confessed to Duffy, hinting that she was beginning to embrace a genetic view of homosexuality. As she met more lesbians, and as fashions became more casual, Barbara realized appearance alone did not render someone a butch. After all, people who saw her dressed in trousers and button-down shirts assumed she was a butch, while she considered herself "very femme."[44]

Barbara Gittings

In addition to conducting pen friendships with poets and writers, Barbara sustained regular correspondence with Barbara Gittings. From the onset of her appointment as *Ladder* editor, Gittings's relationship with the DOB governing board had been rocky. As contentious as her communications with Barbara had been, the two women understood one another and shared a common goal: a desire to make *The Ladder* the best lesbian magazine in the world.

In the spring of 1966, Gittings confided to Barbara that she and partner Kay Tobin Lahusen were having "a major domestic crisis" that could affect production of *The Ladder*. Each issue, she elaborated, was the product of their joint inspiration and criticism. Distressed by Gittings's revelation, Barbara feared the editor's situation would affect the magazine's future. Putting aside the anger she periodically felt toward Gittings, Barbara encouraged her trust by offering support and encouragement: "You are loved for many virtues, admired even for what might be thought flaws."[45]

Throughout the summer, Gittings vented her distress and frustration in dozens of letters sent to Barbara's post office box and in occasional late-night telephone calls. By fall, she had phoned so many times that Helen had begun referring to Barbara as Gittings's "silent therapist." When the conversation turned to Gittings' lack of confidence in her sex life, Barbara boldly informed her that she would have "tried very hard to effect a cure myself" if they lived in closer proximity. Not wanting to be misunderstood, she clarified: "I'm not claiming love for you—beyond the extent of caring very much about you and what happens to you…" Barbara simply thought Gittings would find it reassuring to know she was attractive.[46]

With Gittings's consent, Barbara forwarded some of her letters to Jane Rule for the more experienced woman's advice. Based on what she read, Rule suggested they were "all growing people trying to sort out needs and desires with the confused moral equipment provided." The root of the problem, Rule speculated, lay in Gittings's desire for "power and authority," combined with her fear of the responsibilities. In other words, Gittings needed to resolve issues of dominance and dependence. The message resonated with Barbara, who had been spending a great deal of time contemplating her dependence upon Helen. "I am just as quick to say I am also driven by terrible strengths and hideous weaknesses," she responded.[47]

While Rule found Gittings's situation of concern, she was more intrigued by Barbara's distress at the prospect of her friend's breakup. Barbara attributed her discomfort to the insecurity she had experienced as a child: "the constant moving, the never knowing feeling that started when I was 10. I had to get away from change, so I rejected the word, the idea altogether." Gittings's domestic problems had led Barbara to place the life she led with Helen under a microscope. Rule recognized Barbara's restlessness and discontent were deepening, but Barbara could not admit anything was wrong with her relationship because that would result in change.[48]

Meanwhile, DOB officers tired of Gittings's inability to meet deadlines, complaining that she had not published the convention issue in time to promote the annual meeting. Gittings did not expect to be reappointed to another term as editor of *The Ladder*, but her relationship with the governing board had deteriorated so much that the board replaced her after the August 1966 issue appeared instead of letting her edit the final issue of Volume 10. Because of her efforts to promote a co-ed gay movement, Gittings subsequently received offers to work for *ONE*, *DRUM*, and the New York Mattachine Society's newsletter.[49]

In keeping with her personality, Barbara pragmatically encouraged her colleague to stop complaining and "buck up." "One of the best directed criticisms of the homosexual (both sexes) is that he (read she) lets the emotional problems involved lead him around by the balls (read tits). It just won't cut the mustard, baby, the world is hard and earnest and the only way to mark it up with your personal knife is to work hard and gouge deep."[50] By the year's end, Gittings and Lahusen resolved their differences, and once the need had passed, the former *Ladder* editor's correspondence with Barbara grew uncharacteristically silent. By then, Barbara had immersed herself in the needs of yet another pen friend.

Jody Shotwell

For a number of years Barbara had admired the prose and poetry of a Philadelphia woman named Jody Shotwell. Born Josephine Levy in 1917, she fell in love with another girl during her teen years, but the relationship faltered, in part because of her parents' disapproval. Despite marriage to Gilmore Shotwell in 1942, she found ways to maintain her gay contacts even after she became the mother of three sons. In the 1950s, when the children became old enough for her to leave them with their father, she began publishing stories in *ONE*, *The Ladder* and *Mattachine Review*. Jody knew Barbara Gittings well because they worked together in the New York chapter of the DOB, and she also corresponded with Jeannette Howard Foster.[51]

In the spring of 1965 Barbara decided to send Shotwell a fan letter. The two were kindred spirits, and a warm and playful friendship ensued, energized by their mutual love of lesbian literature and biographical research. When Barbara inquired about elusive short stories or books, Shotwell trekked to East Coast libraries and bookshops to obtain them for her. Barbara returned the favor by reading and commenting on Shotwell's unpublished short fiction. Certain Helen would perceive their correspondence as threatening, Barbara instructed Shotwell to use her post office box and told other correspondents to avoid mentioning Shotwell in any correspondence they mailed to Barbara's home.[52]

Just as Maureen Duffy had challenged Barbara's view of butch and femme, Jody Shotwell complicated her understanding of bisexuality. Before getting to know her, Barbara had equated bisexuality with promiscuity. As a staunch advocate of monogamy, she strongly opposed inclusion of articles on the topic of bisexuality in *The Ladder*, arguing it was inappropriate to publicize "that they sleep around with both sexes (or sleep around with one sex) in a magazine which (I hope to God) is attempting to promote the doctrine of the perfectibility of man." If someone loved both males and females, she believed, it was impossible to be monogamous. Shotwell's explanation that her attraction was to people, not to males or females, made Barbara pause for thought.[53]

Unfortunately, their friendship was cut short when Shotwell received her diagnosis of liver cancer in the fall of 1966. Since Barbara could not visit her friend in the hospital, she asked Gittings to "be a good butch and go cheer up the little thing." Only fifty years old, Shotwell declined chemotherapy and accepted the inevitability of her death, which occurred the following January. Barbara, profoundly touched by the loss, found her mind "completely blank," and once again turned to work as her salvation.[54]

* * *

With each paper romance or pen friendship, Barbara moved one step further away from Helen Bennett and the cozy, sequestered life they had created, and one step closer to a wider world that would require her to play a more public role. Each correspondent contributed to Barbara's ongoing education by challenging her assumptions and opening her mind. With a sharpened focus and a widening array of tools and knowledge, she was prepared for the next phase of her life.

CHAPTER FIVE

٭

The Original Paperback Novel

"I cannot write about anything except Lesbianism and what I write is so impossibly romantic[,] so gaggingly so, that no one in their right mind would publish it."

—Barbara Grier, 1965[1]

When readers of *The Ladder* opened the December 1960 issue, they found an article titled "The Life and Death of a Lesbian Novel." Attributed to Theodora, the essay relayed the sad tale of an author's experience with a paperback publishing house. Eager to sell a book manuscript after having it rejected by more reputable firms, the protagonist signed a "full rights" contract with a lesser company, granting it carte blanche on changes. A few months later she spotted the paperback original book at the newsstand with "a hideous cover… and a foolish author's name…and a title totally unrelated to the story." Reading it confirmed her worst fears; the rewrite amounted to a "general demoralization of all the main characters." Aspiring writers should learn from her example and never sign away all rights to their work, concluded the author, who, in fact, was Barbara Grier.[2]

In her ongoing search for lesbian literature, Barbara had read many paperback original (PBO) books like the one described in her essay. Her appreciation for the genre was rooted in a time when lesbians seldom appeared on the printed page. Prior to the 1950s, lesbian characters occasionally surfaced in esoteric literature but had little impact on the common reader. *The Well of Loneliness* by Radclyffe Hall (1928) offered a notable exception. Condemned for its bold portrayal of lesbianism, the book's publication resulted in one of England's most famous obscenity trials. Despite supportive statements by Virginia Woolf and other writers, the chief magistrate ruled the novel was an "obscene libel" and all copies must be destroyed. After its publication a few months later in the United States, and subsequent prosecution, a New York court ruling found "lesbianism was neither obscene nor illegal, and therefore the book should not be declared so either."[3] Publicity surrounding the book's prosecution heightened its visibility. Widely available in subsequent years, *The Well of Loneliness* resonated with young women searching for portrayals of lesbianism, even if they had little in common with an upper-class British noblewoman.

Everything changed with the emergence of the inexpensive paperback novel. First introduced in the United States in 1939, the pocket-sized book initially offered readers inexpensive access to such reprinted classics as James Hilton's *Lost Horizon* and Emily Brontë's *Wuthering Heights*. Then, in 1950, newsstand distributor Fawcett offered a line of original paperback novels under the Gold Medal imprint. While not strictly a lesbian novel, Tereska Torrès's *Women's Barracks* (1950) was cited two years later by the U.S. House Select Committee on Current Pornographic Materials as morally degenerate because it portrayed female characters having liaisons with one another, as well as with men. In anticipation of postal censorship, the publisher had insisted that Torrès include a critical narrator. While the decision saved her book from being banned from the U.S. mail, it also established a precedent for PBO novels to portray lesbians as deviants and misfits who either recognized the error of their ways or suffered the consequences.[4]

Scared, isolated and convinced they were anomalies, lesbians could at last walk to a newsstand or bus station and see books about lesbian love on display. Even so, it took courage to buy them. As a young girl, the poet and writer Donna Allegra found such books in a drugstore's pornography section and felt "embarrassed and ashamed" when she approached the counter to buy them. Yet she did because "I needed them the way I needed food and shelter for survival."[5] Some women went to other neighborhoods to avoid encountering anyone who might know them, while others buried the books among other items and tried to appear nonchalant as a smirking clerk rang up their purchases. No matter how they acquired them, lesbians of the 1950s devoured the books despite their requisite unhappy endings because they "told us we were not alone."[6]

Obsessively combing newsstands and bookshops for new gay and lesbian paperbacks from such publishers as Ace, Ballantine, Beacon, Dell,

Lion, Midwood, Newsstand Library and many others, Barbara pinched pennies in order to add relevant books to her growing private library. She also cultivated pen friendships with book dealers in New York and Chicago who carried some of the more elusive titles and encouraged them to contact her when they had items of interest. Howard Frisch, of Village Books and Press, was one of Barbara's regular suppliers of gay and lesbian titles. All the while, Barbara knew her activities were pushing the limits of partner Helen Bennett's tolerance.[7]

As Barbara quickly discovered, positive portrayals of lesbian life were rare in lesbian pulp novels. She became convinced that the author Vin Packer (one of Marijane Meaker's pseudonyms) must be filled with self-loathing. In the undeniably well-written *Spring Fire* (1952), published by Gold Medal Books, a lesbian affair between two young college students ends with the older girl's nervous breakdown and institutionalization. A subsequent Packer novel, *The Evil Friendship* (1958), served as another cautionary tale. Based on a New Zealand murder case, it told the story of two lesbian teenagers who together murdered the one girl's mother to prevent her from separating them.[8]

Meaker's novels helped launch Ann Bannon's career as an author. After reading *Spring Fire*, the aspiring author wrote to Meaker, who in turn introduced her to Dick Carroll, editor-in-chief of Gold Medal Books. After reading her novel, he advised Bannon to revise it with a focus on the two sorority sisters, Beth and Laura. The resulting *Odd Girl Out* (1957) told the story of a Midwestern college student named Laura falling in love with a sorority sister named Beth. The relationship falters, but by book's end Laura has come of age: "I know what I am, and I can be honest with myself now," she declares before boarding a train for New York City. After writing a second, less successful straight novel, Bannon realized Laura's story was the beginning of a series, and in the second of five books she introduced the endearing butch Beebo Brinker.[9]

As a comprehensive collector of original paperback novels with gay and lesbian content, Barbara favored authors who presented their subject in a positive and compassionate light. Bannon was one of her favorites because of the letters women had written to Barbara after they read Bannon's novels. Justifying her taste to *Ladder* editor Barbara Gittings, she declared: "[T]here is a place for these books, simple moralistic pie in the sky love stories for Lesbians."[10] Barbara praised Bannon's second book, *I Am a Woman* (1959), noting that it was "very realistic, the writing is excellent for a paperback, and the ending is so very happy that it sets the book almost in a class by itself." Likewise, Barbara appreciated the "understanding and sympathy" Chicago author Valerie Taylor brought to her fictional treatment of lesbian relationships. Taylor was a prolific writer, her works including such titles as *Whisper Their Love* (1957), *The Girls in 3-B* (1959), and *Stranger on Lesbos* (1960). Barbara understood such books were not "great literature," but she sensed their significance to countless lesbians desperate for affirmation of their sexuality in a society that considered them mentally ill, or worse.[11]

In addition to using the Vin Packer pseudonym, Meaker wrote a series of five nonfiction books about lesbian life using the pseudonym Ann Aldrich. Difficult to categorize, the books appeared in pulp format but were neither fiction nor memoir. The first two, *We Walk Alone* (1955) and *We, Too, Must Love* (1958), offered a journalistic portrait of New York City's lesbian subculture from the perspective of participants. Critics accused her of having a conflicted attitude toward lesbians even though she had set out to debunk stereotypes of lesbians. Throughout the book the author used such language as "emotional aberration" and juxtaposed lesbians against the "dominant society of the normal," reinforcing an image of this minority as despised and troubled. In an "Open Letter to Ann Aldrich" in *The Ladder* in April 1958, Del Martin expressed concern that Aldrich's focus on "the bizarre" left readers "with the impression that these represent the sum and substance of the group at large." In addition to sending the author a complimentary subscription to *The Ladder* 1958, Martin invited Aldrich to explain her views to the magazine's readers.[12] Instead of replying to the magazine, Aldrich surveyed its issues and skewered *The Ladder* and the Daughters of Bilitis in her next book, *Carol in a Thousand Cities* (1960). Dismissing the magazine as an amateurish attempt, Aldrich mocked its hand-drawn covers, slashed its short fiction to pieces and dismissed its poetry as sentimental.

Aldrich's cutting remarks struck Barbara hard because both she and Jeannette Howard Foster were writing stories for *The Ladder*. "With her witty knife ever in hand," she wrote in her review of the book, "she slashes to ribbons every story without exception." Barbara, who by 1960 was deeply and emotionally invested in *The Ladder*, was not alone in taking offense at Aldrich's critique of the publication as amateurish in appearance and content. Using *The Ladder* as a vehicle for replying to its critic, Del Martin went on the offensive: "We are not great, Miss Aldrich, but we are also not as ridiculous as you would make us out." Since it was "better to have been mentioned disparagingly than never to have been mentioned at all," she informed Aldrich that the DOB Book Service would make copies of the book available for purchase. Also joining in the fun, Foster applied her skills of literary detection to the challenge of uncovering the author's true identity, but mistakenly concluded she must be none other than Ann Bannon.[13] In the end, *Carol in a Thousand Cities* reached a far wider audience than *The Ladder* ever could and became a promotional tool for the DOB. Letters poured in to its headquarters from lesbian readers of Aldrich's book who eagerly sought more information about the organization and its publication.

The Aspiring Writer

As a young woman who liked books "better than anything" and viewed writers as "Gods of the universe," Barbara yearned to be one, and to live in their world. Helen Bennett supported Barbara's dream because it seemed relatively safe: writing could be done at home, it might generate a little income, and if Barbara were writing fiction, she might spend less time corresponding with outsiders who could disrupt the safe existence they had created for themselves in Kansas City.[14]

As an aspiring writer, Barbara drew inspiration from her mentor Jeannette Howard Foster. Foster, who studied English literature at the University of Chicago, had a short story published in *Harper's Magazine* in 1927. Because of societal taboos surrounding homosexuality, there had been no market for Foster's subsequent lesbian-themed stories, many of them written in the 1930s, so she filed them away. The rise of PBO novels rekindled her hope in the possibility of publication but her work was too romantic and outdated for modern readers. Barbara, however, loved the stories because she was a romantic at heart.

By the mid-1950s, Barbara was churning out dozens of short stories. Much like Foster, she stored them in the back of a closet, referring to her efforts as "a regular fire trap of worthless words." Indeed, Barbara's short fiction, which grew from small incidents she had witnessed or experienced, suffered from her limited experience with the gay scene and the world outside Kansas City, and offered more psychological observation than tension-filled plot.[15]

When several homophile magazines emerged in the 1950s, would-be writers at last had outlets for their creative work. The thirteen stories Barbara published in *The Ladder*, *Tangents*, and England's *Arena Three* between 1957 and 1967 bore such titles as "Golden Rule," "The Marble Statue," "Johnny's Bar," "Noblesse" and "Suspended Ride," and portrayed normalized lesbian life: well-mannered and contented lesbians holding jobs as secretaries and accountants, socializing in bars and restaurants, and living in stable, monogamous relationships. Occasionally, characters wore men's pants and went by such androgynous names as Lee and Darrell, but overall they appeared happy, responsible and unthreatening. Beginning with her first publication, Barbara used pseudonyms to placate Helen's intense love of privacy. Because she wrote so many articles, reviews and stories, Barbara had at least nine pseudonyms, keeping a detailed record of each one she used and where the work appeared.[16]

In her desire to impress established writers, Barbara could not resist the temptation to present herself as a far more accomplished writer than she really was. It gave her a certain cachet to claim authorship, and it fed her ego when they inquired about her writing habits and plans. "You talk about your own books as if there were dozens," Jane Rule observed. "How many have you got?" Pressed to be more specific, Barbara replied that she had written "10 under the name Sloane M. Britain" and "a few others under other names." Aware Rule had a low opinion of PBO novels, Barbara dismissed the books as "just tripe, nothing more."[17] Barbara even claimed to have written children's books, but given her use of pseudonyms and the ephemeral nature of the post-World War II juvenile book market, it is impossible to verify which, if any, juvenile books she may have written.[18]

Historians of lesbian pulp fiction attribute the novels of Sloane M. Britain to Elaine Williams, who joined the Midwood publishing company in 1959, the same year her novel *First Person, 3rd Sex* appeared from Newsstand Library. Midwood, founded two years earlier by Harry Shorten and named for the Midwood section of Brooklyn, merged with Tower books in 1964 to become Midwood Tower. Unlike many pulps of the 1950s, Williams's story of a third-grade teacher's discovery of a passion for "twilight women" ended on a positive note. In contrast, her second Sloane Britain novel, *The Needle*, published in 1959 by Beacon Books, recounted the dismal story of a bisexual, heroin-addicted prostitute. Midwood published the next seven Sloane M. Britain books, but none appeared after Elaine Williams' suicide in late 1963.[19]

When reviewing *First Person, 3rd Sex* for "Lesbiana" in 1960, Barbara described the story as "remarkably free of cliché" and speculated that the author "is probably a woman." The tone of the review does not suggest that Barbara wrote the novel or had any connection with Williams. In a review of *Meet Marilyn*, she praised Britain for portraying "a highly constructive lesbian relationship which emphasizes permanence and reliability in personal life" and pronounced it "one of the better paperback treatments." Britain's later books, among them *Woman Doctor* (1962) and *Insatiable* (1963), showed increased cynicism and a decline in quality. Indeed, when editor Gittings asked Barbara to comment on Britain's death for *The Ladder*, she replied: "express *moderate* regret—she was only a good portrayer of Lesbians about half the time. Some of her stuff stunk (*not* the ones reviewed for Ladder)."[20]

Rule seems to have accepted Barbara's claims of authorship at face value, asking to read one of her original paperback novels. Upon receiving the request, Barbara promised to send a copy of *First Person, 3rd Sex*, but then had second thoughts. "I do poorly enough," she explained to Rule, and did not want to send the work because the publisher had changed the manuscript and added "sex scenes which don't even fit into the story." As a result, the final product was no longer a true reflection of her writing. Barbara blamed herself for selling books "outright, on a full rights contract," but noted this was typical procedure in the original paperback market.[21]

To satisfy Rule's request to read one of her novels, Barbara mailed a copy of *Twilight Girl* (1961), attributed to Della Martin. Although Barbara led Rule to believe it was her own work, in reality it had been written by the Chicago-based husband and wife writing team of Adela and Sebastian "Gale" Maritano. Adela, who had written radio scripts, was a stream-of-consciousness writer who chain-smoked her way through longhand manuscripts her husband then edited and embellished. Together, they published more than eighty original paperbacks under a variety of pseudonyms, among them Della Martin.[22]

Appalled by the novel's tone and writing, Rule urged her friend to aim higher and be true to herself. "I am bewildered at the split in your energies," she exclaimed. How could a woman who worked so zealously for magazines that sought to improve the image of homosexuals sell book manuscripts to publishers who marketed them as sleaze? How could she tolerate a blurb on her book cover stating "This book should be read by everyone bent on combating the lesbian contagion"? Rule informed her friend that the few hundred dollars she claimed to receive for each book seemed such "awfully little money for selling your soul." In response, Barbara justified writing for the pulp market by claiming she gave the money to her mother to pay for such necessities as dentures and her siblings' school-related expenses. If that were the case, however, it was without either sister's knowledge.[23]

Further going on the defensive, Barbara informed Rule that many of the characters in *Twilight Girl* had been based on "people I've seen on the street or in bars or in high school." The story featured Lon (Lorraine), a sixteen-year-old high school student who developed a crush on a female English teacher twice her age. Once spurned, Lon turned to a brash new friend, the purple-haired Violet Soup, who introduced her to the lesbian underworld in Southern California. According to Barbara, the character Violet Soup "was an attempt to poke fun at myself while evoking the memory of French writer Renée Vivien's *The Muse of the Violets*."[24]

Refusing to let Barbara make excuses for poor writing, Rule insisted she needed to stop producing "trash for money" if she wished to become a serious writer. Certain Barbara was intelligent and had potential, Rule accused her of hiding "behind the concept of a simple-minded public to keep from risking being good at writing…You won't learn to write well while you find excuses to write badly." Warning Barbara she ran the risk of becoming the voice she had created for the pulp market, Rule invited her to send a more serious piece of writing to her for a critique.[25]

Even though Barbara had written volumes of letters, dozens of articles and hundreds of reviews, she lacked confidence in her ability to produce fiction. In her eagerness to impress her mentor and friend, she claimed as her own two book manuscripts that had in fact been written by Jeannette Howard Foster. The first, a mystery called *Death Under Duress*, was written from multiple viewpoints and addressed the consequences of unchecked jealousy and license. Barbara had copies of both manuscripts because Foster had been flattered by her interest and lent them to her to read.

Aware of Rule's disdain for mysteries, Barbara informed her she would instead send the second manuscript, *Temple of Athene*, [sic] a lesbian romance set in the 1930s. The plot, loosely drawn from Foster's experiences as a librarian at a Southern women's college in the 1930s, featured protagonist Theodora K. Hart, a professor who fell in love with the school's female president. Barbara claimed she previously had sent the manuscript to the Scott Meredith Literary Agency, who had pronounced the book "absolutely impossible…not sexy enough for paperbacks, and far too flowery for hardbacks."[26]

As promised, Rule gave the manuscript a careful editing. Beginning with praise, she commended the novella's strong plot and primary theme: achieving freedom from emotional obsession. Based on Rule's experiences at the all-female Mills College, she thought the prevalence of lesbians on the fictional Radnor College campus tested the reader's credibility. She also complained about the story's overdependence on cliché, foolish romanticism and lack of understanding of motivation (ironically, all criticisms Foster had received when she originally sent the work out for review). "I hope all these comments aren't depressingly negative or tediously obvious," Rule concluded, advising her protégé to set her stories in environments with which she had greater familiarity.[27]

Instead of taking offense at Rule's suggestions, Barbara replied that a lack of formal training hindered her writing career. Even though she had never attended college, Barbara brashly declared the main character was in fact herself, thanked Rule for her advice, and promised to pay careful attention to her comments when she rewrote the story. In December

1967, after Barbara became Assistant Editor of Poetry and Fiction of *The Ladder*, she published "Temple of Athene" as a serialized story attributed to Hilary Farr, one of Foster's pseudonyms.[28]

Barbara never admitted to Rule that she had misled her about the authorship of books published under the names Sloane M. Britain and Della Martin, nor did she confess to passing off Jeannette Howard Foster's writing as her own. In time, Rule's interest in her efforts to write fiction made it impossible for Barbara to sustain the image of herself as a novelist. In a face-saving move, she informed her mentor that she had decided to stop writing trashy novels, and would instead focus her energies on editing *The Ladder* and transforming it into a feminist literary magazine.

Years later, Barbara seemed to take pleasure in perpetuating the belief that she had been a prolific writer of paperback novels. In recorded interviews from 1978 and 1987, she claimed to have written approximately thirty-two original paperbacks between the mid-1950s and the mid-1960s. Dismissing them as "bad writing," she described two as lesbian novels and the others as mysteries, westerns and romances. According to Barbara, she "cranked out" a novel about every four months and received between two hundred and four hundred dollars per book. To the end, Barbara steadfastly refused to reveal titles written or pseudonyms used, leaving her assertion of authorship as murky as the worlds in the original paperback novels she claimed to have written.[29]

The End of a Golden Age

When Barbara Gittings became editor of *The Ladder* in 1963, one of her goals was to transform the magazine from an in-house service publication into a first-rate lesbian review. At the time, authors remained reluctant to have their work appear in a magazine that featured "For Adults Only" on its cover and was sold alongside pornography at the newsstand. "My last hope for this loser named DOB," Gittings informed Barbara, "is that *The Ladder* gets into places where the right people will see it." Once that occurred, she predicted, "more right people will start coming to DOB—and if they're not completely deterred by the stodginess they'd see now—soon the balance of the membership would start to shift."[30]

Gittings's attempt to raise *The Ladder*'s reputation also included a campaign against references to books she considered trashy, because she believed they kept good authors from submitting their work for publication. When Del Martin inserted an ad for the DOB Book Service's selections in *The Ladder* without consulting its editor, Gittings exploded, accusing her of "purveying this trash." Someone in DOB, Gittings charged, had made "a big 'deal' with Midwood Tower," one that "duped" the Book Service "into carrying a lot of books it might not take if it had the option of selecting single titles after examination."[31]

When *Arena Three* editor Esme Langley wrote to *The Ladder*'s editor in 1964 to inquire about Midwood Tower as a possible publisher for her lesbian novel, Gittings could not contain her anger. Any author who published with them, she warned, "may as well forget about ever selling to a better house—unless he/she uses a different name."[32]

Using Langley's inquiry as proof, Gittings informed Barbara it was time "to be more selective and drop the trash" from "Lesbiana" and her annual review of lesbian literature. If Barbara refused, the editor would remove reviews of such books for her. Such a step would have decimated Barbara's column because fully eighty-nine percent of the titles included in "Lesbian Literature in '63" consisted of original paperback novels published by such publishers as Beacon Books, Brandon Books, Midnight Reader, Midwood and Nightstand Books. Even the least discriminating reader would have recognized the sleaziest works by their titles, which included such keywords as "perverted," "twisted" and "warped."[33]

Barbara believed future researchers would appreciate her inclusiveness, while Gittings countered that most readers of *The Ladder* did not care. Marshalling support for her viewpoint, Gittings contacted pulp novelist Yvonne MacManus, who, as Paula Christian, had written such books as *Edge of Twilight* and *Love Is Where You Find It*. MacManus shared the editor's low opinion, ranking Midwood with Neva Books, Brandon and the "rest of those lurid, fly-by-night sensational outfits" who published "badly-written near-pornography." No one, she insisted, would ever take an author seriously who had previously published with Midwood. Ironically, MacManus submitted a novel to Midwood that none of her regular publishers would accept; however, she chose another pseudonym rather than besmirch the reputation of her primary pen name, Paula Christian.[34]

Class and educational differences surfaced as Gittings continued to debate the merits of original paperback novels with Barbara. "I simply don't see *The Ladder*'s function as pandering to the taste of the lowest common denominator," Gittings contended. "Why shouldn't it by-pass or try to elevate the taste of the dog-cat-bat reader, instead of catering to her comic-book level...What the poor schnooks need...is to have another lesbian periodical which will feed them exactly what they want." Infuriated by such comments, Barbara argued she would be doing a disservice to many of her readers if she arbitrarily eliminated all Midwood Tower books from her column. "Every fool," she explained, "realizes that Lesbian paperbacks

are directed by the publishers to serve a male audience a vicarious thrill."
Yet the paperback market had served an important purpose by providing
shy and isolated lesbians with glimpses of another world and "novels
without too much sex and a happy ending." Midwood Tower was not
the "worst of the paperback boys at all," Barbara continued. "Like other
semi-readers in the field," she condescendingly concluded, Gittings was
"choosy by lack of immersion."[35]

As the argument escalated, Barbara realized Gittings would not
concede and begrudgingly informed the editor that in the future she
would omit the "damned paperbacks" and only review hardcover books
for *The Ladder*. "I feel that I am drinking the ocean in order to pee into a
funnel," she wryly observed.[36]

Barbara remained undaunted by Gittings's refusal to publish reviews
of PBO novels because she had other outlets for them. Her reviews of
gay male literature had appeared regularly in *Mattachine Review* since
1962. Then, in the spring of 1965, the homophile organization ONE,
Inc., splintered because of irreconcilable differences between its business
manager, Dorr Legg, and Don Slater, editor of *ONE* magazine. Branded
a thief after removing the magazine's mailing list from the Los Angeles-
based headquarters, Slater introduced a new publication, *Tangents*, in
October 1965. Sensing opportunity, Barbara immediately contacted him,
offered a story Gittings had rejected, and indicated her willingness to
provide reviews. A few months later, a gleeful Barbara informed Gittings
that her rejection of Barbara's work was "possibly the kindest thing you
ever did." Not only was Slater publishing her story "Johnny's Bar," but
she also had been given complete control over a monthly book review
column titled "Reader at Large," which ran from October 1965 until the
magazine ceased in late 1969.[37]

* * *

As a young woman, Barbara Grier steeped herself in the world of the
original paperback novel and, like countless other gays and lesbians, valued
them as printed affirmation of gay and lesbian existence even though they
often reinforced negative stereotypes. "I would welcome a return to the
boom days a few short years ago," she confessed to Yvonne MacManus
in 1966, "when you and two or three others in the field were making
life easier for thousands and thousands of desperately lonely people in
isolated small towns throughout this country." Elaborating, she noted
that "[n]one of the better houses are buying lesies [*sic*] anymore, which
is why about all you see on the subject comes from those dirty-book

houses in the West."[38] Irrespective of whether or not Barbara published in the pulp fiction market, she possessed an intimate knowledge of the genre's authors, their books, and what they meant to the scores of readers desperate to find themselves reflected in print media. As literary historian Yvonne Keller notes, original paperback novels helped "put the word *lesbian* in mass circulation as never before."[39]

Despite aspiring to write PBO novels, Barbara knew the mid-1960s represented a watershed moment in the life of the lesbian original paperback. Its golden age, she observed, had begun in 1950 and spanned into the mid-1960s. Beginning in the freer climate of the late 1960s, sexually explicit gay male paperbacks boomed, overwhelming the market for lesbian-themed pulp novels. Now that books were "PLENTY dirty," Barbara reasoned, "male voyeurs just don't bother with the 'good' ones—and there just aren't enough literate female homosexuals to provide a selling audience…"[40]

Pragmatically adjusting her goals, Barbara set out to craft a new identity—as an editor, and ultimately publisher, of stories and books for lesbians. Transitioning from a life of virtual activism into a much more public role, she endeavored to feed women's hunger for literature that affirmed their existence.

CHAPTER SIX

~∾

Changing Times

"I do not really know much about the internal bickering of the hierarchy and wish to know even less, but the whole point of it is that in the changes, that baby must not get lost in the mess."
—Barbara Grier to Jane Rule, 1968[1]

When searching for someone to replace Barbara Gittings as editor of *The Ladder* in 1966, Del Martin asked Barbara Grier to consider the post. Declining, she quipped: "Since I cannot spell or punctuate worth a damn I think it an unreasonable request."[2] As devoted as she had been to writing for *The Ladder*, Barbara had no training in journalism and was not even a member of Daughters of Bilitis. Given Helen Bennett's concerns about privacy, she thought it best to remain behind the scenes.

After Barbara declined the position, Martin turned to graphic designer and DOB stalwart Helen Sandoz, who used the name Helen Sanders within the organization. Thirteen years Barbara's senior, she had grown up in Oregon, the daughter of a hotel maid. Moving to San Francisco as a young woman, Sanders became active in the Mattachine Society and Daughters of Bilitis. As president of the latter group, she signed her real name when the DOB filed for a state charter in 1957, but otherwise used her pseudonym. Sandy, as she was known to friends, met her life partner, Stella Rush, when she attended ONE, Inc.'s Midwinter Institute in Los Angeles. Stella had worked at North American Aviation during World War II and came out as a lesbian in December 1948, but entered the gay movement cautiously because she did not want to lose her civil service position. "It took going through waves of fear," she explained, before she began writing for *ONE Magazine* in 1954 under the pseudonym Sten Russell.[3]

Eager to help the new editor get off to a good start, Barbara wrote to offer her assistance. "She just drove me crazy," Sanders remembered years later, nevertheless recognizing that Barbara had useful connections. Barbara, who thought Sanders was a "nincompoop," prepared a full critique of each issue, chastising Sanders for spending too many pages on a story, not publishing other work, or placing stories in the wrong order. At times Barbara became so obsessed with the content of *The Ladder* that she sent daily special-delivery letters. Even though Sanders chafed at Barbara's criticism, she welcomed the assistance because committed volunteers were difficult to find. "Barbara Grier has been exceedingly cooperative," Sanders informed Martin the following October. She not only submitted material—and lots of it—she also urged others to write for *The Ladder*. Sanders, who had a demanding advertising position with Sears, Roebuck & Co., increasingly relied on Barbara to generate content. Like former editor Gittings, Sanders faced the challenge of editing *The Ladder* in one city, producing it in another and doing virtually everything with volunteer labor. Pointing to numerous subscriber complaints about late or missing issues, Sanders addressed concerns about subscribers' right to privacy and persuaded the DOB governing board to approve the use of a commercial distributor.[4]

Security of the mailing list had been a sensitive issue for the DOB since *The Ladder*'s inception. In the 1950s, subscribers had feared job loss or discrimination if they were linked to a homosexual publication. Aware of such concerns, *Ladder* editor Phyllis Lyon in 1956 had reassured readers: "Your name on our mailing list is as inviolate as the provisions of the Constitution of the United States can make it." During the course of the magazine's sixteen-year existence, other editors periodically informed subscribers their names were safe. In reality, the DOB was not as careful with its mailing lists as it wanted members and subscribers to believe. A person could subscribe to *The Ladder* without being a DOB member; therefore, the organization maintained two lists. DOB officers filed the list of members in a locked filing cabinet at DOB headquarters, but a number of people had access to *The Ladder*'s subscription list, including volunteers who typed and applied the magazine's mailing labels each month. On several occasions, Gittings asked for and received copies of the subscription list so she could recruit people to write for *The Ladder*.

She also sent personalized letters to women who lived within a sixty-mile radius of San Francisco, urging them to attend *Ladder* work parties. When she discovered *The Ladder* was losing money because it had to pay return postage for all undeliverable copies, she edited the list for accuracy, culling names that could not be verified.[5]

Restless Energy

For years, Barbara had funneled her abundant energy into writing, book collecting, the homophile movement, other people, a series of clerical-level jobs and her home life with Helen Bennett. Despite all of these commitments, she felt a deepening void. Beginning in 1966, Barbara confronted the growing realization that something was missing in her relationship with Helen, and struggled with "the knowledge that I must break out of bounds and the knowledge that I could not live with guilt."[6]

Before the end of the year, Barbara had resumed her correspondence with Pamela Rust. When Jane Rule advised her to proceed carefully, Barbara responded that she had no expectations. Yet, as the weeks passed, she allowed her feelings to rekindle. "I got a letter from Pamela today," she informed Rule in late November, "the Pamela I first met this way... Simple truth—I care still, I will go right on caring about her as long as I live."[7] Rust, however, had moved on with her life.

Rule attributed Barbara's actions to restlessness: "You feel tempted all over again...You have an appetite for some new person to discover, for the energy that comes with discovery, for the liveliness of mind and body." Emboldened by Scotch and the deepening intimacy of their pen friendship, Rule assured Barbara it was normal to want to enjoy something or someone new, and urged her to "accept the erotic, not necessarily therefore act on it." Aware of the constraints that bound her friend's life, Rule encouraged her to "[b]e restless. Use me. I am a good safety valve, being a goodly number of miles away."[8]

Rule's directness inspired Barbara to admit that she had feelings for her mentor and friend. Struggling to express her emotions to the woman she had grown to admire and trust, Barbara marveled over their ability to connect. "One of the things I cannot quite get over is that I have, with you, a relationship utterly unlike anything I have ever experienced before." In retrospect, Barbara believed those feelings explained her anger about Rule's seduction of Pamela Rust. "I recognized...I was almost equally as furious for not having been Pamela." Summoning her courage, Barbara declared that "given the necessary circumstances, I would welcome and encourage you…I felt that strongly the one short night in your company." Gently but effectively, Rule dampened Barbara's romantic rhetoric by explaining she did not intend for them to fall in love. "Kidkin, what I suppose I'm trying to teach you, as I try to teach myself, is some method of dealing with erotic energy, which, without denying or destroying it, renders it more happily comic than tragically dangerous."[9]

As she had done in the past, Barbara submerged herself in activity. One project involved editing friend Jody Shotwell's novella for serialization. Shotwell, who would die from cancer in January 1968, had written numerous short stories for *ONE Magazine*, but had no suitable outlets for her longer pieces. The first of six installments of Shotwell's "The Shape of Love" appeared in the May 1967 issue of *The Ladder*. In addition to her regular column in *Tangents* and her articles and reviews in *The Ladder*, Barbara told Rule she had published her twenty-ninth paperback original novel.[10]

The Lesbian in Literature

From 1966 through 1968, DOB president Shirley Willer threw her full energy into the Daughters of Bilitis. Willer and her lover, Marion Glass (whose DOB name was Meredith Grey), traveled the nation organizing new DOB chapters and revitalizing existing ones. While their visits to Boston, Cleveland, Philadelphia, Phoenix, Dallas and other cities served as a stimulus, local women's efforts determined a chapter's success or failure.[11] As an organizational leader, Willer became the primary conduit through which a wealthy closeted woman gave tens of thousands of dollars to the cause. Over a period of several years, the mystery donor referred to as "Jenny" and "Pennsylvania" conveyed her wishes to Willer and sent $3,000 money orders to a different DOB member each month, with the understanding that she would turn it over to her local DOB chapter.[12] The donor's priorities included enhancing the publication quality of *The Ladder*, aiding chapters as they set up offices and newsletters, and funding publication of Barbara Grier's *The Lesbian in Literature*.

In the spring of 1967, Barbara devoted herself to preparation of a book-length bibliography of lesbian literature. The inexpensively duplicated checklists she had compiled with Marion Zimmer Bradley were woefully outdated, yet the DOB continued mailing them to individuals and libraries requesting information about lesbianism. When the DOB's anonymous donor learned of the situation, she allocated $6,000 to transform the checklists into an updated and more comprehensive paperback book. "I am personally sure that she is crazy," Barbara confided to Rule, "but I am not knocking her insanity at the moment."[13]

Gene Damon's reputation as a lesbian literary critic made her the logical person to prepare the publication. In pithy commentary, Barbara offered insights into lesbian literature well in advance of literary scholars who would make it their specialty in decades to come. She chose 1966 as the cut-off date for inclusion and proceeded to organize citations in alphabetical order. Since the DOB wanted to make the book available by fall, she omitted annotations, substituting a coding system to indicate the degree of lesbian content: "A" for major lesbian characters, "B" for minor lesbian characters, "C" for "latent, repressed Lesbianism," "T" for trash, and asterisks (*, **, and ***) to denote literary quality. In keeping with Barbara's goal of inclusiveness and comprehensiveness, *The Lesbian in Literature* (1967) ranged in coverage from such early American novelists as Charles Brockden Brown to noted twentieth century authors, and also included "yesterday's better forgotten drugstore items."[14] Its compilation was no small feat for a woman who lacked scholarly credentials and was not paid for her effort. Helen's careful proofreading earned her credit as co-editor under the pseudonym Lee Stuart. When Barbara's copies of the book arrived in July, she proudly shipped one to Rule.

Rule's reaction to the book disappointed Barbara. The Canadian considered Barbara's rating system "better than the ghastly comments of earlier lists," but found the number of pages "devoted to keeping worthless titles alive" appalling. Rule, like Barbara Gittings before her, thought her friend's time and effort would be better spent if she stopped reviewing original paperback novels and focused on nonfiction titles. Barbara went on the defensive once again, explaining that *The Lesbian in Literature* was "not the Lesbian in good literature, or so-so literature, or in some certain portion of literature." Moreover, the inclusion of nonfiction would render the bibliography impossible to compile because of the burgeoning literature on the subject of homosexuality. As for the trash, inclusion of the "T" category warned readers away from inferior literature. Unconvinced, Rule relentlessly questioned Barbara's judgment: "You are willing to write trash, to keep files of it, and publish lists of it. If you were frankly cynical about the whole thing, it would make more sense to me. But you seem to feel you're devoting a good part of your life to serving the cause of your minority." The book, Rule concluded, was yet one more example of proof that she and Barbara operated under different moral codes. Unable to agree, Rule suggested that "perhaps kindness is found in silence."[15]

The class differences that periodically affected Barbara and Rule's relationship were especially apparent in Barbara's unwillingness to concede. Informing her friend that silence was not a solution, she reiterated that lesbian literature of the best quality was not always the best written.

Indeed, if quality of writing determined inclusion in the bibliography, it would contain two hundred or fewer titles. Pointing to Radclyffe Hall's *The Well of Loneliness* as an example, Barbara argued it was "dreadfully over-written, and corny and several other things. It is psychologically and even physiologically unlikely—but it is still a very big and important title in Lesbian literature." Readers, like books, had many different purposes and she therefore compiled *The Lesbian in Literature* to meet their diverse needs.[16]

To ensure the widest possible number of people learned of the compilation, Barbara sent complimentary copies to local libraries and used some of Helen's connections through the American Library Association to get the book mentioned in *Library Journal*, read by thousands of librarians. She took immense pleasure in college and university library orders because these purchases meant long-term preservation and wider access for *The Lesbian in Literature* as well as *The Ladder*. Barbara's faith in the power of print to open minds was affirmed when a sociology professor from Anderson College, founded by the Church of God, contacted her for assistance in selecting fictional treatments of lesbianism to use in a course and invited her to speak to his students. While she declined to appear due to the travel involved, Barbara recognized significant change was occurring if a faculty member at a conservative religious college could ask a lesbian to lecture on his campus.[17] It was among the first of many invitations she would receive during the next four decades.

A Question of Ethics

In the 1950s, Barbara and Jeannette Howard Foster had devoted countless hours to detecting the presence of homosexuality in novels and to speculating on the sexual orientation of their authors. As times changed, some people found fault with their assumptions. In September 1967, Chicago novelist Valerie Taylor expressed displeasure with what she perceived as misleading statements contained in an article on poetry by Lennox Strong and Terri Cook (pseudonyms for Barbara and Helen). "One grows a little tired of these evaluations in which one line out of a hundred or a thousand is seized upon to prove that So-and-So is one of us." Expanding on Taylor's comment in a subsequent letter to the editor, Jane Rule criticized Gene Damon for doing likewise in "Lesbiana." As a writer addressing lesbian experience in her novels, Rule had wearied of mainstream reviewers who focused on her book's "sensational subject matter," not her writing ability. "When a Lesbian magazine not only imitates but exaggerates such distortions," she argued, "it does nothing for the cause it professes."[18]

With Gene Damon's reputation at stake, Barbara prepared a well-reasoned reply to Rule's criticism of the "Lesbiana" column for publication in the January 1968 issue of *The Ladder*. Noting there was a difference between the "academic student of literature" and the "ordinary reader," Barbara argued that failing to review original paperbacks would be a disservice to the majority of readers who chose books because of lesbian content, not literary quality. "There are, whether Miss Rule realizes it or not," she noted, "many regular readers of Lesbian material who don't read anything else."[19]

Tension mounted when a poem by one of Rule's friends mysteriously appeared in the June issue of *The Ladder*. Rule, who had shared the poem with Barbara, knew the poet, Lori Whitehead, denied submitting it to editor Helen Sanders. While Barbara never admitted she told Sanders to publish it, she acknowledged that, in her zeal, she may have shared the poem with the editor and left the rest to fate. Expressing regret that she had exposed a friend to Barbara's "dishonesty," Rule declared she was ashamed to have her name associated with *The Ladder*. The poem's publication in a lesbian magazine, she fretted, would impede the budding poet's ability to publish it "in reputable big magazines, which care about previous publication and copyright niceties." Stunned by the accusation she was "a common thief" and by Rule's threat of legal action, Barbara denied knowing how the poem came to appear in the magazine. She chided Rule for stirring up "such a tempest" without first checking with her. "I take my work as seriously as you take yours," she concluded, "however less the quality."[20]

Shaken by the incident, Rule could not help questioning her friend's veracity. "Why would I do something dishonest? you demand...yet all the time you're suggesting things and doing things that seem to me highly doubtful." In particular, Rule questioned Barbara's use of pen names and post office boxes, also citing how she reversed the charges on a call to Rule so Helen would not know of it. "I understand better the lies to Helen than I do some of the other things...But then it's hard for me to believe that you wouldn't lie to me if it was important for you to do so." Rule, who saw traces of her younger self in Barbara, wanted to help her friend. Reflecting on individuals who had cared enough to curb her arrogance, Rule explained: "I suppose I cast myself in a similar role with you, wanting to belt enough dishonesty out of you so that you can use your head and your heart without blowing up the world you care about."[21]

Responding to each of Rule's concerns, Barbara attempted to dispel her friend's image of her as a liar. "Try looking at it from my side," Barbara urged. "You still have me stuck back (in your head) in the days of Pamela—and Pamela was a good lesson and a turning point." At the same time, she was flattered to learn of Rule's concern for her. "I have never known whatever could possibly interest you at all in me." Indeed, Rule asked herself the same question, yet remained intrigued by and drawn to Barbara's native intelligence, inquisitiveness, enthusiasm, ambition and wit. Resigned that some of their differences would remain unresolved, Rule apologized for her part in exacerbating their conflict, called for a truce and shifted to a more constructive approach: offering Barbara guidance in improving *The Ladder*'s quality and broadening its appeal.[22]

Advice from "Poet Goddess" Jane Rule

With their conflict over the unexplained publication of Whitehead's poem behind them, Jane Rule and Barbara resumed their ongoing conversation about books, authors, poets and publishing. Committed to helping Barbara, who had been named *The Ladder*'s Assistant Editor of Poetry and Fiction in July 1967, Rule joked that she could not "yell" at Barbara for writing nine-tenths of the magazine until she helped her find better material.[23] Barbara's ability to write from multiple perspectives ensured few readers realized that one person had written the numerous articles, stories and reviews by Marilyn Barrow, Gene Damon, Irene Fiske, Dorothy Lyle, Vern Niven and Lennox Strong, as well as numerous letters to the editor attributed to a variety of contributors. It amused Barbara when Rule critiqued articles without realizing she had written them.

Sending a peace offering along with New Year's wishes for 1968, Rule informed Barbara that her friend, Canadian poet Helene Rosenthal, would be willing to let her poems be published in *The Ladder*. A bisexual married mother of two, Rosenthal's first book of poetry, *Peace Is an Unknown Continent*, was scheduled to appear in the spring. "Though I know the bisexual turns you off," Rule wrote Barbara, "I imagine these poems—with their tenderness for the female and their restless, trapped anger in reference to male[s]—may appeal to a good many readers..." Delighted beyond belief at the prospect of a recognized poet allowing her work to appear in *The Ladder*, Barbara responded immediately. "The way to my heart," she exclaimed with glee, "is through usable manuscripts." Twelve Rosenthal poems, ranging from erotic to poignant, appeared in the February/March 1968 issue and marked the beginning of Rule's sustained influence on the DOB publication.[24]

Barbara anticipated great improvements in the coming year if Rule continued to persuade writers to submit their stories, poems and essays to *The Ladder*. "[S]hip all the Helen[e] Rosenthals you can dig up to me," she urged. "You know a good many beginning borderline writers, and obviously they are all gay (don't growl too long) or nearly so, and I want a 'piece of the action.'" Rule agreed, believing *The Ladder* would be an ideal outlet for writers to "'dump' the best of their work which, by virtue of subject or idiosyncrasy, would not be published by larger magazines."[25]

In addition to encouraging authors to submit pieces to *The Ladder*, which paid nothing for the items it published, Rule offered advice on how to communicate with prospective contributors because she thought Barbara was too apologetic when soliciting material for *The Ladder*. Attributing this attitude to her many years of interacting with "defensive, frightened people who aren't primarily interested in writing," Rule encouraged her friend to project an air of confidence, "to sound as if you believe that it's not beneath good writers to appear in the magazine." Most of the writers she knew were "much more concerned about the quality of work in a magazine than they [were] about its orientation." "[Y]ou've seen the magazine filled with amateur, anonymous stuff," she observed. "It doesn't have to go on being like that."[26]

Rule, who had not previously reviewed for *The Ladder*, also offered to write a model book review so Barbara could see how one could offer more than "an account of the plot with sexual emphasis underlined." Perhaps most important, Rule made *The Ladder* an outlet for some of her writing. After having spent two hours with several reference books to decipher Rule's "Three Letters to a Poet," with its references to Greek mythology, astrology and Canadian history, Barbara pronounced the prose "much too complicated for the magazine," yet she chose to run the piece because she loved Rule's writing for the same reason she loved poetry: "the joy of the sound. The words don't have to make sense." Beginning with the May-June 1968 issue, Jane Rule became a familiar name to readers of *The Ladder*.[27]

Once Rule began paying closer attention to *The Ladder's* contents, she sensed class conflict occurring on its pages, "a battle between middle class, middle-aged conservatism and the 'swinging' younger generation." While Rule's perceptions were correct, what she failed to realize was that Barbara had manufactured some of the tension in an effort to spark controversy and generate interest in the magazine. It was not uncommon for her to write letters to the editor that represented opposing viewpoints. Two examples appeared in January 1968 in response to a Jane Kogan illustration featured on the November 1967 cover. A departure from the magazine's standard line drawing and photographic covers, the Cubist-inspired image depicted two women, one touching the other's breast. The first letter to the editor objected to the artwork on the grounds it implied "that Lesbians were occasionally delinquent sexually," while the second letter asserted it was "refreshing to see the old conservative rag, *The Ladder*, does know that there is a very swinging new generation just outside the door."[28]

Outside Disruptions

Barbara had a two-fold solution for achieving civil rights for all: voting and education. "If I dislike what my government does, on any level," she argued, "I express it when I vote." Because of her conviction that voting offered the key to lasting change, Barbara joined a campaign in March 1968 to register African Americans to vote in an upcoming fair housing referendum. Thus far, Kansas City had avoided race riots, and Barbara believed the referendum could keep the city peaceful. It was not to be. Fallout following the assassination of Martin Luther King, Jr. led to riots on April 9 that left five dead, more than one hundred arrested, and others hospitalized. From the vantage point of her apartment in the southern part of the city, Barbara attributed the violence to youth, "just ordinary high school kids, shouting and pushing and singing 'Sock it to me, BLACK POWER' and other uplifting mottos of the same ilk."[29] The reports of riots on both coasts, as well as her observations of the local scene, reinforced Barbara's commitment to education rather than direct-action causes.

Despite Barbara's distance from her family, their drama further disrupted her world. In the spring of 1968, Philip Grier, who had remarried her mother two years earlier, suffered a debilitating stroke. Unable to cope due to her own failing health, Dorothy Grier turned to her children for assistance. As the sisters sorted through their parents' financial affairs, it became apparent their father, whom Barbara referred to as a "profligate bastard," had drained their mother's modest savings to pay his accumulated debts. Burning with deep-seated resentment for the man who had shattered her childhood innocence and mistreated her mother, Barbara left the mess for her younger sister Diane to resolve.[30]

While Barbara fumed about family matters and civil unrest, Jane Rule channeled her discontent into a story titled "My Country Wrong." Set in Vietnam-era San Francisco at Christmastime, it featured a lesbian contemplating the morality of war and the mortality of children during her visit home. Declaring no one would want to publish a story with such a pacifist message, Rule included a lesbian love scene because she knew Barbara would want to publish it in *The Ladder*. Rule's description of the story arrived within days of Robert F. Kennedy's assassination in the early morning hours of June 5, 1968. The story left Helen in tears, and

Barbara could think of nothing else. It was "so frankly opposed to this idiot war" and could be interpreted by some as "politically anti-U.S.," she reflected, but it also was "a requiem Mass" for a dying country, one that Rule "obviously loved ardently." Declaring it "the best thing you have done in the short story line," Barbara scheduled "My Country Wrong" for publication in the August issue, eager to show *Ladder* readers that "Yes, we are timely, yes, we are topical, and still, by God or whatever, we are literary."[31]

Meanwhile, as DOB president Shirley Willer and companion Marion Glass traveled the country on behalf of the DOB, they sensed tension between the national governing board and local chapters that felt less allegiance to the national office and wished for greater autonomy. To address these concerns, Willer and Glass developed a proposal to disband the DOB's current organizational structure in favor of a loose confederation of chapters known as the United Daughters of Bilitis, and scheduled a vote on the matter for the 1968 biennial convention in Denver on August 9.[32]

In the weeks leading up to the convention, DOB members learned about the proposed reorganization when DOB member and avowed feminist Rita Laporte launched a campaign to defeat it. The estranged daughter of a prominent New York attorney, Laporte had enlisted in the Women's Army Corps after graduating from Swarthmore College, but was discharged because of her homosexuality. Masculine in appearance, she attributed her feminist views to childhood experiences when her parents gave preferential treatment to a younger brother because of his gender. Upon learning about her homosexuality, the family had her committed to a psychiatric hospital, and upon her release offered the unrepentant Laporte a monthly income as long as she remained as far away from them as possible. Moving to Oakland in the mid-1940s, she explored her sexual orientation while working as a streetcar motorwoman, peach pitter, raisin packer, bottle factory employee and taxi driver. Intelligent and articulate, she also earned a law degree from Boalt School of Law at the University of California, Berkeley. Laporte only sporadically attended DOB meetings, in part because of her unwillingness to abide by a provision in the organization's Statement of Purpose indicating members should adopt a "mode of dress and behavior acceptable to society."[33] Eager to defeat the Willer and Glass proposal, Laporte took the DOB membership list from San Francisco headquarters and mailed members a mimeographed letter denigrating their plan for reorganization.

DOB-Denver, 1968

Race riots rocked Chicago and Miami in August 1968 as Republican and Democratic delegates gathered to nominate their respective candidate for Lyndon Baines Johnson's replacement as president. In this tense atmosphere, Barbara and a reluctant Helen boarded a train for Denver to attend the fifth national meeting of the Daughters of Bilitis. On the way there, Barbara broke an incisor on her bridge and consequently "went with less facial expression than usual, and did little talking."[34]

A realist, Barbara knew her limitations, especially when it came to organizational politics. Neither she nor Helen had previously belonged to DOB or had any interest in the "internal bickering of the hierarchy." The DOB people, Barbara explained to Rule, "aren't my kind of people, they are promoting different things in different ways. They like meetings…and panels and discussions and all the hoopla that is basically a form of politics or lobbying and never does do a damned thing." A fervent believer in print, Barbara thought one good issue of *The Ladder* would accomplish far more than all of their meetings and conferences and groups combined. "As far as I am concerned," she noted on more than one occasion, "nothing any of the organizations do amounts to a damn except for their publications."[35]

The trigger that prompted Barbara to attend the meeting was Helen Sanders's announcement that she wished to be relieved of her duties as editor of *The Ladder*. Fearing for her beloved publication's fate, Barbara decided that she could edit the publication if Sanders continued supervising technical details, especially the layout and proofreading. Allowing her imagination to soar, Barbara dreamed of developing *The Ladder* into a tool that could play an even greater role than it already did in fostering self-acceptance and changing public perceptions in a world where being queer was "not a serious topic, but a snide remark."[36]

When DOB president Willer convened the biennial convention on August 9, she faced a small assembly of just fourteen women (a few others arrived later). In one of the first items of business, Sanders declined the position of *Ladder* editor and the members present selected Barbara as her replacement. As thrilled as she was with the appointment, Barbara was not impressed by what she observed during the meeting. "This organization represents several thousand women with nothing basically in common but their sexual preference for their own sex," she informed Rule. She was intrigued by her encounter with Martha Shelley, "a draft card burning type ready to change the world TODAY," and impressed by Priscilla Royal and Karen Wilson, two San Francisco delegates who assisted with *The Ladder*'s circulation. After sharing a lunch with them, Barbara realized they recognized "that the magazine's potential is far beyond the organization's potential as a moving force in the world." Impatient with seemingly endless discussions, Barbara and Helen skipped the rest of the meeting and returned to Kansas City so the new editor could begin work on her maiden issue.[37]

With *The Ladder*'s fate determined, the remaining delegates turned their attention to the Willer and Glass proposal for reorganization. Eager to defeat it, Laporte had come to the meeting with proxies from a majority of the New York and San Francisco DOB chapter members. In the end, delegates chose to defer action until the 1970 meeting, when they hoped more members would participate. When Willer (the current DOB president) and Glass resigned in disgust, Laporte stepped forward to become DOB president.[38]

Barbara had not met Laporte prior to the Denver DOB meeting, but knew of her longstanding interest in the butch-femme stereotype within lesbian culture because of essays she had written for *The Ladder*. Their brief encounter left Barbara convinced the new DOB president's manic behavior would discourage anyone from volunteering to assist with the magazine. Her assessment was reinforced by comments made by *Ladder* circulation volunteers Wilson and Royal. They were, Barbara observed to Rule, "very bright, loathe her [Laporte], and are too young not to say so at every opportunity." Indeed, Royal took proactive measures to protect herself and her friend because she did not trust Laporte. Slipping into DOB headquarters, Royal removed all their information from the DOB files and retrieved address plates from the printer so she could destroy both of their entries.[39]

Because Barbara had doubts about Laporte and regarded the DOB as outmoded and overly bureaucratic, she dreamed of the day when her beloved magazine could become independent. From her perspective, the changes implemented in Denver signified *The Ladder* had "subtly moved more and more out of the control of the national organization."[40] Indeed, both Helen Sanders and Shirley Willer severed their connections to the DOB but remained loyal to the magazine, the former by helping with production and the latter by channeling money from the DOB's mystery donor to *The Ladder*'s account. With her growing army of volunteers, Barbara had reason to be optimistic.

As someone connected to the DOB through its publication, Barbara eschewed organization politics and increasingly believed enough readers existed to support an independent publication. "The organization can go to hell," she proclaimed to Rule, but "[t]here are so many reasons for making the magazine good." As someone drawn to the magazine's literary content, Barbara knew she could edit a publication that would appeal to "the non-militant, not really committed characters," but she also planned "to keep our hard-core lifelong readers happy" while offering "a market for writers who have something to say in this field and who are working toward a writing reputation." Ever the publicist, she also intended for *The Ladder* to serve as "a good public relations image for homosexuals." "I have rather some grandiose plans," she concluded, "but I believe I can make it [*The Ladder*] work."[41]

CHAPTER SEVEN

≈

The Ladder: Theft or Liberation?

Gene Damon is my Editor, I shall not loaf,
She maketh me to lie down in exhaustion;
She driveth me to drink the still's waters,
She restoreth my comma; She leadeth me in the paths
Of doublespacing for her printer's sake.
Yea, though I walk through the valley of the shadow
Of Lesbos, I will feel no leisure, for she is with me
Her whip and her staff they confront me.
She prepares a table before me in the presence of many manuscripts.
She annointest my typewriter with carbons; my ribbons runneth ragged.
Surely subscriptions and advertisements will fall on us all the days
Of publication, and we will dwell in the house of THE LADDER forever.
— *Anonymous [1971]*[1]

Barbara Grier's dedication to *The Ladder* made her an ideal choice to serve as editor, yet she had significant liabilities. An isolate, she preferred working behind the scenes in her Kansas City home. As she explained to Florence Jaffy, research director for Daughters of Bilitis, "I am as public a person as the fishes in the deep. I loathe public meetings, loathe all political action and controversy."[2] Barbara's preference for hierarchal organization also conflicted with the growing feminist emphasis on cooperation and collaboration. Finally, she erroneously assumed she could edit *The Ladder* without becoming enmeshed in DOB politics.

After becoming editor in 1968, Barbara had more frequent contact with the DOB's national governing board. From her perspective, the national officers' failure to adapt the organization to the changing cultural, social and political scene of the late 1960s placed *The Ladder* in jeopardy. "The sad thing is," she wrote to Jane Rule, "I am dealing with a lovely bunch of illiterate people. I like a lot of them, and yes, they can read, it is just that they are all ORGANIZATION people—they have gray flannel minds to match their gray flannel suits—and they are either militant (let's burn queers in the streets) or lazy (let's all have a fuck-in to show how liberated we are)."[3] In Barbara's opinion, no one, with the possible exception of her predecessor as *Ladder* editor, Helen Sanders, cared as much about the magazine and its readers as she did.

Barbara had reason to be concerned about *The Ladder*'s fate. The DOB's new national president, Rita Laporte, seemed obsessed with eliminating everyone from the organization who had supported the Shirley Willer and Marion Glass proposal for the DOB's corporate reorganization. One of Barbara's contacts in the New York DOB informed her Laporte had written officers there suggesting they "vote to KILL THE LADDER" because she "did not trust that sneaky Gene Damon, and Sandy and Lois Williams either." Alarmed to the point of hysteria, Barbara spent hours on the phone and at her typewriter conferring with DOB officers in San Francisco, New York, and Los Angeles because she wanted to ensure the future of her precious magazine. "Rita," Barbara declared, "sincerely is quite mad, and I mean ready to be put away."[4]

Sanders believed one solution was to incorporate the magazine as a separate entity. During her editorship, she had learned sponsors existed who would be willing to support the magazine if it separated from the DOB. Evidently, some women wanted to give money for the publication but had no interest in supporting its parent organization. "If a donor gives a substantial amount of money for TL [*The Ladder*]," Sanders argued, "then I think we must be able to guarantee that this donation will, indeed, go to that specific purpose."[5] Nine governing board members supported separate incorporation, but they were no match for Laporte's opposition. Citing legal knowledge gained while studying at the University of California, Laporte informed board members that they knew nothing about the legal ramifications of separate incorporation. If the magazine incurred debt, she argued, a creditor could sue DOB and force it into bankruptcy. "If we want real safety," she teased, "we'll have to say good-bye to *The Ladder*. No, we'll have to disband DOB and cease publishing anything. After all, we've been recommending bedroom crime for a long time and that ain't legal."[6] In their uncertainty, the governing board decided to let the issue rest until the DOB's next biennial meeting in 1970.

Watching the DOB machinations from a distance, Barbara vowed "to see this mess through," but as soon as things were smooth again to look for a replacement editor because of her partner, Helen Bennett. The job wasn't hard "but obviously these people seem to refuse to function in their own cages without drawing me into [them]." The frequent long-distance phone calls at all hours of the night were making Helen "nervous to the point of hysteria," because she simply wanted to live without interruptions of any kind. "When I go away in my head to think," Barbara confided to Rule, "she knows, and I know it, and she cannot help resenting it."[7] Under the circumstances, Barbara believed it would be best if she relinquished the editorship once *The Ladder* stabilized.

Since former editor Sanders had worked so closely with Barbara, she understood the new editor's personal constraints and therefore offered to serve as production assistant for *The Ladder*. Sanders knew Barbara's intensity made her difficult to work with, but she also recognized Barbara's ability to produce results. "Sometimes when I go to my mailbox and I see a letter edged in blue and salve-green," Sanders confessed, "I reach in with trepidation because I know it is an edict from Gene Damon." Yet time and time again, Gene Damon's efforts had kept the publication going during lean times. Now that the baby was "hers," Sanders urged the DOB board, "Let's not kill it with doubts, fears and past dreads."[8]

Vision for Change

Shortly after assuming her responsibilities as editor, Barbara learned that *The Ladder*'s stated circulation of one thousand was misleading because many on the subscription list received complimentary copies. According to former editor and DOB president Del Martin, there were fewer than six hundred paid subscribers, and the magazine's five dollar subscription fee fell far short of covering printing and distribution costs which by 1968 were a minimum of one thousand dollars per issue. Consequently, the magazine had grown dependent on the generosity of its anonymous donor, but since she was linked to the DOB through former president Shirley Willer, the future of her contributions looked dubious. As someone who had spent much of her working life in business settings, Barbara recognized the necessity of cultivating other sources of income if *The Ladder* were to continue.

Magazines typically generated money from the sale of advertising, but in the late 1960s few companies were willing to have their products associated with lesbian and homosexual publications. Undeterred, Barbara ramped up her pursuit of potential advertisers, but declared she would not "push trash," for example, advertisements for pornography or sex toys. "I never minded making money for me, or for my sisters, when it was needed," she explained to Rule (referring to her claims to have written for the original paperback market), "but I won't sell *The Ladder* to anyone."[9]

Despite the time and energy Barbara devoted to selling advertisements, they were slow to materialize. The first non-DOB-related advertisement appeared more than a year later when Vantage Press advertised *Sex Cage* by Ilonka. Authors, including Isabel Miller (*A Place for Us*, reissued in 1971 as *Patience and Sarah*) and Robin Morgan (*Sisterhood Is Powerful!*), also advertised in *The Ladder*. Other companies willing to do business with a lesbian magazine included the Magic Turban, a hair product manufactured in Brooklyn, New York, and Laurelwood Antiques in San Jose, California. By the spring of 1971, *The Ladder* also published ads for such women's journals as *Radical Therapist*, *Ain't I a Woman*, *Arena Three*, *The Great Speckled Bird* and *off our backs*. In lieu of payment, however, editors of such magazines often returned the favor by placing advertisements for *The Ladder* in their publications.[10]

Since Barbara could not rely on advertising revenue to sustain the magazine, she decided to increase subscription revenue. She began by asking the many attorneys, doctors and ministers who had for years received complimentary copies to become paying subscribers. By mid-October, approximately forty had complied in response to her persuasive barrage of letters. She also worked to make *The Ladder* more visible to the reading public. Convinced everyone read Ann Landers, Barbara submitted a letter containing information about the DOB. If Landers failed to publish it, she planned for a *Ladder* volunteer to write "a ringer letter" inquiring about organizations for lesbians.[11] To grow subscriptions, Barbara believed she needed to appeal to rural and urban residents, to eighth-grade graduates as well as people with doctorates, and to readers of all ages. One way of doing this was by developing a reputation for publishing material of interest to the non-literary reader as well as quality material for the woman who loved fiction and poetry.[12] A realist, she understood the need to publish material of interest to DOB stalwarts as well as the rising tide of lesbian feminists. She also wanted to include something for the men who read the magazine.

In Barbara's opinion, publishing the works of well-known writers in *The Ladder* would convince others that the publication was a credible venue for their work. Launching a volley of letters, she solicited contributions from hundreds of prominent psychologists, leading religious authorities, and a variety of well-known women writers. Many of her letters went unanswered, but some yielded results. A child psychologist who practiced in a metropolitan school district in California submitted an article on cross-cultural sex roles, but felt it was too risky to have her "professional name" associated with *The Ladder*. Likewise, a college librarian who had been president of the Los Angeles DOB chapter used a pseudonym for her article on "The Homophile and Income Tax Inequities."[13] Because Barbara wanted readers to know the qualifications of pseudonymous authors, she included brief summaries of their educational attainments at the end of each article.

As Gene Damon, Barbara had spent many years reviewing gay male literature; therefore, she was well positioned to ask gay men to write for *The Ladder*. Aware some DOB members would object to the men's presence in the magazine, she minimized their visibility by using ambiguous pseudonyms and initials rather than first names when publishing their work. Their receptiveness to her overtures encouraged the editor's desire to widen the magazine's appeal by including "more male H stuff." She began by publishing some "sexless poetry" and reviews of gay male literature in "Lesbiana." Articles essays, and stories followed, and when readers turned the pages of *The Ladder*, they found the work of such respected writers as Reverend Robert Wood, author of *Christ and the Homosexual* (1960), writer and editor Joseph Hansen (writing as James Coulton), eminent sexologist Vern Bullough, and gay activists Frank Kameny and Leo Skir.[14]

In keeping with the changing times, Barbara believed the time had come to end *The Ladder*'s prudery. "We will print anything good, regardless of approach," she promised. "I have never liked the tendency to act as if Sex hadn't yet been discovered." Amused by Barbara's enthusiasm, Rule found it ironic that a magazine "dedicated precisely to *sexual* rights" had "a prudery that even *Redbook* would laugh at." Wasting no time in introducing a little sex into the magazine's pages, Barbara published Rule's short story "House Guest," which described two drunk women lying on the couch "kissing into an opening desire, the longing of body for body."[15]

More Advice from "Poet Goddess" Rule

Jane Rule enthusiastically supported Barbara's goal of transforming *The Ladder* into a quality magazine with broad appeal because she wanted to see more publication outlets for writers of good fiction and poetry. True to her word, Rule assisted Barbara in evaluating poetry submitted for publication and served as a trusted sounding board. Given the limited number of outlets available to poets, Barbara received many more poems than she possibly could publish. Beginning in the fall of 1968, she selected what she perceived as the best of the lot and mailed them to Rule for blind review. The first batch included several by Judy Grahn, a poet Rule praised as having a true tone and "a real voice." For years, Barbara had insisted *The Ladder* should only promote positive portrayals of lesbianism, but when Lori Whitehead submitted a poem filled with "despairing anger," Rule convinced the editor that the magazine's integrity depended on her willingness to present "any emotionally valid work of merit." That, she stressed, is what would encourage writers to submit their work there because they will see it is not necessary to remain within "the positive superficiality that dominates popular fiction."[16]

In general, Barbara followed Rule's recommendations, but there were exceptions. Sometimes she published poems Rule disliked because she wanted to reward loyal *Ladder* volunteers or because she liked a poem's sentimental message. Instead of rejecting a poet's work outright, Barbara turned the situation to her advantage, asking her to contribute typing or proofreading skills to support the work of *The Ladder.* She rewarded a poet writing as Maura McConnell by publishing many of her poems and, in time, the woman became Barbara's unpaid secretary. Other aspiring contributors became an army of volunteer reporters who helped Barbara expand the monthly "Cross Currents" column by sending her news about gay and lesbian events in their communities.

In her role as mentor, Rule did not hesitate to critique Barbara's plans for the publication. Insistent that *The Ladder* build its reputation for publishing quality literature rather than political rants, Rule chided Barbara whenever she sensed an imbalance in coverage. She believed the magazine would become more acceptable to up-and-coming feminist writers if Barbara de-emphasized the focus on lesbians as a sexual minority. Taking Rule's advice to heart, Barbara published very little of her own work (with the exception of editorials and reviews) after August 1968. Nevertheless, despite her eagerness to broaden the magazine's appeal, Barbara ignored Rule's suggestion that she replace the title of "Lesbiana" with something more innocuous, like "Books" or "Book Reviews," because that represented too significant a departure from her goal of improving the lives of lesbians.

Through blunt yet loving comments, Rule attempted to curb and refine Barbara's brash personality. Rule was close enough to Barbara to recognize that the "street tough" persona of her youth too often guided her actions and statements. In general, Barbara accepted Rule's criticism without complaint because of her admiration for the Canadian writer. On the few occasions when she vented anger or frustration, Rule simply waited, and equilibrium soon returned to their relationship. "You are who you are," Rule wrote after one of their disagreements, "which is sometimes a great blessing, sometimes a great trial. That is the experience of a friendship that grows as steadily and soundly as ours does. You don't ever need to apologize to me about who you are."[17]

Sisterhood Is Powerful!

With the emergence of the feminist movement in the mid-1960s, the personal became political for many American women, including lesbians. Some members of DOB, among them Del Martin and Phyllis Lyon, threw their support to the National Organization for Women (founded in 1966) because they wanted it to advance the cause of all women. Never a joiner, Barbara remained focused on her print-based activism while increasingly embracing feminist sentiments. As she explained to Barbara Gittings in 1966, "I do feel that woman [sic] can THINK as WELL AS LOVE."[18] After reflecting on the inequality of the sexes, Barbara concluded lesbians had more in common with heterosexual women than they did with gay men because the latter benefitted from male privilege despite their sexual orientation.

Like Rule, Barbara became involved with a local women's liberation group and was eager to compare notes with her Canadian friend. The Kansas City Women's Liberation Union (WLU), Barbara observed, "is full of silent brooding women." Struggling to understand how these confused "upper middle class children" had managed "to grow up so uncombed, unkempt, unloved and frightened," she responded in the best way she knew how, feeding them homemade "chili sauce, pickled okra and love." Though she was only in her late thirties, Barbara encouraged the women to view her as an elder sage: "I look reassuringly like all their fantasy school teacher grandmothers," she explained to Rule. Convinced that women's liberation groups were filled with "burgeoning Lesbians in various conditions of 'coming out,'" Barbara proudly informed WLU members that she edited a lesbian magazine and encouraged them to call her at work anytime. Barbara sent sample copies of *The Ladder* to Rule's group at the University of British Columbia in the hope of gaining more Canadian subscribers.[19]

As someone who had come of age before the feminist movement, Barbara's knowledge of feminism came from reading women's liberation magazines and corresponding with young activists. When lesbian feminist college students discovered *The Ladder* in the mid-to-late 1960s, they were pleased when its editor responded to their queries personally. Encouraged by her show of interest in their lives and activities, they mailed her news clippings, whole issues of feminist publications, and stories and essays they had written. Barbara found it invigorating to exchange ideas with these brash, brilliant and passionate women whom she viewed as "young, on fire," and wanting to change the world.[20] In the process, she received tutorials on leather culture from University of Michigan graduate student Gayle Rubin, on the Feminist Economic Network from Martha Shelley, and on the Gay Liberation Front and Radicalesbians from Karla Jay. Ultimately, Barbara acquired enough knowledge to pass as a feminist, though her awareness of the movement's foundation, goals and complexity clearly outpaced her comprehension of such strategies as lesbian separatism or public demonstrations.

At the same time, Barbara recognized the desirability of cultivating a new generation of writers because their work would keep *The Ladder* relevant to a new generation of readers. Her tendency was to "discover" a new writer, celebrate and publish her work, and correspond extensively. Secure in her role as editor, and comfortable with the typewriter as her medium of communication, Barbara initially mailed carefully constructed prose designed to impress, and it did. Inevitably, she grew comfortable enough to relax her guard, revealing a firm conviction in the efficiency of hierarchy and an inability to comprehend feminist emphasis on consensus and cooperation. Once Barbara's correspondents realized the lack of common ground, they moved on to other causes and people, but she still considered them part of her web of contacts.

Steeped in decades of caution and paranoia, and living with a woman whom she dubbed "president of the super paranoid society," Barbara needed time to adjust to younger feminists' freer approach to life. She was alarmed when Jill Johnston, columnist for *The Village Voice*, revealed electronic music composer Pauline Oliveros's lesbianism by writing about her 1971 "marriage" to cellist Lin Barron, a student at the University of San Diego, where Oliveros taught. "One thing that disturbs me," Barbara explained, "is that the unspoken code is now being broken freely...it used to be you could safely trust any other gay person even if they hated you[,] and you them[,] not to reveal your identity in print (anyone in the movement, that is), but it's not that way now..." Barbara admired Johnston's boldness, but she worried that the University of San Diego would fire Oliveros: "She could not have attracted more attention if she had taken Fay Wray's place in KING KONG's right paw."[21] Relieved to learn Oliveros had given her consent for the story, Barbara nonetheless thought Johnston might be moving too quickly for the times.

With the rise of feminism and gay pride in the late 1960s and early 1970s, fewer contributors felt compelled to use pseudonyms when writing for *The Ladder.* Indeed, such writers and poets as Martha Shelley, Rita Mae Brown, Judy Grahn and Jane Rule became part of the growing trend of coming out in print. Though she did not fully understand their motivations, Barbara admired their freedom to be themselves. Shelley, she explained to Rule, was "a young wunderkind." A prolific author who wrote intelligently and without pretense, the Brooklyn feminist's passionate essays, poems and artwork infused *The Ladder* with feminist rhetoric. Ironically, she contributed so often that Barbara encouraged her to select a pen name for some of her pieces so it would look like the magazine had many women writing for it.[22]

Because of Barbara's visibility as editor of a nationally circulated lesbian magazine, feminist activist Robin Morgan contacted her in 1969 with an invitation to contribute an essay about the DOB for a forthcoming women's liberation anthology. "I have been for some time very concerned about the ironical strain of Puritanism as regards homosexuality" within the women's movement, Morgan explained. "I want your piece to open some squeezed shut eyes, to break down their barriers and fears, to teach them about the honor and beauty of a kind of love our depraved society condemns." Barbara, impressed and amazed that she now lived in a world where Morgan felt free enough to describe herself as "a practicing bisexual" to a complete stranger, set to work immediately. Her essay, "The Least of These: The Minority Whose Screams Haven't Yet Been Heard," appeared in the 1970 anthology *Sisterhood Is Powerful!*, along with essays by such feminists as psychologist Naomi Weisstein, *Sexual Politics* author Kate Millett, congresswoman Eleanor Holmes Norton, civil rights activist Florynce Kennedy, and poets Rita Mae Brown, Sylvia Plath and Lynn Strongin.[23]

Using language shaped by her coming of age in the 1940s and 1950s, Barbara portrayed lesbians as "the most hidden, the least noticed of any minority group…the most disadvantaged minority." In addition to the "vituperative treatment handed out [to them] on a daily basis," she noted many women's rights groups also shunned lesbians because they feared being branded with the negative stigma associated with homosexuality. "The Least of These" illustrates Barbara's obsession with factors that circumscribed lesbian lives: the inability to marry, the lack of economic protection and invisibility. Years of correspondence with isolated and closeted women had left her keenly aware of "the constant feeling so many of these kids carry around of being outcasts," a condition she desperately wished to eradicate. Offering the DOB as "the only boat for the exhausted and mistreated Lesbian to crawl onto," Barbara included the address for DOB headquarters and waited for letters to arrive from readers.[24] By the time the essay appeared, however, *The Ladder* had jettisoned away from the DOB and Barbara had become an outcast from the very organization she had so recently championed.

"Theft" of The Ladder and Its Aftermath

After becoming editor of *The Ladder* in 1968, Barbara's knowledge about publishing increased, along with confidence in her abilities. Consequently, she was prepared to fill the void when Helen Sanders announced in late 1969 that she could no longer assist with production because the demands of her job, relationship and work on *The Ladder* had taken a toll on her health. Drawing on her network of contacts, Barbara found volunteers ready to assist with technical aspects of production, but it was impossible to replace Sanders's understanding of DOB politics. Since Barbara's sole connection to the DOB had been through *The Ladder*, as editor she concluded that the organization was an impediment to efficient production of the magazine. Thus, her ties to DOB grew weaker with each passing month.[25]

Over time, DOB president Rita Laporte learned to appreciate what *The Ladder* meant to women living beyond the reach of DOB chapters, and she and Barbara established a good working relationship grounded in their shared work ethic and mutual desire to expand the magazine's reach and impact. Increasing visibility for herself, the DOB and *The Ladder*, Laporte spoke to high school, college and university classes and appeared on television to promote the DOB. The resulting avalanche of letters written to the DOB by "16, 17, 18, 19 and 20 year olds" distressed Barbara because of the organization's longstanding requirement that one must be twenty-one in order to become a member.[26]

Under her leadership, Laporte intended for the DOB to embrace feminism. In an essay appearing in the November 1968 issue of *The Ladder*, she described herself as "the woman I am: one long-resentful of her oppressed condition." Tackling oppression on multiple fronts, she subsequently had a letter published in *Playboy* criticizing that magazine for its portrayal of homosexuality as an inferior condition. Additionally, she superintended the publication of a promotional pamphlet, "What Is D.O.B.?" In keeping with her goal of making the DOB relevant to heterosexual as well as lesbian feminists, Laporte stressed that lesbians understood "what it meant to be oppressed as women." Upon receiving copies, members of the New York DOB chapter sensed the brochure "seemed to present a radical change in D.O.B. policy. For all intents and purposes, this pamphlet was the public relations [tool] for a feminist group that happened to allow Lesbians to join their ranks."[27]

In the wake of the Stonewall riots in June 1969, homophile organizations with roots in the 1950s struggled to adjust to changing times. In April 1970, the Eastern Regional Conference of Homophile Organizations announced the intent to suspend its constitution and by-laws for a year. As time neared for the DOB's upcoming annual meeting, to be held in New York City July 10-12, 1970, Barbara and Laporte both believed that the DOB faced a similar fate. Worried about *The Ladder*, Barbara concluded its future depended on the re-election of Laporte. Concocting a scheme, Barbara launched a letter-writing campaign in which she urged magazine subscribers to join DOB as national members to be eligible to vote, and then asked them to give her their proxies for the upcoming election. "I need as many proxy votes as I can get," she confided to *Ladder* contributor Lee Lynch, "to ensure the continuation of TL [*The Ladder*], and where it is concerned, I have neither pride nor qualms."[28]

When her efforts failed, Barbara considered other options, among them transforming *The Ladder* into an independent publication. She and Laporte were neither the first nor the only women to think that the magazine would have greater impact if it separated from its parent organization. Former editors Barbara Gittings and Helen Sanders both thought the DOB took the magazine for granted and saw the merit in having *The Ladder* operate as an independent publication. As early as 1965, DOB research director Florence Jaffy had predicted "there will have to be a divorce between D.O.B. with its social service activities…and the kind of quality magazine you [Kay Lahusen] and Barbara [Gittings] are getting out." Jaffy further predicted a breakdown of the national organization, in part because of its inability to change with the times.[29]

In early June 1970, Barbara gleefully announced to Rule that "the magazine is going to get a divorce from DOB," and "it is going to be about Lesbians and women in that order and in about a 60/40 split." Even though she anticipated "female homosexuals," by whom she meant long-time DOB members, "will be unhappy," she predicted "there are more women's rightists…than not."[30] Neither she nor Laporte could predict how *The Ladder*'s mystery donor would respond, but both women were willing to take the risk.

The New York chapter's officers were taken aback when they received a letter from Laporte informing them that none of the DOB's current national officers or candidates for office would attend the annual meeting. Shortly thereafter, they received an additional shock upon learning Laporte had gone to the DOB headquarters, removed *The Ladder*'s mailing list along with back issues and some supplies, and transported everything to Reno.[31]

Although Laporte alone was physically responsible for removing the mailing list and other *Ladder* materials, Barbara willingly took credit for the action because the two women had planned it together. Barbara claimed that once she became aware that "the kids," as she called her younger readers, were no longer content with "the establishment magazine," she knew the time had come to sever ties to its founding organization. Through her voluminous correspondence with readers, she perceived that many in her vast network felt an allegiance to *The Ladder* and her as its editor, but had virtually no sense of connection to the DOB, which many lesbians living in rural and small-town environments regarded as a social club for city dwellers.

Unable to contain her excitement about *The Ladder*'s liberation from the DOB, Barbara confided in Rule: "*The Ladder* is going to the moon and DOB (for all I care after two years of hard slavery) can go to hell." In her opinion, the organization had become "more of a handicap than a help," and she looked forward to being in total control. Begging and borrowing from the magazine's most loyal supporters, Barbara moved forward in classic Gene Damon style, soliciting new subscriptions, calling in favors from friends, and declaring her allegiance to a "wonderful lesbian magazine originating from Reno called *The Ladder*."[32]

DOB co-founders Del Martin and Phyllis Lyon had been inactive in recent years as they increased involvement in the National Organization for Women and other causes, but upon hearing the news about The Ladder, they decided to help DOB through a difficult time by attending its national meeting. Attendance was sparse, with only thirty individuals present, including five from Boston, three from San Francisco, two from Los Angeles, and twenty from New York. While some attendees criticized the national DOB office as dysfunctional and outdated, others believed a national DOB could still exist if the organization would "stop wasting time and energy."[33]

Tempers flared when Marion Glass blamed attendees for the organization's problems because they had voted down her and former president Shirley Willer's plan for restructuring the DOB two years earlier. She further charged the New York DOB chapter with responsibility for what happened with *The Ladder*, since its members had played a major role in electing the strong feminist Rita Laporte president in 1968. Unwilling to condemn Barbara, who had done so much for the organization's magazine over the years, Glass underestimated Gene Damon's role because she believed the editor was in "a great state of turmoil" and in all likelihood had "followed the policies laid out to her by the national officers which you elected."[34]

When Martin offered a motion to disassociate *The Ladder* from DOB, several members voiced objections, noting "[i]f we disassociate, we are giving an enormous money-making potential to someone out in Reno, and are giving up a good magazine." Such comments reveal how little people understood about the magazine's revenues and expenses. Others countered that Laporte could not be prosecuted because she had taken *The Ladder* in her official capacity as DOB president. After a lengthy debate, members voted twenty to three (with three abstentions) against taking legal action to recover *The Ladder*. With that, the DOB formally separated from *The Ladder* on July 12, 1970, and encouraged local chapters to run necessary legal notices to protect themselves from future debts or libel that might be incurred by the independent publication.[35]

Disenchanted by the squabbles, former DOB president Helen Sanders resigned from the organization. Whereas she had once taken pride in the DOB's accomplishments, Sanders was deeply disturbed by the back-biting and distrust that plagued its functioning. "I see very little love in the bitch-fights that go on in the homophile movement," she explained. "Perhaps we need to love ourselves before we can love anyone else in the cause."[36]

The DOB governing board urged local chapters to compensate for the loss of its national publication by enhancing the quality of their chapter newsletters. In response, members of the San Francisco chapter inaugurated a newsletter called *Sisters*. As its co-editors quickly learned, putting out the kind of publication DOB members had come to expect required intense devotion to the cause. "One or two women cannot go it alone," a fatigued co-editor admitted. They needed help with everything— writing articles, typing, proofreading and especially financial support.[37]

Indeed, Barbara suspected her most vocal critics belonged to the San Francisco DOB chapter, which "can be considered to be full of haters of me, which automatically makes them hate TL." Convinced they were not forwarding her mail "out of sheer spite and vindictiveness," she declared "there are many of them that would cut my throat on sight even if GOD were standing there telling them it would doom all Lesbians…" To test her theory, she asked one of her correspondents to send a letter to the DOB inquiring how she could subscribe to *The Ladder*. As Barbara anticipated, the DOB replied with an explanation that *The Ladder* "is now a women's liberation magazine, with some lesbian news & focus," and if the young lesbian wanted a gay women's magazine, she needed to subscribe to *Sisters*, the San Francisco DOB chapter's new publication.[38]

In separating *The Ladder* from the DOB, Barbara and Laporte lost some subscribers and the magazine's major donor, the mystery woman who had sunk thousands of dollars into the publication. Unwilling to go down without a fight, Barbara duplicated seven thousand brochures and mailed them to single and divorced women listed in *Who's Who of*

American Women in an effort to generate new subscriptions. Relentless in her efforts, the great promoter was thrilled when *Writer's Digest* finally included a listing for *The Ladder* in the spring of 1971.[39] Drawing upon her well-honed survival skills, she secured donations of paper, envelopes and postage (sometimes courtesy of unknowing employers), and with new subscriptions and donations, managed to keep the magazine afloat. With determination, hard work and the support of an army of volunteers, she set out to make each issue better than the last.

In October 1970, a young lesbian and ex-nun named Jeanne Córdova became involved with the Los Angeles chapter of the DOB. Elected president of the chapter, she became aware of a split between the agenda of her feminist peers and the older DOB establishment. Córdova, who realized members would not re-elect her because of her feminism, decided she would appear less threatening as editor of the chapter's newsletter, *The Lesbian Tide*. After she had been editor a mere six months, however, critics began complaining about her inclusion of feminist and anti-war material, calling it socialistic and communistic.[40]

Córdova, who had heard much about Barbara's "theft" of *The Ladder*, viewed herself as a protégée. Like Barbara, she concluded her magazine could not grow as long as it was attached to the DOB. In plotting the separation of *The Lesbian Tide* from the organization, Córdova chose a different path because she did not want to be accused of theft. "Why don't we call for a vote," she asked her supporters, and "get the magazine voted out of DOB."[41] The plan worked, and by its seventh issue, *The Lesbian Tide* was independent and well on its way to becoming an even more political publication.

The Feminist Ladder

"I'm tremendously excited about the new transformation of THE LADDER," wrote feminist activist Robin Morgan to Barbara in September 1970. "It's a most important development for all of us—Lesbians, 'bisexuals,' and straight women—that the magazine will now relate consciously to ALL women, and to the women's revolution for human rights." As a new reader, Morgan could not fully comprehend just how far *The Ladder* had come in fourteen years, from an organizational newsletter to a way-station on the path to achieving lesbian identity, to a polished feminist publication with lesbian emphasis.[42]

Like *The Ladder*, Barbara had traveled a long way since the mid-1950s. Initially, she had embraced the DOB's focus on the education and assimilation of the lesbian into society, but her study of feminist literature, interaction with the Women's Liberation Union, and correspondence with dozens of college-age lesbian feminists had convinced her "the first basic struggle is women's rights and until that is handled properly nothing much else is going to happen in the areas of liberating underdogs." While Barbara had a few reservations about Laporte's most strident rhetoric, she relished her missionary zeal, commitment to the cause and work ethic.[43] With Laporte focused on polemics, and Barbara on literature, they made a formidable team.

With a hard-driving personality some likened to World War II's General George S. Patton, Barbara wholeheartedly threw herself into the challenge of building a successful magazine with feminist appeal, one dedicated to raising "all women to full human status…whether Lesbian or heterosexual." As a middle-class Midwesterner and a Republican, Barbara considered herself "a maverick feminist" whose major virtue was the ability to work like a Trojan. "I am a real radical," she explained to Lee Lynch, "but not a revolutionary."[44] With enough effort, she believed the existing socio-cultural-political system could be made to work for gays and lesbians.

As an independent publication, *The Ladder*'s new mission was evident in numerous articles about patriarchal attitudes, gendered wage discrepancies and male chauvinism in art. After years in which white, middle-class, professional women had dominated its pages, the magazine now reflected greater diversity of age and class, if not race. Feminist symbols and slogans such as "You've Come a Long Way, Baby" dominated covers and cartoons that also enhanced the magazine's visual appeal.

Laporte's frequent contributions, appearing under her own name and the pseudonym Hope Thompson, further aligned the magazine with feminism while at the same time raising questions about the future of feminism as an inclusive social movement. In an editorial titled "Can Women Unite?" she highlighted pitfalls facing the women's movement, among them heterosexual "hatred" of lesbians, the "only really 'respectable' scapegoats left, and heterosexual women's deeply ingrained concern with pleasing men."[45]

Other evidence of the shift in tone surfaced in "Cross Currents." Drawing on the many news items sent to her by lesbian college students, Barbara filled the column with women's liberation movement news and notices on feminist books. As readers scanned its pages, they increasingly encountered such words as "militant" and such phrases as "abortion reform," "discrimination against women," and "women's liberation." Even more strident feminism surfaced in polemical essays written by frequent contributor Wilda Chase. She considered it "ironic that feminists have always been accused of being lesbians" because some radical feminists believed lesbians were in the forefront when it came to a woman having "a healthy respect for herself as a *primary* human being rather than a *secondary* one, i.e., an appendage to a male." Admonishing lesbians who hesitated to embrace feminism, she urged: "Snap out of it, sisters, and get with it! *Demand* your rights to your whole human dignity."[46]

During her editorship, and especially after the magazine's separation from the DOB, Barbara intentionally transformed *The Ladder* into a feminist publication because she wanted it to be as relevant to a new generation of readers as it had been to her when she discovered it in 1957. Yet Barbara had come of age in a pre-feminist era, and try as she might, she never fully understood younger readers and their beliefs. She was baffled by Rita Mae Brown's request that members of her collective receive credit for essays Brown had written. Even though she complied, Barbara had little sympathy for "this young new left shit in women's liberation that is anti-elitist...anti-leaders and even anti-credit." Barbara also found it distressing when women's bookstores expected her to send them free copies of *The Ladder*. "I suffer from a bombardment of pseudo-socialist women's liberation groups *taking for granted* that I will send them—as one gratuitously put it—a *complete* back file of *The Ladder*... and 5-10 copies of each successive issue FREE! I may begin a magazine editor's lib movement."[47]

Death of The Ladder

From the fall of 1970 until early 1972, Barbara edited *The Ladder's* content, Laporte and her partner, Paula Buckingham, supervised its layout and production, and Kathy Mengle and Marcia Ross handled circulation from their home in Reno, Nevada. When the magazine became separated from its parent organization, Barbara anticipated facing several major obstacles. Immediately after the break, they lost DOB member-subscribers who wanted the magazine to retain an exclusive focus on lesbian and gay topics, while some feminists refused to subscribe because they believed that associating with lesbians hindered their cause. Additionally, some young women living with their families hesitated to subscribe to a lesbian magazine because they had not come out to their parents.

Jane Rule had been ambivalent about *The Ladder* until Barbara became editor in 1968, but once it separated from the DOB she relented and submitted a number of short stories her agent had been unable to place. Since *The Ladder* was "opening up a bit," Rule decided it had become a suitable place for some of her friends to publish, beginning with prominent feminist Kate Millett, whose older sister had been her roommate at Mills College. "I didn't press her," Rule explained. "I told her why I published in *The Ladder* and that you would very much like something of hers." Since Millett's *Sexual Politics* had become a Book-of-the-Month selection, Barbara understood that an essay by her would be an "historical leap for the magazine."[48] Once Barbara received a tentative commitment from Millett, Rule and Barbara both dropped her name when they invited other authors to submit work.

Eager to see improvement in *The Ladder's* literary quality, Rule offered brutally honest critiques of poetry and stories. She told Barbara if a particular writer were "light years away from something publishable," leaving Barbara to nurture or discourage the contributor as she saw best. Rule had little tolerance for articles filled with "penis hatred," and challenged Barbara's decision to publish male poetry because it might "strain the magazine in range." She also attempted to keep Barbara's weakness for sappy, romantic poetry in check. "No, babe," Rule replied after receiving one of numerous batches in the mail, "those poems won't do at all. I know you are tempted by the sentiment, but there is nothing else." If Barbara felt passionately about contributors or their work she did not hesitate to exercise her editorial prerogative. She published the poems of Paul Mariah, who founded *Manroot* magazine in 1969, even though Rule questioned the inclusion of work published by men. Overall, however, Barbara absorbed her mentor's criticism and advice and used it to improve the magazine substantially.[49]

Encouraged by the promise of work from Millett, Barbara inundated a number of leading feminists with letters and copies of the magazine. She optimistically believed feminist author and philosopher Ti-Grace Atkinson, Caroline Bird, author of *Born Female* (1968), and others would comply with her requests. "We are literally fighting now to bridge the most difficult gap of all," she wrote Robin Morgan, whose presence in a magazine previously identified as lesbian would make a huge difference. Morgan subscribed and committed to write, as did Millett, but their pieces never materialized. Pauline Oliveros was one of the few who delivered an essay, though others supported *The Ladder* by providing free advertisements for it in *RAT*, *Radical Therapist*, and several other women's liberation newspapers.[50]

In keeping with the times, Barbara also included movie reviews and introduced a regular art column by Sarah Whitworth, curator at the Whitney Museum of Art, titled "Journeys in Art."[51] Racial diversity proved more elusive. Aside from news items in the "Cross Currents" column, women of color seldom found themselves in issues of *The*

Ladder. Thus, Barbara was euphoric to publish Anita Cornwell's "Open Letter to a Black Sister: Women's Liberation Is Our Thing Too!" in the fall of 1971. Cornwell, who grew up in South Carolina, graduated from Temple University and became a journalist and freelance writer. In two subsequent articles, also appearing in *The Ladder*, she critiqued racism in the women's rights movement and urged her sisters to save themselves by working together.[52]

Rule's association with *The Ladder* was not enough to encourage established and well-known prose writers to submit their work to the lesbian feminist magazine. With the changing times, mainstream publications were increasingly receptive to feminist poets and authors, and some paid their contributors. As an all-volunteer endeavor, *The Ladder* remained unable to pay authors with anything but complimentary copies of the magazine. Consequently, *The Ladder* evolved into a venue where new lesbian writers broke into print. During Barbara's four years as editor, she published such up-and-coming writers and poets as Rita Mae Brown, Dolores Klaich, Judy Grahn, Helene Rosenthal, Martha Shelley, Alma Routsong writing as Isabel Miller, and Lee Lynch writing as Beverly Lynch, Lynn Flood, Carol Lynk and Ellen Gold.

Throughout her editorship, Barbara focused on *The Ladder*'s content, not its production; therefore, when Laporte withdrew from the editorial team early in 1972, Barbara was forced to reevaluate the magazine's future. Without financial resources and technical support, she knew it would be impossible for her to continue even though *The Ladder* still filled an important need in the lives of many readers. Thinking like a librarian, she decided to continue the magazine through volume sixteen so the issues could be bound together as one volume, and to publish as many stories, essays and poems as possible. As a result, the final two issues of *The Ladder* contained over thirty items written by such familiar names as Mickie Burns, Lynn Strongin, Anita Cornwell, multiple items under Lee Lynch's pseudonyms, as well as material from such new contributors as Sarah Aldridge.

* * *

As one of Barbara's closest friends, Rule understood how all-consuming Barbara's work on *The Ladder* had been. Realizing she had a right to carve out a new and different life for herself, Rule assured her friend that "four years of your life is enough, more than enough, given no pay, difficult people to deal with, general flak." She made no effort to talk her friend out of the decision, but instead praised her accomplishments.

Under Barbara's editorship, she elaborated, *The Ladder* had become "so much better a magazine, one to be really proud of." Unable to envision another person who possessed the knowledge, vision and dedication to fill Barbara's shoes, Rule declared, "I'd rather see it fold than go downhill. There are now some other places where at least some of the material in the magazine could be published, something not true a few years ago, and so, though nothing else will exactly serve its purpose, it won't leave the kind of silence it would have before women's lib."[53]

Indeed, *The Ladder* had filled a critical void in the lives of lesbians from the mid-1950s to the early 1970s. Working from the nation's heartland, Barbara had dedicated herself to sustaining and transforming her beloved magazine into a resource that met the needs of women from multiple walks of life. Though it ceased with the August/September 1972 issue, *The Ladder* paved the way for creation of a publishing company whose reach would span the globe.

CHAPTER EIGHT

❧

Donna, A Whole New World

Donna is in every way a whole new world.
—*Barbara Grier, 1974*[1]

When Donna McBride picked up the phone at the Kansas City Public Library one day in 1967, she heard a strong voice on the other end: "You're new, aren't you? Get a pencil and write down these titles." Donna, who worked as a library tech in the literature department, had been warned by co-workers about the woman who asked for "those books." Dutifully recording the lesbian titles Barbara Grier requested, Donna knew she wanted to read them too.[2] Like many young Midwestern lesbians, Donna had led a closeted life, but that was soon to change.

Donna's Story

In many respects, Donna McBride and Barbara Grier had much in common. As a young girl, Donna had learned from her parents' example that "you have to work your butt off to survive." Her mother, Hazel Williams, had dreamed of being a dancer and yearned to travel to exotic places. Instead, she married Donald Merle McBride in the waning years of the Great Depression and gave birth to their only child on July 3, 1940. Merle's job as a truck driver provided a steady income, but the family led a far from a privileged existence. One day Hazel gave Donna a cookie and placed the toddler in her crib. Hearing a cry just a few minutes later, she ran back into the room to discover that a rat, attracted by the cookie, had bitten Donna's finger.[3]

During the early years of World War II, the McBride family moved to San Diego, where Merle worked until he was drafted in late 1944 and sent to the Pacific. Donna and her mother returned to live with in-laws in Kansas City, Kansas, where Hazel took a job driving a forklift in a nearby B-25 bomber production plant until the war's end. After the family reunited in 1946, the three moved to Merle's hometown of Harrisburg, Missouri, where Merle joined his brothers in a lime-spreading company. A steady provider, he took a job with the Armour meat-packing company a few years later.

Loved and well cared for, Donna grew up with a positive outlook and approached life with optimism despite her parents' economic struggles and occasional marital problems. She gave little thought to socioeconomic class because she and her school friends all seemed to wear dresses made from feed sacks, but hers were beautifully smocked by her mother. Like Barbara, Donna grew up relatively free from religious influences. Donna's father, a nominal Southern Baptist, and her mother, a Roman Catholic convert, seldom attended church. When they sent Donna to Catholic school in the third grade, she focused more on connecting with her peers than on religious teachings, and did not absorb negative messages about sexuality.

Surrounded by loving aunts, uncles and cousins, Donna never felt like an only child and grew to regard her mother as a best friend. Donna also formed a deep attachment to her paternal great-grandmother, Ida Cordelia Rupard, affectionately known as "Ma." Life as the wife of a hard-scrabble dirt farmer had not marred her gentle and loving personality. Donna treasured her affection and never forgot Ma's advice: "You might as well do what you want to because when you get to be my age you will realize that none of it matters."[4]

Like many young lesbians of her generation, Donna experienced a number of youthful crushes, with her first occurring at age six when she fell in love with an older woman of nine or ten. A tomboy, Donna became conscious of her lesbianism when she was fourteen after experiencing crush after crush on girlfriends, finally realizing her feelings for them might be more than friendship. After the McBrides settled in Kansas City, Kansas, in 1952, she grew aware of people making jokes about "queers" and saw magazine articles about the evils of homosexuality. Over the next decade she made friends with girls, fell in love with them, and then ran away so they would not discover her terrible secret.[5]

When Donna enrolled as a freshman at Central College (now Central Methodist University (in Fayette, Missouri), she searched the library for information about homosexuality. After reading Vin Packer's novel, *The Evil Friendship*, she shuddered with horror and declared, "Not me!" This and similar books convinced Donna she must keep her feelings for women carefully hidden.[6]

A bright student, Donna loved learning and graduated in three years with a bachelor's degree. After graduation, she taught French and English to high school students in Pilot Grove, Missouri, for one year, but soon concluded that she was not meant to be a teacher and that she wanted to live in a larger community.

Resigning her teaching position, Donna found employment at Business Men's Assurance in Kansas City, Missouri. When she joined the company-sponsored softball and basketball teams, Donna sensed the presence of other lesbians on the teams, but at the time no one felt safe or comfortable admitting their lesbianism, even to other lesbians. Then Marilyn Coe, a new employee, joined the team and Donna felt an immediate attraction to her and vice versa. Thrilled to realize the feeling was mutual, they began an exciting, romantic courtship. When other team members went for drinks or meals, Donna and Marilyn stole moments together, going from holding hands to becoming lovers, each other's first. They were "scared to death" every step of the way.[7]

In the mid-1960s, the Australian government encouraged immigration to the continent by paying the passage for people who pledged to work there a minimum of two years. Seizing the opportunity to see the world while running away from their closeted existence in Kansas City, Donna and Marilyn left for Australia in February 1966 by way of Hawai'i, Japan, Hong Kong and Fiji. When they arrived in Sydney, the two naïve young women rented rooms in Kings Cross, a tenderloin area respectable during daytime but full of prostitutes at night. Employment proved more difficult to find than they had anticipated, and by the time Donna secured a position with Prudential of England she was down to her last thirty dollars.

Donna and Marilyn's relationship floundered, so instead of remaining the full two years, they decided to cut short their stay in Australia. As soon as the two women had saved enough to book a return passage, they sailed for the United States, arriving in May 1967. After a brief stint at the Kansas City Public Library, the two women, no longer partners but still good friends, enrolled in the University of Missouri's Graduate Library School. They graduated a year later, and with Master of Library Science degrees in hand, returned to the Kansas City Public Library to take positions as reference librarians.

From her seat at the reference desk, Donna watched with fascination and growing curiosity as Barbara Grier "hit the library entrance at full throttle." In her low-heeled shoes, she clicked her way to the literature department or to the library catalog. Not yet comfortable with the thought of coming out as a lesbian, Donna wanted to talk with Barbara, but refrained because it might expose her secret. Instead, the librarian discreetly followed her around to discover which books Barbara examined and, during evening shifts, examined them herself. On other occasions, she took Barbara's *The Lesbian in Literature* from the shelf and searched for copies of books it mentioned.

Donna had never seen a copy of *The Ladder* before she went to work at the library. At the time, the library kept it and similar publications behind the reference desk to prevent their theft and defacement. Donna saw the delight in Barbara's face as she hand-delivered the latest issues to Donna's closeted supervisor, Betty, whose discomfort was obvious. Yet when Betty became interested in Donna, she used the magazine as a tool for seduction, suggesting the younger woman might find it of interest. In time, the two women became lovers, and Donna mistakenly assumed her supervisor desired a long-term relationship. Once, during a heated argument about their future, Betty exclaimed: "I can't be [out] like Barbara Grier."[8] The comment prompted Donna to compare her lover's unhappy demeanor with Barbara's visible confidence and enthusiasm. Pondering her future, Donna knew she would be much happier with Barbara, or someone like her, because of her positive approach to lesbianism and life.

Shortly after this self-revelation, Donna summoned her courage, phoned Barbara and volunteered to assist with *The Ladder*. At the time, she regarded Barbara as a strange but intriguing woman. "She would come stomping into the library," Donna recalled, "run around and walk out with a great armload of fourteen or fifteen books every week. She was so precise. Everything about her was exact: all of her movements, speech patterns, and everything." Meanwhile, Barbara regarded Donna as a "frightened rabbit." Aware she terrified her, Barbara sometimes took pleasure in tormenting the younger woman "just for the sheer joy of it," but soon realized she could not be mean to someone who was "extremely sweet and very patient."[9]

Withdrawing from Helen

By the time Donna began volunteering for *The Ladder*, its editor had gained a reputation among members of the Kansas City Women's Liberation Union as someone who knew how to get things done. Barbara, who did not attend many WLU meetings, was nonetheless pleasantly surprised to discover she could sit "literally cheek to jowl on a floor with some 35 women in a room that won't handle 25 comfortably" and feel at ease. During the chaotic gatherings, she found herself "listening to women I probably would have ignored in other circumstances." When they shared their personal stories during consciousness-raising sessions, Barbara felt stunned by the "degree of bitterness" and "amounts of pain" they unleashed. She also was horrified to learn that women thought they had been raised to compete with and even to hate one another. Unable to identify with their emotions, the pragmatic Barbara responded by addressing their immediate needs, and before long, she was "spending way way too much time" on their behalf. She approached her contacts in television and radio to arrange interviews for WLU members and persuaded local merchants to donate flooring and other items to the WLU's childcare center. "For some inexplicable reason," she observed, they were "less well versed on gutter survival than I am."[10]

As the group's only "public lesbian," Barbara found herself vulnerable, or, as she put it, "ripe for 'trouble'" when she interacted with lesbians in the process of coming out. No matter how fearful women felt, "taking steps into the light" was exciting and empowering. As they explored their sexuality, some perceived Barbara as safe and supportive, shared their confusion with her, and sometimes wanted her, as an older woman (in her mid-thirties), to bring them out as lesbians. In time, she grew particularly fond of one, a twenty-three-year-old recent college student named Penny. "I knew a great many people like her when I was about 16," Barbara confided in a letter to Lee Lynch. "When I met her she was in dysfunction...no job, money troubles, the usual head troubles."[11]

The realization that she wanted to sleep with the younger woman rocked Barbara's world. She had spent years promoting fidelity in *The Ladder* because of her belief that lesbians had to live lives beyond reproach. While she had succumbed to pen romances in the 1960s, she had never crossed the line to physical infidelity to Helen Bennett. As flattering as it had been to receive letters from grateful women who praised Gene Damon for her efforts to validate their existence, she wisely knew they were responding to the aura of Gene Damon, not to the flesh-and-blood Barbara Grier. The sensual and attractive Penny, however, represented a real-life test of Barbara's convictions. Working within the constraints of her relationship with Helen, Barbara carved out a time to be with Penny, and was angry yet relieved when the younger woman changed her mind about entering into a relationship with Barbara. Even though nothing physical had happened, Barbara knew that she would one day "break all my rules or none of them...and I wait quite terrified and happy at the same time watching myself turn into a human being."[12] That time was not long in coming.

Falling in Love

With Penny as the catalyst, Barbara realized that she had, in fact, fallen in love with Donna McBride. One day in early March 1971, when volunteer Donna arrived at Barbara and Helen's apartment with the mail from *The Ladder*'s post office box, a very serious Barbara greeted her at the door. Taking Donna's hands, Barbara revealed that she had a crush on her.

Uncertain where her feelings would lead, Barbara confessed to Jane Rule, "I am in love with her and have been for a long time." After interacting with so many troubled women over the years, Barbara found it refreshing that Donna was "singularly lacking in neuroses…a reader but very active (tennis and horse and so on)…ex-Catholic agnostic." Donna also possessed two important traits for dealing with Barbara—she was calm and stubborn. In love with Donna but unable to leave Helen because she saw that as an act of betrayal, Barbara acknowledged: "Where it goes I do not right now know. I am neither unhappy nor insane…and will behave as well as possible."[13]

As Donna's feelings for Barbara deepened during the summer and fall of 1971, she was stunned to discover that, in reality, the woman who exuded so much confidence lived a highly constrained life. Barbara dreaded Helen's anger if she accidentally broke a dish because, according to "Helen's Rules of Order," there could be no mistakes or errors. Barbara's solution was to strive to live each day exactly like the one before. She also resorted to living a dual life through her post office box because she could not be herself under Helen's watchful, and at times jealous, eye. "I was publicly lesbian, but led an isolated, closeted kind of life," Barbara reflected.[14]

Under the rigid regimen she and Helen had maintained for nearly twenty years, Barbara lacked comprehension of what it meant to act on impulse. Donna, however, thought impulsiveness made life exciting. One day as Donna drove them through the Rosedale section of the Kansas City area, Barbara casually mentioned she had always wondered what was up a particular street. Immediately turning in that direction, Donna introduced Barbara to the first of many real-life adventures. The two women soon learned they were not clones of one another, and could have lively discussions, and even disagreements, that did not damage their relationship.[15]

Rule, who had seen Barbara through her earlier paper romances, sensed this time was different and wished the two friends could spend a few hours talking together. "You are caught between a clear morality and a clear desire," she observed, "unable to live with yourself if you inflict hurt, yet trapped in that requirement and unwilling." Challenging Barbara to look inward, Rule suggested she reflect on how much of her reluctance to leave Helen "has to do with morality, how much has to do with the nourishment you take from such security...and, how much your love of Donna is romanticizing sexual restlessness." Acknowledging Barbara had matured substantially since she went to live with Helen at age eighteen, Rule speculated that the relationship no longer offered enough space to accommodate the person Barbara had become.[16] After imparting this advice, Rule departed for a holiday in England, leaving Barbara to figure out the future on her own.

As they worked together on *The Ladder*, Barbara and Donna discovered a shared passion for books, the women's movement, cats and life. Unlike others Donna had known, Barbara did not poke holes in Donna's enthusiasm, but instead treated her as intelligent and witty. Donna collected mail at the post office box, indexed the magazine and wrote book reviews Barbara incorporated into "Lesbiana." They enjoyed laughing together over things large and small. After years of being closeted, Donna blossomed in the freedom to be herself.[17]

Emotionally, Barbara had been growing away from Helen for years, but the decision to leave her safe haven proved more difficult than she anticipated. She continued to care deeply for Helen, the woman who had taught her self-discipline and how to channel her vast energy into productive outlets. Donna represented an unknown future. Just beginning her career, Donna lived in an efficiency apartment and carried graduate school debt. Barbara also suffered lingering self-doubt because of her stillborn relationship with Pamela Rust. Alarmed by her feelings for Donna and feeling guilty about the stolen moments they had shared, Barbara thought moving to another part of the city would create distance and diminish her feelings. In the fall, Barbara became ill from the stress of her conflicted feelings toward Helen and the disruption of changing apartments. Years later, Barbara laughingly explained she thought Donna would go away as a result of the move.[18]

On November 4, 1971, Donna, Penny and other women from the Kansas City Women's Liberation Union celebrated Barbara's thirty-eighth birthday with an impromptu gathering at The Alternate, a lesbian bar in Kansas City, Missouri. In Barbara's eyes, it was "a people's bar... men, women, children, lovers, singles, helpless, helpful, homeless, homebodies...all came together, races, places and religions...believers and infidels...in some kind of communion of place and time and spirit. It had a kind of special magic."[19] Helen, who was not comfortable with the bar scene or the WLU, did not attend, instead working her regular shift at the University of Kansas City Library. Despite the happy occasion, it was a time of uncertainty for Barbara as she grappled with her feelings for Donna, the possibility of leaving Helen, and the unexpected loss of her current clerical position, which had provided the fringe benefit of free postage for her voluminous *Ladder* correspondence.

Donna intuited Barbara would not have fallen in love with her if she had felt fulfilled in her relationship with Helen. She also knew Barbara had grown dependent on Helen for a sense of financial security. A younger woman at the beginning of her career, Donna could not compete as a wage earner, so she set out to improve her position. Because she no longer had to spend energy hiding her lesbianism, Donna applied it to her career and soon became Head of Technical Processes at the Kansas City Public Library.

By November, Rule had returned to Canada from her holiday in England, and once again Barbara sought her advice. Addressing her friend by the affectionate nickname Kidkin, Rule acknowledged the complexity of the situation and encouraged Barbara to approach the decision "as a choice rather than an inevitability out of your control." Only then, she surmised, could Barbara avoid succumbing to another "helpless dependency" and have a chance at true happiness. From her perspective, Barbara appeared to care for Helen as a friend, staying with her out of a sense of obligation. "Not loving isn't good enough," Rule observed. Additionally, Barbara had spent many years pouring her life's energy into validating the lives of hundreds of correspondents. Now it was time "for each to carry what is hers to carry, no more. We are all tied together, but our hand and toe holds [*sic*] have to be our own."[20]

Fully aware Barbara had a happy relationship with Helen even though it was "very, very narrow" and isolated, Donna periodically lured Barbara away during the winter of 1971-72. "She would kidnap me on certain afternoons to her apartment," Barbara remembered, "and say, 'There is your orange juice,' which I insisted on drinking every morning, and 'There is your cat,'" hoping to persuade Barbara to stay. Each time, Barbara went home a day or two later and resumed her life with Helen as though nothing had happened. Then, on Friday, January 28, 1972, Donna left work early, picked up Barbara at her home one last time, and together, they embarked on what Barbara later described as "the most romantic adventure of my life." It was not without a few challenges. After an unsuccessful search for a larger apartment, a hysterical Barbara stood in Donna's tiny apartment and said, "You'll have to take me home, I can't stay." Donna calmly replied, "I will drive you home, but this is the last time, there is no returning." The finality worked, and that day marked the end of Barbara's relationship with Helen.[21]

Donna and Barbara continued their search for a rental the next day, and found a duplex apartment owned by the Greens, a Jewish refugee couple. Because the new apartment had less space than the home she shared with Helen, Barbara made room for her beloved collection of more than twelve thousand books by destroying some of her files of correspondence, including letters sent to her by Jeannette Howard Foster. All told, Barbara came into her new relationship with her books, clothes and one-hundred-thirty-one dollars.[22]

Reactions to the New Relationship

Not one to shy away from difficult topics, Barbara sat down at her typewriter and began composing letters to inform friends near and far of the major change in her life. "Sorry to hit you with a bombshell," she wrote Barbara Gittings in early February, "but I've known you too long to mickey mouse [*sic*] around. Helen and I have separated…it's all perfectly amiable [*sic*] but it's permanent." Rather than go into details about the breakup, Barbara claimed she was "too shy just yet to talk about this much," and turned to other subjects.[23]

When Barbara left Helen, most of her friends took the news well, but a small number of women associated with *The Ladder* "got terribly upset" upon learning she had broken up her twenty-year relationship for another woman. Holding Barbara to a higher standard because of her years spent promoting monogamous "lesbian marriage" as the highest ideal, some viewed her as a hypocrite, and one woman informed a mutual friend that she was "a menace to every decent Lesbian couple." Rita Laporte claimed she did not object to Barbara's decision to leave Helen, but a rift grew between the two women and they soon parted ways. From Donna's perspective, Laporte became upset with Barbara's secretiveness about Donna in the months leading up to her life-altering decision. Beginning with the April/May 1972 issue, Laporte's name no longer appeared as one of *The Ladder* staff; however, her pseudonym, Hope Thompson, remained listed as Production Editor through the final issue and several of her articles appeared between April and September. Their relationship damaged by hard feelings, Barbara and Laporte did not communicate again until shortly before Laporte succumbed to pancreatic cancer in November 1976.[24]

Barbara's family viewed her situation sympathetically because life with Donna meant they could see more of her. Shortly before her mother's death in April 1972, Barbara took Donna to the hospital to meet Dorothy Grier. As Donna leaned over to lift Dorothy into a more comfortable position, the older woman looked into her eyes and smiled. "I always said Barbara needed a big strong woman." At the same time, Barbara reconnected with her sister Diane, also a lesbian, and her partner Geyne, and visited her youngest sister before Penni moved with her husband to Saudi Arabia for his job. It was difficult for the younger siblings to bridge the gap of years and the impact of Barbara's estrangement from them during their childhood, yet shared memories of their much-loved mother and everyone's fondness for Donna helped them reconnect.[25]

For many years Donna had refrained from revealing her lesbianism to her parents, but after moving to a new apartment with Barbara, she wrote them a letter explaining she had met the woman with whom she intended to spend the rest of her life. In response, Hazel McBride informed Donna that Barbara was not welcome in their home. Years later, Donna suspected her mother may have been a lesbian, since she had married Merle McBride, whom she had known only a few months, shortly after her best friend married. "At least I did the right thing, I married your father," Hazel told Donna. "I never let her come between me and my family." Hazel's refusal to accept the fact that her daughter loved a woman led to years of estrangement, and the two did not speak to each other for the next seventeen years. More accepting of his daughter's sexuality than was his wife, Donna's father phoned from time to time.[26]

In contrast with her family, Donna's friends at the Kansas City Public Library pleasantly surprised her by responding supportively to her news. When she confided in a favorite colleague that she was a lesbian, her friend's response was: "I know that, you talk about Barbara the same way I talk about John."[27]

Helen Bennett responded to the change in her life by maintaining appearances and routines despite Barbara's absence, almost without missing a beat. When feminist activist and writer Robin Morgan phoned just a few days after Barbara's departure, Helen "did not feel free to explain" the separation.[28] In the coming months and years she responded politely to Barbara's efforts to sustain contact, but remained emotionally distant. Reclusive after two failed relationships, Helen never embarked upon another, and instead devoted herself to work, to her feline companions and to caring for her aged parents until their deaths. Barbara, who phoned Helen periodically and visited her home when she and Donna passed through Kansas City, learned Helen had died in 2003.

Building a Life Together

In June 1973, while taking a drive, Barbara and Donna found and fell in love with "a very large, new, five room house on a level 5 acre tract 40 miles east of Kansas City[,] some 8 miles south of the tiny village of Bates City." After moving to the property the following September, Donna named it 20 Rue Jacob Acres, in honor of Alice B. Toklas and Gertrude Stein's address in Paris. Barbara loved to tell people they lived "at 40th and Plum…40 miles out in the country and plum [*sic*] back in the woods." They turned the second bedroom into a library for Barbara's books, "with floor to ceiling shelves in the same walnut used throughout the house." The country kitchen was "big enough to entertain an army." As a city person, Barbara delighted in every new activity. "Since moving in last September 1, we've had the fun of building a fence, preparing a patio bed, putting in a lawn, trees and clothesline poles, and now that winter is here we are working on making the basement into a recreation area."[29] After Donna barely avoided a serious injury while loading a piece of equipment onto a truck, Barbara insisted that Donna teach her to drive so she would be prepared to take Donna to the hospital.

Barbara and Donna thrived in their relationship and in the life they were creating on the land. From the beginning, they possessed an ability to turn ordinary situations into fun occasions. One day while making their long daily commute to and from Kansas City, they found themselves caught in a huge traffic jam on I-70. When "Tangerine" began playing on their radio, they got out of the car and began dancing. "It was a lot of fun," Barbara noted. "People should do things like that more often." Life was good. Their days were full as they returned home from their jobs to plant trees, manage a garden with over one hundred types of plants, and preserve the resulting produce. "We are bronze, well-muscled and often very tired, but it is a lovely kind of tiredness," Barbara wrote in June 1976. "It is sometimes hard to remember I am supposed to be a bookworm."[30]

When Barbara and Donna fell in love, they both discovered a whole new world. After years of yearning for someone who loved her and wanted to build a life around their relationship, Donna had found emotional security, along with direction and purpose. Living with Barbara gave her the freedom to live openly, and happily, as a lesbian. Besides, loving Barbara was fun because she embraced life enthusiastically and fully. Donna would never have survived the relationship, however, if she had not been Barbara's intellectual peer. After years of sitting at her typewriter and living vicariously through books and a post office box, Barbara found her life with Donna enriched by travel, friends, activities and adventure. "I learned that I could carry on a conversation in person," she explained, "instead of by mail, and that I can socialize without vomiting."[31]

Her more active life represented a dramatic change for Barbara, one that did not occur overnight. She compensated for her unease by appearing gruff, relaxing only when she showed off her library and archives. It took time for Barbara to grow comfortable entertaining guests. Maida Tilchen's partner, Barbara Anne Allen, felt so intimidated by meeting the legendary Barbara Grier that she dropped her camera lens while attempting to photograph her. When New Yorker Karla Jay arrived early for an interview with Barbara, she had to wait in her car until Donna intervened. However, with Donna as the catalyst, a serious and intense Barbara gradually learned to relax, occasionally be frivolous, and even to love hosting guests—or, as she described it, "petting, feeding, entertaining, and bedding people down for the night."[32] Together, they made a formidable team and a companionable partnership as they embarked upon a nearly four-decade journey grounded in the movement for lesbian visibility and equality.

CHAPTER NINE

～❧

The Birth of Naiad Press

"Now, as you know, there are difficulties about getting this sort of thing published, even by the new women's presses, who seem hung up on the idea of fiction as tracts with social significance...I have decided to try printing the story myself and selling it as a paperback book."
–Anyda Marchant, 1974[1]

By the fall of 1973, Barbara Grier and Donna McBride had settled into their new home at 20 Rue Jacob Acres and were commuting eighty miles daily (round-trip) to work in Kansas City. In the year since *The Ladder's* demise, they had paid off the magazine's debt and begun compiling an index for all sixteen volumes. Given her role as *The Ladder's* final editor, Barbara continued to spend time on what she fondly referred to as "Ladder work," especially responding to letters, mentoring lesbians embarking on publication ventures, and using the mailing list (for a fee) to promote lesbian publications. Because of her extensive correspondence, Barbara had her pulse on the development of lesbian publishing, but she had no plans to embark on a career in book publishing until an aspiring author named Anyda Marchant and her partner, Muriel Crawford, presented Barbara and Donna with a new opportunity.

* * *

Throughout the spring and summer of 1973, Barbara spoke of resuming publication of *The Ladder*, but her interest waned as lesbian feminism gained momentum and dozens of magazines emerged to fill the void left by the departures of *The Ladder*, *ONE*, *Mattachine Review* and *Tangents*. Bearing such proud and at times defiant names as *Amazon Quarterly*, *Big Mama Rag*, *Common Lives/Lesbian Lives*, *Dyke*, *Lavender Woman*, *Lesbian Connection*, *Lesbian Tide*, *off our backs*, *Sinister Wisdom* and *Womanspirit*, these new publications fed a rising spirit of freedom, pride and visibility.

The Furies, a lesbian collective founded in 1971 by twelve lesbian-separatists in Washington, D.C., published a monthly newspaper of the same name. Nationally distributed, it tackled such weighty issues as sexism, patriarchy, socioeconomic class and corporate capitalism. Barbara absorbed information from former *Ladder* contributor, now Furies member, Rita Mae Brown, about the collective's inability to generate sufficient advertising revenue and the difficulty in finding a printer willing to publish a lesbian newspaper. By the publication's final issue (May-June 1973), most members of the collective had moved on to other endeavors.[2]

In the early 1970s, a number of small presses arose to publish the pamphlets, chapbooks, poetry, novels and nonfiction that further defined the lesbian feminist movement. Barbara devoured news about these presses, the women who ran them, and the products they produced. Typically undercapitalized, the women who ran small presses often relied on donated labor and supplies and attempted to conduct business according to feminist principles. The earliest, the Women's Press Collective (WPC) of Oakland, was founded in 1969 by poet Judy Grahn and her lover, Wendy Cadden. Specializing in works created by women who had been disenfranchised by their race or class, the WPC produced its first book, *Woman to Woman*, on a mimeograph machine in 1970. Martha Shelley, also a former *Ladder* contributor, kept Barbara informed about the WPC's struggles to pay the direct costs of publishing plus "rent, overhead on the shop, payments to writers and artists, and a certain percentage for reprints." After publishing twenty-four books, the WPC disbanded in August 1977, for both personal and economic reasons. According to Martha Shelley, Grahn and Cadden "got burned out because for years they had been working and working and never making any money…They were always living in poverty."[3]

In contrast, Daughters Publishing Company (Daughters, Inc.) had a more solid financial foundation. Co-founders June Arnold, a writer, and her lover, Parke Bowman, an attorney, both invested significant personal resources in the company, which began in Vermont in 1973. Unlike the working and middle-class women involved with other feminist publishing collectives, Bowman came from a background of privilege. Barbara admired Bowman's efforts to operate Daughters as a profit-making business, but paid less attention to Arnold's vision of the press as a tool for revolutionary struggle. During the company's five-year history, Bowman and Arnold gained a reputation for publishing such innovative and high-quality literary fiction as Rita Mae Brown's *Rubyfruit Jungle* (1973), Arnold's *The Cook and the Carpenter* (1973) and *Sister Gin* (1974), and Bertha Harris's *Lover* (1976). Filled with sex, anger, love and desire, these books challenged readers to think more deeply about aging, alcoholism, anti-gay prejudice, sexism, gender roles and socioeconomic barriers.[4]

The Diana Press Collective began in Baltimore in 1972 as a commercial instant print shop, but by the following year had ventured into book publishing when Rita Mae Brown inquired if Diana would print her second book of poetry. Like The Furies and the Women's Press Collective, Diana Press lacked financial resources. Barbara learned from Brown that she had paid three hundred dollars for paper to print *Songs to a Handsome Woman* (1973), and members of the collective donated their time with the understanding that revenue from sales of the two thousand copies printed would be used to repay the author and to compensate the women of Diana for their labor. Barbara was intrigued by Diana's cost-recovery model, which stipulated that the publisher and author would divide net profit.[5]

Barbara held Diana Press in high regard and was flattered when, in 1974, Coletta Reid, a key player at Diana, contacted her for advice on how the press could become financially stable. Based on her knowledge of the used-book market, Barbara advised Reid to reprint paperback originals from the "golden years" that were no longer covered by copyright, beginning with the Beebo Brinker novels of Ann Bannon as well as the "better novels" of Valerie Taylor and Paula Christian. In Barbara's opinion, the three women authors "were so popular as to achieve a kind of cult glory," so their books were guaranteed to sell well. When Diana needed money to purchase paper for print runs, Reid asked Barbara to tap her network for potential donors. As she correctly assumed, Barbara knew women who were "committed & might have some money they can spare for a year."[6]

After the American Library Association awarded its third Gay Book Award to Jeannette Howard Foster for *Sex Variant Women in Literature*, readers had difficulty obtaining copies of the out-of-print book. Responding to demand for the book, Reid informed Foster that Diana wanted to reprint her book, but hinted the press might need a subsidy. Consulting with Barbara about the possibility, Foster quipped, "All these 'queer' new non-commercial presses must be operating on a *broken* shoe string [*sic*]." After she received her attractive paperback copy of the book in May 1976, however, Foster pronounced it "an absolutely PERFECT job!"[7] Eagerly awaiting her royalties, she remained blissfully unaware of the challenges wracking Diana Press. Succumbing to criticism, financial difficulties, internal dissension and even vandalism, Diana suspended publishing in early 1979.

Anyda Marchant and the Origin of Naiad Press

Naiad Press grew out of an author's desire to see her fiction in print. Two decades older than Barbara Grier, Anyda Marchant was born in 1911 in Rio de Janeiro, where her family had moved in the aftermath of the American Civil War. Southern aristocrats, they left the United States rather than live through a devastating and demoralizing period of post-war reconstruction. As a young woman, Anyda used the initials of her full name, Anne Nelson Yarborough De Armond Marchant, to create the name by which Barbara and Donna knew her. When the Marchants returned to the United States, they settled in Washington, D.C., where the young Anyda remembered attending parades for women's suffrage with her mother. Her feminist consciousness sparked, it never occurred to Anyda that certain avenues remained closed to women because of their sex.

Marchant matriculated at George Washington University in the late 1920s, earned B.A., M.A. and LL.B (Bachelor of Laws) degrees in the 1930s, and while still a law student, served as a research assistant to Alice Paul, women's rights advocate and author of an Equal Rights Amendment introduced in Congress in 1923. Several additional factors fed Marchant's feminism. In 1940 she became an assistant in the Library of Congress, succeeding the male manager of her section when he was drafted into the army. Upon his return in 1945, she refused to go back to a lesser role and instead accepted a position in South America. When she returned to the United States three years later, Marchant became one of the first female attorneys in the firm of Covington & Burling, and during her career she was admitted to the bars of Delaware, Maryland, Virginia, the District of Columbia and the U.S. Supreme Court.[8]

While associated with Covington & Burling, Marchant met and fell in love with legal secretary Muriel Crawford. The two began a lifelong relationship during Thanksgiving vacation, 1948. Cautious and closeted, Crawford feared job loss and rejection by the Episcopal Church if anyone discovered the nature of their relationship. Consequently, the two led deeply closeted lives, maintaining "a false front to everyone: family, friends and business associates." They made their home with Crawford's elderly aunt until 1965, when they purchased a home in Rehoboth Beach, Delaware. Marchant was serving as legal counsel for the World Bank when a heart ailment forced her to take disability retirement at the age of sixty.[9]

As a young woman, Marchant struggled to reconcile her fierce physical desires for women with her upper-middle-class existence. While still a teen, she decided to free herself through writing. As she soon discovered, committing the most intimate details of her sexual encounters to paper became an "avenue to freedom from the psychic shackles of my youth."[10] A novel Marchant wrote in the late 1920s never appeared in print, but years later she incorporated portions of it in *Misfortune's Friend* (Naiad Press, 1985). Marchant published scholarly prose in the 1930s and 1940s, including *Aviation in Colombia, Chile and Brazil* (1939), as well as a biography of Brazilian entrepreneur Irineu Evangelista de Sousa, published by the University of California Press in 1965. Marchant eagerly looked forward to resuming her fiction writing career in retirement.

Marchant and Barbara's pen friendship took root in 1971 when Marchant first wrote to Barbara in her capacity as editor of *The Ladder*. Despite differences in age and class, they found common ground in discussions of books, writing and current events. Both eschewed political activism and demonstrations, preferring instead to effect change through literature and education. They also thought it foolish for lesbians to join with gay men in the fight for their rights because "the interests of men, in mixed groups, will always prevail over the interests of women." When Barbara announced *The Ladder*'s demise in 1972, Marchant sent a small "goodwill offering" to assist with final expenses and any "future venture you may undertake."[11] Barbara reciprocated the gesture of friendship by offering to critique Marchant's novel, which already had been rejected by a mainstream publisher.

As she did with many aspiring novelists, Barbara read Marchant's manuscript, *The Choice*, and then offered optimism and encouragement. "There are no barriers in terms of Lesbian themes in books these days," she concluded, implying there would be a market for the book. Thus encouraged, Marchant submitted a second, less overtly lesbian novel, "one of those read-between-the-lines things," to Dun and Lapham Agents for Writers. While waiting for their decision, Marchant finished yet another novel and mailed it to Barbara for a candid assessment. This time Barbara offered less hope: "You plot enormously," she observed, "and it would be hard to place such an introspective piece at a time when [sic] publishers seem to favor novels filled with 'hot house sexuality.'"[12]

Years later, Barbara would claim January 1, 1973, as the day Naiad Press began. At the time, however, she was focused on raising money to pay *The Ladder*'s residual debt, selling back issues and sending out mailings for lesbian magazines using *The Ladder*'s mailing list. When *The Ladder* ceased, she sustained its identity by continuing to use *Ladder* stationery and retaining its post office box in Reno. "There is still some good chance," she wrote Marchant in March 1973, "that we may be able to start TL [*The Ladder*] again in the fall." The following December, Barbara's first of many "Dear Friends" letters told about her hysterectomy, the new home she and Donna had purchased near Bates City, Missouri, and the joy of building fences and planting trees. She made no mention of starting a lesbian press, but did promise to inform everyone when *The Ladder* resumed publication.[13]

Throughout, 1973 Marchant searched for but failed to find a publisher for her novel. After rejection by mainstream presses, she sent it to Daughters, Inc., but they declined to publish the book because Marchant "was not confronting the real issues facing women today." Diana Press also returned the manuscript, noting she wrote "for a social and economic class that has already had too much of this world's attention." After concluding that the newly emerging women's presses "seem hung up on the idea of fiction as tracts with social significance," Marchant decided to explore the possibility of self-publishing her novel, *The Latecomer*.[14]

By the mid-twentieth century, lesbian self-publishing had a long tradition that included Leonard and Virginia Woolf's Hogarth Press, created to publish small volumes with little chance of publication by a commercial publisher. Gertrude Stein and Alice B. Toklas created the Plain Edition imprint and issued five volumes from 1931 to 1933, when mainstream recognition of their fifth title, Stein's *The Autobiography of Alice B. Toklas*, rendered self-publication no longer necessary. Decades later, Alma Routsong, who wrote under the pseudonym Isabel Miller, experienced similar commercial success after initially self-publishing one thousand copies of her lesbian novel, *A Place for Us* (later reissued as *Patience and Sarah*), and selling them on the streets of New York City and by mail.[15]

Marchant also found inspiration in the example of Jeannette Howard Foster, who had paid a year's salary to Vantage, the subsidy press that published *Sex Variant Women in Literature* (1957). Nevertheless, when Marchant contacted subsidy publisher Exposition Press in the early 1970s, she was stunned to learn they required an eight thousand dollar payment to print her novel. Searching for an alternative, Marchant purchased a copy of *The Publish-It-Yourself Handbook* and asked Barbara to assist in bringing her self-publication plan to fruition. "I have the greatest confidence in you and your experience in this sort of thing," Marchant informed her. "I shall take your advice completely." Marchant planned to protect her privacy by using the pseudonym Sarah Aldridge and by having Barbara serve as the contact person for advertisements, orders and correspondence. "I do not want any trace of my own name and address to appear," she instructed.[16]

In the spring of 1974, Marchant informed Barbara and Donna that she had chosen Naiad as the name of her publishing venture because it was, in a sense, an anagram of her name. Having a private press, she predicted, would "be our answer to the editorial policies of other book publishers and magazines." In addition to publishing her own "Great Works," she expected Naiad to build a reputation as "being the publisher of a certain type of lesbian novel. Just that. No other type of fiction or nonfiction…"[17] In other words, Marchant wanted a press dedicated to publishing classic lesbian love stories much like the ones she wrote. In deference to Barbara's experience as a collector, editor and publisher, she invited input on how to realize that vision.

Letting her imagination flow freely, Barbara dreamed of many projects for Naiad, among them a new edition of *The Lesbian in Literature*, reprints of early pulp favorites, the publication of Jeannette Howard Foster's early lesbian novels, and a revival of *The Ladder* magazine. Marchant, elated by the prospect of publication of *The Latecomer*, and anticipating Naiad as a venue for publishing her other novels, enthusiastically concurred. "Yes, yes, yes to everything you say…If all goes well with the printing press, I shall be sending you a check for $1000 as a subsidy for all these endeavors."[18]

One of Marchant's first tasks was to find a printer willing to typeset a lesbian novel. While in Florida, where she and Muriel Crawford wintered each year, Marchant discovered Rose Printing, a Tallahassee-based firm, and contacted them about printing *The Latecomer*. Founded in 1932 by Sam Rosenberg, Rose Printing had developed into one of the largest printing companies in northern Florida. Eventually, Naiad would become one of Rose's largest customers after the Southern Baptist Convention. Rose always made sure that no Naiad books were visible when the Baptists came to call.[19]

Having learned much from her years of editing *The Ladder* and corresponding with numerous authors, Barbara offered Marchant advice on print runs, bookstore discounts and where to place review copies, always with the understanding that final decisions were the author's to make. Upon learning of a proposed print run of one thousand copies of

The Latecomer, Barbara cautioned it might take two or three years to sell them, but in the end Marchant succumbed to the lure of a price break for a larger order, and optimistically requested two thousand copies. Convinced publicity was the key to selling that many copies, Barbara employed her powers of persuasion and her network of connections to arrange for announcements and reviews of *The Latecomer* to appear in *Amazon Quarterly, Lesbian Tide* and *Sisters.* She also promoted the book through a direct mailing to the nearly four thousand people from *The Ladder*'s subscription list, ensuring that all the energy she had poured into the magazine would not languish, but instead yield results for her newest venture.[20]

The Promoter

As a longstanding reviewer of lesbian books, Barbara knew female writers remained virtually invisible in mainstream marketing and review outlets. According to Sherry Thomas, co-founder of Old Wives Tales bookstore and publishing company Spinsters Ink, few who shopped at her bookstore in the 1970s had heard of writers like May Sarton or Marge Piercy, let alone lesser-known lesbian authors.[21] Aware of this deficit, Barbara devoted hundreds of hours to her typewriter to ensure that editors of lesbian magazines and newspapers knew about Marchant's *The Latecomer.* Barbara knew reviews, whether good or bad, triggered sales.

A firm believer in promotion, Barbara explained her approach to Marchant. "I continue a regular program of 'fallout' on those that have so far dragged their feet…and eventually, they will all mention us…and we will have saturated [the market]." Always eager to obtain maximum impact with minimal cost, Barbara suggested she could generate national publicity for the book by writing a letter to *Playboy* magazine. She thought the most effective approach would be to read the magazine until she found an entering wedge that allowed her to write a letter to the editor in which she would include the address of Naiad Press.[22]

As publication day for *The Latecomer* approached, Marchant could not contain her excitement. "Muriel and I are getting the heebee-jeebees waiting for the books," even though they had taken great pains to ensure people did not connect Anyda Marchant to Sarah Aldridge. In her eagerness to see her book acknowledged as a credible piece of fiction, Marchant sent publication announcements to *Publishers Weekly, Paperbacks in Print* and *Cumulative Book Index,* and to bookstores in Baltimore and New York City. Book orders and payments arrived at *The Ladder*'s old post office box in Reno, where a volunteer retrieved and forwarded them to Barbara for bookkeeping and banking. She then sent orders on to Marchant and Crawford, who prepared the books for mailing in brown paper envelopes with no return address. At Crawford's request, the two women drove to post offices in neighboring communities to ensure no one detected their involvement in distributing a lesbian book. Euphoric as orders for *The Latecomer* arrived, Marchant vowed to publish her second novel, *Tottie*, as soon as one thousand copies of the first book had sold, a feat which took nearly three years to accomplish.[23]

Barbara correctly anticipated *The Latecomer* would receive some negative reviews. Some women objected to Marchant's aristocratic tone and could not relate to the story. A small number still harbored hostility toward Barbara because of her involvement with the "theft" of *The Ladder*'s mailing list, and therefore did not want to support her new effort. Addressing the issue in a letter to *Lesbian Connection*, Barbara acknowledged some of the negativity stemmed "from the unhappy few out there who don't love us anymore."[24] Some reviewers also attacked Marchant's work as racist. Descended from a slaveholding family, she employed language that reflected outdated values.

Barbara was not overly concerned because she welcomed all reviews as a form of free publicity. "*Off* [*sic*] *Our Backs* will give it a VERY bad review," she predicted, "but the mere fact that it is an available Lesbian novel will sell it." Marchant was not to worry because even if romance were a "no-no" among lesbian feminists, *The Latecomer* would sell well because it is "what the people want." While negative reviews troubled Marchant, Barbara declared: "I am out of my tree with glee over your review in *Spokeswoman*." She was certain the review would send "closeted ladies" running to their mailboxes with orders for the book. When Marchant continued to fret, Barbara adopted a sterner tone: "Stop rankling over the review in SPOKESWOMAN. Bright women like the things you like… but the world isn't being run by bright people just now so we just have to live with it."[25] Positive or negative, Barbara assured, reviews would sell the book.

Despite her optimistic outlook, Barbara encountered a roadblock when the women from Seattle's It's About Time Women's Bookstore relayed complaints from buyers about the book. They had assumed it would be good because Barbara promoted it, but instead they found it "poorly written, full of role stereotypes…[with] no grip on politics and was classist." In addition to no longer carrying the book, the women informed Barbara they planned to destroy it and they wanted her to replace it with complimentary copies of *The Lesbian in Literature*. Arguing that "it is not a tract, so it doesn't need a 'grip on politics,'" Barbara reasoned art and politics did not have to be married. A pragmatist, Barbara suggested the bookstore use *The Latecomer* as giveaways, but if they did not like that idea, she urged them to return the books to Naiad rather than destroy them.[26]

Searching for Direction

Despite the pleasure she had found in her new life with Donna and the publication of Naiad's first book, Barbara felt mildly depressed in the autumn of 1974. After years of living as a hermit, she struggled to adjust to the drastic change in her lifestyle. Socializing did not come easily, and without *The Ladder* as her central focus, she felt adrift. The loss of her clerical job at the All Packaging Company in late September compounded matters, because she had more time to fret. In characteristic style, Barbara busied herself with projects on her home and property. "I never run out of work," she informed Marchant: "incidentally, it is against my puritan nature to do so."[27] She also immersed herself in what she had come to call "*Ladder* work," responding to letters that kept trickling in to *The Ladder*'s last editor, working on an index of the magazine, and compiling a new edition of *The Lesbian in Literature.*

The preparation of an index for *The Ladder* remained first and foremost on Barbara's mind. As a frequent user of libraries, she knew the value of having books and magazines well indexed. Working without the benefit of computerization, she and Donna chose to index each volume separately. The final product was printed on inexpensive paper and stapled together by a team of volunteers who collated it around a pool table. Despite the less-than-ideal format, the index proved invaluable because such standard reference sources as *Readers' Guide to Periodical Literature* did not include material from *The Ladder* and other small publications. Aware it would not be a bestseller, Barbara set the price of the index at ten dollars to recover printing and mailing costs. When a few librarians complained about the format, and accused her of "profit-mongering," she went on the defensive. The project, she proclaimed, had lost them money and would have been junked if not for the labor invested.[28]

Based on letters from readers, Barbara knew a market existed for a new edition of *The Lesbian in Literature.* An ambitious work, the update of the 1967 edition included novels, short stories, poetry, plays and biography dealing "wholly or in part with Lesbianism." Barbara coordinated the project, which relied on Donna (writing as Jan Watson), former *Ladder* circulation manager Kathy Mengle (writing as Robin Jordan), and multiple volunteers from coast to coast who scanned their assigned publications for lesbian items, jotted them down on slips of paper, and mailed them to Barbara. Influenced by the language of feminism, Barbara referred to *The Lesbian in Literature* crew as "a 'loose' collective of women spread all over the U.S." As in the first edition, she retained the coding system that indicated extent of lesbian content and the "T" signifier for trash. In response to feedback on the first edition she also inserted some important nonfiction titles.[29]

Contrary to the image of success that Barbara attempted to project, Naiad Press was cash poor and depended on volunteer labor and Marchant's willingness to pay the costs associated with publishing her novels. As they moved forward with publication of *The Lesbian in Literature*, Barbara fretted about the costs of printing, binding and postage, even though Marchant assured her Naiad would print the book using income from the sale of the Sarah Aldridge books. To save money, Mengle typed the final copy, and another volunteer provided cover art. Barbara's frugality was so legendary that when she solicited bids for printing the bibliography, Jean Wallen, a local woman, quoted affordable rates because she thought of Naiad as "a pauper's organization."[30]

Employing the same techniques that had kept *The Ladder* afloat for years, Barbara remained on alert for free items or donated supplies, and when she had jobs she routinely used her employer's Wide Area Telephone Service (WATS) line to reduce the burden of costly long-distance phone calls. She also devised a scheme in which women placed collect calls to her using coded words, and then she rejected the calls. For example, when volunteers in Reno called for "Barbara Bread," it meant they had received between one hundred and two hundred dollars in orders. Yet times were changing, and when Barbara attempted to obtain free review copies from emerging feminist presses, some told her they rejected the idea as a male concept, and also believed women should be willing to pay one another for their products.[31]

Echoes from The Ladder

Barbara mistakenly assumed her correspondence would wane once she published the last issue of *The Ladder*. Instead, it blossomed as she responded to young women eager to connect with one of their lesbian foremothers, in part because Barbara took her correspondents seriously and expressed interest in their activities, and also because she peppered her letters with irreverent wit. "You're a treat," author Bertha Harris enthused from her New York apartment in 1975. Feeling besieged by "Amazon this and Amazon that" and the political intensity of her lesbian feminist friends,

Harris confessed: "I MISS THE LADDER, I MISS THE LADDER, I MISS THE GOOD OLD LADDER!!!…I miss Ann Bannon and Beebo Brinker…and sentences that begin, 'It was my first week in New York, and I was lonely.'" She was one of many who had looked to Gene Damon, as a public lesbian, and found understanding. "Thank you," she continued, "for rescuing me from Doom and Despair over 'not being understood'— your sense of humor not only rolled the clouds away but allowed me to lie down on the floor and laugh like hell at myself."[32]

For several years after *The Ladder* ceased, Barbara continued to mention the possibility of its revival because it was impossible to let go of the magazine to which she had devoted so much of her energy. Moreover, it had given her direction and forged her identity as an authority on lesbian literature. She perpetuated the myth of *The Ladder* as a living entity by retaining its bank account and post office box in Reno and typing her correspondence on *Ladder* stationery. Yet when Kirsten Grimstad, co-author of the *New Woman's Survival Catalog*, offered to organize a benefit for *The Ladder*, Barbara quickly backpedaled. Reviving *The Ladder*, she explained, depended on revenue generated by sales of *The Lesbian in Literature*, so proceeds from a benefit should be applied to the cost of publishing that work instead.[33]

Because of her visibility as a lesbian pioneer, Barbara received invitations to speak at a number of conferences organized in the mid-1970s. Chicagoans Marie J. Kuda, Valerie Taylor, and women from Lavender Press and Mattachine Midwest had convened the first Lesbian Writers Conference in September 1974. Energized by a weekend of workshops, coffeehouse readings and examining lesbian and feminist books on display, lesbian writers departed with the knowledge that they were part of a larger movement.

When Kuda, who had corresponded with Barbara since 1969, invited her to keynote the second conference the following September, she was unaware that the well-known bibliographer, editor and reviewer lacked public speaking experience. "Your fantastic 'floor to ceiling' background would make for a terrific talk," Kuda declared. The young woman's enthusiasm for lesbian literature and her flattery appealed to Barbara's ego: "I find the whole thing delightful fun…having enough ham in me to enjoy a captive audience."[34]

Despite her bravado, Barbara was terrified at the prospect of speaking to an audience of lesbian writers. She could hear her heart pounding as she stood to deliver "The Possibilities Are Staggering" to a sea of expectant faces. Her nerves calmed as she described the isolation lesbians had experienced in the 1950s and 1960s. "When you are close to a movement," she told her audience, "as presumably all of you are, it's hard to realize that most of the women who come out[,] come out alone." The vast majority of women who had subscribed to *The Ladder* lived isolated lives in small towns. Even though the magazine no longer existed, they continued writing to her with pleas for validation, information and recognition. "For the isolated ones, the frightened ones," she informed the writers, "we're their only hope."[35]

After the talk, Barbara found it difficult to cope with emotional responses from women who credited Gene Damon and *The Ladder* with saving their lives. Responding abruptly, she left them wondering how they had caused offense and what they could do to make things right. One woman traveled to the conference from Canada to meet Barbara and be with a group of lesbians for the first time in her life. She, like others, wanted to express her appreciation to the woman whose letters had been "like manna from Heaven!!....Only someone completely isolated, as I was, could understand what it meant to me! I owe her so much—at the very least, my sanity—perhaps even my life." Like many of Barbara's correspondents, she thought she had a special connection and felt rebuffed by the awkward personal encounter. Writing to Kuda afterward, the Canadian queried, "Is she usually rather abrupt?"[36]

When lesbians set out to queer the college curriculum in the mid-1970s, they often started in the library, where they discovered *The Ladder* and *The Lesbian in Literature*. When they wrote to editor Gene Damon, they encountered an incredible resource in Barbara Grier. In addition to flooding them with correspondence, Barbara and Donna hosted those who traveled to Missouri to interview her or see the famous library of lesbian books. Visits from lesbian feminists Beth Hodges, Karla Jay, Joanna Russ, Maida Tilchen and lesbian musician Margie Adams, among others, heightened Barbara's sense of her status as a foremother and helped her bridge the gap between the homophile and lesbian feminist movements.[37]

In response to demand on college campuses, graduate students played a leading role in developing early gay and lesbian studies courses. Many originally began as pass/fail courses, while others were housed outside the traditional curriculum in free universities until they could be absorbed by women's studies and related programs. Initially, the curriculum often featured guest speakers. Shannon Hennigan, who pioneered a course on lesbian sexuality at Sacramento State in 1971, brought Del Martin, Phyllis Lyon, Rita Mae Brown, Judy Grahn and other lesbian luminaries to campus, while academician Gayle Rubin and freelancer Lyndall Cowan turned to Barbara for advice in developing courses in lesbian literature. Uninhibited by her lack of a college degree, she joined a panel of ministers, medical doctors and professors at the Kansas State University Educators' Conference on Lesbianism and Male Homosexuality in October 1975. On this occasion, Barbara appeared as Gene Damon, giving two sessions on homosexuality in film as well as a lecture on "Homosexuality in Literature."[38]

The following month, Barbara and Donna traveled to New York City at the invitation of the Gay Academic Union (GAU), founded in 1973 to oppose discrimination against all women and gay people in schools and universities. In an attempt to calm Barbara's anxiety about her first airplane flight, Bertha Harris encouraged her to think about "the wonderful sexual power of the lifting, soaring, landing—just relax into it." Barbara also fretted about the prospect of meeting so many strangers. "I am simply too chicken to go to Sodom by the Sea by myself. I am not too many years from my hermitage and I have not yet adjusted to human beings in mass quantities." After the Chicago experience, Barbara knew Gene Damon needed a bodyguard because she was "not equipped mentally to cope with weeping women," and she would have declined the opportunity if Donna had been unable to accompany her.[39]

The GAU conference, which convened on the Columbia University campus, made an indelible impression on Barbara because she had the opportunity to speak face-to-face with many of her long-time correspondents. They included fiction writers Mary Phoebe Bailey and Alma Routsong (who wrote as Isabel Miller), *Ladder* art columnist Sarah Whitworth, essayist Anita Cornwell, and some of Barbara's newer pen friends, including Dolores Klaich and Gayle Rubin. In a program that featured Charlotte Bunch, Bertha Harris, Kate Millett, Ti-Grace Atkinson, Frank Kameny, and Julia P. Stanley, Barbara participated in a panel on "Images of Lesbians in Fiction." Other sessions addressed such topics as gay psychological counseling, gay religion, economic issues, gay activism, and language, class and sex.

Aware of the history they were making, Barbara provided Marchant with a detailed portrait of every person she saw. Publishers June Arnold and Parke Bowman invited her and Donna to a party held in the Daughters, Inc., loft, which Barbara thought screamed "money, money, money." She admired Arnold's elegant appearance and "quick bright eyes" and categorized Bowman as a "tweedy, horsey type," but found both "so left as to lean slightly even in conversation." Arnold, she noted in passing, wanted to organize a conference for publishers. The following evening when they went to Bonnie and Clyde's, a lesbian bar, Barbara "got nicely drunk and amused myself and everyone else…happily star struck and liked it."[40] Barbara and Donna also found time to take Dorothy Grier's ashes to

Central Park, thus fulfilling Dorothy's wish to return to the much-loved city of her youth. The trip, Barbara's first to the Big Apple, whetted her appetite for travel, marked the beginning of a love affair with New York City, and reinforced her commitment to the spread of lesbian literature.

The Ladder Anthologies

With Naiad in its infancy, Barbara threw herself into a new project: working with Coletta Reid to anthologize some of *The Ladder*'s best writing. Diana Press already had anthologized material from *The Furies*, so the project seemed like an ideal sequel. After reading the entire run of *The Ladder*, Reid selected enough pieces to fill three volumes: *The Lesbians' Home Journal* (short stories), *The Lavender Herring* (essays), and *Lesbian Lives* (biographies). Barbara was thrilled when Reid suggested they split royalties fifty-fifty, because she sensed an opportunity to recoup some of the money she and Donna had lost during *The Ladder*'s final year of publication. When Reid asked to obtain permissions from *Ladder* authors, she was stunned to learn Barbara had written forty-two of the one hundred and ten stories and essays under a variety of pseudonyms. The next most prolific authors represented were Beverly (Lee) Lynch and art columnist Sarah Whitworth, with eight items apiece.[41]

After years of building up her reputation as Gene Damon, Barbara thought the time had come to shed that persona. Feminists of the 1970s stressed authenticity and criticized the idea of anyone hiding behind a false name. No longer compelled to protect her partner, Barbara relished the idea of finally seeing her name in print and thought the three Diana Press anthologies of material from *The Ladder* represented an ideal opportunity. Reid, however, preferred for Barbara to use Gene Damon because of "the selling power of that name." Disappointed and frustrated, Barbara challenged Reid's decision: "I am terribly desperately tired of being, from time to time, accused of 'hiding' behind a pseudonym, it wouldn't make me so FURIOUS if it weren't for the fact that in the early 1950s I was announcing my Lesbianism to everyone, both vocally and by deed...I've believed in Living Propaganda all my life...I am very PROUD of being a Lesbian."[42] In the end, Barbara's name appeared on the cover of all three volumes while the essays were credited to her pseudonyms.

Barbara was still searching for something to fill the void left by *The Ladder* when Anyda Marchant decided to print her second novel. Sales of *The Latecomer* had not reached five hundred copies, and some reviews had been harsh, yet she thought a second book would spark sales of the first. Barbara, busy with arrangements for *The Ladder* anthologies, asked

Mengle to assist with promotion and sales of *Tottie*, but personally handled complaints about the book's content and appearance. In response to a negative review, Barbara assured Marchant the reviewer "belabors you for sins you do not commit. She assumes that your characters are 'emancipated women' and belong to the 'new literature,' which is a cockamamie bunch of something I wish we had more of for our garden…" Undisturbed by the responses to her work, Marchant informed Barbara, "I try to exercise patience with my sisters, especially if they are younger than I and less acquainted with the world."[43]

New Directions for Naiad

When she first conceptualized Naiad Press, Marchant envisioned it as a means of publishing her novels, and possibly a few other similar works. Once the press had released two books, authors began contacting Barbara about the possibility of publishing their manuscripts. "What flavor of tale do you want me to use with these?" Barbara inquired when she forwarded a few of the proposals to Marchant in the fall of 1975. "I get 2-3 or so a month." Reflecting upon the matter, Marchant instructed Barbara to inform those who inquired that Naiad was a new press and could only publish work if an author covered the initial outlay. In other words, Marchant envisioned Naiad as a subsidy press for lesbians. "Obviously neither you nor I would be doing it for money," she explained to Barbara, "though it is conceivable that sometime in the future we might have operating funds." If Barbara were not interested in this alternative, Marchant elaborated, they would continue publishing one book a year, and "the selection for 1976 is already made."[44] After giving the matter some thought, Barbara decided to see how far she could stretch Marchant's vision.

Recognizing the necessity of reducing production costs, Barbara set out to find a less expensive printer for Naiad's next few books. While at the Lesbian Writers Conference in Chicago, she had discovered Salsedo Press, operated by a mixed collective of women and men. Hoping to secure advantageous prices, she painted a picture of Naiad's silent partners as elderly, ill and living on a fixed income.[45] Both Marchant and Crawford had retired (Marchant due to disability), but they were far from impoverished invalids and instead remained active enough for periodic travel to Europe on the *Queen Elizabeth 2*.

Salsedo published four books for Naiad in 1976. In addition to a third Sarah Aldridge novel, *Cytherea's Breath*, Naiad released *Speak Out, My Heart*, a lesbian coming-of-age story written by long-time *Ladder* volunteer Mengle and published under the pseudonym Robin Jordan.

Barbara wanted to publish the book as a token of appreciation for Mengle's work. Marchant and Crawford, who expected repayment, advanced money to cover the book's production and Mengle kept costs low by typing the camera-ready copy. That same year, Barbara arranged for the publication of the first English-language translation of Renée Vivien's *A Woman Appeared to Me*. Jeannette Howard Foster had translated the French lesbian's work as a birthday gift for her, and Gayle Rubin provided a scholarly introduction. Naiad also published an anthology of the book columns Barbara had so lovingly written for *The Ladder*. Maida Tilchen, who reviewed *Lesbiana* for the Canadian *Body Politic*, praised her style of reviewing as "personal, never pedantic, and always enthusiastic and stimulating. Even her biting comments are usually more amusing than cruel."[46]

Satisfied Naiad could sustain itself well enough to publish her books plus a few other titles, Marchant decided the time had come to incorporate. She initially envisioned that Naiad Press would have three officers holding equal shares: herself as president, Barbara as vice president and general manager, and Muriel Crawford as treasurer. Barbara loved the idea of having a title, even though the position came without promise of payment for services. By May 28, 1976, when Marchant filed the incorporation paperwork in her home state of Delaware, she had expanded the Board of Directors to four by giving Donna a ten percent share. Donna attributed her smaller percentage to Marchant's unwillingness to accept the daughter of a truck driver as a peer.[47] Barbara's subsequent claim that Naiad had been founded on January 1, 1973, likely was part of an effort to portray the company as a pioneering press, or at least the peer of other feminist presses.

Barbara with her paternal grandparents, Glycine and Charles J. Grier, near Charlotte, Michigan, circa 1934.
Courtesy of Donna McBride

Barbara Grier with her parents, Philip and Dorothy (Black) Grier, circa 1939.
Courtesy of Donna McBride

Barbara, circa 1942.
*Courtesy of Donna McBride
and Penelope Grier Martin*

Penelope and Diane Grier, ages 3 and 7,
Woodland Park, Colorado.
*Courtesy of Donna McBride
and Penelope Grier Martin*

Barbara, Diane Grier, Penni Grier, circa 1945.
Courtesy of Donna McBride and Penelope Grier Martin

Isabel Miller and Barbara Gittings at the "Hug a Homosexual Booth," 1971. *Photo by Kay Tobin Lahusen. Courtesy of Barbara Gittings and Kay Lahusen Gay History Papers and Photographs, Manuscripts and Archives Division, The New York Public Library*

Marion Zimmer Bradley, 1994. *Photo by Robert Giard. Courtesy of Jonathan Silin and the New York Public Library*

Jeannette Howard Foster, Pocahontas, Arkansas, 1977. *Photo by Tee Corinne. Courtesy of the Tee A. Corinne Papers, Special Collections and University Archives, University of Oregon Libraries*

Del Martin, 1975. *Photo by Joan E. Biren*

Jane Rule and Pamela Rust. *Courtesy of Pamela Rust*

Cover, Sloane Britain, *First Person, 3rd Sex*.
Courtesy of San Francisco Public Library

Cover, Della Martin, *Twilight Girl*.
Courtesy of San Francisco Public Library

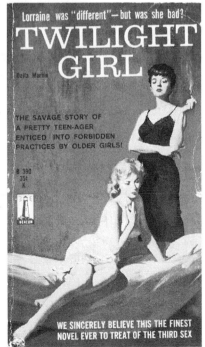

75¢

The Ladder
a Lesbian Review

acme

November, 1967

Jane Kogan cover of *The Ladder,*
November 1967.
Courtesy of San Francisco Public Library

Cover, Barbara Grier, *The Lesbian In
Literature, 3rd Edition.*
Courtesy of Donna McBride

THE LESBIAN
IN
LITERATURE

•
new
revised
• 3rd edition
• 89 photographs

BARBARA GRIER

Rita Laporte image used for Aug-Sept 1969 issue of *The Ladder*.
Courtesy of San Francisco Public Library

Jody Shotwell.
Courtesy of Donna McBride

Barbara Gittings and Randy Wicker in picket line, 1966. *Photo by Kay Tobin Lahusen. Courtesy of Barbara Gittings and Kay Lahusen Gay History Papers and Photographs, Manuscripts and Archives Division, The New York Public Library*

Tee Corinne, 1980. *Photo by Joan E. Biren*

Donna McBride, age 3.
Courtesy of Donna McBride

Donna McBride with her mother, Hazel McBride, early 1970s.
Courtesy of Donna McBride

Donna and Barbara, 1972. *Photo by Marilyn Coe*

Donna, Penny Yeargin, Barbara, 1971. *Courtesy of Donna McBride*

Barbara and Donna in Tallahassee, 1982. *Photo by Joan E. Biren*

Women in Print, 1976. *Photo by Ruth Mountaingrove.*
Courtesy of Ruth Mountaingrove Collection, Vol. 15_cs49-007,
Special Collections and University Archives, University of Oregon

Sherry Thomas in the new Spinsters Ink offices, 1976. *Photo by Joan E. Biren*

Helaine Harris and Cynthia Gair at WinD Office and Warehouse, 1977. *Photo by Joan E. Biren*

Katherine V. Forrest, circa 1984.
Photo by Tee Corinne.
Courtesy of Katherine V. Forrest

Rosemary Curb speaking at Charis Books
& More, Atlanta, 1985. *Courtesy of Linda
Bryant and the Rubenstein Library and University
Archives, Duke University*

Barbara, Ann Bannon, Donna on tour, Hinsdale, Illinois, summer 1982.
Courtesy of Ann Bannon

Barbara on a NWSA panel, 1980. *Photo by Joan E. Biren*

Gloria Greenfield with Rolodex, 1981. *Photo by Joan E. Biren*

Barbara at Naiad Press booth with Katherine V. Forrest and Lee Lynch, 1982.
Courtesy of Lee Lynch

Muriel Crawford. *Courtesy of Donna McBride*

Anyda Marchant. *Courtesy of Donna McBride*

Anyda and Muriel. *Courtesy of Donna McBride*

Barbara and Nancy Bereano at 1987 March on Washington.
Courtesy of Donna McBride

Collage of *Lesbian Nuns:Breaking
Silence* covers.
Courtesy of Carol McCafferty

Collage of Naiad Press book covers
featuring artwork by Tee Corinne.
Courtesy of Carol McCafferty

Donna and Barbara, Bates City—40 miles east of Kansas City. 1970s.
Courtesy of Donna McBride

Cover of Sarah Schulman's *The Sophie Horowitz Story,* 1984.

Nancy Manahan, Margaret (Peg) Cruikshank, and Barbara, American Booksellers
Association Conference, 1985. *Courtesy of Nancy Manahan Collection, the Jean-Nickolaus Tretter
Collection in GLBT Studies, University of Minnesota Libraries*

Linda Bryant, Charis Books & More. *Courtesy of Rubenstein Library and University Archives, Duke University and Linda Bryant for Charis Books*

Donna and Barbara at NWSA. *Courtesy of Donna McBride*

"What is this *@! younger generation coming to?!" 1993. Cartoon by Pat Tong.
Courtesy of Katherine V. Forrest Papers, San Francisco Public Library

Publishers Panel, 1999, Charis Books & More. Left to right: Lisa Moore, Mary Bricker-Jenkins, Carol Seajay, Barbara, Joan Drury, Barbara Smith, Nancy Bereano.
*Courtesy of Rubenstein Library and University Archives, Duke University and
Linda Bryant for Charis Books*

Barbara and Teapot.
Courtesy of Donna McBride

Devoted fans of the Lady Vols, Barbara and Donna, 2006. *Photo by Deb Wehman*

Naiad and Bella Books, 2006. The last Book Expo America attended by Barbara and Donna. Janette Wagner, Barbara, Becky Arbogast, Donna, Linda Hill.

Barbara on Danube Cruise, 2010. *Courtesy of Donna McBride*

Donna's favorite photo of Barbara, on the Danube 2010.
Courtesy of Donna McBride

CHAPTER TEN

❧

Building Naiad: A Personal and Business Challenge

"Donna says I eat, sleep, drink and dream about Naiad."
–Barbara Grier, 1977[1]

In the summer of 1976, Barbara Grier and Donna McBride rented a Scamp travel trailer and drove to Camp Harriet Harding, southwest of Omaha, Nebraska, to join approximately one hundred thirty women for the inaugural Women in Print conference. Omaha, chosen as a mid-point between the two coasts, seemed an unlikely place for this assembly of illustrators, printers, publishers, bookstore owners and editors of lesbian and feminist magazines and newspapers, many meeting face-to-face for the first time. Writers were not invited, and the few who attended (for example, novelists Parke Bowman and Bertha Harris) came in other capacities. Some attendees were new to publishing, working on mimeograph machines in their basements, while others did contract printing on temperamental Multilith machines. Whether young or old, professional or novice, they were all tired of having women's ideas distorted, trivialized, or rejected by the mainstream press.

Serving as gatekeeper and conference organizer, Daughters, Inc. publisher June Arnold had assembled a veritable Who's Who of the Women in Print movement. On the first evening, women assembled in a large circle to introduce themselves and the organizations they represented. They included Charlotte Bunch from *Quest* magazine, Cynthia Gair and Helaine Harris from Women in Distribution, Carol

Seajay and Carla Javitts representing A Woman's Place Bookstore in Oakland, Joan Pinkvoss and Barb Wieser from Iowa City Women's Press, graphic artists Tee Corinne and Honey Lee Cottrell, and publishers Coletta Reid and Casey Czarnik from Diana Press and Martha Shelley from the Women's Press Collective of Oakland. *Sinister Wisdom* co-founders Harriet Desmoines and Catherine Nicholson also attended, along with representatives from *Womanspirit,* the *off our backs* collective, and many other publications. After years of working in relative isolation, all these women met, and names on paper came to life. By the time they left the conference, these pioneers in feminist publishing were secure in the knowledge that they belonged to a national movement, one dedicated to creating a woman-centered publications network.[2]

In her forty-third year, Barbara was a full generation older than many of her peers in publishing, and she had dreaded the meeting since spring. "I am scared of the shit that is surrounding the upcoming summer meeting in Omaha, Nebraska," she confided to freelance editor and critic Lyndall Cowan, "in which we are all invited to examine our revolutionary purity in publishing."[3] Despite her years of corresponding with authors, editors and people involved with publishing, Barbara felt intimidated by the prospect of meeting people face-to-face. As her brief forays into public speaking venues confirmed, Barbara had an Achiiles' heel when confronted with face-to-face interactions.

Donning her Gene Damon persona, Barbara compensated for her insecurity with bravado. As she approached the registration table, she nodded toward Tee Corinne and asked, "Who is that beautiful woman over there?" Barbara recalled later that she could feel the artist radiating love over everyone, "a good kind of natural caring that women need to be able to feel and project."[4] Conversation revealed they had a mutual friend in Martha Shelley. When Barbara invited Corinne to prepare artwork for two of Naiad's forthcoming books, she agreed on the condition that Barbara sit beside her and share stories of lesbian history while she drew. Pleased with the result, Barbara asked Corinne to become Naiad's cover artist.[5]

As time grew short during the first evening of self-introductions, *Quest*'s Charlotte Bunch leaned over to Barbara and said, "You're next, Barbara, keep it short." Standing, she briskly announced, "I am Barbara Grier, and I'm here because I represent Naiad Press and, I suppose, to some extent, *The Ladder.*" At that, the women spontaneously burst into applause, giving Barbara the first public recognition of her years of work for *The Ladder.*[6]

Eager to do their part, Barbara and Donna had signed up to cook breakfast the following morning. Other members of their crew included

Corinne and her lover, Honey Lee Cottrell, who had been separated due to Cottrell's work-related travel. When Barbara banged on the door of their camper at the crack of dawn, Cottrell bellowed: "You motherfucker." Unfazed by bawdy language, Barbara embraced her new nickname, "Mother-fucker Grier."[7] Barbara also enjoyed the freedom women felt to hold hands, kiss and celebrate their existence, but she and Donna were less comfortable when they donned their bathing suits to go for a swim in the pool and discovered they were the only two who had dressed for the occasion. In an act of sisterhood and compassion, conference organizer Arnold left and soon returned in a swimsuit.

As *WomanSpirit*'s Ruth Mountaingrove snapped photographs during the conference, she observed a split among some of the attendees. There were the "feely" participants who were more focused on the spiritual and artistic dimensions of print culture, and also the more political women who regarded the printed word as a weapon. Attendees who came out of feminism expected lesbian publishers and booksellers to conduct business according to feminist values of consensus and collaboration. "It was such a heady time," bookstore owner Carol Seajay later recalled. "There was a strong political belief that we had to control the means of production...a woman writer printed on a women's press, sold in a women's bookstore."[8]

Participants left the Women in Print conference invigorated and infused with the sense they were partners in a grand cause, one deeply invested in the written word. Determined to do her part to strengthen the feminist media system, lesbian activist Marie J. Kuda inaugurated a monthly WIP newsletter that continued much of the following year. Seajay, who learned during the conference that her application for a business loan had been approved, returned to San Francisco and opened the Old Wives Tales feminist bookstore as a collective with her then partner, Paula Wallace. Seajay also initiated a new monthly publication, *Feminist Bookstore News*, which she edited for the next twenty-four years. The publication, which became the "industry bible for lesbian and feminist booksellers," contributed to a sense of connectedness among businesswomen unable to afford long-distance telephone calls.[9] Like the others, Barbara Grier left the conference infused with a new goal: to transform Naiad Press into a leading movement publishing company that was committed to working with women printers, typesetters, bookbinders and illustrators in the production of women's books.

As 1976 came to a close, Barbara and Donna reflected upon what had been a very fine year. In addition to Naiad's release of four volumes, they were delighted when the three Diana Press anthologies of stories and essays from *The Ladder* arrived in mid-December. Increasingly recognized as an expert on lesbian literature, Barbara had begun receiving more invitations to speak at conferences and on college campuses. Unlike Helen Bennett, Donna encouraged Barbara to embrace these opportunities, eased her entry into a more public role, and ensured they had fun along the way. When the fall issue of *Sinister Wisdom* arrived in her mailbox, Barbara was stunned and flattered to find it dedicated to her—editor, correspondent, bibliographer and preserver of lesbian history. "What moves me," wrote guest editor Beth Hodges, "is the woman Barbara: not-very-humble, not-so-patient, but infinitely generous. For twenty years you've been encouraging lesbian writers and lesbian readers by sharing your time, your love, your energy, your knowledge."[10] Long years of this tireless labor of love had finally born fruit.

On a personal level, the year had been tinged with loss, but overall it was very satisfying. Barbara did not lament the passing of her father, Philip Grier, but she had reconnected with former *Ladder* colleague Rita Laporte shortly before her death from cancer.[11] Donna remained on staff with the Kansas City Public Library while Barbara worked in the credit department at Macy's Department Store, and together they had taken significant steps toward improving their property. Even when decorating their "20 Rue Jacob Acres" home for the holiday season, Barbara remained conscious of her longtime goal of heightening lesbian visibility: "It is a good time of the year, solstice or Christmas or whatever one calls it... We have intertwined women's (Lesbian) symbol in lights on our door and our neighbors come and ask what it is and we tell them, slowly in patient language but without blinking..."[12]

The Bookstore Scene

Barbara watched with glee as gay and feminist bookstores spread across the nation beginning in the 1970s. Infused with optimism, idealism and a sense of possibility, women joined together to sell gay and lesbian books not carried by regular stores. The earliest queer bookstores, beginning in 1967 with Craig Rodwell's Oscar Wilde Memorial Bookshop (New York City), tended to cater to gay men, but feminism soon sparked the creation of women's bookstores. Collectives like A Woman's Place (Oakland) and the Amazon Bookstore Cooperative (Minneapolis) led the way, many of them beginning as volunteer-based ventures and with a commitment to eliminating the hierarchical structure characteristic of many male-dominated businesses. By the decade's close, there were approximately seventy-eight women's bookstores in the United States and Canada working to bring greater visibility to women poets and writers.[13]

In 1974, Linda Bryant and friend Barbara Borgman opened Charis Books in the Little Five Points district of Atlanta, an area populated by gun shops, pawn shops, liquor stores and seedy bars.[14] Charis offered a safe alternative to sexually oriented adult bookshops by providing space where the out and the closeted alike could attend readings, join gay book discussion groups, and find ads for gay-owned businesses. Customers no longer had to lurk furtively in the stacks of a chain bookstore as they paged through the one or two gay books tucked unobtrusively away on the shelves. Later, the store expanded from its original focus on women's literature, leftist theology and children's books to include lesbian books, women's music and gay pride items. Becoming part of a print-based gay and lesbian ecosystem, Charis supported gay and lesbian community development and served as an incubator for the development of gay and lesbian political consciousness.

During her early years with Charis Books, Bryant had limited knowledge of lesbian books, and initially questioned whether Naiad's "fluffy, lightweight" novels qualified as literature. After reading several titles and seeing customer reactions to them, however, she realized they played an important role by providing "the affirmation and experiential kind of thing that would let lesbians be entertained and know that they were not alone." In time, Charis became one of many stores that set up a standing order for whatever Naiad Press published, but Barbara continued calling regularly with news about new titles, authors and the community of booksellers. Buyers from other stores jokingly boasted of using income from the sale of Naiads to support their line of more literary or political lesbian material.[15] Unfazed by the implied insult, Barbara was delighted to live in a world where lesbian books flourished.

The Lecture Circuit

Barbara, who had grown up starved for attention, felt like a celebrity when she and Donna traveled to California in March 1977 for several speaking engagements. With Donna at her side to manage travel arrangements and provide moral support, Barbara gained confidence and quickly grew into her role as a public advocate for lesbians. On the campus of San Francisco State University, Barbara spoke to Lyndall Cowan's Lesbian Literature class, and women snapped up the supply of Naiad Press books Donna offered for sale. While in the Bay Area, Barbara appeared at the Full Moon Coffeehouse and Bookstore, visited Laura X, founder of the Women's History Library at the University of California, Berkeley, and enjoyed a five-hour visit with poet Elsa Gidlow, one of her longtime correspondents.[16]

Barbara also gave a speech at the San Jose State University Women's Week celebration in which she urged everyone to come out of their closets. According to two appreciative participants, Barbara's passionate remarks dispelled the notion of "Old Dykes" as "old foggeys [sic] of a bygone age of conservatism, traditionalism, & appeasement." While staffing a booth, Donna saw an older woman with a bouffant hairdo taking Barbara's advice to come out of the closet. Then she noticed a young man saying filthy things to the woman. Striding over to confront him, Donna commanded him to "Leave!" When he informed her it was a public place and he did not have to leave, she told him to "Get the hell out of here now!" and kicked him in the shin with one of her cowboy boots when he refused to budge. Seeking retaliation, he returned with the campus police. Unintimidated, Donna inquired if they wanted to know what he had said to the woman. Upon hearing the crude comments, the older policeman blanched, admonished Donna, and then led the offensive man away by the scruff of his neck. Donna was jet-propelled to heroine status because of her willingness to confront the bully.[17]

The following month, Barbara accepted an invitation from Gayle Rubin to speak at the University of Michigan. Rubin had first written to Barbara six years earlier when she decided to write her honors thesis on lesbian literature. When Rubin remained undaunted by her initial terseness, Barbara recognized a kindred spirit and gave her the equivalent of a private tutorial through the mail. Rubin grew to regard her as a "Professor of Lesbian Studies" even though there was no such position anywhere in the country in 1971. By inviting Barbara to speak on her campus, Rubin hoped to build support for the organization of a women's studies program and to establish lesbian studies "as a valid political and intellectual topic for women's studies." With this in mind, Barbara spoke on "The Lesbian Movement: 25 Years of Literature & Life." She also delivered the talk at Michigan State University, before taking Donna on an odyssey to see people and places associated with her childhood.[18]

Love Is Work Too

When Barbara and Donna purchased the house and five acres forty miles from Kansas City in 1973, it had seemed like a utopian ideal. Donna, who had grown up on a farm, loved working the land. By the summer of 1976 they had over one hundred items growing in their garden, including seventeen different kinds of beans and peas. Planting hundreds of trees, they made self-sustainability a goal. The more outgoing of the two, Donna felt at home among local farmers, who reminded her of family members, and she enjoyed welcoming people to their home. Barbara, on the other hand, loved the rural location because of its remoteness, and asked travelers to give ample warning before their arrival.

In the spring of 1977, several unanticipated developments turned Barbara's world upside down. The three years of a long daily commute to Kansas City, combined with ambitious plans for developing their property and Barbara's obsession with her movement work, began taking a toll on the couple's relationship. During the winter months they left for work in the dark and returned home long after sunset. Numerous chores filled the remainder of their short evenings and weekends, leaving little or no time for recreation and relaxation. Donna increasingly found the routine depressing, while Barbara seemed content to fill her life with work, work and more work.

Matters worsened when Macy's fired Barbara for using the company's WATS line to make unauthorized phone calls related to her movement work and Naiad Press business. Dismissed with cause, she was ineligible for unemployment benefits at a time when the couple needed both of their incomes to cover expenses. The next blow occurred when longtime Reno volunteer Kathy Mengle informed Barbara and Donna that as much as she loved them, she needed to move forward with her life and could no longer continue as a Naiad volunteer. To ease the transition, she agreed to work into the summer months, if needed. Reading between the lines of Mengle's letters, Anyda Marchant sensed resentment and wanted to know if Barbara had informed the dedicated woman of their plans to pay her in the near future.[19] In reality, Mengle's decision involved more than the question of compensation. By her own admission, Barbara could be demanding and difficult, and Mengle had survived longer than most, in part because of the geographic distance separating them.

Mengle's announcement convinced Barbara that the time had come to move Naiad's entire operation to Missouri, and with Donna's consent, she planned the transition. "What we envision now," Barbara informed one of her correspondents, "is that I will have to simply devote every minute of my life" to Naiad. She asked Mengle to prepare a work manual of Naiad routines "in enough detail so that granny simpleton can use it," and asked her to maintain the *Ladder*/Naiad post office box for another year.[20] Even though five years had passed since the last issue of *The Ladder* appeared, lesbians kept finding the magazine and writing to Gene Damon with pages of questions and she did not want them to go unanswered. Barbara gave little thought to the impact her work on behalf of *The Ladder* would have on the couple's personal finances.

Barbara had been giving her labor to lesbian publishing for two full decades by the time Marchant proposed she receive some compensation. With an eye on Internal Revenue Service requirements, the retired attorney weighed tax implications for various options before authorizing a payment of one hundred dollars a month, noting that she could deduct it as a business expense. In response to Marchant's request that she log the time spent doing Naiad work, Barbara replied, "That is easy...Donna says I eat, sleep, drink and dream about Naiad." The payments began in September 1977.[21]

In the middle of the Naiad-related upheaval, Barbara faced yet another adjustment when Donna accepted a sales representative position with the Midwest Regional Office of Computer Library Services, Inc. (CLSI), a Massachusetts-based company founded in 1971 to develop computer applications for use in libraries. The job, which began in late June, paid well but required extensive travel throughout Nebraska, Kansas and Missouri, as well as occasional trips to Boston.[22] Donna had read that if a person worked for ten years in one place, she would likely spend the rest of her life there. Unable to envision herself at the Kansas City Public Library for the remainder of her career, Donna had decided it was time for a change.

Barbara found it difficult to be home alone while Donna traveled. She missed her companionship, suffered from insomnia, and lacked a personal governor. "Without my keeper here," she confided to Marchant, "I stay up all night. I also work all day." Confined to their house with the cats, she focused almost exclusively on the business of Naiad Press and poured out her anxieties to her correspondents. After Sandia Belgrade, one of *The Ladder*'s loyal supporters, received one of Barbara's emotion-filled missives, she offered to come to Missouri for a month to assist with packing and mailing books so Barbara could manage the publicity, correspondence and payments. Barbara, who sometimes failed to comprehend the power of her words, admitted she had been "rather full of a sense of panic" when she wrote, and assured Belgrade and others who wished to help that they could do their best work for Naiad without leaving home. "It is getting like the old days," she mused. Firmly entrenched in the volunteer model that had worked so well during her editorship of *The Ladder*, Barbara believed that "if I sit at this typewriter long enough I will gather a marching army of loving/dedicated/working women," and together they would make the world a better place for lesbians.[23]

As Barbara frantically threw herself into the work of Naiad, Donna contended with the pressures of her new position. As much as she liked the CLSI product and her work-related travel, she soon realized she was not cut out to be a salesperson. When she returned home from her travels at week's end, she faced the demands of caring for the five acres and helping Barbara with Naiad-related tasks, leaving little time for relaxation or enjoyment. During Donna's absence, Barbara's reclusive tendencies resurfaced. On the rare occasions when a lesbian couple from Springfield invited them to spend weekends at a nearby lake, Barbara found herself "just itching" to stay home so she could keep working, and at times her intensity manifested itself in a short temper.[24]

Donna's efforts to cultivate friendships uncovered a basic difference in the two women's social outlook. In a self-reflective moment, Barbara acknowledged: "I do not agree with her view of people...she likes them more genuinely than I do...she likes people in mass quantities and to entertain and talk mindlessly about everything." When Kathy Mengle told Barbara and Donna that she was leaving her partner for another Naiad volunteer, Barbara became angry because she blamed the relationship for Mengle's decision to cease working for Naiad. In response to Donna's assertion that Mengle and her friend had a right to their happiness, Barbara "snapped back 'NO,'" but later admitted she had not meant the words spoken in anger. She also realized Donna had spoken the truth in saying "You only like people you can use."[25]

By fall, Donna had developed a crush on one of their friends and contemplated ending her relationship. She briefly pursued the other woman, who turned out to be attracted to someone else, but Donna never moved out of the home she shared with Barbara.[26] Instead, her work-related travel provided the space she needed to reevaluate her life and relationship during this difficult period.

"I am very frightened, and somehow stunned," Barbara wrote Marchant in mid-October, "trying to unscramble the abrupt collapse of a known world." The main problem, as she understood it, was that Donna was unhappy with her and "[t]here is some question about whether we are to last forever." In her panic, Barbara also turned to Helen Bennett, "my oldest friend on earth," to see if she would take her back, but Helen said no. A tired and "minorly drunk" Barbara poured out her anxieties to longtime friend Jane Rule, who speculated Donna's new job had "let her measure the limitations of the life you'd been leading before." Attributing part of their relationship troubles to Barbara's financial dependence on Donna, Rule urged her friend to find a job "that is as important to you as your work without pay has been, not just a clerical job." Otherwise, she predicted, Donna would feel guilty for asking Barbara to sacrifice the work she loved for employment that merely paid the bills. At forty-four, Rule observed, Barbara was not too old to merge her professional and personal interests in one job, and she could tap into her vast network of publishers and editors for assistance in finding something suitable. Encouraging Barbara to write frequently as she worked through this difficult period, Rule concluded: "We've done a lot of growing up together over quite a stretch of time, and neither of us has ever taken our friendship lightly."[27]

When Barbara left Helen in 1972, she told Donna she "would not come to live with her for less than forever...period, no compromise." Through counseling and honest conversation, the two women worked through their difficulties in the fall of 1977. When they consulted with a minister at the Kansas City Metropolitan Community Church, Donna expected him to listen to her description of the relationship and then explain to Barbara the error of her ways; however, he surprised her by stating that neither woman was blameless. He helped Donna realize that she hated conflict and needed to voice the things that bothered her before losing her temper. He explained to Barbara that she needed to listen carefully to her partner, who had been dropping clues about her pain. He also helped Barbara recognize that she was channeling her excess energy into the movement instead of dealing with problems in their relationship, and that this tendency was "damaging and hurting Donna."[28] As much as Donna loved their place in the country, she felt trapped by responsibility and needed more time to play.

Initially, Barbara reacted to these revelations in her characteristic dramatic style. She announced the abrupt termination of her movement activities to friends near and far: "I will not be speaking. I will not be writing to as many people. I will not be spending time working with anything (including NAIAD and housework and anything) when I should be with Donna...and I will be out of the way when I should be out of the way...the trouble is, will I know what to do when?" As drama yielded to day-to-day reality, Barbara realized Donna had never asked her to give up the movement work. With love grounded in the ability to make each other laugh, they agreed to compromise. Donna encouraged Barbara to become a more people-oriented person, while she became more involved in the work of Naiad. Recognizing that the rural property demanded too much of their time, Barbara and Donna put their home at 20 Rue Jacob Acres on the market in November 1977 so they could move closer to Kansas City and the airport. Barbara also returned to the workforce by taking yet another clerical-level position.[29]

By the following fall, Barbara and Donna had settled into their new home on Weatherby Lake, just north of Kansas City, which they christened Llangollen after the Ladies of Llangollen, two women who rejected marriage and made their home together in Wales for more than fifty years. With their relationship back on an even keel, Barbara resumed movement work, made all the easier by Donna's ability to coordinate travel plans and drive. "I must be Barbara's vitamin pill," she good-naturedly noted in a 1979 interview, "because she takes all my strength and uses it."[30] In the spring of 1979, they traveled to Washington, D.C., where

Barbara addressed the D.C. chapter of the National Organization for Women's Sexuality Task Force, met many "old line LADDER women," and connected with Carol Anne Douglas, Helaine Harris, Cynthia Gair and Joan E. Biren. The publication of Barbara's speech, "Neither Profit nor Salvation," in Karla Jay's *Lavender Culture* prompted a few angry responses from closeted teachers who resented her insistence that all gays and lesbians needed to come out of their closets. Barbara, they argued, had no comprehension of the risk involved, the loss of job, church, work and custody of children. "Can teachers really 'come out' anywhere?" one woman demanded. "It's not as simple as you think."[31]

When the National Women's Studies Association convened in Lawrence, Kansas, in May 1979, Barbara spoke on a panel about research on single women, along with historian Lee Chambers Schiller. Thrilled to find so many lesbians present in NWSA, Barbara encouraged Marchant to take out a membership for the press so Naiad could exhibit at the following year's conference. As conference attendees traveled to and from the airport, dozens stopped at Llangollen to see the collection that Barbara touted as the "largest private library of homosexual literature in English in the world."[32]

Defining Naiad's Market

In the mid-1970s, the women involved with Daughters, Inc., Diana Press, Naiad Press and Out and Out Books envisioned themselves publishing work with intrinsic rather than commercial value. According to *Sinister Wisdom* co-founders Harriet Desmoines and Catherine Nicholson, mainstream publishing houses existed to make profit, while lesbian presses existed "to make revolution." In words that were music to Barbara's ears, they pronounced lesbian literature as "central to sustaining the reality we create together…When we treat our presses as the real presses and we fight for them with every weapon we have and we give our best work to them, we refuse legitimacy to the patriarchal press."[33]

Lesbian writers differed when it came to the question of women's presses profiting from their labor. Maureen Brady of Spinsters Ink thought the pursuit of monetary gain jeopardized the special relationships lesbian and feminist presses cultivated with writers and readers, while author Rita Mae Brown contended that "[t]he more money lesbian presses make the more authors they can publish." Desmoines and Nicholson believed a combination of commercial businesses and federal agencies stood poised to destroy women's presses, pointing to presses that had been plagued by mysterious vandalism as well as IRS and postal harassment. Both the right and left wing, they continued, were attempting to absorb the feminist movement. To illustrate their point, Desmoines and Nicholson cited the six-figure payment to Susan Brownmiller for the paperback rights to *Against Our Will: Men, Women, and Rape.* Calling for unity of women in print, they declared that the solution to breaking down "the patriarchal elitism of print" lay in making it a priority to use women typesetters, press operators and bookbinders in the production of books.[34]

From the beginning, Marchant viewed Naiad as distinctly different from other movement presses. A voracious reader, she was familiar with the focus of Daughters, Inc., Diana Press and the Women's Press Collective of Oakland on the "political possibilities and political meanings of books." A product of her class and generation, Marchant remained firmly wedded to the idea of the novel as a work of art, not a weapon. "Of course we are feminists and we support all sorts of activism in favor of feminism," she explained in 1977, "[b]ut supporting activism is one thing and turning our books into propaganda is another." When asked to compare her company to other presses, Marchant found it easier to explain what Naiad would not publish: "tragedies depicting the hopeless quality of lesbian love… caricatures of non-women and menaces to society; lesbians as objects of ridicule; and, down at the bottom, straight pornography for the titillation of male appetites." Responding to an early charge that Naiad simply published romance novels, Marchant declared: "We are publishing for women who want real novels—you can call them romantic if you want to." Advising Barbara to maintain a certain aloofness from other presses, she opined that writers who "would please the critics that have called our books trash can, with my best wishes, go to Diana and Daughters for their way into print."[35]

Barbara approached publishing differently than a majority of her lesbian-feminist peers. Standing outside the periphery of feminist politics, she eschewed consensus-based decision-making, preferring instead a hierarchical organization with herself responsible for the day-to-day business decisions. Since Naiad lacked the large capital investment that funded the beginning of Daughters, it had more in common with Diana when it came to finances, including use of the cost-recovery model. Yet, after witnessing the feminist movement turning against its own during Diana's involvement with the Feminist Economic Network holding company, Barbara vowed "to turn my back on the movement and walk away." She was committed to Naiad Press, but not to "the mickey mouse" [*sic*] politics that consumed the energy of so many lesbians in publishing.[36]

Volunteers and Naiad

When Marchant prepared Naiad Press' taxes in the spring of 1977, she informed Barbara that three of the six books published had paid for themselves: *Speak Out, My Heart*; *A Woman Appeared to Me*; and her own *The Latecomer*. Nonetheless, the bottom line showed the press continuing to lose money. Unless Naiad began generating profit, the Internal Revenue Service would re-classify it as "an activity purely for self-satisfaction" and deny its status as an incorporated business.[37]

After Naiad had published three Sarah Aldridge novels in as many years, Barbara persuaded Marchant that the press should publish an original novel by pulp fiction novelist Valerie Taylor. *Love Image*, which Naiad published in 1977, was "a romantic potboiler about a young [lesbian] movie star." Describing the book to cover artist Tee Corinne, Barbara explained, "You know while you are reading it that it's all crap...but it's such fun crap." When Taylor received Naiad's cost-recovery contract, she insisted money had to change hands for the agreement to be valid. Musing that Taylor must be "fishing for an advance," Marchant condescendingly instructed Barbara to "send her fifty dollars for next week's groceries."[38]

Barbara also harbored dreams of publishing contemporary poetry. When she contacted Marchant about the possibility of issuing a volume of poems by Chocolate Waters, however, Marchant responded with an emphatic no. Her vision for the press consisted of novels, biography and poetry only if the poet were already established, and preferably deceased.[39] Working within these parameters, Barbara next proposed an English-language translation of Renée Vivien's *The Muse of the Violets* (1977), translated from French by Margaret Porter and Catherine Kroger.

Looking ahead to 1978, Naiad planned to publish two books, another Sarah Aldridge novel and *Berrigan*, a first novel written by a young Colorado woman who assisted Barbara by typing and mailing invoices and writing reviews. Vicki P. McConnell, who published under the pseudonym Gingerlox, found Barbara to be a woman of "extreme contrasts: at once ingratiating and charming, with another side that could emerge with whiplash rapidity." After telling her that *Berrigan* "did everything but launch airplanes off the page," Barbara mailed Naiad's cost-recovery contract to McConnell. Reviewing it with dismay tinged with anger, the young feminist informed Barbara that she was not a "naïve first-publishing over-eager author" and detailed the changes she expected to see. Marchant resolved the conflict, and McConnell went on to publish four books with Naiad. In reality, Naiad's contract was quite similar to the one Diana Press used, stipulating that royalties were paid after payment of bills for advertisements, printing and distribution.[40]

By the end of 1978, costs continued to outrun inventory and Naiad had lost slightly more than $2,400. "This means," Marchant explained, "that we have just two more years in which to prove to the IRS that we are a business and not merely dilettantes in the publishing world." If the press could not show a profit, she lamented, it would become necessary "to go back to reporting everything as a personal hobby of mine," something the publisher found "irritating beyond measure."[41]

Faced with the challenge of turning a profit while assuming responsibility for Naiad's distribution and marketing, Barbara relied on time-tested techniques that had worked for her as editor of *The Ladder*. A mistress in the art of composing "begging letters," her appeals in *Lesbian Connection* and other publications generated sympathy for a press seemingly poised "at the sink or swim point." For those unable to give money, she suggested donations of equipment and supplies ranging from staplers and paper cutters to paper, pens, envelopes and stamps. Barbara also implored publications like *Albatros, Lesbian Voices, off our backs, Plexus, Sinister Wisdom* and others to run free ads for Naiad books.[42]

In addition to promoting Naiad Press books, Barbara recruited dozens of volunteers to inform her if they found books containing lesbian characters or themes. Naiad had published a second edition of *The Lesbian in Literature* in 1975, and she envisioned a third edition would be necessary within five or six years. Barbara grew to depend on the discoveries of women like poet Shebar Windstone, gay men like historian and reviewer Eric Garber, and countless others. She even persuaded her former lover, Helen Bennett, to gather citations for the bibliography. Over time, her intense focus on the books and abrupt personality alienated a few of her volunteers, but many others excused her behavior because they shared her love of lesbian literature.[43]

By the mid-1970s, Barbara had cultivated a following among lesbian college students who had read *The Ladder*. Because of her visibility as the magazine's editor during its final four years, they viewed her as a pioneer and showed their appreciation of her efforts on their behalf. Barbara used their gratitude to Naiad's advantage. When she requested a free advertisement in *off our backs*, Janis Kelly replied, "You can have any kind of ad you want and print it IN MY BLOOD…I simply cannot express to you how important *The Ladder* was to me in 1967-68-69 when I was doing gay organizing at Cornell University." At the time, Kelly thought the nascent women's movement on campus had rejected her because she was a dyke, "so it was nice to find support from *you*." While not technically a volunteer, Tee Corinne agreed to do cover art and copy for Naiad for just fifty dollars per book. Reflecting on her effectiveness in making these and other appeals, Barbara admitted she had begun to feel "like a bloodsucker...I am draining friends."[44]

Women responded to Barbara's call for assistance because she appealed to their desire to make a difference. "We are simply trying to make enough money," she explained, "to keep on publishing Lesbian books that will otherwise never be published."[45] A church secretary and former *Ladder* subscriber typed manuscripts and contracts that others edited. Vicki P. McConnell handled invoices and payments, and Barbara also recruited women who lived in major cities to promote books at local women's centers, gay bars and bookstores. Other former *Ladder* subscribers and young lesbian feminists showed their appreciation for her courageous cultural work by helping get review notices of Naiad books placed in magazines and newspapers.

Once women began working with Barbara, some enthusiastic volunteers discovered how temperamental and demanding she could be. By her own admission, she was a slave driver: "I brutalize, ignore, mistreat, and generally savage my slaves," she jokingly boasted when describing her management style. While not willing to pay Naiad volunteers as staff, Marchant thought the company should at least pay minimum wage for "some of the donkey work." Otherwise, she fretted, overworked volunteers might turn resentful and even sabotage the press. Indeed, she reminded Barbara, Kathy Mengle was "nursing a deep resentment" when she wrote a negative review of *Berrigan* and sent it to *Ms. Magazine*. Advising Barbara to be on her guard, Marchant cautioned: "You cannot tell what little viper is awaiting the opportunity to do you dirt!"[46]

Barbara knew from her vast correspondence with other movement workers that Naiad was not alone in relying heavily on donations and volunteers. In the 1950s and 1960s, homophile publications would not have existed without the selfless dedication of people who gave their time to the cause. People living in isolation could connect with the movement and feel a sense of purpose through their volunteerism. Indeed, the Michigan-based *Lesbian Connection*, founded in 1974, had received good responses to its pleas for money as well as offers from lesbians willing to handle printing and provide computer access.[47]

Yet some women challenged Barbara's perspective on volunteerism. Writing from San Francisco, Lyndall Cowan questioned Barbara's willingness to work for free. "I am curious as to why getting paid for the work you do for the 'movement' is not a priority...the 'volunteer' concept is defeating us."[48] Like other feminists, Cowan knew that patriarchal culture had systematically devalued women's labor for centuries. Thus, while many women still gave their labor to undercapitalized women's presses, bookstores and magazines in the late 1970s, they increasingly questioned the practice. Barbara, however, had devoted years of free labor to movement publications, and mistakenly assumed others shared her single-minded commitment to building Naiad into a successful lesbian press.

As Naiad Press matured, Marchant's discomfort with Barbara's efforts to recruit an army of volunteers increased. An attorney well versed in tax law, she felt "a little uneasy about our getting volunteer help. I know you have a pretty heavy burden. But, you know, if we were a non-profit undertaking, that would be fine. Then you would be in the same position as you were with TL [*The Ladder*]. But since we look forward to at least making our expenses and perhaps enough of a profit to impress the IRS...I don't like the idea." Until the press could afford to compensate its volunteers, she suggested giving volunteers copies of Naiad books. Despite her awareness that the press needed to acknowledge the value of volunteer labor, it did not always translate into payments. Although Naiad had depended heavily on Mengle's volunteer labor for several years, she rationalized: "In Kathy's case we have been able to make some recompense to her, if not much in money, at least in publishing her work."[49]

Honing Naiad's Approach

It was in this context that Naiad Press developed from a self-publishing venture into a publishing empire. At Naiad's inception, Anyda Marchant had envisioned the press as a vehicle for printing her books plus a few others as rewards to authors who aided the press in its work. Operating on a cost-recovery basis, she lent the press money to cover the cost of typesetting, printing, binding and distribution of her first book, and then repaid herself from income generated by sales. She subsequently subsidized the publication of several additional books, but always reimbursed herself from their sales. When her books began to make a small profit, she invested the royalties back into the company to offset the cost of publishing her next book.[50]

Barbara approached her role as general manager of Naiad Press much as she had editorship of *The Ladder*, promoting lesbian literature and conducting extensive correspondence. As Naiad's primary interface with the public, she conveyed Marchant's wishes to authors and bookstores. As the company's president, Marchant at the time had the final say in the selection of new manuscripts. She also prepared author contracts and offered editorial commentary on manuscripts received. Barbara soon discovered that authors often had high expectations for the young press and mistakenly assumed it would function much like a commercial business. Those who previously published in the pulp or academic markets, for instance, expected advances and royalties.

As Naiad's chief publicist, Barbara recognized the importance of having its books included in standard reference sources and reviewing media. She dedicated herself to securing a listing for Naiad in *Literary Market Place* because she thought it would "make us officially a REAL publishing company in the eyes of the publishing world." When they refused her application, she accused its publisher of "BLATANT anti-Lesbian discrimination" even though she knew Naiad had been excluded because it published too few titles. Ultimately, her powers of persuasion and persistence worked, and Naiad gained a listing. Taking the long view, Barbara projected that achievements such as this eventually would lead to "the kind of world we seem to envision," a world where lesbians could find books about themselves as easily as they could books on any other topic.[51]

Barbara considered it an even greater coup when library review media began including Naiad Press books. Acting without Marchant's prior authorization, she distributed one hundred complimentary copies of Naiad's fall 1977 releases in the hope of garnering notices and reviews. She welcomed the assistance of children's book author and librarian Dorothy M. Broderick in unlocking the review column of *Library Journal*, and in return offered to recruit support for Broderick's run to become the first lesbian president of the American Library Association.[52]

In addition to securing public recognition for Naiad and its books, Barbara continued her efforts to cultivate good relations with the women she viewed as the company's primary customer base. Continuing a habit begun during her many years with *The Ladder*, she made it a priority to answer every letter sent to her or the press, with the exception of obscene requests. Her curt answers to some suggest Barbara had grown weary from years of correspondence with isolated women and those who had recently come out as lesbians. "I believe that we will succeed primarily because we are more efficient and more considerate of the idiot requests…and you SHOULD SEE some of them…unbelievable what we get asked…"[53]

After the Women in Print conference in 1976, Barbara was convinced of the political necessity of using women's labor to produce women's words. "I believed," she later wrote, "that one of my obligations was to PUT MY MONEY WHERE MY MOUTH IS…to give my business, all of it, to women's businesses, to Lesbian businesses, and so I did." She began by asking the Iowa City Women's Press (ICWP), a lesbian collective, to print twenty thousand promotional flyers for Naiad. She also requested estimates for printing several titles and found them anxious to obtain the work. Her idealism tempered by Midwestern practicality, Barbara anticipated a mutually beneficial partnership.[54]

As someone who came of age before second-wave feminism swept the nation in the 1960s, Barbara remained "a bit wary of the collective [way of] functioning," and was at times at odds with the priorities and needs of the women in Iowa City. Her job, she believed, was to "find ways to cut costs so that more of the money we make can be put where it belongs into the production of more books...that is, entirely, our goal...PUBLISH BOOKS." When Barbara complied with Marchant's instruction to send partial payments to both ICWP and Salsedo Press in Chicago for work they had completed, the ICWP responded with a lesson in the economics of small press publishing. As a slightly older and larger press, they explained, Salsedo had easier access to credit than the women of Iowa City. "It is not politics or giving of support; it comes down to month to month survival economics." Elaborating, they explained that ICWP women had devoted themselves virtually full-time to Naiad's two books during the summer and workers needed income so they could pay their rent and buy food. After Barbara paid them in full the following October ($1,179), the collective was ready to move forward with the printing of more books for Naiad Press.[55]

Once books were published, small presses struggled with the challenge of marketing and distributing them. In the early years, they often relied on word-of-mouth and distribution of flyers. At first, many small publishers had bought access to *The Ladder*'s mailing list, but this began to change in 1973 when Helaine Harris and Cynthia Gair, both formerly associated with the Furies Collective, founded Women in Distribution (WIND) to serve "as a central clearinghouse for lesbian-feminist presses and journals." Publishers shipped copies of their books to WIND, which the distributor marketed to bookstores through catalogs. This method heightened awareness of small-press books and eased the work of bookstores by becoming a one-stop shop for all who depended upon lesbian and feminist press books. As a businesswoman, Harris appreciated Barbara's willingness to share her skills, which included "how to deal with collecting overdue accounts in a professional manner."[56]

When WIND filed for bankruptcy in July 1979, Barbara recognized the impact its cessation would have on small bookstores. Taking immediate action, she composed a "Dear Friends" letter to inform her network of the potential consequences for all associated with women's press publishing. "We will all have to work very hard to make up for this loss," she encouraged. "One of the reasons for WIND's failure," she concluded, was "an abundance of accounts receivable of long duration, which is a polite way of saying that some of our community did not pay their invoices without long, long periods of delay." As a veteran of collections work, Barbara was determined to prevent this from happening to Naiad. Detailing everyone's responsibility, from bookstores to publishers, she admonished readers to take action rather than "sighing about how sad it all is." They could correct the mess, she insisted, if everyone worked together. "It is such an uphill battle so much of the time," she wrote the women of the Iowa City Women's Press, "but it is for love and belief we do it all. I want so much for us all to succeed so that women will always know that they can make it...they can do what they damned well please whenever they please...that life is something to shape and hold in our own hands."[57]

With WIND out of business, Naiad moved into the work of distribution, and by mid-July Barbara had made arrangements to distribute Joan E. Biren's book, *Eye to Eye*, and Tee Corinne's *Cunt Coloring Book*. When Marchant learned of the latter, she cautioned: "I expect we had better be careful about two things, taking on too many distributions, and too much sensational material. We must guard our reputation for being a sobersides outfit." Marchant also fretted about Naiad's growing reputation for heckling bookstores into prompt payment. "This is not appropriate as regards Naiad's image," she instructed her general manager. Instead, Marchant preferred that Barbara require prepayment for stores that lacked a good payment record. Tightening the reins a bit further, she reminded Barbara that their original plan for 1979 had been to reprint *A Woman Appeared to Me*, yet they had undertaken far more. Unless they proceeded more cautiously, she warned, the press could be in danger of foundering.[58]

* * *

Despite Barbara's obsession with work, Donna persuaded her of the necessity to take a vacation. In early October, they traveled to Eleuthera, an island in the Bahamas that soon became one of Barbara's favorite places on the planet. They spent "four wonderful days there...swimming, snorkeling, running, walking on the miles of pink sand beaches, eating and sleeping." Upon returning home, however, Barbara felt guilty for taking time away from the movement and work, and immediately composed a "Dear Friends" letter confessing their grievous sin: that they had "committed the unconscionable act of having taken a vacation."[59]

CHAPTER ELEVEN

༈

Naiad: A Flourishing Lesbian Press

*"I love you, pussycat and you must not be worried about anything...
it will be fine...we will sell the house and I will come and live with
you...you will come and kidnap me...along with 20,000 books and
7 rooms of furniture."*
—Barbara Grier to Donna McBride, 1980[1]

If not for Donna McBride, Barbara Grier might have spent the
remainder of her life in Missouri. Instead, the couple moved to
Florida in 1980 because Donna needed a change of scene. She loved the
product she sold for Computer Library Services, Inc. and admired the
company's founder, but as a lesbian felt like an outsider in a heterosexually
dominated work environment. Additionally, her partner did not cope well
during Donna's week-long absences, when Barbara tended to work round
the clock until she hit an emotional low point. After the harsh winters of
1978 and 1979, both women were ready to live in a milder climate, so
Donna searched for jobs in Florida. That location had the added benefit
of placing them in closer proximity to business partners Anyda Marchant
and Muriel Crawford, who wintered each year in Pompano Beach. By
April 1980, Donna had landed a position as associate director of the Leon
County Public Library in Tallahassee, with a starting date in mid-June.
Barbara announced her partner's new position in a "Dear Friends" letter
that May.[2]

In the weeks before Donna's departure for Florida, the couple
maintained a hectic schedule, which included attending the second annual

National Women's Studies Association conference in Bloomington, Indiana. Barbara went to the conference prepared "to oil the right waters, trouble the ones that need it, and generally make the world function." She loved the NWSA's energy, especially being among "a very large happy functioning group of women, primarily Lesbians, and sharing our work, our dreams and plans."[3] Back in Missouri, she and Donna put their Weatherby Lake house on the market and pragmatically agreed Barbara would remain behind until it sold.

Barbara coped with the separation by sending Donna daily letters filled with endearments as well as news about their kitties and details about work she was doing in the house, yard, garden and for Naiad. Barbara fretted because she didn't know what to give her "Sweetie Pie" for her birthday, before deciding: "I may ship myself...that seems best to me." Overcoming her concerns about finances, Barbara scheduled a flight to arrive in Tallahassee on July 4. "I am so happy about getting to come and see you...it's sad to waste money, but that is no waste of money...life is now...not later...I have to keep remembering that."[4]

Upon moving to Florida, Donna had found temporary quarters in an apartment across the street from Rose Printing, the company that published *The Latecomer*, Naiad Press's first book. During Barbara's July visit, the couple went house hunting and found a lovely contemporary home on two wooded acres northwest of Tallahassee near Lake Yvette. After returning to Missouri, Barbara grew increasingly discouraged yet tried to put a positive spin on their extended separation: "I have a wonderful collection of love letters from you now...I like that." As days passed without an offer on their house, Barbara's gloom deepened. "I alternate between terror and hope...possibly without reason...it's just knowing that we have almost no control over our lives and very little lifetime left...the combination is frightening." A woman who thrived on action, she hated the sense of "treading water."[5]

Barbara's work as a credit counselor did little to alleviate her frustration and impatience. As was her custom, she remained alert for opportunities to type Naiad correspondence during lull times at work but found it difficult under the eyes of her watchful supervisor, whom she referred to as the "Ayatollah." Angered by the homophobia and "general loathing of women" in her workplace, Barbara informed Donna she intended to line up at least four applicants for a position there, "including Deborah Butner...who is very well qualified...and very black and very female... chuckle...make the mf's squirm a bit."[6]

Phone bills mounted as Barbara and Donna's home lingered on the market. In August, Barbara spoke at a conference in Memphis and arranged for Donna to manage the book table. As thrilled as they were to see each other, it was "a strange situation" because they had to concentrate on being public, "ordinarily an easy thing to do."[7] Eager to reunite, Barbara joined Donna in Florida in September even though their Missouri house had not yet sold. A major undertaking, the move involved their household, business and enormous library. "Our journey," Barbara wrote afterwards "was hilarious and frightening...35 miles an hour much of the way" with Donna driving a twenty-two-foot truck with a trailer attached to it while Barbara followed in the car with the two cats. Once in Florida, Barbara spent a "nightmarish" two weeks searching for and finding a minimum-wage department store job while she and Donna handled shipments of Naiad's fall releases. Eager to re-create aspects of the countryside they had enjoyed while living at "20 Rue Jacob Acres" outside Bates City, they also found time to plant a garden, trees and ornamental bushes. By year's end, Barbara had found a better job working with the Florida Department of Education, one that offered a number of benefits, including the vacation time she needed for her growing Naiad Press responsibilities.[8]

State of Lesbian Publishing

As Barbara surveyed the lesbian publishing scene in the summer of 1980, she predicted a bright future for Naiad Press. "We are the largest press now operating functionally in the business. DAUGHTERS has issued no new titles for a year or so...DIANA has gone to hell (where they belong) in a hand basket...and the next largest presses are FEMINIST PRESS...[and]...MOON BOOKS...even more specialized than we are, and are not per se or even really much at all interested in the Lesbian market." Persephone Press had just three titles in print, and in Barbara's opinion, the lesbian-feminist founders were "new babies, nice kids, and they will someday be real competition on a friendly basis with us."[9]

Despite her interactions with others in the Women in Print movement, Barbara was a maverick, standing on the periphery of lesbian-feminist politics. A veteran of childhood poverty, she found the hand-to-mouth existence of the Women's Press Collective unacceptable. Like Parke Bowman of Daughters, Inc., Barbara had come of age in the pre-feminist era. She saw nothing wrong with a top-down management style and operating a successful for-profit business, especially after decades of giving her labor to the movement. Convinced she was right, Barbara forged ahead fearlessly with her plan to increase access to lesbian books.[10]

Prior to 1981, when Naiad Press released eight titles, its publication output varied from one to four books each year, and had no clear specialization. In addition to the Sarah Aldridge novels, Naiad offered readers three volumes by French writer and poet Renée Vivien, a novel by 1950s pulp novelist Valerie Taylor, and the work of two first-time novelists. Reacting to Marchant's displeasure at "Naiad's being accused of being lily white," Barbara responded almost immediately with a manuscript by Ann Allen Shockley for a collection of short stories about interracial relationships that her black friends in Kansas City had read and enjoyed. In less than two weeks, Marchant had drawn up a contract for *The Black and White of It*, which appeared in 1980, along with Lillian Faderman and Brigitte Eriksson's *Lesbian-Feminism in Turn-of-the-Century Germany* and Pat Califia's *Sapphistry: The Book of Lesbian Sexuality*.

Shepherding Sapphistry

Barbara gained numerous insights into the world of publishing when she shepherded Califia's *Sapphistry* into print. After years of plowing income from one book into the next, she anticipated that a book about lesbian sexuality would sell well and hoped it would earn enough to propel Naiad from a volunteer-based operation onto a more solid commercial footing. Aware that sex educator Betty Dodson's self-published *Liberating Masturbation* had sold more than one hundred thousand copies, Barbara enthusiastically predicted *Sapphistry* "ought to make us all [including the printers and bookbinders] very rich." Far from being a prude, Marchant proposed that Naiad print at least four thousand copies, more than double the normal print run.[11]

Califia had written much of *Sapphistry* in the mid-1970s, but mailed Barbara additional chapters on self-loving, partners and sexual problems during the summer of 1979. "My heart is in my mouth," Califia confided after sending the most controversial chapter of all, the one on variations in sexual expression that included sadomasochism (S/M). At the time, few within the lesbian-feminist community discussed this topic. The chapter had to be written, Califia explained, because of people who claimed "they didn't know any lesbians who did any of 'those things.'"[12]

Barbara's knowledge of sadomasochism came through her correspondence with Gayle Rubin. In 1978, the University of Michigan doctoral student's dissertation research took her to Berkeley, California, where she met Califia. Hinting to Barbara and Donna that her life had taken a new direction, Rubin introduced the subject of S/M in one of her letters to the publishers: "Did I tell you I may do leather bars?" Uncertain of their response, she steeled herself before coming out to them as a sadomasochist. Unfortunately, her letters arrived when Barbara was preoccupied with other matters, and she sent one of the more generic "Dear Friends" letters in reply, which Rubin interpreted as avoidance or discomfort. Yet as soon as Barbara heard from a mutual acquaintance that Califia and Rubin had formed a lesbian feminist S/M support group named Samois, she sent a warm letter assuring Rubin that she "had known forever."[13]

Because she viewed Barbara as "my lesbian mother, my teacher, my friend," Rubin felt safe in sharing how much more difficult it was to come out as a feminist sadomasochist in 1980 than it had been to come out as a lesbian in 1970. She thought "the usual feminist gay liberation lines on such things [as sadomasochism, prostitution, and pornography] were disguised prejudice." Indeed, Rubin and Califia felt alienated from the lesbian-feminist community after they became among the most vocal critics of the Women Against Violence in Pornography and Media movement, founded in 1977. Headquartered in San Francisco, WAVPM campaigned against pornography and the degradation of women in mass media. While they ensured the feminist agenda addressed pornography, they also contributed to the divide between feminist advocates of free speech and those who fought to eliminate debasing images.[14]

Staunch advocates of the first amendment, Barbara and Donna sympathized with Rubin and Califia's reaction to the anti-pornography movement. They had not forgotten the days when the only images gays and lesbians could find of themselves were in publications often deemed pornographic. "The women who have me most frightened now," Barbara confided to Jane Rule, "are the pornography witches," and she feared WAVPM's next target would be women like Tee Corinne, who had self-published the *Cunt Coloring Book* (1975), and Honey Lee Cottrell, co-author with Corinne of *I Am My Lover* (1978).[15] Despite her sympathy for Califia and Rubin as underdogs, Barbara had never been one to protest in the streets. Instead, she preferred to change the world one book at a time, beginning with the publication of books like *Sapphistry*.

Barbara responded enthusiastically to Califia's completed manuscript, praising the author for reassuring women "whose sex life is and will remain…secret and unspoken…that we KNOW THEY ARE THERE, AND THAT THEY EXIST AND THAT THEY are part of our world." Although she did not realize it at the time, the book's inclusion of the chapter on variations in sexual expression foreshadowed the emergence of S/M as a lesbian subculture. However, as the book's editor, Barbara thought something was missing. "Forgive my being so horribly middle class, middlewestern and full of terribly mundane even archaic views," she wrote, "but the book doesn't talk of love though it must, must, of course, be very much dealing with it throughout and you are very loving in your handling of everything in the book." Barbara envisioned a discussion of the kind of love she had discovered in early lesbian fiction, "that devoted fire...that often non-specific but very very sexual (though often, most often unexpressed, unacted upon) intensity." Since the final chapter of the book dealt with sexually transmitted diseases, Califia agreed to add something more upbeat, though informing Barbara, "I feel more awkward writing about love than I do about sex."[16] In its final form, *Sapphistry* concluded with a one-page chapter on passion.

In the months leading up to the book's publication, Barbara's relationship with Califia ran hot and cold. The author had reservations about Barbara's plans for Corinne to create ten illustrations, one per chapter. Barbara felt certain the artist's images would increase sales. Previously close, Corinne and Califia had grown apart because of the latter's involvement with Samois. "Tee is scared shitless of sadomasochism," Califia explained to Barbara and Donna, and "thinks it is caused by unhealthy childhoods." Succumbing to Barbara's powers of persuasion, Califia consented to use of the illustrations as long as she had the right to refuse any that violated the tone of the manuscript.[17]

After Califia's essay, "A Secret Side of Lesbian Sexuality," appeared in the December 1979 issue of the *The Advocate*, Barbara phoned at two a.m. and threatened to cancel publication of *Sapphistry*. "It was hard to tell which upset her more," Califia recalled, "the fact that I had publicly revealed my identity as a leather person ('You might as well tell people you are a murderer!') or my statement that S/M was so important to me that I would rather be marooned on a desert island with a male masochist than a vanilla dyke."[18] When Barbara calmed down, she pragmatically suggested Califia avoid writing essays that would offend the lesbian community, at least until the book appeared. "I can't hobble my career as a free-lance writer and sit here in limbo," Califia replied. Citing responses from "other women who are tired of being berated by sex-negative stars of the lesbian movement," the author forged ahead with more articles and work on a new book. Recognizing the futility of arguing the point, Barbara accepted the situation because any kind of publicity, whether positive or negative, would sell the book.[19]

Naiad encountered another obstacle in *Sapphistry*'s production when Barbara sent it to Harriet Desmoines and Catherine Nicholson for estimates on typesetting and paste-up charges. "After many hours of soul-searching and discussion with each other," the *Sinister Wisdom* co-founders replied, "we have decided that we cannot in good conscience typeset and paste-up Pat Califia's *Sapphistry*." They found the book "well written, highly readable, and thorough" but objected to the "Variations" chapter and could not produce a book advocating what they considered to be a "patriarchally inspired and encouraged," emotionally and physically dangerous practice. Standing on different sides of the feminist sex wars, Barbara pragmatically took the Califia project elsewhere but continued sending other Naiad typesetting jobs to the women of *Sinister Wisdom*.[20]

Since 1977, the Iowa City Women's Press (ICWP) had filled most of Naiad Press's printing needs. Initially, the ICWP contracted out for binding because the collective did not possess binding equipment. Barbara knew from experience that male printers and bookbinders sometimes refused to work on sexually explicit material, so the printing of *Sapphistry* and such books as *Labiaflowers* (a new edition of Corinne's *Cunt Coloring Book* issued by Naiad in 1981) heightened her conviction that the ICWP needed to expand its operation to include binding "so that no part of OUR operation is jobbed out to anyone except women...this means that no stupid fundamentalist asshole can decide on the whim of the moment to sabotage our books...which would, could, kill us."[21]

Naiad's relationship with the ICWP was complicated by the fact that both operations lacked sufficient capital. Cash poor, Naiad paid printing bills in installments, and on occasion the owners covered printing and typesetting costs with personal loans to the company until bookstore payments arrived. With Barbara and Donna's move to Florida, the ultimate sale of their Missouri home at a loss, and the purchase of a new residence, they had no disposable income to pour into Naiad. Marchant and Crawford lived a comfortable life in retirement, yet had limitations on the amount of money they could pour into the press. Meanwhile, the women of ICWP needed timely payments. "It is not politics or giving of support," a member of the ICWP collective explained. "[I]t comes down to month to month survival economics." Instead of the small sums Barbara sent them, they requested larger amounts so they could cover payroll and large printing bills.[22]

Determined to see *Sapphistry* succeed, Barbara marshaled her network of volunteers. Mailing them advance copies of the book, she explained: "[W]e need reviews of this in as many styles and lengths as can be managed in every possible periodical known to the feminist world." While it was impossible to control lesbian-feminist responses to the book, Barbara cloaked it in respectability by planning a book release party at Old Wives Tales Bookstore. She also included an introduction by Phyllis Lyon and blurbs for the back cover written by Jane Rule and Joan Nestle, co-founder of the Lesbian Herstory Archives. As Barbara told Carol Anne Douglas of *off our backs*, "I am prouder of publishing this book than anything we have done" because of "how desperately good sexual information is needed."[23]

As anticipated, Califia's book prompted controversy and debate among lesbian-feminists. The Woman to Woman Feminist Book Center in Denver removed *Sapphistry* from its shelves, and a store in Madison, Wisconsin, chose to keep the book behind the counter, but the majority of Naiad's bookstore customers had no reservations about stocking it. Letters from readers like Ann Arbor resident Christine Jenkins further reinforced Barbara's conviction that Naiad served a silent majority. "I know you've gotten flack for publishing it," she wrote, "but there are *many* women who feel affirmed, excited, and included by *Sapphistry*." Jenkins and her friends in Ann Arbor were appreciative of Naiad's work "even though you don't read our letters in *off our backs* & *Big Mama Rag*, or at least not very often."[24]

Barbara did not realize it at the time, but discussions surrounding the publication of *Sapphistry* foreshadowed broader conversations about sexuality that would become known as the "feminist sex wars." In the early 1980s, anti-pornography rhetoric simmered within the lesbian-feminist community even as pro-sex lesbians gained increased visibility. Following *Sapphistry*'s publication, for instance, Califia and members of Samois published *Coming to Power* (1981), a book arguing for "recognition of the pleasures of S/M against a lesbian-feminist stance that saw S/M as oppressive to women." *On Our Backs*, the first all-female produced erotica magazine, debuted in 1984, and the erotic art of photographers like Tee Corinne and Honey Lee Cottrell also gained heightened visibility in the 1980s.[25] Naiad Press's willingness to publish *Sapphistry* underscored its commitment to the first amendment, if not the pro-sex camp.

Flourishing as a Business

It was not long before Donna decided that she had erred in taking the Leon County Public Library position. Her co-workers' personal dramas left her feeling as though she had "stepped into a Southern gothic novel," while encounters with racism left her cold. Steeped in Midwestern culture and values, she had difficulty adjusting to the seemingly slower pace of life. After discussing their options, Donna and Barbara decided the best one was to make Naiad Press successful enough to support them both financially. They were encouraged by the fact that *Sapphistry* and Ann Allen Shockley's *The Black and White of It* had exhausted their initial print runs. In the quest to build an economically viable press, Donna and Barbara pushed to expand the number of books published each year. "Anyda's romantic books go on selling and selling and selling," Barbara explained. "The bookstores blast us every time we let one of them go out of stock briefly." The same was true for Valerie Taylor's *Love Image*, even though Barbara considered it not "a good book, but it is entertaining and it is important to entertain." Readers have "the right to read," she asserted, "an old library axiom and I believe it very strongly."[26]

In addition to Sarah Aldridge romances, Barbara envisioned Naiad growing large enough to publish an occasional volume of biography, contemporary poetry, or literary work even though such books were not profitable. Donna's insight, business acumen, instinct, work ethic and can-do attitude made it possible to realize this dream. When she was not at work in the library, Donna provided input on book manuscripts, packed books for shipment, built bookshelves for their extensive personal library, and even did much of the assembly of a large storage unit for unsold book stock.[27]

Barbara and Donna recognized one way to make the press more cost-efficient was by reducing production costs. In late 1980 when the ICWP sent Naiad an estimate for printing and binding two novels, Barbara replied that she could no longer afford to do business with them because of their lack of competitive pricing. A commercial printer, she informed Jane Rule, could save Naiad as much as forty-five percent per book. Stunned when Barbara wrote to notify them of the decision to take business elsewhere, the ICWP women replied: "Though we understand the reasons, we feel it extremely unethical and a breach of faith for you to abruptly break such a long-standing verbal commitment with us." They had good reason for concern because Naiad was a major customer. By 1981, after producing three reprints and four new Naiad titles in less than four months, the ICWP women had begun referring to themselves as "the Naiad Press factory."[28] Losing Naiad would not bankrupt the press, but it would make survival much more tenuous. Succumbing to their argument, Barbara reversed the decision for the time being, but remained on alert for other reasons to break the agreement.

Propelled by her determination to transform Naiad into a company that could support at least two paid employees, Barbara believed in projecting a larger-than-life image. When Naiad made its first appearance in *Literary Market Place* in 1981, she crafted the entry to suggest a much larger company than the two-person operation it actually was. In addition to listing herself and Donna as employees, she used multiple pseudonyms to suggest there were other officers and employees in the company. Together, Barbara and Donna forged an ambitious agenda calculated to put Naiad on the map: the release of eight titles in 1981 and ten more the following year. Providing something for everyone, they published

Jane Rule's *Outlander* for literary readers and Victoria Ramstetter's *The Marquise and the Novice* for lovers of the gothic novel. In addition to pulp novelist Valerie Taylor's *Prism* and Tee Corinne's sexually explicit *Labiaflowers*, Naiad customers could order reference works, including J. R. Roberts's *Black Lesbians: An Annotated Bibliography* and a new edition of *The Lesbian in Literature*. The latter contained a stunning sixteen-page inset of grouped photos of such classic and current writers as Mary Wolstonecraft, Virginia Woolf, Natalie Barney, Hilda Doolittle, May Sarton, Elsa Gidlow, Audre Lorde, Mary Oliver, Chocolate Waters and many others. Naiad's future looked even brighter for the upcoming year.

Barbara dreamed of publishing an original novel by Rule, her Canadian mentor and friend. For years she nurtured their pen friendship, and she felt rewarded when Naiad became the exclusive publisher of Rule's reprints in the United States. Nonetheless, Barbara yearned for more: "I want to get NAIAD large enough to do one of your [original] novels, and to do it justice. All we have to do is make the time move to our seasons." She had every reason to believe *Outlander*, which came off the press in time for Rule's fiftieth birthday celebration on March 28, 1981, would sell well for Naiad because Rule's name had become "a household word" as a result of her writing for the Canadian publication, *The Body Politic*. "[T]here is a special market for your work above and beyond the ordinary reading public," Barbara explained, "those hundreds of women who read you for your content rather than your talent."[29]

Barbara dedicated herself to promoting *Outlander*. In addition to sending out seventy review copies and persuading pen friends to write reviews for more than a dozen periodicals, she mailed flyers designed by Tee Corinne "all over the U.S., Canada, England and Europe." As Barbara and Donna had hoped, *Outlander* was an overwhelming success and only two hundred copies of the original print run of four thousand remained by mid-June, when they approved a second printing of five thousand copies. Barbara was delighted when "bookstores from all over Canada" bought the book. After hearing such good news, Rule was surprised to learn *Outlander* had not yet reached the break-even point in terms of cost recovery, in part due to the high cost of printing with the ICWP. Barbara optimistically thought Robin Morgan's "kiss on the brow" review in the July 1981 issue of *Ms. Magazine*, plus the dozens of other reviews in publications ranging from *Village Voice* to *Sinister Wisdom*, would console the author, but this was not the case. Eager for Naiad to release more of Rule's work, Barbara commenced negotiations with Harcourt Brace Jovanovich, Canada, for the right to reprint a second work, *Contract with the World*. "They don't know it yet," Barbara confided to Rule in September 1981, "but the book is coming out in August 1982."[30]

Persephone Press

Barbara envisioned herself at the hub of the lesbian-feminist publishing network, and made it her goal to serve as a clearinghouse for publishing-related news. The information she gained in the process provided her with currency she used when negotiating for power. When Barbara learned through the grapevine that authors Sally Gearhart, Julia Penelope Stanley and Susan Wolfe had not received royalties on books they had published with Persephone Press, she felt it was her duty to relay the news to others who might choose to publish with them. Founded in 1976 by the lesbian-feminist collective Pomegranate Productions, Persephone had published four books by 1980, beginning with a new edition of Gearhart's self-published *The Feminist Tarot*. Located in Watertown, Massachusetts, Persephone bore some resemblance to Naiad's early years because its co-founders, Gloria Z. Greenfield, Pat McGloin and Marianne Rubenstein, subsidized publication of early books with personal loans and donations. In contrast with Naiad, they repaid the loans to themselves and in 1979 chose to have a paid staff, which made it impossible for them to plow income from the sales of books back into the press.

Initially, Barbara envisioned herself in the superior position of an experienced publisher willing to share useful information with neophytes; however, her relationship with Persephone co-founder Greenfield stalled after the 1980 NWSA meeting in Bloomington, Indiana. During the conference, Barbara had offered her help and support, but sources subsequently informed her that Greenfield "had wondered why we felt we might help you and that you (meaning Persephone) intended to 'put them out of business in two or three years.'"[31] The following year Barbara's hackles rose when Greenfield accused her of "disseminating false information" about Persephone. "We were also told that you have said that we have no right to try to make a living on lesbian publishing," the younger woman admonished. "Come on, Barbara. Did you really say something so absurd?" Accusing Grier of jealousy, Greenfield sent copies of the letter to her attorney as well as to current and future Persephone Press authors.[32]

Rallying to defend Naiad and their reputation as publishers, Barbara and Donna responded immediately with a letter establishing their personal and professional credentials. Reminding Greenfield that she was not the only one who had grown up without privilege, they suggested that "there are those who would pit us against one another...There must be people jealous of both of us, and therefore would choose to see us fight." They acknowledged being upset to hear several Persephone authors had not received their royalties, especially since one of the books in question, *The*

Coming Out Stories, edited by Susan J. Wolfe and Julia Penelope Stanley, had been "an enormous best-seller." It was hard for them to believe it had not made back its costs. In response to Greenfield's accusation that they objected to Persephone having a paid staff, Barbara and Donna clarified they were not opposed to a press supporting its workers and in fact had plans for Barbara to become Naiad's first full-time paid employee, effective January 1982. "Since we have long been providing at least partial income to many other women's businesses, it will be a pleasure to provide a part of our own." The letter concluded by informing Greenfield that Barbara and Donna were only mailing copies of their reply to the women she had initially copied.[33]

From a distance, Barbara watched as Persephone developed its reputation as the publisher of books that would play an important role in feminist identity formation during the early 1980s. The women associated with both presses wanted to foster lesbian sensibility by publishing lesbian writing, but while Naiad focused on storytelling, Persephone set out to "build a women's revolution."[34] Titles such as *This Bridge Called My Back: Writings by Radical Women of Color* (1981) and *Nice Jewish Girls* (1982) prompted new conversations as contributors to these volumes challenged established constructs. Despite its success in publishing innovative and provocative writings, Persephone Press closed its doors in 1983. According to feminist scholar Julie Enszer, its failure "was due to being overleveraged with debt and making common small business mistakes—including not paying the IRS for payroll taxes." Additionally, the Persephone collective's efforts "to respond to many ideological viewpoints, which at times conflicted with one another and with the business of publishing," made survival virtually impossible.[35] Barbara, speculating that Persephone's end left Audre Lorde's *Zami: A New Spelling of My Name* in limbo, called the author immediately to see if Naiad could publish the book, but Lorde had already signed with Crossing Press.

Women in Print, 1981

The second WIP Conference convened at the National 4-H Center in Washington, D.C., on October 1, 1981. A magnificent gathering, it was attended by more than two hundred and fifty women, including such lesbian luminaries as Michelle Cliff, Barbara Smith, Audre Lorde and Adrienne Rich. In response to a pre-conference planning survey, Barbara stressed that she hoped the outcome would include "HARMONY, COMMUNICATION, MAKING SURE WE SEE TO IT THAT WE ALL SURVIVE...IT IS A CATASTROPHE WHEN A SINGLE

STORE CLOSES." As much as she loved to work, Barbara also urged the organizers to "HAVE AT LEAST ONE RAISE HELL AND LAUGH TIME...DRINK BEER AND WINE, SING SONGS, SPREAD TALL TALES...ETC. REMEMBER WE LOVE EACH OTHER AND THAT WORLD CHANGING CAN AND SHOULD BE FUN." Many other respondents agreed survival was a key theme, but they stressed the necessity of deepening the political and ethical dimensions of their work.[36]

In her eagerness for Naiad's silent partners to meet other members of the Women in Print community, Barbara arranged for Marchant and Crawford to attend a conference party. "At Barbara's behest," Marchant noted in her diary, "I was introduced as one of the Naiad Press women and also as Sarah Aldridge [her Naiad pseudonym]. That is as far out as I want to go now." Upon reflection, Marchant found herself "perched on a divide, always just outside a culture, an ethos, a belief, a community." At seventy, she found most of the conference attendees "quite young, wearing jeans and long hair." She and Crawford left the party early, but were pleased with the number of women who had complimented her books. "I don't say this to anyone but M[uriel]," she wrote, "but Sarah Aldridge's novels will one day be seen as classics, true classics."[37]

Much more structured than the Omaha conference five years earlier, the 1981 WIP meeting featured nearly sixty workshops on technical and business aspects of publishing, politics and ethics, and according to Spinsters Ink publisher Sherry Thomas, "political fights out the wazoo." At the same time, in an overview of the meeting for *off our backs*, reporter Fran Moira recalled detecting "an atmosphere of decency, caring, and hard work—that was far from devoid of humor." Class and race both emerged as pressing issues, with six Jewish women questioning why they had not met as a caucus as the third-world women had, and with white women attempting to take responsibility for their own racism. When attendees sat in a basement conference room listening to Pat Parker, Barbara Smith and other women of color reading new work, poet and feminist Adrienne Rich stood up and said, "Lock the door." Acknowledging women in the movement had limited disposable income, she nonetheless raised ten thousand dollars for Kitchen Table: Women of Color Press by instructing everyone to take out their checkbooks and write a check, declaring that collectively "[w]e have the means to make our movement stronger." As the donated amount confirmed, Rich's message resonated with many of her listeners.[38]

Barbara had left the first WIP Conference convinced that she must use women printers and women bookbinders to produce Naiad Press books. By the end of the second conference, she and Donna concluded they had been "demented for having done so." Some of the smaller women's stores still regarded Naiad's simple matte-finish covers as politically correct, but the majority of bookstore women they spoke with argued more professionally produced books would sell better. Barbara and Donna already were aware of the problem with Naiad bindings. According to Donna, the binding on *Sapphistry* had been so poor that she had to spend hours regluing many of the books before shipping them. When they received hundreds of improperly bound copies of Valerie Taylor's *Prism* in February 1982, Barbara demanded an explanation from the ICWP. She knew the poor quality was not intentional, but she also understood it could not continue if Naiad were to flourish. Quickly evaluating the situation, Barbara concluded that "quite clearly women not only will not pay more, they will not tolerate bad quality." Tired of apologizing for books that fell apart before readers finished them, she cut ties with the ICWP and moved Naiad's business back to Rose Printing Company in Tallahassee. "Naiad and its potential is my life and blood," she explained to those who questioned her commitment to lesbian feminism. "Any threat to it makes the years I've spent in this movement...wasted."[39]

Naiad's First Paid Employees

"Four weeks from yesterday," Barbara wrote to Rule in November 1981, "I become a full-time NAIAD PRESS employee, small wages, but what a joy...what a joy. We are also trying to plan for Donna's freedom." As planned, Donna quit her library position at the end of May 1982, in time for the NWSA meeting in Arcata, California. "[I]t is only right after this many years and this much work," Barbara reasoned, but nonetheless it was scary to know their livelihood would depend on the press. As they forged ahead, Barbara felt a sentence from Sheila Ortiz Taylor's *Faultline*, one of Naiad's best-selling books that year, accurately described their life: it was a time "when the process started to bubble back toward chaos."[40]

Barbara and Donna learned about Sheila Ortiz Taylor from people who had heard her read from a novel-in-progress at local Tallahassee bars. Taylor, who taught English at Florida State University, had not yet found a publisher for the book. By this point in Naiad's history, Barbara had wearied of receiving unpublishable manuscripts in the mail, so she had low expectations. Finally, because so many people told her she must take a look at it, Barbara phoned Taylor very early one morning in 1981 and said, "Oh hell, send me the damn thing." She had never read anything quite like this comedic novel about the adventures of Arden Benbow, a "Chicana, Indian, white mother of six children and 300 rabbits," a six-foot-tall black drag queen and an aging ex-hooker running a trailer park for tourists in Mexico. Uncertain if it would appeal to Naiad readers, Barbara sent the manuscript to Marchant, who loved the book and immediately issued Taylor a contract.[41]

After seeing Marchant's reaction to the book, Barbara's confidence soared. She had dreamed of publishing a book as popular as Rita Mae Brown's *Rubyfruit Jungle*, and thought *Faultline* possessed that potential. "It's so far beyond any novel we have seen that I cannot contain my excitement," she explained to Rule. "FAULTLINE will make us rich," she further boasted to Marion Zimmer Bradley. Never one to wait for success, Barbara persuaded noted authors Doris Grumbach, Bertha Harris and Rita Mae Brown to write blurbs for the back cover, and she marshaled her army of trusted friends and volunteers to review it for a host of publications. Rule, whose review appeared in *The Body Politic*, hoped Barbara's ambitions for *Faultline* would come true because it would put Naiad "in a much better position to negotiate with other writers for good books."[42]

Barbara and Donna had great fun planning a book tour that took Taylor from Tallahassee to Humboldt, California. With Donna behind the wheel of a Suburban jam-packed with books, the threesome traveled across the country so Taylor could do readings and sign books, sometimes for only two or three people. While Naiad never invested huge sums in this or subsequent author tours, they knew everyone—author, publisher and bookstore—benefitted from these appearances. The California trip also included exhibits and readings at the NWSA conference in Arcata and the American Booksellers Association (ABA) meeting in Anaheim. It was an exhilarating time now that Naiad had grown large enough to be a presence at these and other conferences. Still, Barbara and Donna were stunned when Naiad took in orders worth $14,000. "I couldn't write them fast enough," Barbara recalled.[43] In addition to the direct sales, Naiad gained visibility and made invaluable contacts.

Barbara also utilized her international connections to market Naiad books overseas. Determined to get Taylor's *Faultline* "into the hands of every woman in America (and all over the world too)," Barbara capitalized on her contacts with European publishers, and through skill and persistence, she negotiated the book's publication in England, Germany, Spain and France. The International Feminist Bookfair, which Barbara and Donna attended regularly, offered an excellent opportunity to finalize "sales of various books around the world" and to initiate the sale of others. As a result of these proactive efforts, readers in Canada, Europe, Australia, New Zealand, Mexico, South America and Japan had access to Naiad Press books. Barbara also worked hard to sell the mass-market paperback rights for some of Naiad's more popular works. She asked Rita Mae Brown to persuade someone at Bantam to take a look at *Faultline*, and she tapped contacts at Avon Books and other mass-market publishing companies with similar requests. She even sent a copy to Lily Tomlin, perhaps hoping for a movie tie-in. While the latter dreams never materialized, it was not for lack of effort.[44]

Naiad briefly ventured into the mass paperback market when it introduced its less expensive, smaller-format Volute Books, named for a type of shell Barbara liked to collect. For years, Barbara had yearned to return popular pulp-fiction writers to print, so in 1982 Naiad issued Valerie Taylor's *Return to Lesbos, Journey to Fulfillment* and *A World Without Men* as Volute titles.[45] In her quest to get Rule's books into the hands of readers, Barbara also reprinted Rule's *Desert of the Heart* in the Volute format. In the process, she tested the patience of Rule's agent, Anne Borchardt, but seemed to know just how far she could go without invoking legal penalties. Upon learning Naiad had used the Talon Books edition to produce its offset reprint of Rule's book, Borchardt tactfully informed Barbara that she "forgot to pay them an offset fee. I am sure this was an oversight on your part." When Naiad still had not paid the invoice more than a year later, David Robinson of Talon Books vented his anger: "Well, you do owe us for the type, lady, and if you do not pay, we will send a collection agency after you, and report you to every other publisher whose work you have used." Undaunted by his hostile tone, Barbara informed Robinson that she had made her living in the credit and collection field, and that "Simply declaring that you are owed money does not make it so," and she considered the case closed.[46]

After deciding Naiad also should reissue the very popular Beebo Brinker novels in the Volute format, Barbara used the skills she had refined as a collections agent to track down their elusive author, Ann Bannon. One day in 1981, Bannon, whose real name is Ann Weldy, answered the phone at six a.m. and heard a commanding voice on the other end say: "This is Barbara Grier, G-R-I-E-R, of Naiad Press, N-A-I-A-D." After telling Bannon a bit about her company, she announced her intention of publishing the novels as Volute reprints for a new generation of readers. Lest her effusive praise go to the author's head, Barbara paused to explain: "Now, I'm not trying to tell you you're Marcel Proust. I know better than that. These books are not great literature, but they are emotionally, socially, and historically a part of Lesbian development in this country and in this century."[47] Thunderstruck and pleased at the interest in her work, Bannon succumbed to Barbara's optimism and powers of persuasion.

At Barbara's request, Bannon drove to San Francisco later that year and sat in the back of a crowd assembled to hear Taylor read from *Faultline*. Dressed as a college professor, Bannon assumed no one would recognize her. After the reading Barbara spoke a few words about the Volute reprint series and then asked who else members of the audience would like to see in print again. When the crowd called out Ann Bannon's name, Barbara asked if they would like to meet her, and the novelist found herself speaking to a friendly and curious audience. Afterward, she realized Barbara had wanted to "out" her, but she had no hard feelings because she understood that "one of Barbara's missions in life was to out everyone who could possibly be LGBT." Later, Bannon joined Barbara, Donna, writer Lee Lynch and a few others for coffee. As they walked toward the restaurant, Barbara said, "I can't believe I'm walking down a street in San Francisco with Ann Bannon!" to which Bannon replied, "I can't believe I'm walking down a street in San Francisco with Barbara Grier!"[48]

In July 1983 Bannon embarked on her first author tour. With Donna as the patient and supportive chauffeur, and Barbara as "an indefatigable spark plug of energy," they traveled 3,600 miles in thirteen days, visiting seven bookstores, giving radio and print media interviews, and attending a three-day lesbian and gay conference. "Ann Bannon is a real trooper," Barbara boasted, aware her author had recently gone through a divorce. "[S]he has as much energy and stamina I think as I do...and that is remarkable. I thought I had the corner on the market." Throughout the tour, Barbara urged Bannon to exchange her professorial attire for more butch clothing. "I think she may have expected me to be a more 'Beebo Brinker' type of person," Bannon reflected years later.[49]

Curious Wine

Another fortuitous event occurred during the *Faultline* book tour when Barbara, Donna and Ortiz Taylor visited Sisterhood Bookstore in the Westwood area of Los Angeles. During the reading, Barbara noticed a woman with a blond Afro watching and listening intently. After the author's reading, Barbara spoke for a few minutes about Naiad Press. Impressed by what she heard, Katherine V. Forrest approached her and said: "I have this book." By this point in the tour, Barbara was tired. "God help anyone who gets me when I'm really tired," she explained years afterward. As Forrest recalls, her "steely blue stare cut me off at the knees, a stare that sneered, 'I've heard this a thousand times.'" "Tell me," Barbara said, enunciating each syllable, "does anything HAPPEN in this book?" After hearing a bit more about the life-affirming love story between two women, Barbara instructed Forrest to send the manuscript to her, and upon reading it, she and Donna discovered quite a few things happened in *Curious Wine*, which Naiad published in April 1983.[50]

By mid-May 1983, Donna realized *Curious Wine*'s first printing of eight thousand copies would be exhausted by the time she and Barbara returned from the ABA convention at the end of the month. Surprised by the book's success, they ordered a second printing of another eight thousand copies, and it continued to sell well for years. When pondering why the book sold so well, Barbara speculated it was "safe sexuality."[51] *Curious Wine* resonated with young lesbians in the early 1980s, especially those in rural and small-town America, because of its eroticism and its portrayal of two women who recognized what they wanted and had the strength to reach for it. In addition to finding validation of their feelings in print, women used the book as a way to find out if someone were gay. "Have you read *Curious Wine*?" they asked prospective dates. Or, if they saw someone sitting on a bench reading it during lunch hour, they exchanged meaningful glances before striking up a conversation.

As Forrest soon discovered, Barbara loved to arrange book tours. In 1987, her "Dreams and Swords" express visited nine stores in ten days. While Forrest signed books, Barbara and Donna circulated the store, selling Forrest's book along with other Naiad books. On one occasion Barbara got bored, so she helped the store's owner by selling "a cat book just for exercise." On another occasion, Donna, Barbara and Forrest were on their way to an appearance in Baltimore. As the rain pelted down in torrents, they had a flat tire. Jumping from the car, Barbara ran into traffic, frantically waving her arms until a Volkswagen Beetle skidded to a stop. "This is an EMERGENCY! We have a flat tire!" Pointing to Forrest, watching in amazement from the car, Barbara continued: "I have an AUTHOR in that car! We have to be at a bookstore in FIFTEEN MINUTES! You WILL take us, WON'T YOU!" Mutely agreeing, the driver carried them to the Twenty-Third Street Bookstore, where Forrest found nearly two dozen women assembled to hear her read from *Daughters of a Coral Dawn*. Donna appeared about an hour later after fixing the tire and checking them into the hotel. Calm, cool and collected, she showed no sign of the crisis other than the damp bills extracted from her billfold for a purchase.[52]

Soon after Forrest became a Naiad author, she found herself assuming the unexpected yet critically important role of the press's supervising editor. During the first decade of Naiad's existence, Barbara and Marchant had edited the books they published. As neophytes in publishing, they had much to learn. In part because of Jane Rule's urging, Barbara decided the time had come to hire a professional editor. As Barbara soon realized, Forrest was not only a wonderful novelist, but also a fine editor. "I do not know why," Barbara told Rule, "she does not know why, but the results are obvious and wonderful." As someone who understood the importance of the independent press in publishing minority voices, Forrest accepted the role of supervising editor because she regarded Barbara as a fearless pioneer in lesbian publishing, someone committed to publishing worthwhile books even if they had no promise of commercial success.[53]

Highsmith and Wilhelm

As Naiad continued to grow, Barbara dreamed of restoring to print some of her favorite novels from the 1930s and 1950s. She especially loved Patricia Highsmith's *The Price of Salt* (1952), written under the pseudonym Claire Morgan. In an era when lesbian pulps portrayed their protagonists suffering a painful death or committing suicide, she offered a well-written and realistic lesbian love story about a young woman questioning her identity. At the time, many acknowledged it as "the first gay book with a happy ending," and Highsmith was inundated with letters from "girls and boys too, the young and the middle-aged, but mostly the young and painfully shy" writing "from somewhere in Canada, from towns I never heard of in North Dakota, from New York, even Australia" to thank her for giving them a book about same-sex lovers who not only survived but also had the promise of a happy future together.[54]

When Barbara became convinced that Highsmith's agent had allowed the book's copyright to lapse, she launched into action. Tapping into her vast network of correspondents, she contacted Jacqueline Lapidus, who worked in the French office of *Reader's Digest*. Eager to assist, Lapidus replied: "Yes, you were right to ask me to help you find Highsmith—I am always willing to do whatever I can to help you out, it's the least I can do for a great lesbian bibliograph[er] front-line fighter and publisher of *Yantras*, no?" From Lapidus, Barbara learned that Highsmith was "alcoholic, difficult, and supercloseted to the point of paranoia." With that in mind, Barbara mailed a carefully crafted letter to the author, then living in France: "You will not remember, but I wrote to you in 1965…[and] today I run a publishing company, THE NAIAD PRESS." Employing a combination of flattery and persuasion, Barbara praised *The Price of Salt* and argued the time had come to reprint it, along with any other novels Highsmith might have written as Claire Morgan.[55]

In a cautious reply, Highsmith indicated that "*Salt* was written when homosexuality was a secret thing, liable to prosecution, and the picture is different now," and that she did not like "to associate myself with protest movements...I believe in equal rights and pay, abortion, and that's about it." Undeterred, Barbara explained Naiad Press was noted for keeping books in print and for getting them reviewed. She urged Highsmith to remember the women "who deserve to have the right to find that book I first read so many years ago." Name dropping, she noted with pride that Naiad was reissuing Jane Rule's books to "much more extensive notice than they did originally."[56] Barbara's powers of persuasion prevailed, and by June 1983 she felt like turning cartwheels in the street after securing the reprint rights for *The Price of Salt*, which Naiad released as a trade paperback in early 1984. Highsmith, who insisted on publishing under her original pseudonym, Claire Morgan, wrote a short afterword for the book, which enabled Barbara to copyright it as a revised edition in case any questions arose about the book's original copyright.

"Bulldog Grier," as she referred to herself, also was on a quest to discover what had happened to another of her favorite authors, Gale Wilhelm, whose books *Torchlight to Valhalla* and *We Too Are Drifting* had been published by Random House in the 1930s. In fact, her longstanding admiration of Wilhelm had led her to write a poem titled "Iniquity" and to dedicate it to Wilhelm for *The Ladder* in 1960. As she informed Eric Garber, one of her loyal bibliographic friends and confidantes, "I am simply nuts about her." After publishing six novels in the 1930s and 1940s, Wilhelm moved with her companion, Kathleen Huebner, to a home in the Berkeley Hills. In the pre-Internet age, Barbara was unable to locate Wilhelm and asked friends near and far to assist her. Acting on tips provided by bibliographers Lyndall Cowan and Garber, she contacted people who had known Wilhelm, ranging from her dancing teacher to novelist Helga Sandburg.[57]

Forging ahead, Barbara made plans to return Wilhelm's work to print. Since the author's copyright had lapsed, there were no legal prohibitions in 1984 against publishing *We Too Are Drifting* without the author's consent. Finally, in April 1985, Barbara received a letter from "A Friend" giving her Gale Wilhelm's address in Berkeley, "if you're still looking for her." Wilhelm was a gracious host when Barbara and Donna visited her the following month while in California to attend the ABA and Women in Print meetings, but Barbara must have sensed some anger generated by Naiad's publication of the book without first consulting the author. In the ensuing weeks, she worked hard to soothe Wilhelm's anger over having her work reprinted without her permission, sending roses and first editions of Wilhelm's two novels, along with Forrest's loving review of the *Torchlight to Valhalla* reprint. From Huebner's perspective, Barbara and Donna had "done Gale very proud." The reprint, she believed, had "furnished this year with joy and pleasure and light. I thank you personally for this accomplishment." Barbara's critics, on the other hand, raised questions about Naiad's right to reprint the work, and suggested Wilhelm would not receive satisfactory royalties because of Naiad's cost-recovery contract.[58]

Mentoring Others

As a veteran publisher, Barbara considered herself well positioned to mentor, coax and advise other women who wished to succeed in the business. In reality, her success stemmed from a combination of native intelligence and the mentoring she received from women like Jeannette Howard Foster and Jane Rule. As a publisher who had learned by experience, Barbara attempted to mentor other women in the movement, but their relationships often were complicated by her infallible conviction that success depended on doing things her way.

Nancy Bereano worked for Crossing Press when she met Barbara in 1981 at the second Women in Print conference. Several years later, after she had been fired from Crossing Press due to creative differences, Bereano phoned Barbara to let her know she planned to start her own press. Based on their brief acquaintance, Barbara correctly sensed Bereano was a force to be reckoned with, and she wanted her to succeed. "Congratulations," Barbara perfunctorily replied before launching into advice mode: "You still have time to put down money for a booth at ABA." Bereano had limited resources, yet she realized Barbara was right. Registering for a booth gave her a deadline and goals, and by the following spring Firebrand Books announced the release of three books. Bereano based Firebrand's contract on the one Crossing Press had used, but Barbara was the first person she contacted when it came to percentages, foreign rights and other technical aspects related to publishing. "Barbara Grier was as supportive of me as she was of many other lesbian presses," Bereano recalled. "She genuinely believed that the more lesbian publishers there were, all would be good as long as she was kingpin." While the two never became close personal friends, Barbara had an affinity for Bereano, who was just nine years younger, and they spoke often by phone. "I was closer to her than [to] women in their forties," Bereano noted, since "people look at the world based on the age they were when passing through a certain time." Even when they disagreed, the Firebrand publisher found it difficult to remain angry with Barbara, whom she viewed as "very dear, perceptive, astute, combined with a set of blinders that only her reality existed."[59]

As a publisher, Bereano emphasized quality over quantity, building Firebrand's reputation with such titles as Alison Bechdel's *Dykes to Watch Out For*, Dorothy Allison's *Skin: Talking about Sex, Class and Literature*, Audre Lorde's *A Burst of Light*, Leslie Feinberg's *Stone Butch Blues*, and Joan Nestle's *A Restricted Country*. Barbara praised her achievements, but informed Bereano she could make more money if she stopped publishing the literary books. She also took the younger publisher's public comments about Naiad's quality in stride. When appearing on a panel sponsored by Charis Books in Atlanta, Bereano criticized Naiad Press for scaling down "the reach" of lesbian publishing and determining "what the public thought of as lesbian literature" because it "had gotten there first and had gotten big." While the public nature of the comments angered Donna, Barbara unapologetically replied, "Yes, I publish for the sixteen-year-old reader."[60]

After Sherry Thomas purchased Spinsters Ink in 1982, she traveled to upstate New York to finalize the transaction. While there, she stopped in Ithaca to visit Bereano, who told her: "You've got to be friends with Barbara because she will give you the shirt off her back if you're part of what she wants to do." One call to Barbara launched a series of regular phone calls in which Barbara told the novice publisher where printers were, who would work with Spinsters Ink and who would not. Recognizing that Barbara considered her way as "the only way," Thomas also understood that the older woman shared information with many people because "she really wanted a movement as big as it could possibly be."[61]

Barbara and Donna also encouraged women to open new businesses. In 1982, they met used-bookstore owner Joan Denman when they traveled to Huntsville, Alabama, to promote *Faultline*. Using her powers of persuasion, Barbara encouraged Denman to consider opening a feminist bookstore in Tallahassee. When Denman's personal relationship ended before the store could open, Barbara appeared unfeeling when she informed mutual friends that no matter what had happened, they had to help Denman "get it together" because Rubyfruit Books must open, and it did in 1983. Barbara invited Denman to accompany her and Donna to an ABA meeting, where she introduced Denman to *Feminist Bookstore News* editor Carol Seajay and other key players in the feminist publishing world. Denman quickly realized Naiad was a major force in bringing lesbians into her bookstore. For example, a carload of lesbians each month made the ninety-minute drive from Fort Rucker, Alabama, to Rubyfruit Books in Tallahassee to acquire Naiad's latest releases along with new lesbian books from other publishers. "We could have sold more," Denman reflected, because "there was a real hunger for lesbian writing at the time."[62]

Through monthly contact by phone and regular visits each year, Barbara and Donna grew close to the owners of independent bookstores selling Naiad books. They especially enjoyed visiting Harriet Clare's Dreams and Swords in Indianapolis, a store that filled a significant void in central Indiana. Prior to opening her own bookstore in 1982, Clare had managed a B. Dalton bookstore and sold feminist books from her car and at a local women's bar. It took two years before the store's income was sufficient for the single mother of two to pay herself a salary of two hundred dollars a month. Customers remember Dreams and Swords as "the place to go"—not just for books but also for information and conversation. If you were new in town, wanted concert tickets, or needed to know where the next lesbian pitch-in was going to be held, you checked the store's bulletin board. Poet and novelist May Sarton, who gave a reading there in mid-October 1986, declared it heavenly, "such an open-armed, welcoming place, with a tiny room at the back where one can read or talk."[63]

Barbara's idea of mentoring businesswomen involved a combination of positioning people to do what she considered best for the movement and Naiad Press, and reaching out to women who felt ostracized or marginalized because of their minority viewpoints. After bookstore employee Dawn Oftedahl was ousted from Amazon Books, the Minneapolis-based women's bookstore, during a restructuring in 1990, she was touched by Barbara's "supportive and so genuinely caring" response and her offer to help find another position. Carol Seajay had a similar experience when she announced her departure from Old Wives Tales. Barbara phoned her at home and wanted to know what she planned to do next. "You know too much," Barbara insisted. "We can't afford to lose you." Upon reflection, Seajay realized the movement had lacked mentors. Without older generations to provide guidance, there was a void, "and Barbara stepped in and filled this role," imperfectly, but with zealous intent.[64]

* * *

By 1984, Barbara and Donna had built Naiad Press into a major force in women's publishing. Having survived its first decade, the press had matured to the point of having two full-time paid employees to oversee the production of ten or more titles per year. Yet growth had come with hard feelings within the lesbian-feminist community as Naiad severed its ties with the ICWP and shifted to commercial printer Rose Printing Company. Additionally, authors like Jane Rule, who had experience with other publishers, questioned Barbara's approach to business. "I know you thrive on crisis," she counseled her friend, but "[y]ou need to be quieter, slower, in the important decision-making processes. You need time for more feedback or the very greatest virtue of what you're doing, which includes everyone involved, will be sacrificed."[65]

In contrast, Barbara felt like pinching herself when she surveyed Naiad's progress. The Volute reprints had not proved profitable, but they had ensured a new generation of readers could know and love Beebo Brinker. The popularity of *Outlander, Faultline* and *Curious Wine*, combined with affordable reprints of Rule's stories, essays and novels, brought increased visibility in the early 1980s. While bookstores had dozens of presses to choose from, Naiad cultivated a reputation for being steady and reliable when it came to delivering new books on a regular basis, and bookstores rewarded them with business. In late 1981, Naiad's core list of bookstores had numbered two hundred but, by the end of 1984, had more than doubled. Many of the bookstores serving the feminist, gay, and lesbian communities in the 1980s enjoyed a mutually beneficial relationship with Naiad Press. Barbara's proactive advocacy of lesbian books through review outlets and her "Dear Friends" letters brought customers into stores. Acknowledging Barbara and Donna as good businesswomen, Richard Labonté, co-founder of A Different Light Bookstore in San Francisco, praised their ability to set a publishing schedule and stick to it, as well as their nurturing of a wide range of writers.[66] When Barbara put out feelers for possible author appearances, she received so many requests it was impossible to fill all of them.

The women who loved Naiad Press books were an eclectic group, one that defies labels. Some had come of age at a time when gays and lesbians lived in social isolation, inundated with negative messages about homosexuality. Naiad books served as a lifeline for them and others who sought positive validation of their existence and who hungered to know who they were. No matter what their background, they read books like *Curious Wine* because the stories captured how they had felt the first time they fell in love.

In the 1980s, Naiad enabled new authors like Sarah Schulman and Lee Lynch to launch their writing careers, and brought renewed exposure to novelists from the 1930s and 1950s, whether they welcomed it or not. Barbara spread the work of Naiad Press authors around the globe by cultivating her talent for selling world rights. She also worked hard to discover a book for which she could sell the mass paperback rights to a larger publisher after the Naiad edition appeared. She thought she had found it in *Faultline*, but Warner Books declined to purchase the rights for a mass paperback edition. Acquisitions editor Mario Sartori encouraged Barbara to try again if she found a book with wider appeal. Soon after, she approached him with a new possibility, an anthology about lesbian nuns Naiad had scheduled for release in 1985. It would, she predicted, bring Naiad "the kind of instant notice that will put us in bookstores all over the country."[67]

CHAPTER TWELVE

৵৩

Lesbian Nuns: Breaking Silence

"I have a way of refusing to see difficulty, on the grounds that if you ride right over the top of it, it'll disappear."
—*Barbara Grier, 2006[1]*

While attending the 1981 National Women's Studies Association meeting in Storrs, Connecticut, Margaret Cruikshank introduced Rosemary Curb and Nancy Manahan to each other and urged them to compile an anthology of lesbian convent stories. Former nuns, they each had contributed an essay to Cruikshank's anthology, *The Lesbian Path* (1980). Pointing to *This Bridge Called My Back: Writings by Radical Women of Color* (1981) and *Nice Jewish Girls: A Lesbian Anthology* (1982), she argued the time had come for lesbian nuns to add to the evidence that lesbians were everywhere. Curb, a high-energy professor of English and women's studies, responded cordially but noncommittally while privately dismissing the suggestion as "way off the charts for me."[2] Manahan, on the other hand, thought such a project might aid in her quest for closure. In letters exchanged after the conference, a warm friendship emerged as the two women discussed the emotional roller coaster they had experienced since leaving the convent.

The exchanging of coming out stories has a long history among lesbians and gays, yet for much of the twentieth century the naming of oneself as a lesbian was a radical and dangerous act in a society that privileged heterosexuality. In the 1970s, however, stories rose to the surface as lesbians recognized the urgency of breaking the silence that obscured their existence. It was a time of energy and vitality, recalls Ruth

Baetz, author of *Lesbian Crossroads* (1980), and "it seemed like everything we did was important...every person we came out to, every time we marched in a gay pride march, everything we wrote."[3] Momentum grew, and by 1983 seven book-length anthologies of coming out narratives had appeared in print.

In keeping with their goal of increased visibility for lesbian books and Naiad Press, Barbara Grier and Donna McBride were on the alert for a prospective cross-over title. Upon learning about Cruikshank's idea for an anthology of lesbian convent stories, Barbara instinctively knew it had potential to be Naiad's breakthrough book. As she told *Feminist Bookstore News*, "It had Catholics, nuns, sex, it would be banned in Boston, it was [going to be] brilliant and wonderful." Barbara knew that Americans were fascinated with nuns and their sexuality. It was, after all, an era in which collectors of nun memorabilia purchased nun wind-up toys, cookie jars and even salt and pepper shakers, and nuns figured prominently in cartoons, calendars and greeting cards. Moviegoers formed impressions of nuns based on such films as *The Nun's Story* with Audrey Hepburn (1959), the iconic *The Sound of Music* (1965) and the bizarre *The Blues Brothers* (1980). *The Singing Nun* starring Debbie Reynolds (1966) and *The Flying Nun* television show of the 1960s also had fueled interest in and curiosity about the lives of nuns.[4]

Late in the summer of 1981, Barbara phoned Rosemary Curb to let her know Naiad would be interested in publishing a book about lesbian nuns. The two women were not strangers. Curb, who was interested in feminist theater, had corresponded with Barbara about Lorraine Hansberry's letters to *The Ladder* because Barbara was searching for evidence to prove the playwright was a lesbian. Curb had also enjoyed Barbara and Donna's hospitality, visiting their home while traveling from Rollins College in Winter Park, Florida, to Atlanta for a conference, and by the end of the visit had agreed to write a blurb for one of the forthcoming Naiad Press books. Rosemary considered Barbara to be "one of the most energetic leaders of the lesbian movement," and she was flattered by the "incredible show of faith" in a book yet to be written.[5] Her reserve soon melted and she and Nancy Manahan set to work.

The Making of Lesbian Nuns

Once Curb and Manahan committed to the project, their first challenge was to locate lesbian nuns and former nuns who were willing to reveal their thoughts and experiences in print. At a time when many lesbians still lived in closeted isolation, lesbian ex-nuns felt doubly closeted because they thought second-wave feminists would criticize them for having been in the service of a patriarchal church. Admitting one had been a nun, Curb explained, was "sort of like admitting that you had recently been released from prison." Thinking strategically, Curb and Manahan solicited essays from such nationally known lesbian ex-nuns as activists Jeanne Córdova (editor of *The Lesbian Tide*, 1971-80), Jean O'Leary (founder of Lesbian Feminist Liberation, and later co-founder of National Coming Out Day), and Virginia Apuzzo (executive director, National Gay and Lesbian Task Force), names they knew would lend credibility to their endeavor. They placed announcements about the project in such publications as *The Lesbian Connection* and Seattle's *Out and About*, and reached out to others through sessions held at women's music festivals, bookstore gatherings and academic conferences.[6]

When Manahan had sat under an oak canopy with nineteen former nuns at the 1981 Michigan Womyn's Music Festival, they experienced "a taste of that community feeling again" as they discussed "the pain of denying, betraying, or being separated from the sisters we loved." When Curb and Manahan held additional gatherings in women's bookstores and people's homes, participants often looked at one another and said, "Oh, it was like that for you too." During these meetings, Manahan focused on the healing power of the women's conversations, but the more political Curb found herself wanting "to move the consciousness raising" to "Let's storm the barricades."[7]

In 1983 Naiad Press sent Curb and Manahan a contract for the book, and Barbara assured them she would "throw an inordinate amount of weight behind it." She also vowed to "promote it intently" and anticipated that "it will sell incredibly well." Since neither woman had published a book before, Manahan asked her brother, an attorney, to review the contract. Seeing nothing out of the ordinary, he advised them to trust each other because they were "all in this movement together." With that, they signed the contract, which, among other things, gave Naiad "full, exclusive and sole right" to make arrangements for serial publication, translations, abridgements, public readings, radio and television interviews and motion picture rights. A notation in the contract stipulated that Naiad would inform Curb and Manahan "whenever a proposal for such an arrangement is offered and to consult with the Editors in regard to the terms of such proposal."[8]

As feminists and educators, Curb and Manahan compiled their book collaboratively, spending many hours on the phone and in correspondence with one another and their contributors. As academics who previously had published essays in an anthologies, both knew they needed to provide contributors with release forms. Since Naiad had not previously published an anthology, Barbara sent them one Diana Press had used when it serialized essays from *The Ladder*. "I really do not care what kind of form you use," she explained, "as long as it covers you and covers us." The permission slip each woman signed granted Curb and Manahan the "rights to the autobiographical essay and any photographs, drawings, statements, or other materials" for "exclusive use in the anthology."[9] At the time, the form seemed routine, and none of the signatories realized Curb and Manahan's contract with Naiad Press had precedence over their individual permissions.

Few contributors to the book anticipated the media firestorm *Lesbian Nuns: Breaking Silence* would generate. Some viewed the collection of stories as a print-based sisterhood written for themselves and a small audience of lesbians, feminists and Catholics, while others expected it to "gather dust in a corner of some feminist bookstore and soon be forgotten." A few correctly assumed the subject of lesbians and sex would attract significant media attention. "My expectations," recalled Sister Eileen Brady, "were that the book was going to be huge, so I wrote an article that I could show to my family and one that I expected many people I knew to see." With the media's fascination with nuns riding bicycles and going to baseball games, she reasoned, "then this surely would [attract attention], especially combined with a sex theme."[10]

While Curb and Manahan focused on collecting stories from potential contributors, Barbara remained focused on her campaign to get more mainstream recognition for lesbian books. She fervently believed that "if women do not take the initiative[,] the day is coming when the trade press will catch on and once again take an opportunity away from our community for economic and political independence. It is NOT a joke to recognize that you really DO control the world when you control what gets into print."[11]

Curb and Manahan structured the manuscript they submitted to Barbara in May 1984 to resemble the coming out process, moving from the personal (individual stories of religious life, desires and fears) to the political. Many of the forty-nine essays included then-and-now photographs. After the book's publication, the image of a bare-chested ex-nun, Joanne Morrow, later became a source of controversy, as did Tee Corinne's book cover, though Barbara had conferred with the co-editors before using it. "If you and Tee want to use that magnificent photo of Betsy Snider leaning against the fence post, looking so jaunty with her habit tucked up and tennis shoes on," Manahan replied to Barbara's query, "Betsy says she would be honored." Katherine V. Forrest's jacket blurb also prompted some accusations that she had sensationalized the book's content by portraying nuns as "alien in their dramatic garb" and by referring to the anthology as "myth-shattering," "explosive" and "among the most controversial books of this or any other year."[12]

Once Barbara received the completed manuscript, she made its publication and promotion a priority; therefore, she was perturbed when several contributors expressed second thoughts about their stories appearing in print. Acknowledging it was natural to have second thoughts, Barbara informed them that it was too late to make any changes because the manuscript had already gone to the typesetter. Shocked by Barbara's treatment of the women, Curb complained that "it sounds as if we are sort of 'steamrolling' over the wishes and feelings of our contributors. That is something Nancy and I have never done."[13]

The Promotion of Lesbian Nuns

More pragmatic than political, Barbara was so intent on Naiad's survival and success that risk-taking had become a way of life. In the movement, but not of it, she had little patience with lesbian-feminist politics of the 1980s because they clashed with her management style and decision-making process. While she straddled some generational differences, she lacked a nuanced understanding of feminist priorities and communication style. According to Margaret Cruikshank, "feminism & sisterhood & consensus were not a part of her method of operation."[14] Unable to anticipate, let alone comprehend, the backlash that some of her pragmatic business decisions engendered, Barbara found herself caught in the crosshairs of the 1980s sex wars and lesbian-feminist politics because of her promotion of *Lesbian Nuns: Breaking Silence*.

From the beginning, Barbara knew the book would sell well, but as an experienced publicist and businesswoman, she left nothing to chance. Unlike the trade press, which could afford to pour money into a prospective best-seller, Naiad budgeted virtually nothing for marketing and instead depended on Barbara's ability to get books noticed. Recognizing that women's studies professors and students represented a primary audience for the book, she urged Curb and Manahan to create interest in the forthcoming book by offering a session titled "Lesbian Nuns: Breaking the Silence," at the 1984 NWSA meeting. It would, she predicted, sell hundreds of books and lead instructors to adopt it as a text for their courses. As she anticipated, many women attended the session, eager to hear nuns and ex-nuns speaking out on sexuality, spirituality and politics.[15] At the meeting, Barbara "bragged about what a success *LN* would be" and asked Curb and Manahan if they would like to appear on *Donahue*, a popular television talk show hosted by Phil Donahue, a proposition Curb considered "in the same category as 'How would you like to fly to the moon?'"[16]

Barbara knew getting a book discussed on a popular daytime television show was a boon to sales. As a former bill collector, she knew the key to opening doors was to speak with authority and confidence. In 1983 she picked up the phone and called Phil Donahue's office in Chicago about *Lesbian Nuns: Breaking Silence*. An employee named Jose informed her it was too soon to get the anthology into the show's pipeline, but promised to assist her if she called back closer to the book's release. Nearly two years later, when the book neared publication, Barbara phoned again, this time learning that *Donahue* had moved to New York City and that José was no longer with the company. Fortunately, another employee provided the information she needed, and in late January 1985, a producer for *Donahue* phoned to schedule an hour-long interview. Upon learning Naiad was a small press with no tour budget, the show offered to pay all costs associated with the joint appearance of Curb and Manahan.[17]

During the summer and fall of 1984, Barbara took steps to guarantee media saturation because she knew from experience that advance hype guaranteed sales. Determined as she was to change "the face and reputation of Lesbian-feminist publishing," her expectations for the book escalated daily as she worked to make it the "most successful book to come out of the movement."[18] Expanding beyond the gay and lesbian communities, Barbara sent pre-publication copies of the manuscript to key periodicals whose early reviews would attract notice, and to the hosts of several television and radio shows. Unabashedly proud of the book, she offered it to Quality Paperback Book Club, Book-of-the-Month Club, the Literary Guild and the LGBT-focused Century Book Club, but only the latter made it a selection. As she had done with previous books, she embarked upon the sale of world, serial and mass paperback rights. In her typical hyperbolic style, Barbara further piqued interest in the title by mailing provocatively worded flyers to approximately thirteen thousand individuals on the Naiad Press mailing list.[19]

Barbara's persistence and powers of persuasion yielded results. By the end of January 1985, she had arranged for the sale of serial rights to several publications, including *Christopher Street*, *Forum*, *Ms. Magazine*, and the *Philadelphia Gay News*. On one day alone, she took great pleasure in selling twelve thousand copies of the book to Waldenbooks and B. Dalton bookstores, neither of which typically featured gay and lesbian titles. They must have *Lesbian Nuns: Breaking Silence* on their shelves, she insisted, because after Curb and Manahan appeared on *Donahue*, everyone would be asking for it. Later that spring, Mario Sartori offered $65,000 to obtain the rights for a mass paperback edition to be issued by Warner Books. When some news releases inflated the amount to six figures, Barbara saw no reason to issue a correction. As a result of her efforts, Barbara sold world rights to publishers in Australia, Brazil, England, France, Germany, the Netherlands, Ireland, Italy and Spain. She also sold movie rights to ABC-TV for a film that never materialized, and granted Walt Disney Productions permission to use the book as a prop in the film *Down and Out in Beverly Hills*. At the height of the book's promotion, which far surpassed any of Naiad's previous efforts, Barbara acted first and informed the co-editors afterward. "I had to make a lot of nutty decisions while you were away, Rosemary," Barbara wrote in late January 1985, "but it has been fairly clear that this is, in the words of Sheila Ortiz Taylor, 'the main chance' the book [has] to change the world."[20]

Returning home to Tallahassee after a visit to New York City to see an adaptation of Lee Lynch's "Swashbuckler" performed at The Wild Café, Barbara heard her name being paged in the Jacksonville airport. Upon checking with the Naiad office, she learned that a woman from St. Louis kept calling and saying she "would give anything to talk with Barbara Grier." When Barbara returned the call, the voice at the other end said: "I want the nuns." "Do you?" Barbara intoned. "And who are you?" The woman, who turned out to be the assistant producer for *Sally Jessy Raphael*, had learned about the nuns from her senior producer, José, formerly associated with *Donahue*. "I want them first," she declared. With that, Barbara realized she and Donna had a "hot property" on their hands.[21]

Both *Sally Jessy Raphael* and Gary Collins's *Hour Magazine* talk shows taped interviews with Curb and Manahan in March, and from the first question, it was clear people were curious about lesbian nuns. The experience reinforced the necessity for Curb and Manahan to develop strategies for coping with all kinds of questions, ranging from the salacious ("Where do nuns go to make love?") to the curious ("How many lesbians are there in convents?") to the intrusive ("What was your lover's name?"). They had not anticipated the hostile callers to radio talk shows and the hate mail sent to them in care of Naiad Press.[22]

Shortly before their appearance on *Donahue*, the co-editors learned the live studio audience consisted of residents from a conservative Catholic neighborhood in Queens who had been given tickets but not told of the day's topic. At the top of the hour, Phil Donahue, in his characteristic showmanship style, held up the book and declared, "Lesbian nuns! This shouldn't be on television, should it?" The crowd went wild. Curb and

Manahan, accompanied by contributor Sister Esperanza Fuerte, who remained behind a screen, faced audience members who called the book an insult to the Catholic Church and pointed to biblical injunctions against homosexuality. In response, the calm and composed co-editors emphasized three main points: the book's scholarly merit, the need to alleviate isolation for lesbian nuns and the ending of women's oppression. Late in the show, Donahue paused to introduce Curb's daughter, Lisa. Upon learning that the lesbian "monster" was mother to a child who looked like Alice of *Alice's Adventures in Wonderland*, the audience softened.[23]

Contributor reactions to the *Donahue* interview ranged from exhilaration to anxiety. A closeted sister expressed gratitude to Curb and Manahan for being "in the public speaking for us," and another, who initially had some misgivings about the publicity, described *Donahue* as a "triumph." "We were everywhere," she recalled, "on morning news, talk shows, Phil Donahue. It was time. We were like pioneers." When contributor Mary Mendola gave workshops at Dignity National, an organization for gay Catholics, she ended each talk by asking how many in the audience were familiar with *Lesbian Nuns: Breaking Silence*. "It was like every hand went up," she noted, and there were approximately three hundred people attending her sessions.[24]

In contrast, those who had envisioned the book as a minor publication were appalled and frightened to see their lives paraded so publicly. "I've lived in alternate states of anxiety and fear," confided one contributor. A few worried that straight colleagues or family members might discover the book and recognize their stories, and one told of receiving pornographic phone calls in the middle of the night. Some, like Wendy Sequoia, had written their essays several years earlier and had given no thought to the book's potential impact on their careers. It was difficult enough trying to establish oneself as a respectable massage therapist, she explained, "let alone being known as a lezzie ex-nun!"[25]

Requests for newspaper and magazine interviews with the book's co-editors came fast and furious. Kay Longcope, of *The Boston Globe*, flew to Florida for an in-depth feature interview with Curb. Longcope, who in 1987 would be chosen as the journalist to whom Congressman Barney Frank "came out," had been covering civil rights issues since the 1970s. "Kay says I'm going to be FAMOUS," Curb reported in her diary.[26] The prediction proved true, as journalists called from the *Chicago Sun-Times*, *The Detroit News*, *Newsweek*, *People* magazine and *The Washington Post* as well as from such gay publications as *The Advocate*, *Washington Blade* and *Gay Community News*. Within the first six months of the book's release, Barbara's promotional efforts had netted more than eighty television appearances and radio interviews and over two hundred book reviews and articles, an amazing number for any book, and before the end of the first year, the latter figure had soared to four hundred fifty. *Gay Community News* writer Patricia Gozemba believed no other group's coming out had had "the same kind of revolutionary impact. This was a real gate crasher."[27]

Catholic leaders initially tried to ignore the book so it would get less attention, but they faced a formidable foe in Barbara Grier. In addition to television, radio and print media coverage, the book was being featured on tabletop and window displays at B. Dalton and Waldenbooks, as well as in airport kiosks and local drugstore book racks. After Longcope's story appeared in the *Boston Sunday Globe* on Saint Patrick's Day, Catholic leaders took action to suppress interest in the new release.[28] Speaking for the Archdiocese of Boston, Rev. Peter V. Conley, without having read the book, denounced it as "sensational," "bizarre," and "prurient." Pressure from the Archdiocese led Group W, the nation's fifth largest consortium of television stations, to rescind an invitation for the co-editors to appear on *People Are Talking* in Baltimore and Boston, and to cancel *Hour Magazine* segments in five major urban outlets. Twenty out of forty-five television affiliates refused to air Curb and Manahan's appearance on *Sally Jessy Raphael* during Holy Week. Meanwhile, the Detroit Heart Association chose not to use thirty free tickets to the *Sonja Show* when the topic of the day's program was announced, leaving the television audience sparsely populated.[29] Oprah Winfrey also cancelled Curb and Manahan's appearance on *The Oprah Winfrey Show*, not because of content, but because her rival, Phil Donahue, had edged her out of the first live interview with the ex-nuns.

Testing the Limits of Community

In late April, several of the book's contributors learned Naiad Press had sold four excerpts from *Lesbian Nuns: Breaking Silence* to *Forum* magazine, a soft-core pornographic magazine published by Bob Guccione's Penthouse, Ltd. News of the sale, breaking as it did in the midst of the feminist sex wars, sparked immediate controversy. At the time, Catharine MacKinnon and Andrea Dworkin, among the most prominent voices in the feminist anti-pornography movement, were leading a campaign for citywide anti-pornography ordinances on the basis that pornography fostered violence against women. On the other end of the spectrum, pro-sex feminists countered that protection historically had been used as a ploy to control women, especially lesbians, who refused to comply with patriarchal demands. As the historian Carolyn Bronstein explained in *Battling Pornography*, pro-sex feminists "worried that an attack on pornography at a time when politically powerful religious conservatives had declared their intent to restore morality to the nation…was likely to result in counter-feminist ends," especially censorship and an erosion of women's freedom to express themselves sexually. These viewpoints framed and informed the months of debate that followed as some lesbian-feminists excoriated Naiad's decision while others suggested that "the rhetoric about 'good taste' and 'right to privacy' and 'offensive material'" sounded remarkably like the phrases "being used by the Catholic Church in its attempt to ban or discredit it."[30]

With the rise of politically powerful religious conservatives after the 1980 election of Ronald Reagan as president, sex-positive feminists became concerned that Women Against Pornography legislative campaigns would yield counter-feminist results. At a Barnard College conference in 1982, Barbara's friend, scholar Gayle Rubin, had criticized the anti-porn movement for demonizing sexual expression while claiming it spoke on behalf of all feminism.[31] Although they had not taken a strong vocal stand against censorship, Barbara and Donna believed that if conservative groups co-opted feminist anti-pornography rhetoric for their own ends, lesbian erotic magazines such as Susie Bright's *On Our Backs*, a magazine of lesbian erotica premiering in 1984, and erotic photographs by such photographers as Tee Corinne and Honey Lee Cottrell could become targets of prosecution.

Barbara was proud of the publicity and early sales garnered for *Lesbian Nuns: Breaking Silence*, and also of Naiad's sale of serial rights to *Forum* magazine. So when the February 15, 1985, issue of *Publishers Weekly* announced the sale, she mailed copies of the announcement to thousands of customers on Naiad's mailing list. At first glance, many who read the piece failed to recognize its significance. As lesbian-feminist activist Susanna J. Sturgis noted, she was "not the only one to gloss right over this bit of information because I had no idea what *Forum* magazine was." On the other hand, anti-pornography activist and anthology contributor Jan Raymond immediately recognized the magazine's name and phoned Barbara. Outraged, Raymond demanded to know what had led a leading lesbian publisher to do business with a pornographer.[32]

After news of the *Forum* sale broke on the front page of *Gay Community News* in late April, the furor over Naiad's actions escalated into accusations of exploitation and betrayal. Lesbian-feminists questioned Barbara's ethics, motives and politics and accused her of sensationalizing and objectifying women's stories for commercial gain. Cheryl Moch, a founding member of the Jewish Feminist Organization, reasoned Guccione "did not buy

portions of *Lesbian Nuns* because of his concern for women religious."
A lesbian nun writing from Jamaica argued that Naiad's handling of the
book was counter to her understanding of lesbian goals, which were "to
wake up every day feeling good about ourselves and to share our plight
with those who may gain a greater degree of understanding and empathy."
Instead, two others declared, Barbara had put "love of money ahead of
women." Calling for a boycott of Naiad unless it cancelled the *Forum* deal,
they declared that Naiad "can kiss our business goodbye forever!"[33]

Curb and Manahan's apparent reluctance to denounce Naiad Press
led some critics to accuse them of complicity. In reality, they were
distressed by their publisher's decision, but attributed her lack of feminist
sensibility to the fact that she had come "out of the gay movement—not
the feminist movement." Manahan believed Barbara had committed a
"terrible mistake," but wanted to put her anger aside because she knew it
would destroy her (Manahan) as well as the book's potential for positive
impact. "Not everyone," Curb admitted, "has the privilege of feminist
consciousness-raising and women's studies." Indeed, Curb found herself
struggling with self-doubt about her "classist and elitist assumptions"
about readers after Barbara argued that if publishers "address only
the middle and upper middle class [readers], the waitresses that [poet]
Judy Grahn writes about won't see this." After much agonizing, the co-
editors concluded it would appear "unsisterly" to denounce their lesbian
publisher just prior to the book's publication, and they hoped its powerful
educational message would eclipse the controversy.[34]

Barbara's tendency to exaggerate, combined with her quick temper
and arrogance, exacerbated the *Forum* controversy. Even as critics
raised their voices to complain about Naiad's promotional efforts, she
continued flooding media outlets with news of the book's unprecedented
sales. After reporting to *Publishers Weekly* that the first printing would
be ninety thousand paperback and ten thousand hardback, she informed
Curb and Manahan that "The real press run today is 37,500...I WILL
PERSONALLY KILL YOU BOTH if you tell anyone that figure."
According to Carol Seajay, of *Feminist Bookstore News*, it was not an
uncommon practice for publishers to inflate reports of their press runs
because the higher numbers created an impression of success and fueled
sales.[35] Unfortunately, those unfamiliar with the publishing process
envisioned money flowing into Naiad's coffers when, in reality, the press
desperately needed revenue from the advance sales of serial, world and
mass paperback rights to cover the cost of the book's first printing. Even
advance sales to bookstores could not guarantee solvency, because a
publisher's relationship with them resembled a consignment system in

which the store had ninety days to pay for books, some of which might be returned unsold. Publishers, however, had only thirty days to pay printers, typesetters, designers and shipping costs.

Feminist Backlash

With her anger fueled by painful encounters with women who questioned her commitment to feminism, an incensed Curb contemplated suing Naiad for damaging her reputation and credibility as a feminist academic. Upon learning Barbara had made a verbal agreement with ABC-TV for a movie, Curb took action. In a meeting in late May, attorney Barbara Price mediated as Barbara, Donna, Curb and Manahan hammered out an agreement giving the co-editors veto power over future serializations and allowing contributors to withdraw their essays and pictures, or to change their names in the forthcoming mass market paperback.[36]

When the June 1985 issue of *Forum* appeared on the newsstands in late May, it kindled even more anger about Naiad's sale of the excerpts. The magazine's cover, which featured a scantily clad man and woman clasped in a passionate embrace, announced the stories contained inside. "Sex Lives of Lesbian Nuns" was prominently featured at the top of a list that included "Standing Intercourse" and "Are You Kinky Enough?" Inside, excerpts from three women's essays appeared next to advertisements for X-rated videos and dildos. As contributor Helga Dietzel explained, contributors objected to the publication because they had "a different respect and honoring of ourselves," not because they were prudish. Magazines like *Forum*, she elaborated, "have a different form of energy, one that is not compatible with feminist goals."[37]

Emotionally charged debates about publishing ethics dominated the third Women in Print conference when it convened at the University of California, Berkeley on May 29, 1985. Unsigned leaflets bearing the words "NAIAD EXPLOITS" greeted conference attendees when they arrived the first morning. In a "hastily arranged and heavily attended morning session on the ethical and legal issues" of publishing contracts, more than two hundred women listened as Barbara defended her actions to an overwhelmingly hostile crowd. Tricia Lootens, writing in *off our backs*, regarded the session as "useful, if painful."[38]

After years of striving to get Naiad's authors reviewed in national forums, Barbara explained, she had sold serial rights for several pieces with the sole intent of reaching more women with lesbian stories. She believed this exposure had opened doors to other, more positive opportunities, among them the sale of mass paperback rights to Warner Books. Moreover, Barbara argued, the *Forum* sale extended access to lesbian literature to an underserved population. An estimated fifteen percent of *Forum*'s more than 600,000 readers consisted of women reading copies of the magazine acquired by their fathers, husbands and brothers, and some of them were closeted lesbians. Indeed, *Forum* did publish a regular sex advice column that occasionally published queries from lesbians, and as Barbara knew from the hundreds of letters she had received over the years, closeted wives, daughters and sisters could read a men's sex magazine without raising questions about their sexuality. Some lesbians in the military also informed Barbara that they could have male pornography in their barracks, but lesbian publications were regarded as contraband.

In response to Barbara's declaration that profit from the book's sale would fund the publication of additional Naiad titles, writer and activist Victoria Brownworth proclaimed that "taking money from the male pornography monolith—even to support feminist projects"—was never right because it connected "your politics with theirs." "What an actress!" recalled one contributor, convinced Barbara had sought out *Forum* magazine simply to make money. Even if one did not question Barbara's intentions in making the sale, *Lesbian Nuns* contributor Mab Maher argued, "the damage done to women contributors was cause for outrage."[39]

Barbara's lack of social skills, abrupt manner, and impatience with the feminist focus on consensus and collaboration compounded her difficulties. An admission that she had made a "dumb mistake" seemingly fell on deaf ears, as did her attempt to explain the releases contributors had signed, because she was talking about legalities when her critics were focusing on politics. "My whole life," Barbara declared before she left the room with Donna, "has been to get as much of the Lesbian-feminist message around the world as possible."[40]

The question of the contract became a pivot around which much of the discussion revolved. Lesbian-feminist publishers, lacking the capitalization of mainstream presses, assumed substantial risk in an environment where bookstores could not be relied upon to pay in a timely manner. As the session continued, it became evident Naiad was not the only press that had violated author assumptions about the rights to their words. Novelist Elana Dykewomon told of a similar experience when Daughters, Inc. had sold an excerpt from her book, *Riverfinger Women*, to Harper & Row for inclusion in an anthology titled *The Woman Who Lost Her Names—Selected Writings by American Jewish Women* (1980). "I didn't realize I had signed away my right to say no," she observed. Building on this comment, Firebrand Books publisher Nancy Bereano urged authors to take responsibility for obtaining consultation when signing contracts. She did elicit some applause when she attempted to put the issue in a larger context of lesbian-feminist publishing by citing Naiad's role in the movement's history and the challenges facing lesbian and feminist presses in a capitalistic world. "Naiad," she concluded, "made it possible for me to exist."[41]

After extended discussion, a subset of four conference attendees adjourned to draft two documents pointedly directed at Naiad Press. Written by Joan Pinkvoss (formerly of the Iowa City Women's Press and co-founder of Aunt Lute Book Company), Sherry Thomas (publisher of Spinsters Ink), and Marjory Larney and Paula Moseley (both of Acacia Books), the documents addressed the need for more detailed contracts and better communication between publishers, editors and writers. "We believe," the women stated, that "our responsibilities should be first dictated by our individual and collective political commitments and only secondarily by our business requirements." The "1985 Women in Print Publishers Accords" stressed that publishers "should assume a responsibility in relieving the inexperience of our writers" and needed to be "caretakers of the integrity of our authors' and contributors' works." The "Statement on Feminist Publishing Ethics" focused on the question of consent in the sale of stories to *Forum* and argued that in the case of a windfall, publishers had "a direct obligation to fairly share the proceeds with contributors, legal contracts notwithstanding."[42]

When Carol Seajay reprinted both documents in the *Feminist Bookstore News*, she urged readers to note that neither was an official WIP statement. Read during the closing session of the conference along with a number of other statements, the "1985 WIP Publishers Accords" was never moved, voted on, or passed by WIP attendees. Moreover, she observed, the document's title was misleading because twenty-one of thirty publishers attending the meeting had chosen not to sign. Nonetheless, the documents were widely circulated and discussed in the lesbian-feminist press.

As a war of words played out on the pages of gay and lesbian publications during the summer of 1985, Curb and Manahan saw their book become a pawn in an argument about lesbian publishing. While a number of publications covered the saga of *Lesbian Nuns*, *off our backs*, based in Washington, D.C., ran article after article hammering Naiad Press for its role in promoting the book. The months of painful testimony and mutual criticism appearing on its pages showed that Naiad's decision to sell serial rights to *Forum* had touched a raw nerve not only among the book's contributors but also among lesbian- feminists nationwide. A letter from "Mary Brady," whose story had been sold to *Forum*, charged that "the ethic of the bottom line has corrupted even the lesbian press." Another contributor, writing as "Margaret," described the "incomprehensible" sense of betrayal she felt because Barbara "had given me so much over the years with her publishing, had validated my lesbianism, had fed that hungry part of myself." Several contributors, especially those active in the anti-pornography movement, likened the serialization to rape. "We are all defamed," wrote Jan Raymond and Pat Hynes, "by even the most indirect association with this piece of trash called *Forum*."[43]

Barbara's critics, who included contributors to the anthology, lesbian separatists, and members of Women Against Pornography, dominated the discourse; however, Barbara was not without support. Following the conference, Arleen Olshan, co-owner of the bookstore Giovanni's Room, and psychologist Mary Cochran gave an interview in which they expressed "their pain on observing Barbara's public humiliation after all that she and Naiad have contributed to lesbian culture." Before the advent of *Lesbian Nuns*, Olshan noted, Naiad "was criticized by many for publishing 'soft' works, predominantly novels by such writers as Valerie Taylor, Jane Rule and Ann Bannon." According to Cochran, threats to censure Barbara's boldness would "discourage individuals in their innovative spirit." Calling the incident a learning experience, both expressed confidence in Naiad's ability to "handle this, because they're the strongest of the women's presses." In a similar refrain, Mary Gabriel, of the gay and lesbian Century Book Club, lamented the "unfortunate tendency of the lesbian/feminist community to view issues in terms of absolutes" and its quickness to dismiss Barbara's decades of supporting, nurturing and sustaining lesbian literature.[44]

The size of the backlash and the unwillingness of feminists to view Barbara's actions in the larger context of her decades of activism stunned feminist print activist Helaine Harris. "I truly believe from experience," she wrote, "that one of the most telling characteristics of an oppressed group is that members of that group spend a great deal of time oppressing each other." Feminists, she continued, had been discussing such issues as pornography and the ethics and business of publishing for at least fifteen years. "I'm not quite sure why Naiad Press is getting all the heat, but I suspect it has something to do with being the most successful sitting duck."[45] To some degree she was correct. Barbara's strategic positioning of the press and the books it published did result in longevity and success; however, it alienated her from some of the women she initially had intended to serve.

Barbara attempted to assuage angry contributors to *Lesbian Nuns* by issuing apologies, but trust had been breached and some questioned her sincerity. A serialized contributor who had tried unsuccessfully to withdraw her story from the book before it went to press settled for five hundred dollars, the amount *Forum* had paid Naiad for her story. Another woman sought redress by asking for a private meeting with Barbara in which she asked her to read a "Chapter of Faults" admitting guilt. Donna, concerned for Barbara's safety, stood warily by as she went to the meeting alone. At the request of this same contributor, Barbara also donated money to a battered women's shelter.[46]

Convinced Barbara had sold out for money, some of her peers in publishing felt there was no going back. "She not only crossed it, betrayed the writers involved…" noted Sherry Thomas of Spinsters Ink, "but she didn't apologize for it." Rumors spread that Naiad had earned half a million dollars or more from *Lesbian Nuns*, which made Barbara's treatment of the co-editors and contributors appear all the more egregious. Indeed, the book did well. Barbara's talent for marketing serial and subsidiary rights generated nearly $150,000, and the gross income from the first printing (before deducting printing, typesetting, and distribution costs as well as discounts to bookstores) was nearly $350,000. Yet many of Barbara's peers found fault with Naiad's path to success. Prior to the *Lesbian Nuns* controversy, Thomas explained, there was an unspoken agreement that publishers "didn't poach each other's authors…At that point we felt we could poach Naiad authors because she had crossed a line."[47]

Calls for a boycott of Naiad Press never resulted in a coordinated effort, yet sales slowed by late summer as a result of the controversy. Undaunted, Barbara and Donna focused on the future by bringing out books both old and new. Nonetheless, Barbara did begin to question whether the lesbian-feminists who had condemned her were, in fact, her people. As Barbara had anticipated, the debates over Naiad and the *Forum* sale gradually faded. In December a reader of *off our backs* asked the editors if it would be possible to "declare a moratorium" on comments, letters, editorials and essays about *Lesbian Nuns*. In her opinion, there had been "[e]nough already." With that, the controversy seemed to fade and readers turned their attention to such topics as the politics of lesbian motherhood and gay adoption.[48]

In keeping with her approach to life, Barbara refused to dwell on the controversy, and instead focused on the work of Naiad. In addition to reprinting Jeannette Howard Foster's *Sex Variant Women in Literature*, Barbara took great pleasure in reissuing Gale Wilhelm's long out-of-print *Torchlight to Valhalla*. Other releases in 1985 included Sheila Ortiz Taylor's second novel, *Spring Forward/Fall Back*, Elisabeth Nonas's *For Keeps* and a trade edition of Jane Rule's *Desert of the Heart*.[49]

The Legacy of Lesbian Nuns

Curiosly, while heated arguments dominated meetings and filled the pages of lesbian periodicals and newspapers, countless readers in middle America knew virtually nothing about the controversy and instead focused on the book's empowering content. Audiences across the country continued to be captivated, inspired and touched by Curb and Manahan's appearances. In September 1985, the co-editors traveled to Ireland, England and the Netherlands. Upon their arrival in Dublin, they found themselves on the front page of Dublin's daily newspapers when customs officers seized copies of their book and their hotel refused to lodge them because they were lesbians. Forging ahead with this and other overseas tours, taken together and individually, Curb and Manahan also had appeared in France, Italy, Norway and Australia by the end of 1986.

Oblivious to controversies, whether they originated within the Catholic Church or the lesbian-feminist movement, thousands of readers across the decades have benefitted from the book. Sixteen-year-old Julie Enszer read *Lesbian Nuns: Breaking Silence* in Detroit in the mid-1980s, standing in the aisles of her local Waldenbooks. After reflecting on what she had read, Enszer confided in her father that she had discovered her true identity—she was "a nun." Puzzled by his daughter's statement, he inquired, "What do you mean? We're not Catholic, we're not even religious."[50] Hearing that, it dawned on her—she was a lesbian.

As an activist and former nun, Jeanne Córdova reflected a quarter century after the publication of *Lesbian Nuns: Breaking Silence*: "Occasionally our books go mass market and reach people that the movement, or our bookstores, could never reach." When social worker Mary Gay Hutcherson came out in late 1993, the forty-something woman read everything she could find for insights into her sexual identity—Naiad novels, coming out stories, pamphlets and more. She learned about Curb and Manahan's book from members of her women's book co-op. It meant the world, she later recalled, to know that "even nuns were lesbians...[it] made me feel like we are everywhere." Comedian Kelli Dunham found a copy at her public library after she left the convent in 1995, the first explicitly gay book she had ever read. It was, she recalled, "One of the things that got me through those first months." Even today, Dunham gives copies to young queer-identified people so they can understand what earlier lesbians experienced. Removed from the emotion of the book's controversial launch, she can focus on its message: "I feel like storytelling is more important than arguing about politics."[51] More than a quarter century after the book was first published, it still appears on college reading lists and is referenced in periodical articles.

With her flair for promotion and her desire to get lesbian books into women's hands, Barbara brought unprecedented visibility to *Lesbian Nuns: Breaking Silence*. Yet success came with a substantial cost to all involved in the book's production and raised numerous ethical issues about the conduct of lesbian and feminist publishers. In response to friends who asked Jane Rule why she allowed Naiad to publish her work, Rule focused on Barbara's ability to manage "the business side of such a big sale without going under." Naiad was the only lesbian press, Rule argued, "handled by someone with some real business sense and real determination to be successful." Nevertheless, she acknowledged, *Lesbian Nuns: Breaking Silence* probably had been the wrong book for Naiad because of Barbara's inexperience and insensitivity to protecting the rights of people too inexperienced to know how to protect their own." Certain that her friend could learn an important lesson from this experience, Rule cautioned Barbara about misuse of power: "I have called you on it because I think it's a real blind spot for you which can make real trouble. Having absolute power does make things more efficient in the short run, but the room for error is too great to take the risk."[52]

Responding as she had to difficulties in the past, Barbara put the controversy behind her, focused on the future, and forged ahead.

CHAPTER THIRTEEN

๛

The Largest Lesbian Publishing Company in the World

"I am particularly enjoying not feeling bound by a set of conventions, more a publisher and less a movement."

–Barbara Grier, 1985[1]

Barbara Grier wanted recipients of her first "Dear Friends" letter in 1986 to know all was well with Naiad Press. Leading with an announcement about the Hollywood film adaptation of Jane Rule's *Desert of the Heart*, she boasted that *Desert Hearts* "will be shown all over the U.S. even in relatively small towns." Other good news included the acquisition of two properties. For years, Barbara and Donna McBride had operated Naiad Press from their home and garage, but Naiad's commercial success, combined with Donna's astute financial management, enabled them to move the business operation into the newly acquired house next door. Barbara attributed the purchase of a second property, a beach house at Alligator Point, to a generous supporter. Located south of Tallahassee on the Gulf of Mexico, the house became a retreat where artists, bookstore owners and others associated with Naiad could stay free of charge.[2]

Given the letter's optimistic tone, one would think Barbara and Donna had remained untouched by the months of controversy surrounding the publication and promotion of *Lesbian Nuns: Breaking Silence*. In reality, Naiad Press had suffered financial losses for several months in late summer and early fall, and Barbara received hate mail and experienced bruising confrontations in print and at conferences. When a writer in

Lesbian Contradiction called her "a pimp, a whore, and a rapist" because of the sale of excerpts to *Forum*, Barbara stoically remained focused on the business and continued sending the magazine review copies of new Naiad titles. The experience taught Katherine V. Forrest, who objected strenuously to having her book reviewed in *Lesbian Contradiction* because of what it had published about her employer, that no matter how ferocious the battle, Barbara would "get up, dust herself off and say, that's over. Let's go to our corners and do business again."[3]

In many ways a paradox, Barbara was idealistic yet pragmatic, tactless yet able to charm, someone whose goal was to nourish all lesbians with books even as she bullied and championed those who played a role in their creation and success: booksellers, authors and editors, and employees.

Ingredients of Success: Booksellers

Throughout the spring and continuing into the summer of 1986, Barbara and Donna made their annual circuit of visits to bookstores and appearances at conferences, including the American Booksellers Association (ABA), National Women's Studies Association (NWSA), and American Library Association (ALA). Barbara, who believed in countering homophobia with visibility, took great pleasure in reserving two and sometimes three full tables in the exhibit hall, usually in a strategic corner location.[4] Naiad also made a strong impression because of its author signings and receptions. The first time Forrest saw the entire aisle at ABA featuring gay pride flags flying from the booths for Alyson Books, Cleis Press, Firebrand Books, Naiad Press and Seal Press, she felt tears of joy. As laughter rang from the gay and lesbian aisle, a tired man staffing another booth suggested they seemed to be having all the fun. "Gay is not a misnomer," Donna informed him.[5]

Barbara felt in her element at ABA, "bounding up and down the aisle from booth to booth like an exuberant child."[6] She took great delight in introducing women to one another. Joining Naiad Press women for dinner in the evening, Forrest watched Barbara at the head of the table, "glorying in her little stable of Naiad writers," while savoring the sense of community, shared purpose and delight in being together with kindred spirits.[7]

Building on a network forged through Women in Print conferences, the ABA meetings, NWSA conferences, OutWrite and other meetings, Barbara and Donna built strong working relationships with dozens of bookstores from coast to coast. When Barbara became a full-time employee in 1981, Naiad Press interacted with 221 bookstores, but by the end of the decade that number had increased to more than 1,100 stores.[8] In the pre-Internet age, when everything was sold through catalogs that accumulated in huge piles around the book buyer's desk, Barbara kept the lines of communication open through regular mailings and phone calls. Indeed, she contacted all of the feminist and gay bookstores at least once, if not more frequently, to alert them to books of interest to their readers. She also remained alert for announcements of new stores joining the ABA, and wrote immediately to introduce them to her company.

Barbara gained international exposure for Naiad Press authors by cultivating relationships with booksellers in other parts of the world. In May 1984, Jane Cholmeley and Sue Butterworth opened Silver Moon Women's Bookshop on Charing Cross Road in London and grew the business into the largest women's bookshop in Europe. As owners of a feminist and lesbian bookshop, they knew more publishing of lesbian and gay titles occurred in the United States than in the United Kindom, so they relied on the services of the well-established Airlift Book Company to supply their needs, along with Giovanni's Room in Philadelphia, which served as a bookshop-to-bookshop supplier.[9]

From the store's opening, Silver Moon sold Naiad titles in great numbers. Cholmeley and Butterworth ordered "substantial quantities" of every title Naiad published, ranging from forty to one hundred copies for an initial order. In addition to selling to customers in their shop, Silver Moon featured Naiad titles prominently in its substantial mail order business serving the United Kingdom and the rest of Europe, along with other parts of the world, excluding the United States. As businesswomen, the owners appreciated Barbara's forthrightness and efficient capitalism. "She was extremely important to us," Chomeley recalled, "as we were to her, as the major UK outlet for lesbian books."[10]

Based on their bookselling experience, Chomeley and Butterworth became convinced sales of light lesbian reading could be significantly increased in the UK and throughout Europe if the books were published as British editions and at a cheaper price, one not subject to currency fluctuations. The two women approached Barbara with their proposal, and in 1989 licensed their first Naiad titles, Katherine V. Forrest's *An Emergence of Green* and Claire McNab's *Lessons in Murder.* Naiad Press could have made more money from direct export sales, but Silver Moon's customers and Naiad authors appreciated having affordable British editions of their books. Finding Barbara "very accessible and willing to help," Chomeley and Butterworth recognized that "as with any woman of a strong character, Barbara could be very demanding. But if you put your point of view to her with conviction, that was fine."[11]

Because Naiad was one of many publishers from whom the stores ordered, Barbara and Donna worked diligently to build their company's reputation for excellent customer service. They made it a priority to fill orders the same day received and no later than the next. "We are efficient," Barbara informed prospective book buyers, "and exist to serve your needs...You may, or may not know it, but a lot of your customers are waiting for these books. We can be your 'rent.'"[12]

While Barbara coordinated direct communication with the buyers, Donna ensured shipments of books were packed with care to arrive on time and in pristine condition. Unlike the majority of other presses, Naiad released books on a monthly schedule instead of having two or three book-release seasons a year. Richard Labonté, who co-founded A Different Light Bookstore in Los Angeles in 1979 and worked with a wide range of LGBT publishers between 1970 and 2000, praised Naiad Press for running "like clockwork." From his perspective, Barbara and Donna ran "the best business, followed closely by Alyson Books...and Cleis Press."[13]

Barbara "was a great phone caller," recalled Linda Bryant, of Charis Books. "[S]he would call you up and tell you about the books that you should order, and we would." Naiad made buying easy by offering stores a fifty percent discount and an easy return policy, a practice that led Labonté to acknowledge Naiad as a cornerstone of his business. Dawn Oftedahl had a similar experience in Minneapolis; the more books Naiad published, the more Amazon Bookstore sold. This was especially beneficial when the store began interacting with more established companies. Harper & Row, Random House and university presses were willing to extend Amazon Bookstore credit because of its volume of sales, much of it due to Naiad Press. In addition to selling books, Barbara also phoned to collect unpaid invoices. While she could be "hard-nosed about payments," Labonté noted, she understood when a store had financial problems, "was gracious about slow payments, and never failed to ship titles." Still, she never missed an opportunity to remind booksellers that "We cannot keep your shelves full unless you pay your bills promptly."[14]

All who interacted with Barbara recognized she was a force. Bryant was able to maintain a good working relationship with Barbara because she understood the publisher possessed a "single-mindedness of purpose that kept her from seeing that other people might have another purpose." It was, Bryant believed, "born of her life and her desire that other people didn't suffer...[and] came out of that deeply good place in her." Oftedahl concurred. "When you peel away the off-putting Barbara, there was a genuine woman there I knew I could count on," a woman who was dedicated to "making sure there were books for lesbians." Though

Barbara sometimes made Bryant "crazy" because she was "always right, always knew what was happening," both she and Oftedahl appreciated her commitment to getting the books out. Linda Bubon, co-founder of Women & Children First Bookstore in Chicago, enjoyed Barbara's sense of humor and the flirtatiousness that surfaced as she coaxed buyers to join her in the promotion of lesbian literature.[15]

At a time when some lesbians and feminists wanted nothing to do with the patriarchy, Barbara "had no qualms about dealing with a male-run bookstore." During her formative years she had devoured and collected gay as well as lesbian titles, and could speak with ease to male and female booksellers. According to Labonté, Barbara phoned regularly to check on stock levels and promote new releases and gossip, but made fast work of those topics so they could discuss the literature, "both then-current titles and books from the past—her knowledge of the field was both eclectic and encyclopedic."[16] On the phone with publishers and bookstores eight hours a day if not more, Barbara sat at the center of a lesbian book publishing network, and she loved sharing the news about the world of lesbian print culture.

Barbara thrived on direct sales to bookstores, but when she could no longer single-handedly manage sales, she trained Alex Jaeger to do the work. When Jaeger joined Naiad Press in 1992, Barbara correctly predicted her theater background would be an asset in sales work. Much to Jaeger's delight, she soon found herself selling books by the case. Preparing herself to pitch an author's latest work, Jaeger was surprised when she encountered buyers who automatically ordered the latest mysteries and romances by the case, or simply said "give me fifty of your new Naiads."[17] In the late 1980s, some stores found it more convenient to order their books through distributors rather than working with individual publishers. Accommodating this trend, Barbara and Donna worked with BookPeople, The Distributors, Ingram and the Inland Book Company, and with Airlift for foreign sales.

Through monthly mailings Barbara raised reader awareness of Naiad titles and urged readers to support their local businesses. Bookstore owners grew accustomed to seeing women enter their shops each month, flyers in hand. In addition to sending regular direct mailings to individual customers, Barbara worked diligently to ensure Naiad titles were reviewed in dozens of lesbian periodicals and newsletters. With a conviction deeply rooted in her early work for *The Ladder*, she flooded periodicals with review copies.

Lambda Rising Bookstore owner Deacon Maccubbin, who shared Barbara's belief in the power of reviews, set out to create the nation's most widely circulated book review publication by paying local gay papers an insert fee. The store's toll-free phone number appeared on every page of the *Lambda Rising Book Report*, which also included an order form and sold advertising to gay and lesbian publishers. Jane Troxell became the women's book buyer at Lambda Rising in 1987, and subsequently started working on the publication. At twenty-three, she was new to the business and considered Barbara Grier as more of a myth than an actual person, but that soon changed. When Barbara phoned and wrote periodically to alert her to new Naiad titles, Troxell enjoyed the publisher's passion for lesbian literature and "did not feel pressure from her to give more coverage to Naiad books." In return, Barbara enjoyed the opportunity to discuss books with someone who understood and appreciated the value of book reviewing. "I miss being Gene Damon," she wrote in 1989. "I miss doing the Lesbiana column."[18]

Ingredients of Success: Authors and Editors

As one of the most visible lesbian publishers, Naiad Press received several hundred manuscripts each year. Upon receipt, Barbara sent them to volunteer Darlene Vendenga and other readers, who reported their reactions and made recommendations concerning publication. Once she decided to publish a book, Barbara sometimes surprised its author with an early-morning phone call. Direct and focused on the business of publishing, she wasted little time exchanging pleasantries. One morning after Amanda Kyle Williams sent a manuscript to Naiad, she awakened to a phone call from Barbara demanding: "How in the hell are we supposed to sell a lesbian spy to an audience who doesn't even believe the government has a right to exist?" Continuing, she informed Williams there was no category for her novel. "Even if we publish," Barbara announced, "we can't win awards with it, nobody's publishing lesbian spy novels." Williams, whose book manuscript already had earned seven rejection letters, thought it unnecessary and highly unusual for a publisher to phone an author with the bad news. Much to her surprise, Barbara accepted *Club Twelve* (1990) and instructed her to send it to supervising editor Katherine V. Forrest for editing. During the next four years of her association with Naiad, Williams learned an important lesson: "When you talked with Barbara, you checked your ego or ended up wounded."[19]

Many Naiad Press authors regarded Barbara Grier as an intimidating force. After Marianne K. Martin submitted her first novel, *Legacy of Love*, to Naiad Press in 1991, she was told to expect a phone call from Barbara on a specific day and time. "I had been nervously pacing," Martin recalled, "but once I heard her voice, that serious 'in charge of your future' tone, my knees buckled and I dropped into a chair." Wasting no time, Barbara announced: "I know you can write. From your first two paragraphs, I know that." Then she launched into a list of stipulations that included cutting fifty pages ("I don't care where") and eliminating some references to spirituality. While the latter referred to the Native American spiritual heritage of Martin's main character, Barbara wanted no "fairy spirits floating through the air" in the book. Martin, who was aware of Barbara's ability to get books into independent and chain bookstores across the country, as well as widely distributed through mail order, did exactly as Barbara asked and went on to publish four books with Naiad.[20]

Barbara's drive and determination enabled aspiring authors to realize their dream of being published. Linda Hill, who had wanted to be an author since childhood, studied Naiad's guidelines before submitting a précis and cover letter. A few weeks later, Hill answered the phone at 7:00 a.m. and her heart practically stopped after she heard a low voice slowly and deliberately say, "Is this Linda Hill? This is Barbara Grier." As a result of the call, Hill realized her dream of becoming a published author when Naiad published *Never Say Never* (1996) and four subsequent titles. Because of her penchant for marketing, Barbara encouraged authors to look ahead to the next book. She knew that once readers found an author they liked, they would want to read her earlier publications. Australian-born novelist Claire McNab thought she had written a stand-alone novel when Naiad published *Lessons in Murder* (1988). Barbara thought otherwise, demanding, "Where's the second in the Carol Ashton series?" Thanks to Barbara's insight, McNab wrote fifteen more Carol Ashton novels.[21]

Like a number of others who published with Naiad, Diane Salvatore aspired to be a novelist from childhood. Despite her success in pursuing a magazine career that included positions with such publications as *Cosmopolitan, Ladies' Home Journal, Redbook* and *Good Housekeeping*, Salvatore did not realize her dream until the 1990s. When no one would publish her first novel, which featured a young straight heroine, she decided to be true to herself by writing about lesbianism. Unable to stomach the prospect of another round of rejections, she sent the book to Naiad, and was pleased when Barbara announced her decision to publish *Benediction* (1991). Even though Salvatore was "still seriously terrified" that being outed would derail her magazine career in New York, she published under her own name because of her conviction that "you would have to be in a gay and lesbian bookstore to find it." As someone working in a commercial environment, she appreciated Barbara's fierce competitiveness and dedication to proving "lesbian fiction had a thriving audience that would support the telling of our stories with cold hard cash." Later, after Salvatore went to work for Random House, she recognized how pivotal a "publisher's push" could be in making the difference "between finding an audience and not." In addition to publishing *Benediction; Love, Zena Beth; Not Telling Mother; Paxton Court* and *One of Our Own*, Barbara functioned much like an agent, introducing Salvatore "to a whole world of passionate and committed independent bookstore owners, a network of other publishers, other lesbian writers, book reviewers and of course a hungry audience of lesbians who depended on Naiad to provide them with stories of their lives in entertaining literature."[22]

In her role as supervising editor, Forrest was surprised by the amount of discretion Barbara gave her with book manuscripts. In thoughtful and thorough critiques, Forrest taught writers to show a scene rather than to narrate it, and how to eliminate text that did not advance the story. Pleasant and helpful, she respected the labor and creativity of authors and assured them she "knew what it was like to have someone's fingerprints all over your work. You don't like it much." Such established writers as Isabel Miller and Jane Rule understood Forrest was helping them put out the best book possible, but others sometimes refused to accept her suggestions. If Forrest mentioned she was having a problem with an author, Barbara's idea of negotiation was to call her and state: "Do what Katherine says or take your book and go." Only later, when a writer complained to Forrest, did she learn Barbara often attributed statements to her that she had never made. Forrest also learned Barbara had a penchant for hyperbole. When Forrest inquired how many manuscripts Naiad Press received, the publisher threw out the number six hundred. Questioned further, she glibly replied: "Everybody knows to take everything I say and divide it by eight." To the contrary, Forrest contended, not everyone did know. Barbara spoke with such certainty that she gave people the impression her pronouncements "had been handed down from Mount Olympus."[23]

Forrest perceived Barbara as a mass of contradictions. On the one hand, Barbara decided to reprint classic works, even though they were not cost-effective, including Patricia Highsmith's *The Price of Salt*, Jeannette Howard Foster's *Sex Variant Women in Literature* and Gertrude Stein's *Lifting Belly*, which received the Lambda Literary Foundation Editor's Choice Award in 1990. Barbara had long dreamed of publishing an original novel by Jane Rule, cultivating her friendship for more than two decades before Naiad finally published *Memory Board* in 1987. She felt similar elation when Isabel Miller, whose real name was Alma Routsong, consented to let Naiad publish *Side by Side* (1990), a sequel to *Patience and Sarah* (albeit with different characters, set in New York City, and at the time of Stonewall).

On the other hand, Barbara kept Naiad Press books to a set page limit and focused on the bottom line, insisting manuscripts be cut ruthlessly to save on publishing costs. While not unique to Naiad, such actions were more in keeping with commercial presses than with the small feminist and alternative presses that were Barbara and Donna's peers in publishing. Most genre fiction ran 208 pages or less, Barbara explained in 1990, and books over 240 pages had to be priced at $9.95, which was "more than the going rate customers will pay." Additionally, since Naiad sold titles to bookstores by the case, the shorter a book, the more copies shipped. After having her manuscript cut to save publishing costs, romance writer Jackie Calhoun learned to write shorter books.[24]

Despite their periodic conflicts, Forrest recalled years later that working with Barbara on a daily basis "was fun." She was "a fabulous person to be around if you were on somewhat equal footing with her," Forrest observed. "She radiated optimism, affirmation, confidence, and if there was a problem, it was just something she was going to ride over."[25]

A number of authors had attempted to publish with mainstream presses before submitting their manuscripts to Naiad. After Calhoun's query letter to Little, Brown failed to yield results, she paged through *Writer's Digest* and found a more receptive publisher in Naiad. Amanda Kyle Williams had a similar experience when trying to find a publisher for her spy novel. Upon learning of her latest rejection, a friend suggested that since her book's protagonist was a female, she should visit a women's bookstore to discover what presses published similar books. Struck by the number of Naiad books on the shelves, Williams adjusted her story, submitted it and soon had a contract. Elisabeth Nonas also found Naiad Press through *Writer's Digest*. Before sending a query letter, she phoned to confirm the company's mailing address. Much to her surprise, Barbara answered the phone and grilled the prospective author: "What have you written? How long is it? What name do you want to publish under?" Once satisfied, she instructed Nonas to mail the manuscript to supervising editor Forrest. "Tell her Granny Grier told you to send this." Almost as an afterthought, she inquired, "What's the book about?"[26]

As someone who had devoted years of literary detection to uncovering obscure references to lesbians in printed works, Barbara took great delight in serving as midwife to their increased presence on the printed page. In the 1970s and early 1980s, Naiad had published coming out novels in which fictional females acknowledged the feelings they had for women and realized others felt them too. Beginning in the mid-1980s, the press became a major force in developing new genres in lesbian literature: lesbian mysteries, westerns, science fiction and erotic fiction. Naiad books normalized lesbian presence in all kinds of settings, including historical periods where lesbians previously had been invisible.[27] In Penny Hayes's *The Long Trail* (1986), for example, readers encountered lesbians living in the Old West. When Naiad published Forrest's *Amateur City* in 1984, it became the first mystery to feature a lesbian police detective. Readers who enjoyed Forrest's Kate Delafield novels subsequently devoured Nikki Baker's Virginia Kelley mysteries, Claire McNab's novels about Australian police detective Carol Ashton, Jaye Maiman's Robin Miller, a romance-novelist-turned-private-investigator and many more in that genre.[28]

By the mid-1980s, Naiad had a reputation for publishing light fiction, whereas Firebrand and Kitchen Table Press, among others, strived to publish serious books. Therefore, Barbara's colleagues in publishing were shocked when Sarah Schulman sold her first novel, *The Sophie Horowitz Story* (1984), to Naiad. "There was tension," Spinsters Ink publisher Sherry Thomas reflected, because Barbara's counterparts in publishing thought she "should stay in her lane." Some critics argued that the dominance of Naiad's lesbian romance novels in the marketplace would make it impossible to nurture good lesbian writers. "We damned her with faint praise," Thomas recalled; yet in 1986 after Spinsters Ink partnered with Aunt Lute Books, Thomas realized Barbara had been right about the necessity of publishing commercially successful books to offset the cost of less-lucrative serious titles.[29] Indeed, while Barbara fed appetites for light fiction and knew Naiad could profit from it, she harbored a desire to publish some of her favorite writers from earlier in the century. It gave her great pleasure to release Margaret C. Anderson's unpublished lesbian novel, *Forbidden Fires* (1996), edited by professor Mathilda Hills. Despite her enthusiasm for the book, Barbara realistically knew few other readers shared her appreciation for its historical significance.[30]

As much as Barbara prized the writing of 1920s-era lesbians, their books tended to be about privileged white women. After comprehensively reading 1950s-era lesbian pulp fiction and corresponding with readers of *The Ladder*, she knew how important it was for Naiad's books to portray blue collar and middle-class lesbians in ordinary settings. "I have been reading your books since I first came out," wrote one of many customers. "At first, I read to get support for my lifestyle but now I read Naiads for fun, companionship, and love…I love how you publish a great range of stories which reflect the great range of your readers."[31]

With its reputation for publishing unabashedly lesbian genre fiction firmly established, Naiad increasingly offered readers books containing realistic characters who could be living next door. Several of Calhoun's romances explored the lives of middle-aged women who had left their husbands for other women, Lee Lynch featured butch-and-femme issues in working-class relationships, and Schulman addressed homophobia in a conservative Jewish family. In 1994, Elisabeth Nonas' *Staying Home* offered readers an early fictional treatment of lesbian parenthood, with characters facing such issues as donor insemination and custody rights.[32] In addition to offering adult readers nourishment and encouragement, Naiad entered the young adult market with the publication of Hilary Mullins's *The Cat Came Back* (1993), a Lambda Literary Award winner and one of the few books available about growing up lesbian.

Naiad Press novelists could not gather without exchanging Barbara Grier stories. As their publisher, she encouraged and admonished, prodded and promoted writers, and left many feeling bruised and battered. Few knew the real Barbara Grier, whose preference was to interact with the world through the medium of lesbian literature. Her intensity and intimidating personality manifested itself in her disregard of time zones. Nearly all of the authors, cover artists, editors and manuscript reviewers associated with Naiad had stories of being jarred awake by her phone calls at the crack of dawn. Answering with the anticipation of learning that a loved one had died, they were startled to hear Barbara's abrasive voice commanding them to "light up the skies!" She talked, they listened. Many came to dread Barbara's calls despite her studied efforts to be complimentary or to inquire about the author's partner or pet.[33]

Tactless and blunt, Barbara's words had the power to elevate a writer's spirits or still her pen for years. According to Lee Lynch, "[S]he praised on one hand and bullied with the other, intimidating both the meek and the strong among us." Barbara did not hesitate to tell a writer she was difficult, had made no progress, and needed more help than any other, while at the same time promising to move heaven and earth on the writer's behalf if she fulfilled her potential. Lynch, a *Ladder* contributor-turned-Naiad novelist, referred to Barbara as her "lesbian mother." Yet years of verbal abuse led to a breaking point, and she did not write another novel for eight years.[34]

Some authors remained with Naiad despite personality clashes and Barbara's insults because she gave them what all writers wanted the most, "the opportunity to see their work in print." For Jackie Calhoun, it was reassuring to know she did not repeatedly have to search for a publisher. Despite moving on, Amanda Kyle Williams recognized that the skills she had gained by working with Barbara and editor Forrest would serve her well in the future, and she emerged from her association with Naiad knowing "how to manage a series, how to craft a series, [and] how much to give a reader in the second book."[35] This knowledge proved invaluable years later when she successfully pitched another series to a mainstream publisher.

A few of Naiad's writers related to Barbara on a different plane because of their long-time friendship, but even they were not completely immune to criticism. "I suppose Barbara needs to give us whacks as writers," Jane Rule observed in 1987, "because she may be a bit wistful about her own writing past and because she needs to keep her own tendency to adulation in line." Writers like Ann Bannon, who had come of age in the 1950s and early 1960s, tended to excuse Barbara's fierce determination because they knew it had taken "someone with her stamina and unquestioning belief in the rightness of her cause to bring a whole new generation of lesbian writers to public attention." As Lee Lynch noted, Barbara forged ahead with the conviction of a martyr, and "did her darnedest to synchronize our revolution. She woke early, slept little, seldom set down her phone because she saw herself in the service of a greater cause, one that tolerated, if not excused, her actions."[36]

One of the greatest areas of contention between Barbara and Naiad authors involved the cost-recovery contract. When Naiad published its first book in 1974, the press was a vehicle for Anyda Marchant to publish her own work, so there was no need for a contract. When Naiad began issuing work by other writers, Marchant, a retired attorney, drafted a relatively simple "full-cost recovery" contract stipulating that royalties would be calculated after the expense of producing the book had been recouped. Both Diana Press and Persephone Press used a similar contract. In the 1970s and early 1980s, women generally accepted the need for a cost-recovery contract because they understood small presses like Naiad lacked sufficient capital to cover the costs of publication (editing, typesetting, cover design, paper, printing and distribution). After the press became more prosperous, however, Naiad persisted in using a cost-recovery contract for most authors instead of adopting the more widespread commercial practice of basing royalties on a percentage of the book's cover price. Under the latter arrangement, publishers are responsible for the cost of distribution, paper, printing, typesetting, cover art, binding, shipping and publicity, as well as payment of salaries and taxes. Historically, commercial publishers compensated for the resulting small profit margins with larger volume of sales.[37]

Those who questioned the Naiad contract encountered a volatile Barbara, who viewed their inquiries as an attack or betrayal. "When I first began to try," Vicki P. McConnell recalled, "she was most offended and accused me of not trusting her." An author as well as an editor, Forrest regarded each of her contract negotiations with Barbara as a battle. When she signed the contract for *Curious Wine* in 1982, Forrest had accepted the necessity of Naiad's full-cost recovery contract, but after the success of *Lesbian Nuns: Breaking Silence* gave Naiad a solid foundation, her expectations changed. When she learned that Nancy Bereano's Firebrand Books based royalties on a percentage of a book's cover price instead of on its net profit, Forrest accused Barbara of "screwing her writers." In reality, Barbara had grown so accustomed to penny-pinching that she approached every business transaction as though "every nickel was her last one."[38]

Few novice writers consulted agents, questioned Naiad's next book option, or understood the clauses governing sale of serial and world rights. Like many presses, Naiad stipulated that an author must give the press the right of first refusal on her next book. Amanda Kyle Williams had eagerly signed the contract for her first book, but after writing four books in a series she wanted to take her writing in another direction. A close review of her contract revealed she had two choices: to send Naiad something so poorly written or so blatantly heterosexual that Barbara would reject it, or to put her writing on hold. She chose the latter path.[39]

Naiad contracts also stipulated that the publisher controlled book cover design and copy. This became a point of contention for women like Nancy Manahan and Rosemary Curb, who objected to their photo on the back cover of *Lesbian Nuns: Breaking Silence* because they felt it implied they were lovers. Other authors were less than pleased about their covers, but did not broach the subject with Barbara. Sarah Schulman, for instance, was uncomfortable with the racialized image of the woman on the cover of *The Sophie Horowitz Story* and with the copy describing her as "up to her Jewish earlobes in murder and intrigue." Barbara, however, remained firmly convinced that sensational copy and covers that could be seen from across the room sold books.[40]

While Barbara insisted on holding authors to their contracts, she had few qualms about breaching an agreement if the outcome would benefit Naiad. One of the clauses in Ann Bannon's contract for the Beebo Brinker novels stipulated that "the Publisher undertakes to inform the Author whenever a proposal for such an agreement [sale of subsidiary rights] is offered, and to consult with the Author in regard to the terms of such proposal." It was not until she received a larger-than-usual royalty check that Bannon discovered Barbara had sold the rights to one of her novels without her prior knowledge, nearly costing the author an opportunity to give the entire series to Cleis Press. Barbara refused Bannon's request to cancel the sale and retrieve the book, declaring Naiad had never once had to take back a sale and she was not going to start. Out of desperation, Bannon went directly to the other press, explained the situation, and received assurance that the book would be returned if she repaid the royalties. Angry that Bannon had taken matters into her own hands,

Barbara threatened to sue. Time passed and no lawsuit materialized, leading Bannon to conclude Barbara's threats "were all bluster." On subsequent occasions when the two women met, the topic never arose.[41]

Ingredients of Success: Employees

After years of managing Naiad Press with a combination of limitless energy, Midwestern work ethic and a corps of volunteers, Barbara and Donna hired their first full-time employee in the fall of 1984. During the next fourteen years, more than thirty-five women worked there, some for a few weeks, others for years. Drawn to the idea of working for a lesbian business, women responded to advertisements for such positions as office or fulfillment managers, administrative assistants, and warehouse, maintenance, and shipping clerks. When they arrived at the "Naiad Island," as employees called it, they found a small family house converted into an office and connected to Barbara and Donna's residence (fondly known as "Two Cats and a Yard") by a path and intercom. They quickly learned the kitchen was the heart of the residence, and every other room in the house seemed to be a library.[42]

As two women operating a lesbian publishing company in a conservative community, Barbara and Donna set out to change people's attitudes about lesbians by leading lives above reproach. "We don't run through the streets, we do not force our lifestyle, our business, or anything else on anybody," Donna explained, but "we don't hide it, and never have."[43] They expected their employees to follow suit. As businesswomen, they stressed the importance of keeping the buildings and grounds neat and clean, and treating everyone with courtesy. They were determined to be good neighbors, even if some equated Naiad Press with a coven of witches. Because of a few hostile encounters with men driving pickup trucks, Barbara was suspicious of strangers. When Marianne K. Martin called to say that her brother-in-law would drop off her manuscript, she was stunned by a barrage of questions: "Who was this guy? What did he do? Where did he live? How long had she known him?" Martin thought it was an overreaction until she realized Barbara lived with the fear of hatemongers who might burn their home and business or, at the very least, make life uncomfortable for two women operating a lesbian press in the South.[44]

Shortly after moving to Tallahassee, Barbara and Donna became friends with a couple who coached a women's softball team. Agreeing to serve as company sponsor, their one condition was an "out-of-closet" policy. "People on the team don't have to be Lesbian," Barbara explained, "just willing to say they are." As a result, the Naiad Press Women's Softball Team suffered from turnover, especially among players who worked for the Florida state government or taught in public schools. Two closeted women who intended to play changed their minds after they learned Naiad would sponsor the team. A year or two later, however, they approached Barbara and Donna to thank them for publishing lesbian material. Naiad books, they explained, had changed their lives. Others on the team discovered they liked "playing for women, women coaches, women sponsors," and they believed Barbara and Donna had "done a good thing."[45]

The women who applied for Naiad Press positions came from varied backgrounds. Some aspired to be authors or wanted careers in publishing. Sue Gambill, who began writing her novel *Heartscape* (1989) during her first year with the company, welcomed the opportunities her position provided to interact with writers, other publishers and bookstore personnel. Others, like Roberta Rostorfer-Stocker, enjoyed attending conferences and continued to do so even after she had left the company's employ. As her position evolved from office manager to Barbara's assistant, Rostorfer-Stocker also learned that while Barbara was not good at hand-holding when an individual had problems, she was a consummate troubleshooter.[46]

Other applicants had recently come out as lesbians and were searching for community and acceptance. What better place to find it, they thought, than at a lesbian publishing company? When Rita Mae Reese first heard of Naiad Press, the only lesbian she had read about in a book was tennis player Martina Navratilova, and the only other lesbian she knew had jumped off a bridge. Somehow Reese ended up on the Naiad mailing list. One day, the flyer included an announcement for a job, and she thought, "What the hell, I'll apply." Operating in characteristic fashion, Barbara phoned her at work, giving Reese the "most baffling interview I've ever had." Barbara never asked Reese one question, but instead made great assertions. "Her voice held so much conviction it mesmerized me." Candis Creekmore had left home at sixteen and was working at a gunpowder plant before she went to work at Naiad. She loved the all-woman environment, the decent pay and benefits.[47]

As new hires soon discovered, the reality of working for "Boss Granny" was far different than they had envisioned. For women who had grown up in an era steeped in collaboration and consensus, Barbara's hierarchical management style seemed overly controlling. Unconcerned if her abrupt ways angered them, Barbara refused to waste time on people who did not like her. "We're not going to get a consensus," she informed them. "I'll make the decisions because this is the bottom line."[48] Consequently, her larger-than-life aura seemed to fill every corner of a room. "I was in awe of her," Reese recalled of the "short, wiry woman with bottle-thick glasses, a bit of paunch, and a serious addiction to telephones." Barbara seemed to be on the phone from the moment she walked into the office until she left at day's end, and once she acquired a cell phone, she would call back to the office as soon as she and Donna backed out of the driveway.[49]

Much like a drill sergeant, Barbara tore employees down with her booming voice and harsh words, and then taught them how to work in her business. When Rostorfer-Stocker began working at Naiad, Barbara and Donna were away on a trip. Shortly after their return, Barbara summoned her into the office and said, "I don't think this is going to work." After requesting and receiving the explanation that she was too inexperienced, Rostorfer-Stocker surprised her employer by saying: "Barbara, I'm not afraid of you, I cut my teeth on someone like you." As a woman who respected people who stood up to her, Barbara gave her a month to learn the job, and at the end of that time they never revisited the subject.[50]

Insistent that excellent customer service be a hallmark of Naiad Press, Barbara demanded "every phone call, every customer letter, every order, every task" had to be performed with the utmost care and concern. Kristen Rouse remembers scurrying around the office "like mice, conscious that if we failed to answer the phone even just once by the third ring, we'd surely get a lecture from Barbara on how Naiad would lose 'thousands of dollars' worth of business' from our loyal customers." Barbara also had no sympathy for illness or tardiness because it impeded the smooth flow of business. When Sue Gambill phoned to say she had been in a car accident, Barbara wanted to know how soon she would arrive at work. In contrast, Candis Creekmore, who worked outside maintaining the property, credited "butch privilege" as the reason she never felt terrorized by Barbara's temperament.[51]

Barbara's plan worked, and many customers felt valued. Each December, Naiad's office overflowed with holiday cookies, cakes, candies and even fan fiction starring the Naiad Press women. In retrospect, Rouse realized prompt answering of the phone had more to do with women's lives than it did with making money. By the third ring, a caller, who might not have anyone else to call, had someone ready to discuss books, movies or what it was like to be a lesbian. While Barbara discouraged extensive personal conversations with customers because Naiad employees were not trained therapists, people nonetheless called the toll-free number when they were sad and lonely.[52]

Employees recognized Barbara was a drama queen with a strong need for attention even though she appeared to be uncomfortable with people and seldom let anyone get close. Barbara wanted publicity for lesbian and feminist books, but at the same time, several employees thought she seemed disturbed when others received more attention than she did. Sue Gambill had written a piece for *Hotwire* about Nancy Bereano and Firebrand Books before she joined Naiad Press in 1986. Upon learning about the article, Barbara insisted that Gambill write one about her and Naiad. On another occasion, after receiving a fund-raising letter from a west coast feminist press, Barbara drafted a letter declaring that Naiad would be closing unless they received donations from supporters. Her employees were surprised by the letter, which they thought was not true. It troubled them when frantic women for whom Naiad was a lifeline sent small amounts of money, explaining that they would buy fewer groceries or make other sacrifices to save the press.[53]

Whereas Barbara was unpredictable and reined in her emotions for no one, down-to-earth Donna was the tether stabilizing the company. Rostorfer-Stocker, who joined Naiad in 1989, recognized that a person could not flare up as much as Barbara did without having a solid base. When she screamed and swore at an employee, Donna would take the woman aside and say, "Don't mind her." Barbara may have had a hard shell, but it was permeable, and Donna protected her soft spot. After putting in a hard day's work of accounting and packing books, Donna was the one who dragged Barbara out the door and forced her to do other things, like camping, fishing and watching football and basketball games.[54]

On good days, employees enjoyed Barbara's sense of humor, her love of practical jokes, her cackle, and the big heart that compensated for some of her bad behavior. Barbara always had a big smile on her face when she told stories about her mother dancing and singing, and everyone could see how much she loved her. Sometimes the staff brought their lunches and ate together, or Barbara and Donna bought them lunch and showed slides of their early years together in Kansas City. These times humanized their employers, especially when Barbara became giggly about such historic moments in their relationship as planting their first garden and buying their first home or truck. Whenever Barbara told the story of the applause she received at the first Women in Print meeting, Donna always got tears in her eyes. Barbara's love of animals also became a hallmark of her personality. She and Donna spared no expense when Rita Mae Reese found a half-dead cat near the warehouse, and on another occasion they gave Alex Jaeger a dog they found on the beach and then fenced in Naiad's backyard so Jaeger could bring the dog to work.[55]

Barbara and Donna also could be quite generous to their employees. Reese arrived broke, having put together just enough money to buy a used car and gasoline for the trip to Florida. Sensing Reese's situation, Barbara followed her to her car at the end of the first day, shoved twenty dollars into her hand, and blustered off before the young woman could respond. Barbara and Donna, who taught that home ownership offered stability, gave one employee the $1,500 down payment as a bonus. They lent another the money to purchase a car. Whenever they returned from extended travels, they gave their employees bonuses, which Barbara called "combat pay." "You work for the bitch of the western world," Barbara liked to boast, "you're going to get paid for it." Even more than the loans or bonuses, twenty-year-old Kristen Rouse valued Barbara's affirming messages. "As an out, young butch from a religious, conservative family, that's something I simply wasn't hearing from anyone in my young life." Barbara let the young woman know it was okay to be herself and declared she would "grow up to become an amazing woman someday."[56]

Some of Naiad's new hires found it difficult to make friends in the lesbian community and attributed it to their employer's reputation for employee turnover. Sue Gambill found Tallahassee-area lesbians surprisingly cool once they learned she worked for Naiad because they assumed she would not be staying long. In time, however, connections developed, in part because Barbara and Donna invited area lesbians to the press once a month to assist with the labor-intensive process of affixing labels to each piece of the monthly mailing. They typically began work at eight in the morning and worked until it was done, fueled by pizza provided by Barbara and Donna.[57]

Unfortunately, Barbara's intense personality made it difficult for many to remain at Naiad. Rostorfer-Stocker, who left Naiad's employ on good terms, knew Barbara "was driven, focused on what she was doing, and she wanted everyone around her to have the same level" of commitment. Other workers found it more difficult to cope with the unpredictability of Barbara's behavior and the fact that she found conflict invigorating and often operated as if the press were in crisis mode. Visitors to Naiad Press were stunned to witness employees carrying on with their work while Barbara screamed at them, told them they were incompetent, and blamed them for making costly errors. When something seemingly minor went wrong, she would swear vehemently and declare, "Oh my God, everything's ruined, what are we going to do," but when something monumental occurred she would remain calm and say, "I've got this." In the very beginning, Jaeger thought she was going to get fired every day because Barbara never hesitated to let her know when she had done something incorrectly. Yet when Rouse backed Naiad's new pickup truck into a mailbox before Barbara and Donna had made one payment on it,

Barbara remained calm, affectionately calling the young woman "Mickey Mouse" and telling her to pay better attention in the future.[58]

When employees chose to leave Naiad Press, most dreaded facing Barbara and Donna to say "I quit." Some left abruptly, either faxing in a resignation or simply disappearing. Leaving was not easy. Once employees gave notice, they felt like they were traitors for quiting. Rita Mae Reese, who worked for the company six and one-half years, decided to quit after Barbara said, "I can't believe you allowed the power to go out." When she reflected on the comment, Reese realized the power had not "gone out," but instead, there were other things she wanted to do with her life. With encouragement from Naiad author Claire McNab, Reese used her Naiad retirement funds to return to college and embark on a new life path.[59]

In retrospect, some of Naiad's employees realized they had learned invaluable lessons during their time at the press. Jaeger left with an ability to work anywhere because of her work ethic and commitment to customer service. As a young woman lacking confidence, Reese saw in Barbara the model of how much a woman could accomplish of what was important to her if she did not stop to ask for anyone's opinion. But she also saw how the relentless pursuit of a goal could leave a person feeling isolated and alienated.

* * *

By the mid-1980s, Naiad Press had become well-known as a publisher of genre fiction. While it continued to publish the occasional serious work, its routine fare still consisted of romances, mysteries, a few westerns and works of science fiction, all featuring lesbian heroines and happy endings. Bookstores thrived because of the foundation that publishers like Naiad provided, but Barbara's impact was also felt in the formation of an LGBT caucus within the American Booksellers Association and the organization of an LGBT aisle in the ABA exhibit hall. She, along with Donna, was a regular presence at the annual Lambda Literary Awards banquet.[60]

Convinced that the goal of worldwide lesbian visibility justified the means, Barbara knew how to get books in the hands of readers, was willing to do the work, and had no qualms about organizing people around her agenda. Unlike Nancy Bereano and other peers in lesbian-feminist publishing, Barbara eschewed the "women's studies" direction because of her commitment to working-class readers and "to the girl out there who had no place else to go." She also knew Naiad could reach more people, find more novelists, and make more money with genre fiction. Whether or not people liked her style and methods, nearly all who came in contact with Barbara in the late 1980s and early 1990s knew she had a single-minded focus: ensuring lesbians could easily find themselves on the printed page. As Lee Lynch observed, "The lesbian skies had been full of storm clouds far too long. She willed the sun to shine on us and shine it did, in the form of book after book, story after story, until she saw a deluge of lesbian literature."[61]

CHAPTER FOURTEEN

❧

Transitions

"Naiad Press is always being written up as having some miracle dust but it is all one simple process...find and address your market and work your ass off regularly, preferably daily."

—Barbara Grier, 1993[1]

Gay and women's bookstores flourished in the 1980s, but by the 1990s they struggled to contend with the impact of a worldwide recession and growing competition from rapidly spreading bookstore chains. Operated by brothers who had opened their first bookstore in Ann Arbor, Michigan, in 1979, Borders rose to national prominence in the 1990s, along with the fast-growing Barnes and Noble. The chain stores' comfortable seating areas, convenient parking lots, competitive pricing and willingness to stock gay and lesbian titles represented serious competition for the independent stores.[2] An astute businesswoman, Barbara Grier ensured that the chain stores sold Naiad Press books, but she recognized that widespread visibility and increased acceptance came with a cost.

Barbara was in denial about the economic recession of the early 1990s. "We do not believe CNN news," she told recipients of a "Dear Friends" letter in late 1991. As if to prove her point, she boasted of a business that was "staying up and growing." Yet just a few months later she admitted that "[g]one, certainly, are the days of spectacular growth." Like other businesses in the United States, Naiad Press had experienced "disastrous lows during the Gulf War." Barbara, who liked to keep her fingers on the pulse of publishing, noted that "at least ten stores have closed their doors at the end of 1991" and "every women's small press with whom we have talked plans to cut back on number of books issued in 1992." Since Naiad had already "spent a fortune" on advance advertising and catalog inserts, she and Donna McBride had no intention of cutting back production for 1992; however, the time had come to review the company's prospects for the future.[3]

As they adjusted to new market conditions, Barbara and Donna began making pragmatic decisions about the press. In December 1992, several weeks before Naiad president Anyda Marchant's eighty-second birthday, Barbara phoned to request that Marchant and Muriel Crawford add codicils to their wills stipulating that their shares in Naiad Press would revert to Barbara and Donna if they predeceased them. Making the request with her customary abruptness and lack of tact, Barbara angered Marchant, who responded by expressing her unhappiness about "the short shrift we (M[uriel] and I) have had financially from the Press, which after all they [Barbara and Donna] would not have had but for us." Indeed, Naiad Press had been Marchant's idea, and her initial investment launched the first books, but Barbara's vision and commitment, combined with Donna's financial acumen and willingness to take risks, produced its successful formula. At the company's inception in 1974, silent partners Marchant and Crawford had welcomed Barbara's willingness to serve as the public face of Naiad. "I was not 'out,'" Marchant explained, "and my real interest was in finding a way into publication for the novels I wanted to write." After mulling everything over, Marchant spoke with Barbara and Donna's attorney, Michael Gruver, and drafted the codicils.[4]

* * *

From the beginning, Barbara had boasted that Naiad Press stood apart from other publishers because it kept nearly all of its titles in print. Once sales declined, commercial publishers typically remaindered books, selling them at greatly reduced prices to clear out their warehouses. In the early 1990s, as the nation coped with a recession, hard times hit book publishing. Barbara grew alarmed when the seemingly stable and highly regarded North Point Press announced its closure after publishing nearly three hundred books. Determined to avoid a similar fate for Naiad, Barbara consulted with other independent publishers and learned they also suffered from diminishing sales and planned to make cutbacks. Instead of decreasing publishing output, Barbara and Donna, after re-evaluating Naiad's policy of keeping books in print indefinitely, decided that the time had come to eliminate slow-moving or inactive titles from their catalog. Initially, in early 1992, Barbara informed authors that books would go out of print when their stock was exhausted, and die a "natural death." "[S]ince they dribble out the door anyway that could be years from now," she predicted.[5]

While the American publishing scene looked lean, if not grim, Barbara felt optimistic about the growing market for lesbian books on the international market. Since the mid-1980s, she had been selling world rights for most of Naiad's mysteries and some of its romances to publishers in England, Germany and the Netherlands. After attending the Fifth International Feminist Book Fair in Amsterdam in 1992, she and Donna returned home excited about the prospects for the sale of gay, lesbian and feminist books in Europe. "The movement there is somewhat behind the U.S.," she observed, "and the audience is growing at the same rate it was in the U.S. say, 10 years ago." Barbara credited the unification of East and West Germany with heightened interest in lesbian titles there, noting "the demand for lesbian and gay material has always exceeded the supply." Mysteries and romances sold well, while there was little or no interest in Naiad's science fiction, fantasy, westerns and "slice of life" stories. Upon returning from the conference, Barbara and Donna projected that fully one-fourth of Naiad's sales, if not more, soon would come from these markets because demand exceeded supply. Consequently, the European market played a role in determining which genres of books Naiad accepted for publication in the 1990s.[6]

Domestically, Barbara had high hopes for short fiction anthologies filled with stories written by Naiad authors. Always alert to marketing opportunities, she knew readers of short stories often wanted to read more work by their favorite authors. "I must say," Barbara wrote, "it is clear that the anthology is the brightest idea we've come up with in a long time to introduce every author's work to an even wider audience." Beginning with *The Erotic Naiad* in 1992, Naiad published an anthology each year through 1999, with a majority offering erotic stories.[7]

Perhaps reflective of the economy, Barbara's "Dear Friends" letters took on a tone of "doom and gloom" in the early 1990s even though Naiad had much to celebrate. In May 1992, the Lambda Literary Foundation recognized Barbara and Donna with its Publisher's Service Award. With Katherine V. Forrest as author and editor, Naiad books earned four Lambda Literary Awards for lesbian mystery between 1990 and 1993. Anyda Marchant and Muriel Crawford received recognition at the National Women's Music Festival, where they were given the Jeanine Rae Award for the Advancement of Women's Culture. And Barbara was thrilled when the Book-of-the-Month Club and the Quality Paperback Book Club chose a Naiad Press book, Diane Salvatore's *Love, Zena Beth*, as a dual selection in early 1993.[8]

Preserving Gay and Lesbian History

Since the 1950s, Barbara had collected everything remotely related to lesbian publishing, including copies of articles, books, magazines and photographs. She had done so with the help of her vast network of correspondents. "Even if you are bored with it all," Barbara admonished them, "please know that from the point of view of archiving material about this small but vital bubble in the lesbian and gay movement called the Women in Print movement, you need to do this for those lesbians that aren't born today." Even with the growing acceptance of gays and lesbians in popular culture, Barbara remained convinced "[h]istory will do its best to ignore us; we need to do our best to make sure it cannot happen."[9]

Barbara had lost a small portion of her collection when she left Helen Bennett for Donna in 1972, but otherwise had comprehensively collected lesbian and gay books, magazines, correspondence, recordings, and ephemera since the mid-1950s. Aware that she could "not protect the stuff forever," Barbara sought homes for her precious documents. Barbara and Donna transferred most of their periodical collection to the June Mazer Lesbian Archives in West Hollywood. They explored the possibility of transferring their remaining library and archival material to several university libraries, but after conversations with longtime publisher Sherry Thomas, they decided their collection should go to the James C. Hormel Gay and Lesbian Center in the newly constructed San Francisco Public Library. In 1992 the Library Foundation arranged for transportation of more than fifteen thousand books along with personal and corporation correspondence, news clippings, pamphlets, images and ephemera from Florida to San Francisco. Barbara loved the attention she and Donna received in October 1993 when they attended the Founders' Day dinner for the Gay and Lesbian Center.[10]

While she had not endorsed Barbara Gittings's and Frank Kameny's protests in the 1960s, Barbara took delight in participating in the Second National March on Washington for Gay and Lesbian Rights in 1987 (the first had occurred in October 1979). When she learned of plans for a third march on Washington, to be held on April 25, 1993, Barbara encouraged everyone she knew to participate. "We will have a banner," she announced, "and it will be visible." She wanted authors, employees and others who planned to march with the Naiad Press contingent to consider wearing Naiad T-shirts. If people were not planning to march with Naiad, she hoped they would march with other organizations. "[W]e believe that it is vital to have every city, every lesbian and gay group, every profession, every craft, every interest to more accurately reflect our incredible diversity. It's good that the world learns from this march that we really are EVERYWHERE."[11]

As was their practice, Barbara and Donna had a full schedule when they traveled to Washington, D.C., in April. Three weeks prior to the march, Jane Troxell, Rose Fennell, Marge Darling and Susan Fletcher had bought Lammas Women's Books from Mary Farmer. Eager for the new owners to succeed, Barbara and Donna "sent enough inventory to stock the store, and staged a book signing with Katherine V. Forrest and other Naiad luminaries." Barbara also promoted the event in Naiad's mailing, contributing to the overflow crowd of lesbian publishers, authors, bookstore women and readers eager to celebrate the store's new ownership. On Sunday, when everyone gathered at the ellipse of the Washington Monument for the beginning of the march, Barbara boasted there were 1.1 million people in attendance, while park police's controversial estimate was three hundred thousand.[12]

Parting Ways

Despite a strong year of sales in 1993, Barbara mailed letters in January 1994 informing twenty-three authors of plans to remove twenty-nine of their titles from Naiad's inventory after years of keeping most of Naiad Press books in print. It was no longer good business practice to keep books in print that did not sell enough to pay for their storage costs. Some books would be given to bookstores to be used as promotional gifts, others would be moved into the bargain book category, and still others would be "gotten rid of altogether." If an author wished to have copies of her book, she could pay the cost of freightage, or they would go to the dump. In a characteristic act of insensitivity, Barbara included two of company president Anyda Marchant's books on the list: *A Flight of Angels*, which had been in print less than two years, and *Keep to Me, Stranger* (1989). "Reaching bargain book status," Barbara blithely explained, "doesn't have diddlyshit to do with the quality of the book." In her mind, the inclusion of Gale Wilhelm's two novels on the list served as ample proof that "[s]ometimes books simply live their lives and die." In reality, Barbara thought that the imperious Marchant had overestimated her ability as a writer, informing people that she considered herself as good as Virginia Woolf and that she refused to be edited.[13]

Galled by Barbara's audacity and the fact that she had not sought her approval, Marchant concluded that Barbara's desire to make money had "completely overwhelmed the original ideal on which the Press was founded." Her anger unleashed, Marchant aired resentments that had accumulated over time, beginning with the shortcuts Barbara had taken during the early years of Naiad's existence. It irritated her that Barbara portrayed her and Crawford as two disabled elderly women, even though that was how she had first introduced herself to Barbara in 1972. Although she was a feminist, Marchant had spent years trying to curb Barbara's lesbian activism because she wanted her company to publish material of interest to all women. Frustrated by her inability to channel Barbara's enthusiasm or to control her ambitions, Marchant informed her partners in April 1994 that the time had come to dissolve Naiad Press, Incorporated.[14]

The Tallahassee firm of Hurley, Morgan & Potts estimated the liquidation value of Naiad Press, Inc. at $78,918 and the fair market value at $263,612 as of December 31, 1993.[15] In the lengthy legal battle that ensued, Barbara and Donna's attorney, Michael Gruver, reasoned that "[t]he real value of the company lies with the talents and contacts of Barbara and Donna themselves." Barbara's efforts until 1982, and Barbara and Donna's collective efforts thereafter, had transformed Naiad Press from a vanity publishing venture into the largest lesbian publishing company in the world. Marchant's initial investment, two thousand dollars to cover the publication and distribution expenses of her books, had been repaid, and both she and Crawford received fees as directors and had benefitted from tax advantages over the years. Therefore, he concluded, Barbara and Donna were "resolute in not permitting their lives' [sic] work be undermined in any fashion and are well prepared to litigate to any extent necessary."[16]

The dissolution of the business became even more contentious as the business partners attempted to resolve the division of real estate that they jointly owned. Marchant and Crawford originally owned a small house in Pompano Beach, Florida, where they wintered each year. The house needed remodeling, and Marchant offered to add Barbara and Donna's names to the title if they would do the work, which included installing new kitchen cabinets and flooring. Several years later, when Marchant and Crawford wanted to move to a larger home in Lighthouse Point, they sold the Pompano Beach house and bought the new property in all four women's names. In addition to the Lighthouse Point property, the partners also shared ownership in the Naiad Press office building and the beach house at Alligator Point. They had purchased the beach house with proceeds from the sale of *Lesbian Nuns: Breaking Silence* and turned it into a tax-deductible business promotion by allowing bookstore owners to stay there free of charge. After reviewing the jointly owned property, Barbara and Donna's attorney indicated that they were willing to sell their interest in the Lighthouse Point property for half of the appraised value, but they wanted Marchant and Crawford to quitclaim their interest in the Naiad Press office building.

Marchant, who responded directly to Barbara rather than communicating through their attorneys, demanded Barbara and Donna transfer their share of the Lighthouse Point house "gratis." She also rejected their offer of $25,000 for Naiad Press, insisting that it must be "at least $100,000" since "over the years as half owners of the corporation we have been jointly liable for many decisions in which we have not been consulted." Marchant was willing to transfer the office building to Barbara and Donna, but insisted that Naiad Press continue selling her current book, *Michaela*, through 1994, and ship her all of the Sarah Aldridge books along with all orders received for these books and the copyright certificates.[17]

As the legal battle continued, Marchant insisted upon an independent audit by Sheldrick, McGehee & Kohler, a firm based in Jacksonville. While the firm's analyst noted that "officer salaries might be slightly in excess of a standard level of compensation," he also observed that additional personnel would "be required to perform those duties" if Barbara and Donna were not working as many hours as they did. Despite Naiad Press's "established reputation in a niche market," the analyst astutely noted the market was "changing to the detriment of companies like NPI, with larger publishers entering the market and having the wherewithal to offer higher author advances." He also noted mainstream outlets had placed increased strain on the women's and alternative bookstore outlets through which Naiad had distributed its product. In conclusion, the firm assessed Naiad's fair market value at $275,000 as of June 30, 1994.[18]

Based on the independent audit, Marchant and Crawford believed an offer of $263,500 would settle both issues, the real property and corporate stock ownership. Rejecting the proposed amount on behalf of his clients, Barbara and Donna's attorney reiterated that Marchant had initiated contact with Barbara because she possessed *The Ladder*'s mailing list, an invaluable asset for anyone wishing to tap the lesbian market. At a time when bookstores did not feature lesbian titles on their shelves, this list had facilitated Barbara's savvy marketing of Marchant's eleven Sarah Aldridge novels. Moreover, the attorney reasoned, Barbara had worked without pay from the inception of Naiad Press until late in 1980, when she began receiving a $100 per month salary. After Donna joined the company in June 1982, their annual salaries rose to $11,000 each, but their compensation remained below industry standard for the next six years.[19]

As the attorneys continued to negotiate back and forth, an impatient Barbara contacted Marchant with a counteroffer, and by January 31, 1995, the two women had reached an agreement: "The Naiad Press, Inc. shall purchase the shares of Anyda Marchant and Muriel Crawford for the lump sum cash price of $125,000 and the quitclaim of the Havana property [the Naiad Press office on the outskirts of Tallahassee]" and that Barbara and Donna would transfer their interest in the Lighthouse Point property for a payment equaling one half of its assessed value. In the final settlement, Marchant and Crawford also received the complete inventory of Sarah Aldridge novels.[20] The transactions were completed on February 22, 1995, at which time Marchant and Crawford tendered their resignations as officers of Naiad Press.

The falling out between the four women was painful and sad. As she did with all adversity, Barbara refused to dwell on it and set her sights on the future. In two sentences of her February 15, 1995, "Dear Friends" letter, Barbara informed recipients that "As of now, The Naiad Press, Inc. is solely held by Barbara Grier and Donna J. McBride," before moving on to the business at hand, royalty payments, the upcoming OutWrite conference and video distribution. In contrast, Marchant spent several years vilifying the way her former business partners had managed the press and trying to counteract what she regarded as the misinformation circulated by Barbara about her beloved company. Upon their resignation from Naiad, Marchant and Crawford established a new company, A & M Books. In 1995, they published the twelfth Sarah Aldridge novel, *Amantha*, followed by her final novel, *Nina in the Wilderness*, two years later. Marchant, who never spoke to Barbara or Donna again, died in 2006.[21]

An Editor Departs

Recipients of the "Dear Authors" letters learned of another change early in 1995, when Barbara announced longtime editor and author Katherine V. Forrest's departure from the press.

When she joined Naiad in 1983, Forrest navigated a dual role—as an author and as an editor. Beginning with *Curious Wine*, her publications sold well. Indeed, eight of her novels appeared on a list of Naiad's fifty best-selling titles, including *Curious Wine* (#2), *Murder by Tradition* (#11), and *Murder at the Nightwood Bar* (#13).[22] In her role as an editor, Forrest had patiently and astutely offered guidance to dozens of writers as she thoroughly and carefully critiqued their manuscripts. Those who worked closely with her knew several mainstream presses had expressed interest in publishing her work.

As her knowledge of publishing deepened, Forrest grew convinced that the time had come for gay and lesbian authors to move beyond their specialized publishing niche and to establish their writing as a legitimate part of the nation's literature. From her perspective, the business was divided into two great camps: men published their mainstream fiction in hardcover, and women published their paperbacks with small presses. When Forrest asked Barbara to publish her books in hardcover, she justified the request by explaining lesbian books would never gain mainstream recognition until they appeared in that format. "You would have thought I had authored the destruction of Naiad Press," Forrest recalled. "It was one of our biggest wars."[23]

Barbara, wedded to the idea that lesbians would not purchase hardcover books because of their higher cost, argued she had positioned Naiad in the correct niche market. When Forrest threatened to leave the press, Barbara acquiesced, albeit in a very public way, informing everyone she was accommodating Forrest's demand. Forrest took great satisfaction in seeing her first hardcover book, *The Beverly Malibu*, reviewed in the *New York Times Book Review*, and her book sold over ten thousand copies in that format. Naively, Forrest thought her success would prove hardcover could benefit Naiad, but Barbara refused to concede the point.

By 1994, Forrest knew she had to leave Naiad if she wanted to continue growing as an author. She also had reached the conclusion that Barbara's early hopes and dreams for the press had been subsumed by a quest to make money. After publishing nine books with the lesbian press, Forrest wanted to join such authors as Dorothy Allison, Ellen Hart and Carol Anshaw, whose publication by mainstream publishers had extended the availability of lesbian literature to many readers who did not know lesbian presses existed, as well as to those reluctant to set foot in lesbian bookstores. Forrest also believed that Naiad's reputation as a publisher of light romances and mysteries inhibited serious authors from submitting manuscripts.[24]

Even though she had witnessed Barbara's seemingly callous treatment of authors over the years, Forrest optimistically expected a different response when she informed Barbara and Donna of her decision to leave. After years of fighting contract battles, Barbara stunned Forrest by declaring she would match Putnam-Berkeley's offer of a three-book deal with a guaranteed $50,000 per book. By this point, however, Forrest felt ground down from years of working with Barbara's abrasive personality, and no longer cared about the money. When she refused the offer, Barbara and Donna insisted on holding Forrest to her contract, and Forrest, in turn, infuriated her publishers by submitting an early novel containing minimal interest to a lesbian audience. In characteristic fashion, Barbara contacted most of Naiad's authors by phone to inform them of Forrest's departure from the press and, in a follow-up "Dear Authors" letter, claimed there were no hard feelings. After Forrest fulfilled her contractual obligations to Naiad, Barbara and Forrest never spoke to each other again.[25]

As time passed, Forrest's anger faded. She recognized Barbara had created "something enormously important, absolutely miraculous for its day" through "sheer force of will," concluding that "it may have taken a personality like hers to accomplish what was needed." Instead of focusing on their unpleasant separation, Forrest chose to emphasize the opportunities Naiad had offered her, as a novice writer, to find her audience. As Forrest subsequently discovered, the mainstream market for gay and lesbian books proved volatile. For a short time, publishers solicited work from gay and lesbian authors because they anticipated their commercial potential and wanted to benefit from it. With their large advances and publicity budgets, they made it difficult for small presses to compete. In the end, however, mainstream presses were disappointed with the sales figures for gay and lesbian books. Her new publisher expected Forrest to be a crossover author, but her books sold no better or worse than they had with Naiad, and as Forrest often joked, her own idea of a crossover market was to gay men.[26]

Christi Cassidy, who came to Naiad Press as an editor in 1988, stepped in to fill part of the void left by Forrest, Naiad's senior editor. Building on her prior experience in New York publishing, and on training provided by Forrest, Cassidy became the sole editor when Forrest departed the press and continued with Naiad until January 2002. A veteran of mainstream publishing, she felt a kinship with Barbara, whom she regarded as a businesswoman. On occasion, Cassidy found herself caught between Barbara and authors, but as a former publicist, she was skilled at compartmentalizing information. Listening carefully, as editors are trained to do, she never felt she had to defend or condemn Barbara.[27]

Film and Video

Naiad's entry into the world of film and video combined two of Barbara's early loves, books and movies. For several years, Barbara had followed with rapt attention filmmaker Donna Deitch's effort to turn Jane Rule's *Desert of the Heart* into a film, dreaming of the day when Naiad could publish a "Read the Book, See the Movie" edition. Rule, delighted to have Naiad bringing her books back into print, hoped "Barbara's linking the new edition of *Desert* with publicity about the movie" would bring the final donations needed to produce the film. In the months leading up to the premiere of the film, Barbara shared her promotional ideas with Samuel Goldwyn Pictures' Hollywood office and tapped her contacts at *Publishers Weekly* and other publications to ensure widespread reviews and notices for the film and Naiad's reprint of the book. When Barbara and Donna attended the film's premiere in New York City in April 1986, Barbara described herself as an adoring fan: "I might well have been Walker Percy's adolescent hero in the long ago novel, THE MOVIE GOER." When the film became available on video, she declared, Naiad would distribute it by mail "to the many who will NOT go into a video store to buy it or even to rent it."[28]

Indeed, Barbara predicted a bright future for lesbian film. Always on the alert for opportunities, Barbara aggressively sought additional film options, and was thrilled when film director Tim Hunter optioned Forrest's *Murder at the Nightwood Bar* (1987) and *The Beverly Malibu* (1989). The latter film was green-lighted in the early 1990s, with Mary-Louise Parker to be cast as Kate Delafield, but "when the Japanese stock market crashed, so did the film."[29]

Remaining on alert for additional book-film possibilities, Barbara seized an opportunity in 1992 for Naiad to become involved in the promotion of Nicole Conn's film, *Claire of the Moon*. Conn, who had a "very close but turbulent relationship" with Barbara, credited its success to her "unwavering belief in the film and her dogged marketing," which resulted in a novelization with over eighteen printings and such ancillary products as T-shirts, prints, posters and even *Claire of the Moon* Christmas ornaments. Eager to prove to the world lesbian movies could do well, Barbara and Donna flew to Portland for the film's world premiere, and Barbara proudly introduced it and its director. Hoping to enlist Naiad Press customers in helping with the promotion of Conn's film, Barbara urged them to "[r]ent those buses, get in the car and drive. Support lesbian movies or, baby, there won't be many more made." In the end, Barbara and Donna never recouped their investment in the film project, but Naiad's novelization of the book "sold like hotcakes."[30]

Interest in lesbian film projects grew in the 1990s, and Barbara sold movie rights to Naiad books whenever possible. "Movies help us all," she explained in 1993, because they bring "us women from all over the country when there is a movie/book tie-in." Barbara had high hopes for film adaptations of Naiad books, among them Forrest's *Murder at the Nightwood Bar*, Camarin Grae's *Soul Snatcher*, Penny Hayes's *Yellowthroat*, and Mindy Kaplan's *Devotion*. Despite her success in the sale of rights, filmmakers found the lesbian market too specialized, and only *Devotion* made it to the screen.[31]

While still president of the company, Anyda Marchant objected to Naiad's venture into video distribution because she thought it appealed to prurient interests, but Barbara and Donna nonetheless moved forward. They anticipated healthy sales for the video release of *Claire of the Moon*, despite its prohibitive cost of $89.95. They then capitalized on interest in the film by offering a second film, *Moments: The Making of Claire of the Moon*, and a six-minute trailer for the film, along with T-shirts, cassettes and CDs. Customers hungered for visual representations of themselves, and soon the sale of such films as *Meeting Magdalene*, *Costa Brava* and *A Midwife's Tale*, among others, accounted for twenty percent of Naiad's income. Indeed, when Barbara and Donna compiled a list of best-sellers by net income, videos held five spots out of the top twenty.[32]

Bookstores Close Their Doors

In the 1990s, Barbara and Donna watched as gay, lesbian and women's bookstores closed in record numbers. Economies of scale made it difficult for them to compete with corporate bookstore chains and the advent of online merchants. As the chains spread nationwide, small businesses like Dreams and Swords in Indianapolis found it difficult to compete with the allure of deep discounts, vast book stock, coffee shops and ample parking space. Recognizing the "days of spectacular growth" for independent bookstores were over, Barbara and Donna anticipated that the stores destined to survive were the ones managed by people who approached them as businesses, not community centers.[33]

As numbers plummeted from a peak of approximately one hundred forty stores committed to selling lesbian books to fewer than three dozen by the year 2000, bookstore owners had to reevaluate their personal goals as well as their business plans. According to Randie Farmelant, writing in *off our backs*, competition from large chains had forced gay, lesbian and women's bookstores and presses "to transform into a world where ideas are commodified." Gays and lesbians who came of age during the 1990s generally felt better about themselves than did their predecessors, and they had less need for books telling them they were okay after celebrities like Ellen DeGeneres began coming out as gay on the cover of national magazines.[34]

When Richard Labonté stepped down as the general manager of San Francisco's A Different Light Bookstore, he attributed his decision, in part, to changing times: "...the passions and the politics which fueled us from the '70s into the '00s have cooled—not personally, perhaps, but politically and culturally." In some instances, the lack of a solid financial base and over-reliance on volunteers had led to turnover, burnout and closure. Common Woman, located in Alberta, Canada, sold its last book in 1992 because it had no one willing to continue managing the store on a volunteer basis. After chain bookstores opened nearby, the lesbian-feminist community was not as faithful as Harriet Clare (Dreams and Swords, Indianapolis) and Simone Wallace (Sisterhood Bookstore, Westwood, California) hoped they would be, and both stores closed their doors by 1999. When the women of Lammas Women's Books bought The 31st Street Bookstore in Baltimore, "it dragged down the entire enterprise." Feminism was no longer in vogue, and online giant Amazon's appeal was growing rapidly. Within two years, the women had closed the Baltimore store and sold Lammas.[35]

In her typical fashion, Barbara offered pragmatic advice to store owners unable to pay their creditors in full: to call up every creditor, explain the situation, and ask if they could pay thirty-five to fifty cents on the dollar. "Her mentorship," Lammas's Jane Troxell recalled, "gave me the ability to get through a tough process."[36]

Some stores extended their lifespan by dissolving their collectives and adopting new business models. Instead of stocking only lesbian books, they acknowledged their customers also read cookbooks and travel narratives, and wanted books for the children in their lives. Responding to the challenge creatively, a few, like Charis Books & More (Atlanta), A Room of One's Own (Madison, Wisconsin), and Women & Children First (Chicago) survive today.[37]

From Naiad Press to Bella Books

After more than a quarter century in small-press publishing, Barbara and Donna decided it was time to contemplate retirement. Barbara never cited her health as a reason, but she no longer possessed the boundless energy that had enabled her to work late into the night. With Donna's knee replacement surgery in 1998, Barbara further realized just how crucial her partner was in making the business work.

Initially, Barbara thought it would be possible to sell Naiad Press. She offered it to Silver Moon Books for one hundred thousand dollars, but Jane Cholmeley and Sue Butterworth declined because they thought the price was too high and "operating a company in the US from the UK made no sense to us."[38] In the end, Barbara and Donna received only one serious expression of interest in purchasing the company. Someone from Kensington Books invited them to New York City to discuss the possibility of adding a line of lesbian books to the company. After Barbara and Donna laughed at his initial offer of fifty thousand dollars, the Kensington representative conferred with his staff and raised it to half a million dollars, but with conditions: Barbara must work for the company for two years, and Naiad had to guarantee the transfer of all author contracts. Unable to accept those terms, Barbara and Donna returned to Florida and, in a flurry of activity reminiscent of Barbara's final days as editor of *The Ladder*, brought out thirty-two new titles in 1999.[39]

When no viable buyer materialized by November, Barbara devised an alternative plan that involved phased retirement and finding a home for Naiad Press authors. She spread the word that she had decided to give away the company because "it was the right thing to do," but from Cholmeley's perspective, this "is what you say when your plan to sell has failed. I would have done the same."[40]

Barbara and Donna had known Kelly Smith since 1992 when she and her lover, Amy Blake, opened A Woman's Prerogative Bookstore in Ferndale, Michigan. Indeed, Naiad had been the first business to give the bookstore credit. By 1998, Smith's interest in publishing had grown, so she left the store in her partner's care and spent a year working with Barbara and Donna. "I figured, if you're gonna learn the business," she explained, "why not learn it from the best." After a year, Smith returned to Michigan, separated from her partner, and founded Bella Books. When Barbara phoned in November 1999 to inform her Naiad was going to slow production in 2000, she inquired if Bella Books would be interested in "taking up the slack."[41] Upon receiving an affirmative response, Barbara and Donna scaled back production in 2000 to just a handful of titles. Naiad published its final books in 2001: Claire McNab's *Death Club* and *Out of Sight*, Nicole Conn's *She Walks in Beauty* and Karin Kallmaker's *Frosting on the Cake* and *Substitute for Love*.

Eager to see Smith succeed, Barbara proposed a non-monetary transaction in which she used her influence to encourage Naiad authors to sign with Bella Books. Mailing them a letter, Barbara indicated authors had the option of having their contracts transferred to the recently established Bella Books or, if an author were not interested, her copyright would be returned. For authors who had wanted to move in new directions but felt bound by the next-book option in their contract, the opportunity was a blessing in disguise. Amanda Kyle Williams, who had written four books for Naiad in the early 1990s, wanted to grow in new directions, but had stopped writing because of the right of first refusal option in her contract. When Williams received Barbara's letter giving authors the option of having their contracts transferred to Bella Books or returned to them, she elected the latter and was free to move forward with her writing career. Within a decade, Random House had accepted her next book, *The Stranger You Seek*. For those who shifted over to Bella Books, the transition was relatively seamless and they kept on writing. Barbara also introduced Naiad's longtime typesetter, Sandi Stancil, to Smith and contacted editors and manuscript readers to see if they would be willing to work for Bella Books.[42] One asset Barbara and Donna did not share with Smith was the Naiad Press mailing list. Originating as *The Ladder's* list of subscribers, the list had been crucial in Naiad's success. Smith, noting that she could not afford a mailing of that size, was satisfied when Barbara continued to promote Bella Books in the "Dear Friends" letters and other Naiad mailings.

Barbara anticipated a bright future for Bella Books, and in the spring of 2000 she and Donna attended the Book Expo America conference "as if we were staff members working for Smith. Barbara enjoyed watching the novice test her wings as a full-fledged publisher, but resented it when people asked how she was enjoying retirement. Even though Naiad Press had significantly decreased its output, the company website created and administered by author Linda Hill ensured steady sales from the backlist.[43]

Barbara and Donna were not the only lesbian publishers to change directions as one century yielded to the next. In July 2000, Nancy Bereano sold Firebrand Books to her distributor, LPC Group and Rising Tide Press, a lesbian press begun by Lee Boojamra and Alice Frier in the early 1990s, also slowed production. After publishing forty-five books during her tenure as head of Spinsters Ink (1992-2000), Joan Drury noted she had "supported it about twenty-five percent." Believing the whole industry was "in big trouble," she attributed economic difficulties faced by small presses to the fact that they published books "for [their] literary or political value, not asking how they will sell." In the coming years, however, Drury anticipated positive developments as "the new generation will be able to take lesbian publishing into a whole new world with all the major technological breakthroughs: e-books, Internet publishing, and so on."[44]

As Kelly Smith soon discovered, the early twenty-first century was a challenging time to embark upon a career in publishing. In need of operating capital, she welcomed Terese Orban into the company as a financial backer and business partner. With Smith functioning as general manager, the press published its first six books in the fall of 2000. Most were "more Naiad than Bella" because the manuscripts had already been in the Naiad Press pipeline. Naiad's authors, Smith explained, had "been programmed to produce the Naiad way," working with a strict word/page limit and limited time for revisions. In the future, Smith wanted Bella authors to have more room to tell their stories and develop characters. She also planned for substantial editing, copyediting and proofreading, areas in which Naiad had been criticized as deficient. While Barbara had been a "mother hen" to her authors, nagging them to meet deadlines that enabled Naiad to produce its monthly quota of books, Smith took a more hands-off approach.[45]

Barbara used her authority and influence to promote Smith and Bella Books in published interviews and through her "Dear Friends" letters. In the fall of 2001, Naiad published its final novels, bringing the company's total output to more than five hundred titles in multiple editions. On January 18, 2002, Barbara mailed her last "Dear Friends" letter and discussed plans for retirement.

Later that year, Barbara and Donna grew concerned as they watched Bella's output dwindle from its anticipated twenty-four new releases in 2001 to nine in 2002, and Bella's book distributor, the LPC Group, filed for Chapter 11 bankruptcy. Barbara, concerned about the press's long-term survival, sensed Bella Books was struggling as well. Smith had anticipated Orban would play a more active role in the press, but in reality, Orban's preference was to be a silent partner whose contributions were primarily financial and advisory, not operational. In Barbara's opinion, Smith loved the selection, reading and editing of books more than their promotion and, as a result, found herself overwhelmed by day-to-day responsibilities.[46]

Meanwhile, Linda Hill became involved with the business side of Bella Books because of her talent for web design and development. As a Naiad author who had created the company's website and served as its webmistress, Hill offered to provide the same service for Bella. At the time, Orban and Smith each owned fifty percent of the company. In recognition of Hill's contributions, they gave her a fifteen percent interest in the company, each woman contributing half from her shares. As she worked on the website, Hill grew frustrated by her inability to obtain copy about forthcoming books, so she contacted Orban. Soon, conversations about marketing books led to discussion of the company's future between Orban and new partner Hill, whose background was in business.[47]

Watching from a distance, Barbara and Donna worried that unless a significant change occurred, Bella would not survive. After years of building the company through close attention to detail and hands-on management, Barbara could not stand back and let it flounder. Inviting Orban to Florida for a weekend strategy session, Barbara proposed that Naiad's office manager, Becky Arbogast, answer Bella's phones and process and ship orders. After Orban returned to Michigan, Smith brought the books to Florida for shipping, but subsequently became difficult to reach. Alarmed, Barbara phoned Orban and declared all would be lost unless Smith was removed from the company. Concluding she must act, Orban arranged for a board of directors meeting to be held in her attorney's office on May 22, 2003. Hill flew in from her home in Massachusetts, and when Smith arrived the partners held a vote and removed Smith from the daily operations of the company. Convinced Barbara Grier had condoned the takeover, Smith, who went on to become the successful editor-in-chief of Bywater Books, never spoke with her again.[48]

When Barbara and Donna first began making plans to retire, they were unaware of Hill's interest in publishing, and she was hesitant to broach the subject because Barbara intimidated her. Hill's desire to become a publisher, however, became evident during the reorganization of Bella Books, and Barbara and Donna were eager to see her succeed. In addition to encouraging Hill to relocate Bella Books from Michigan to Naiad's former office and warehouse in Havana, Florida, they gave her the mailing list and sold Hill and her business partner, Terese Orban, the backlist at approximately five cents per volume. The latter gesture provided Bella Books with a solid financial foundation, generating immediate sales and enough cash flow to print new books. Initially setting out to replicate the Naiad model, Bella printed twenty-four books the first year and thirty-six the second. Hill purchased Orban's Bella Books stock outright in 2005 and Kelly Smith's remaining stock in 2007.[49]

* * *

Because they were impressed with Linda Hill's leadership of Bella Books, Barbara and Donna felt confident lesbians would continue having access to books that validated their lives, and they decided to retire in 2003, two years earlier than expected. As Barbara explained: "We have loved serving your book buying and video needs these last 31 years and we will miss you. It has been wonderful fun. Donna and I will still be around but we are devoting ourselves to building a new home on the Gulf of Mexico and enjoying the remaining years we have together." It was time, she said, "to do some of the other things we enjoy now...collect shells, walk on the beach...go to women's basketball games and other sports."[50]

The day Bella Books moved into the former Naiad Press headquarters was bittersweet for Hill. When reflecting on those years, she realized how much Barbara helped her by stepping aside: "She let me alone, she let me run my business, and as many times as she probably wanted to tell me what

I was doing wrong, she didn't." Instead, Barbara offered encouragement, told Hill what she was doing right, and served as a source of inspiration to the new publisher.[51]

In May 2003, authors, booksellers, editors, publishers and other industry professionals gathered at the Millennium Biltmore Hotel in Los Angeles for the fifteenth annual Lambda Literary Awards. Barbara, seated next to Naiad Press author Karin Kallmaker, appeared surprised when she heard her name announced as the recipient of the 2002 Lambda Literary Pioneer Award. Barbara Grier's commitment "to making lesbians in books visible," the emcee announced, had spanned "almost the entire modern gay movement, from her work with the Daughters of Bilitis newsletter to the founding of Naiad Press." In characteristic style, Barbara muttered to Kallmaker that she would have prepared appropriate remarks if she had known about the award in advance, and then proceeded to deliver a cogent and witty acceptance speech.[52]

CHAPTER FIFTEEN

~⊌

Loss of a Giant

"She thought of our life together as one big romantic adventure. She always said the three most important things in her life were me, the kitties and Naiad, in that order."
  –Donna McBride remembering Barbara Grier, 2014[1]

As someone who believed that "fun is fun, but work is vital," Barbara Grier adapted amazingly well to retirement, yet those who knew her and Donna McBride well understood retirement meant shifting gears, not inactivity. "I will remain busy until the day I fall off my perch," Barbara boasted, also noting Donna had "4,444 craft plans for the future." Almost immediately, Barbara became consumed with plans for Simple Solution, the beach home near Carrabelle, Florida, where they would spend their retirement years. She took great delight in making their home "a tasteful place of cozy, charming, modern, high-quality details."[2]

Barbara and Donna had never been ones to "attack people on the street and scream 'I am a lesbian' at them," but they did not hide their identity. After they began construction of Simple Solution, a man approached one of Donna's former library colleagues and said, "Have you seen that house those two queer women are building?" Unaware the woman's daughter was a lesbian, he was surprised when she replied, "What's queer about them?" Barbara and Donna encountered more overt hostility on weekends when they visited the construction site to check on progress. After some young men called out obscenities as they drove by, Donna yelled, "Come on, Barbara," jumped into her truck and followed their tormenters home.

When a young man and his mother came to the door, she explained, "We are lesbians, we are out lesbians, and we are not ashamed of it...There's no reason that you should be running by my house yelling obscenities at me...I don't have to put up with this." After that confrontation, it never happened again, affirming Barbara and Donna's conviction that people get away with harassment because they think their targets are afraid to confront them.[3]

As an LGBT pioneer, Barbara received numerous requests for interviews. While many of her stories remained constant, her perspective of herself mutated with the passage of time. As she reflected on some of her early efforts, she dismissed herself as "an uptight monster...longing for some kind of civil war to win our rights." While she consented to interview requests about lesbian publishing history, she responded dismissively to the suggestion that someone write her biography. "I know we did wonderful things," she admitted, but she doubted her story would be a best-seller. Ultimately, however, she consented because of her conviction that members of minorities must have a sense of their history or risk elimination.[4]

In retirement, Barbara and Donna embraced their passion for women's basketball which dated to the mid-1990s when they ordered tickets for an NCAA Women's Basketball Final Four Tournament in Minneapolis. After watching the University of Connecticut play the University of Tennessee, they returned home besotted with the Lady Vols. "We wear orange from head to toe, sing 'Rocky Top' (all the words) and follow Pat [Summitt] and her babies everywhere," Barbara exclaimed with pride.[5] Devoted to the team, they attended Southeastern Conference games within driving distance, made frequent treks to Knoxville, and became regular fixtures at Final Four tournaments.

Many people knew the public Barbara Grier, but fewer glimpsed the private woman. As her partner and lover, Donna well knew "she was a romantic at heart."[6] After Barbara left publishing, she became increasingly reclusive, preferring to spend her time with Donna, a few close friends and her beloved kitties. Indeed, cats remained near the center of her universe, with Barbara doting on the antics of Cisco, Max, Thornberry and Sparrow. "I have spent my silly life trying to rescue the world's cats, feeling they all would be best off in my house," she confessed.[7]

Sheila Jefferson, who met Barbara and Donna in the early 1980s, loved traveling with the couple because of Barbara's "ever-present curiosity and sense of wonder at new experiences." Like Jefferson, Helaine Harris appreciated Barbara's "joie de vivre" and ability to see the "positive side to everything." When Harris and her partner vacationed with Barbara and

Donna in Costa Rica, "Barbara was totally excited from dawn to dusk with every living creature from the sloths to the iguanas by the pool trying to eat our lunch."[8]

With their friends Claire McNab and Sheila Jefferson, Barbara and Donna attended numerous book conventions and women's Final Four basketball tournaments. They visited New York, Paris and Scotland, and welcomed the new millennium in Australia. "Barbara was as enchanted as a child" when they stood on their hotel's flat roof to watch spectacular fireworks over the Sydney Harbour Bridge. When McNab and Jefferson spent Christmas in Florida with Barbara and Donna, they received an elaborate printed menu listing three days of breakfast, lunch and dinner— all gourmet cooking. Barbara and Donna enjoyed cooking together, Jefferson recalled, but Barbara insisted on doing the cleanup after meals "because she LOVED cleaning up. She'd spend an hour or so in the kitchen humming away, just completely happy." She also took quiet satisfaction in doing laundry. Sometimes Barbara gave Jefferson a spontaneous bear hug, prompting McNab to declare: "Hands off my woman!" Barbara's hoot of laughter was "so individual, and so wholehearted, that strangers would involuntarily smile."[9]

A highlight of Barbara's final years occurred on September 5, 2008, during the brief window when same-sex marriage was legal in California. In a joyous double wedding ceremony that included close friends McNab and Jefferson, Barbara and Donna were married in Van Nuys, California.

In the last five years of her life, Barbara's body began to slow. As her brisk walk became a stroll, she attributed the increased tiredness to the heart problems that had kept her under a cardiologist's care for nearly a decade. When Barbara and Donna set out for Knoxville to attend the first Lady Vols game of the 2011-12 season, they stopped in Tallahassee to consult with Barbara's physician. Other than a little arrhythmia, nothing seemed amiss, but because she complained of pain in her abdomen, the doctor decided to do some blood work upon her return to Florida.[10]

After quietly observing her seventy-eighth birthday at home on November 4, 2011, Barbara informed Donna she did not feel well and thought she might be having a heart attack. Donna immediately called the ambulance, and soon Barbara was transported by helicopter to a hospital in Tallahassee. After an MRI revealed cancerous spots on her lungs and liver, physicians determined the cancer was too widespread to treat. Barbara died six days later, on November 10, 2011, with Donna at her side. In keeping with her wishes, Barbara was cremated so her ashes could be spread in her beloved Bahamas. There was no funeral service.

* * *

Without a doubt, Barbara Grier had touched the lives of many, both positively and negatively. Some who had felt the sting of her words in the 1970s, 1980s and 1990s realized with time that "her mercurial nature was probably fed by those much bigger battles" that she fought on behalf of lesbian publishing. "Whoever the 'real' Barbara Grier is," novelist and longtime *Ladder* volunteer Vicki P. McConnell reflected after her death, "I am now and always shall be grateful to the very core of my heart for her dawn-to-dusk dedication in working to publish and distribute my four novels, and the hundreds of titles Naiad eventually brought into print." Like Barbara, Naiad author Diane Salvatore was a Scorpio. That knowledge helped her to understand the characteristics contributing to Barbara's success: "she was fiercely competitive, she liked to win, and she was fueled 24/7 by passion for what she was doing." When filmmaker Nicole Conn reflected on Barbara's passing, she thought of "how difficult it is to do ANYTHING in our community because of the limited financing available to lesbian artists." Barbara refused to let such obstacles deter her from ensuring that any lesbian, anywhere, could walk into a bookshop and find herself reflected in print. Naiad author Therese Szymanski credited Barbara with saving "countless lives through Naiad by making lesbians the world over know that they were not (and are not) alone." Despite their earlier differences, author and editor Katherine V. Forrest recognized the significance of Barbara's passing to lesbian culture: "With her forceful personality she was a mover and shaker whose impact on our world of books and lesbian literature can scarcely be overstated. We have lost a giant."[11]

The New York Times, Los Angeles Times, The Washington Post and many other newspapers, magazines and blogs acknowledged Barbara's passing. Heralded as "a pathbreaking publisher who challenged mainstream prejudices to make literature by and about lesbians widely available in the United States and abroad," Barbara was recognized as a risk-taker and as "the premier editor of two generations of American lesbian writers." Contributors to *The Advocate* captured her personality as well as her contributions: "Irascible and cantankerous, with a dry and acid wit, she could make a sailor blush and have you laughing till you cried." Uniformly, those who memorialized her recognized Barbara's passion, determination and commitment. "Barbara Grier was fearless," declared Chicagoan Midge Stocker, the former publisher of Third Side Press. "Her passion was getting lesbian literature into the hands of as many people as possible, because she believed that a climate in which every lesbian could safely live openly would be created by every one of us living openly." "She refused to accept no as an answer," concurred Toni Armstrong, Jr., the former editor of *Hot Wire: The Journal of Women's Music and Culture*. "Barbara Grier, through sheer force of will and commitment, pushed for political rights, respect for early lesbian writers and their 'pulp fiction,' and modern-day lesbian visibility through books…She was a great example of walking the talk."[12]

* * *

From her teenage years, Barbara Grier believed in living propaganda. She thought that if all lesbians and gays lived openly and matter-of-factly, society would be forced to accept them. With that end in mind, she single-mindedly devoted herself to a life of print-based activism. As someone who came out as a lesbian in the 1940s, before the homophile and feminist movements emerged, Barbara lacked their sensitivities. As the politically charged story of her life reveals, late-twentieth-century lesbian publishing was fraught with idealistic expectations, socioeconomic tensions, generational conflict and conflicting goals.

While Barbara was not well-equipped to navigate the intricacies of feminist politics, she and Donna knew how to increase lesbian visibility by conducting business pragmatically, strategically and systematically. Naiad's success prompted some critics to accuse them of not giving enough back monetarily to the LGBT community. In reality, Barbara had given back throughout most of her adult life. The pages of stories, essays and reviews she contributed to the gay and lesbian press in the 1950s and 1960s validated lesbian and gay lives and reassured closeted and isolated individuals that they were not alone. Her comprehensive bibliographies of lesbian literature played a major role in preserving lesbian pulps from obscurity. Aware the correspondence she conducted beginning in the 1950s had long-term historical significance, Barbara not only preserved it but also encouraged other activists to deposit their papers in archives and libraries for future use by LGBT scholars. She fervently believed that members of minorities must have a sense of their history or risk elimination.

With Donna McBride as an equal partner, Barbara Grier devoted three decades to publishing books that validated lesbian lives. "Making people and books meet," she reflected. "What a joyous thing to do… mak[ing] people want to read. That's about as much fun as being God."[13]

ACKNOWLEDGMENTS

Our images of Barbara Grier depend on when we knew her and under what circumstances. I first encountered her in 2005 when I was doing research for a biography of Jeannette Howard Foster. Barbara was one of the few people remaining who had known Foster personally, and I thought she could breathe life into her story. I was correct. Barbara was passionate about lesbian literature and biography, and she refused to let an email grow cold. She took great delight in divulging what she knew and asked for nothing in return. She was enthusiastic, supportive, patient when I misunderstood a point, and generous in making connections. Unknown to me at the time, I was experiencing what it was like to correspond with Gene Damon in the late 1950s and early 1960s.

As a former librarian, and as a historian of women, I share Barbara Grier's belief in the empowering role print culture can play in the lives of women and social movements. I have explored this theme in my previous books, *Cultural Crusaders and the Quest for Women's Equality*, *Sex Radicals and the Quest for Women's Equality*, and *Sex Variant Woman: The Life of Jeannette Howard Foster*. My goal as Barbara's biographer is to present her life as objectively as possible, acknowledging its positive as well as its negative dimensions. In trying to navigate the legends that have grown up around her and the strong, and sometimes emotional, reactions I have encountered in those who knew her, I have combed through thousands of pages of archival material and conducted more than one hundred hours of interviews with people who knew her. Deciphering Barbara's story is further complicated by the myths that she perpetuated about herself, individuals she knew and the company she co-founded.

Because Barbara Grier lived life on her own terms and was not afraid of controversy, she provoked strong reactions among many who interacted with her. Most of the authors, publishers and bookstore personnel with whom I talked had at least one Barbara Grier story. In later years, as some revered her as their lesbian foremother, others found it difficult to forget her willingness to distort the truth and her penchant for making decisions based on the ends rather than on the means. The controversies she engendered by the "theft" of *The Ladder* and sale of excerpts from *Lesbian Nuns: Breaking Silence* would have destroyed a less formidable woman.

This book could not have been written without the assistance and support of many people. My first debt of gratitude is to Donna J. McBride for her efforts to help me see multiple sides of the woman who was her partner for four decades. She patiently answered numerous questions, gave me access to Barbara's collection of Jane Rule correspondence, and provided access to Barbara's copies of *The Ladder*, Naiad Press publications and photographs of Barbara's family and their movement activities. I also am deeply grateful to Barbara's sisters, Diane Grier and Penni Grier Martin, for sharing stories and photographs that shed light on her early years.

Throughout the research and writing of this book, I often found myself wishing I could email or phone Barbara Grier with questions. Fortunately, she had a keen sense of history and from an early age recognized the importance of saving letters, publications and images documenting gay and lesbian life in the second half of the twentieth century. A prolific correspondent, her words survive in the thousands of letters she wrote as well as in a number of published and recorded interviews. Thank you to Maida Tilchen, Manuela Soares, Marcia Gallo, Karin Kallmaker and M.J. Lowe for having the foresight to conduct and preserve audio and video interviews with Barbara, and to all of the individuals who have had the foresight to donate their papers to archives and libraries. Our history is richer for it.

Much of the information in this book is drawn from archival documentation, and I wish to express my appreciation to the archivists and librarians who have collected, preserved and made accessible the primary source materials that make it possible to write gay and lesbian history. It was a pleasure to work with archivist Tim Wilson, of the San Francisco Public Library, whose in-depth knowledge of the Grier-Naiad Press Collection and related collections of papers eased my work. He never tired of my numerous requests, and always went the extra mile in resolving questions.

Many other archivists and librarians also provided invaluable assistance. I would like to acknowledge Peter Berg, Michigan State University; Marjorie Bryer, GLBT Historical Society; Tonya Crawford, University of Missouri-Kansas City Archives; Matt Dilworth and Marcia Sloan, Indiana University East Library; Deb Edel, Lesbian Herstory Archives; Steve Fisher, University of Denver; Sally Harrower, Muriel Spark Archive; Stuart L. Hinds, University of Missouri-Kansas City; Stephanie Iser, Kansas City Public Library; Christina Moretta, San Francisco Public Library; Lindsey O'Brien, Newberry Library; Kerry Schork, University of Maryland Special Collections Department; Loni Shibuyama, ONE National Gay and Lesbian Archives; Saundra Taylor, Indiana University; Lisa Vecoli, Tretter Collection, University of Minnesota; Shaun Wilson and Liana Zhou, Kinsey Institute for Research in Sex, Gender, and Reproduction; Erwin Wodarczak and Candice Bjur, University of British Columbia Archives; and Kelly Wooten, Sallie Bingham Center for Women's History and Culture. Additionally, I am much obliged to staff at the June L. Mazer Archives, the Library of Congress Manuscripts Division, the University of Oregon Special Collections and Archives, the New York Public Library Manuscripts and Archives Division, and the Schlesinger Library for their assistance with my research.

Numerous women and men generously shared a wealth of information about lesbian literature, the homophile movement, the Daughters of Bilitis, lesbian-feminist politics and publishing, and the Women in Print movement. They include Nancy K. Bereano, Jane Cholmeley, Jeanne Córdova, Honey Lee Cottrell, Margaret (Peg) Cruikshank, the late Rosemary Curb, Kelli Dunham, Elana Dykewomon, Maureen Duffy, Julie Enszer, Lillian Faderman, Katherine V. Forrest, Marcia Gallo, Billy Glover, Pat Gozemba, Helaine Harris, Fay Jacobs, Karla Jay, Tom Jones, William B. Kelley, Marie J. Kuda, Joyce M. Latham, Marie E. Logan, Lee Lynch, Donna J. McBride, Nancy Manahan, Ruth Mountaingrove, Priscilla Royal, Gayle Rubin, Carol Seajay, Betsy Schmidt, Martha Shelley, Sherry Thomas, Maida Tilchen, Evelyn Torton Beck, Diana Turner, Ann Weldy, and others who did not wish to be identified by name. Additionally, I am grateful to Sheila Jefferson and Claire McNab for sharing stories of their friendship with Barbara, and to Pamela Rust for discussing what it was like to be one of Barbara's pen friends in the 1960s.

For information about the pulp fiction market of the 1950s and 1960s, I wish to recognize Victor Banis, Ann Bannon, Robin Cohen, Chris Eckhoff, Katherine V. Forrest, Earl Kemp, and Maida Tilchen. Linda

Bryant (Charis), Linda Bubon (Women & Children First), Joan Denman (Rubyfruit), Dawn Oftedahl (Amazon), Simone Wallace (Sisterhood), Jane Troxell (Lammas), Deacon Maccubbin (Lambda Rising), Richard Labonté (A Different Light), and Jim Marks shared valuable insights into the world of gay and feminist bookstores. I also am grateful to Judy Richter, Gloria Barnes, and Paula Susemichael for sharing their memories of Harriet Clare's Dreams and Swords Bookstore in Indianapolis.

I am grateful to the employees, editors, authors and others associated with Naiad Press for sharing their stories. My thanks to Becky Arbogast, Jackie Calhoun, Christi Cassidy, Nicole Conn, Candis Creekmore, Katherine V. Forrest, Sue Gambill, Linda Hill, Alex Jaegar, Karin Kallmaker, Rosemary Keefe Curb, Dolores Klaich, Lee Lynch, Vicki P. McConnell, Nancy Manahan, Marianne K. Martin, Elisabeth Nonas, Rita Mae Reese, Roberta Rostorfer-Stocker, Kristen Rouse, Diane Salvatore, Sarah Schulman, Elizabeth Sims, Kelly Smith, Sheila Ortiz Taylor, Darlene Vendenga and Amanda Kyle Williams.

Barbara's story is enriched by photographs provided by Ann Bannon, Joan E. Biren, Linda Bryant, Katherine V. Forrest, Jane Kogan, Lee Lynch, Donna McBride, Nancy Manahan, Penni Grier Martin, Pamela R., and Pat Tong. I also am grateful for permission to reprint images from the Robert Giard Collection, Ruth Mountaingrove Papers, and the Barbara Gittings and Kay Tobin Lahusen Gay History Papers.

A Faculty Research Grant from Indiana University East not only supported travel to archival repositories, but also enabled me to hire an undergraduate student research assistant. I am thankful to Emily O'Brien for the enthusiasm she brought to the project and for her excellent research skills as she skimmed thousands of pages of documentation. I am especially grateful to I.U. East colleagues Katherine P. Frank, Ross Alexander and Denise Bullock for their interest in the project and their enthusiastic support. Additionally, I would like to acknowledge Shelley Grosjean, a graduate student at the University of Oregon, for her assistance with the Lee Lynch Papers, and Andrew L. McBride, a graduate student at the University of Michigan, for his assistance with Detroit City Directories.

Throughout the research and writing of this book, I have benefited from the support of friends and colleagues. I would like to extend a very special thank you to Carol McCafferty for her amazing ability to retrieve information, much-needed technological expertise, and careful reading of the full manuscript. Maida Tilchen's enthusiastic support, resourcefulness, and constructive critique of each chapter kept me going when I became discouraged. I also am deeply grateful to others who have read portions or all of the text and provided important corrections and excellent suggestions. They include Robin Cohen, Danielle DeMuth, Julie Enszer, Katherine V. Forrest and Donna McBride. I also wish to express my appreciation to Don Weise and Virginia Dodge Fielder, whose editorial pens have enhanced the final product, and to the many others involved in the production process.

Finally, I would like to recognize Deb Wehman for her steadfast support and encouragement throughout the writing of this biography. Together, we visited numerous archives and met many amazing and accomplished women. Deb listened thoughtfully to chapters and made helpful suggestions. Most of all, she put up with the hundreds of hours I spent locked away in my study. Thank you for joining me on this journey.

TIMELINE

1933. November 4: Barbara Glycine Grier is born to Philip S. Grier and Dorothy Vernon Black Grier in Cincinnati, Ohio.

1939. July 6: Barbara's sister, Diane Grier, is born in Detroit, Michigan.

1940. July 3: Donna J. McBride is born.

1943. October 3: Barbara's sister, Penni Grier, is born in Colorado Springs. By this time, Philip Grier has abandoned his wife and family.

Ca. 1946. Barbara's parents divorce and her father marries Marie Upp. Barbara comes out to her mother after she does research on homosexuality at the Detroit Public Library.

1948-50. Dorothy Grier and her three daughters live in Colorado Springs. Barbara has numerous crushes on girls, reads *The Well of Loneliness*, and meets a woman named Peggy, who tells her about Gale Wilhelm's *We Too Are Drifting*. Barbara begins searching used bookstores for lesbian and gay books and starts building her personal library.

1950. The Mattachine Foundation (later known as the Mattachine Society) is founded in Los Angeles by a group of gay men.

Tereska Torrès, *Women's Barracks*, is published.

1951. Donald Webster Cory, *The Homosexual in America*, is published.

Helen L. Burkhardt (Bennett) comes out to herself as a lesbian while she is working as a library assistant at the Kansas City Public Library in Missouri.

Dorothy Grier and her daughters move from Dodge City to Kansas City, Kansas, and Barbara graduates from Wyandotte High School.

1952. February 22: Barbara enters into a relationship with Helen Bennett, sixteen years her senior.

September: Helen Bennett takes a leave of absence from her position at the Kansas City Public Library and enrolls in the University of Denver School of Librarianship. Barbara moves with Helen to Denver and takes a clerical position at *The Denver Post*.

October 14: Helen Bennett's brother, Harold Burkhardt, is killed in a train-car accident.

1953. January: *ONE* magazine begins publication.

Summer: Helen Bennett graduates from the University of Denver School of Librarianship and accepts a library position in Denver.

1954. Barbara Grier and Helen Bennett move from Denver to Kansas City, Missouri, to be near Helen's parents.

1955. January-February: *Mattachine Review* begins publication.

September: Eight women hold the first meeting of the Daughters of Bilitis in San Francisco.

1956. September: Barbara reads a prepublication notice for Jeannette Howard Foster's *Sex Variant Women in Literature*, learns Foster lives in Kansas City, and telephones her. By this time, Barbara has collected nearly one hundred gay and lesbian books.

October: The Daughters of Bilitis begin a monthly publication, *The Ladder*. Phyllis Lyon edits *The Ladder* using the pseudonym Ann Ferguson. Del Martin is president of the DOB.

1957. March: The Lesbiana column (notices of books with lesbian content) first appears in *The Ladder*.

Spring: Barbara subscribes to *The Ladder*.

August: Barbara's first letter to *The Ladder* appears, attributed to "G.D., Kansas City, Kansas." She adopts the pseudonym Gene Damon. During the remainder of *The Ladder*'s existence, she has numerous letters published under multiple pseudonyms.

September: Barbara's first book review appears in *The Ladder*.

November: Barbara's first short story, "Chance," appears in *The Ladder* 2 (November 1957): 8-10, attributed to Gene Damon.

1958. March: Barbara reads a copy of Marion Zimmer Bradley's *Astra's Tower, Special Leaflet #2*, a checklist of lesbian literature, and contacts Bradley to offer assistance in compiling the next edition.

August: Barbara's essay, "Lesbian Marriage," appears in *The Ladder* 2 (August 1958): 12-13, attributed to Gene Damon.

September: The New York chapter of the Daughters of Bilitis (DOB) holds its first meeting.

November: Helen Bennett, using the pseudonym Lee Stuart, and Barbara co-author "The Repressed Lesbian," *The Ladder* 3 (November

1958): 18-20. In subsequent issues, they co-authored such pieces as "Transvestism in Women," *The Ladder* 3 (February 1959): 11-13 and "Renée Vivien, Forgotten Lesbian Poet," *The Ladder* 3 (May 1959): 12-13.

Fall: Barbara begins corresponding with DOB member Barbara Gittings.

1959. February: Barbara's review essay, "The Lesbian in Contemporary Literature," appears in *The Ladder* 3 (February 1959): 16-18, attributed to the pseudonym Lennox Strang. It leads to an annual review of lesbian literature, which she continues until the magazine ceases.

March: Marion Zimmer Bradley self-publishes *Astra's Tower, Special Leaflet #3*, a checklist of lesbian literature. Barbara, along with Jeannette Howard Foster, prepared a number of the reviews.

1960. The Daughters of Bilitis holds its first national convention in San Francisco.

May: Gene Damon's byline first appears on *The Ladder*'s Lesbiana column.

Gene Damon's poem, "Iniquity" (dedicated to Gale Wilhelm), appears in *The Ladder* 4 (May 1960): 12.

July. Del Martin becomes editor of *The Ladder*.

1961. October: Barbara subscribes to *Mattachine Review*.

1962. The Daughters of Bilitis holds its second national convention in Hollywood, California.

1963. March: Barbara Gittings becomes editor of *The Ladder*.

Summer: Barbara Gittings and Kay Lahusen visit Barbara in Kansas City.

1964. Jess Stearn publishes *The Grapevine*, an exposé of lesbianism. The Daughters of Bilitis holds its third national convention in New York City.

Barbara begins correspondence with Jane Rule and with Pamela Rust.

August 20: Barbara meets Jane Rule and Helen Sonthoff when they travel through Kansas City.

1965. Barbara begins correspondence with May Sarton and Jody Shotwell.

Tangents begins publication, with Don Slater as editor.

1966. The National Organization for Women is founded.

February 19-20: The National Planning Conference of Homophile Organizations meets in Kansas City. Barbara meets Del Martin, Phyllis Lyon and Frank Kameny.

Summer: The North American Conference of Homophile Organizations holds its first meeting.

August: The Daughters of Bilitis holds its national convention in San Francisco. Shirley Willer is elected president.

October 28: Philip S. Grier and Dorothy Vernon Grier remarry in Kansas City, Missouri.

November: Helen Sanders becomes editor of *The Ladder*. Barbara changes the Lesbiana column from an annotated list to a narrative review format.

1967. Barbara phones the Kansas City Public Library and speaks to Donna McBride.

The Daughters of Bilitis publishes *The Lesbian in Literature: A Bibliography*, compiled by Gene Damon and Lee Stuart.

July. Barbara, using the pseudonym Gene Damon, becomes assistant editor, poetry and fiction, for *The Ladder*.

1968. August: The Daughters of Bilitis meets in Denver, where Rita Laporte becomes president and Gene Damon is appointed editor of *The Ladder*.

1969. June 28: Stonewall Riot, New York City.

1970. Barbara's essay, "The Least of These: The Minority Whose Screams Haven't Yet Been Heard," appears in Robin Morgan's anthology *Sisterhood Is Powerful!*

July: *The Ladder* separates from the Daughters of Bilitis.

1971. Donna volunteers to help Barbara with *The Ladder*.

1972. January 28: Barbara and Donna start their life together.

Spring: Rita Laporte ceases involvement with *The Ladder*.

April: Barbara's mother, Dorothy Vernon Grier, dies.

August/September: *The Ladder* ceases publication with Volume 16, number 11 and 12.

1973. Helaine Harris and Cynthia Gair found Women in Distribution (WIND).

September. Barbara and Donna move to a home, 20 Rue Jacob Acres, eight miles south of Bates City, Missouri.

1974. March: Anyda Marchant chooses Naiad Press as the name of her publishing venture.

June: Marchant mentions the possibility of making Barbara vice president and general manager of Naiad Press when she files incorporation paperwork.

August: Naiad Press publishes its first book, *The Latecomer*, by Anyda Marchant, writing as Sarah Aldridge. Marchant decides to delay filing incorporation paperwork, and raises the possibility of publishing a new edition of *The Lesbian in Literature* with money from the sale of *The Latecomer*.

September: Lesbian Writers Conference, Chicago. Barbara is functioning as Naiad's unpaid general manager.

1975. Naiad Press publishes the second edition of *The Lesbian in Literature: A Bibliography*.

November: Barbara and Donna attend the Gay Academic Union meeting in New York City.

1976. Naiad Press publishes *Lesbiana: Book Reviews from The Ladder* by Barbara Grier, also known as Gene Damon.

Diana Press publishes *The Lesbians Home Journal: Stories from The Ladder*, *Lesbian Lives: Biographies of Women from The Ladder*, and *The Lavender Herring: Lesbian Essays from The Ladder*.

May 28: Anyda Marchant files incorporation paperwork for Naiad Press in Delaware. The four-member Board of Directors included Marchant, Muriel Crawford, Barbara Grier, and Donna McBride.

July: The first Women in Print conference is held at Camp Harriet Harding, southwest of Omaha, Nebraska. Barbara asks the Iowa City Women's Press to print Naiad Press books.

December: Barbara's father, Philip S. Grier, dies.

1977. Barbara and Donna put 20 Rue Jacob Acres on the market.

September: Naiad Press begins paying Barbara a salary of one hundred dollars per month.

1978. Barbara and Donna move to a home on Weatherby Lake, just north of Kansas City, which they christen Llangollen.

1979. Barbara speaks at the National Women's Studies Association when it meets in Lawrence, Kansas.

July: WIND files for bankruptcy.

1980. June: Donna McBride moves to Florida as associate director of the Leon County Public Library, in Tallahassee.

September: Barbara joins Donna in Florida.

1981. Naiad Press publishes *The Lesbian in Literature*, third edition, with Barbara Grier's name on the cover.

Barbara and Donna attend the National Women's Studies Association meeting in Storrs, Connecticut.

October. Barbara begins full-time work for Naiad Press. Barbara and Donna attend the second Women in Print conference in Washington, D.C.

1982. Donna McBride begins working for Naiad full-time.

1983. Naiad publishes *Curious Wine*. Author Katherine V. Forrest becomes an editor for Naiad Press.

1984. Barbara and Donna hire Naiad's first full-time employee.

Naiad begins developing new genres in lesbian literature: lesbian mysteries, westerns, science fiction, and erotic fiction.

1985. Spring: Naiad publishes *Lesbian Nuns: Breaking Silence*.

May 29: Third Women in Print conference convenes at University of California, Berkeley.

June issue of *Forum* magazine features three excerpts from *Lesbian Nuns: Breaking Silence*.

1987. October 11: Barbara and Donna take part in the Second National March on Washington for Gay and Lesbian Rights.

Naiad publishes an original novel by Jane Rule, *Memory Board*.

1992. Lambda Literary Foundation recognizes Barbara and Donna with its Publisher's Service Award.

Naiad begins publishing anthologies, with a majority offering erotic stories.

1993. Book-of-the-Month Club and Quality Paperback choose Diane Salvatore's *Love, Zena Beth* as a dual selection.

April 25: Barbara and Donna participate in the Third National March on Washington for Gay and Lesbian Rights.

1994. April: Anyda Marchant announces her intention to dissolve Naiad Press.

1995. Katherine V. Forrest leaves her position as supervising editor for Naiad Press.

February 22: Anyda Marchant and Muriel Crawford tender their resignations as officers of Naiad Press.

1999. Naiad publishes thirty-two titles when efforts to sell the press stall.

2001. Naiad Press publishes its final books.

2003. May: Barbara receives the Pioneer Award from Lambda Literary. Barbara and Donna retire.

2006. May 13: Barbara and Donna move to "Simple Solution," the house they built at Hidden Beaches, Carrabelle, Florida.

2008. September 5: Barbara and Donna are married in Van Nuys, California, along with close friends Claire McNab and Sheila Jefferson.

2011. November 4: Barbara celebrates her seventy-eighth birthday at home, then goes to a hospital in Tallahassee, where she dies on November 10.

ENDNOTES TO CHAPTERS

CITATIONS FOR FREQUENTLY CITED COLLECTIONS

Barbara Gittings and Kay Tobin Lahusen Gay History Papers and Photographs, Mss. Col. 6397, Manuscripts and Archives Division, The New York Public Library.

Barbara Grier-Naiad Press Collection, GLC 30, The James C. Hormel Gay and Lesbian Center, San Francisco Public Library.

Eric Garber Papers, GLBT Historical Society, San Francisco.

Florence "Conrad" Jaffy Papers, GLC 33, The James C. Hormel Gay and Lesbian Center, San Francisco Public Library.

Frank Kameny Papers, MSS 85340, Manuscript Division, Library of Congress, Washington, D.C.

Jane Rule fonds, University of Britsh Columbia Archives, Vancouver.

Jean Swallow Papers, GLC 50, The James C. Hormel Gay and Lesbian Center, San Francisco Public Library.

Karla Jay Papers, Mss. Col. 1554, Manuscripts an Archives Division, The New York Public Library.

Katherine V. Forrest Papers, The James C. Hormel Gay and Lesbian Center, San Francisco Public Library.

Lee Lynch Papers, Coll.259, Special Collections and University Archives, University of Oregon, Eugene, Oregon.

Lesbian Herstory Archives-Daughters of Bilitis Video Project, Lesbian Herstory Archives, Brooklyn, New York. The original videotapes are also available online at http://herstories.prattsils.org/omeka/collections/show/36.

Lynn Londier Papers, GLC 1, The James C. Hormel Gay and Lesbian Center, San Francisco Public Library.

The Marie J. Kuda Collection, The Kinsey Institute, Indiana University, Bloomington, Indiana.

Phyllis Lyon-Del Martin Papers, GLBT Historical Society, San Francisco.

Tee A. Corinne Papers, Coll. 263, Special Collections and University Archives, University of Oregon, Eugene, Oregon.

PROLOGUE

1. Barbara Grier to Dear Friends, July 24, 1983, shared with the author by Donna McBride; Gayle Rubin, interview with the author, June 10, 2012.
2. Grier to Jane Rule, August 11, 1985, Jane Rule fonds, Box 30.
3. Cain, Paul D. *Leading the Parade: Conversations with America's Most Influential Lesbians and Gays* (Lanham, Md.: Scarecrow Press, 2002), 150. Nancy K. Bereano discussed Naiad's quality and Barbara's response in Bereano, phone interview with the author, January 23, 2012.
4. Jane Rule to Barbara Grier, January 4, 1985, Jane Rule fonds, Box 30.
5. Cain, *Leading the Parade*, 145.
6. Maida Tilchen, interview with Barbara Grier, Bates City, Missouri, June 1977, shared with the author by Tilchen; Carol Seajay, who described Barbara as an "opportunist," thought she did "unscrupulous things for all the right reasons," Seajay, interview with the author, January 8, 2012.
7. Manuela Soares interview with Barbara Grier, November 27, 1987, Lesbian Herstory Archives-Daughters of Bilitis Video Project.

CHAPTER ONE

1. Sandy Boucher, *Heartwomen: An Urban Feminist's Odyssey Home* (New York: Harper & Row, 1982), 229.

2. Mrs. Doris Lyles [Pseud.], "My Daughter Is a Lesbian," *The Ladder* 2 (July 1958): 4-5.

3. *1933-34 Williams' Cincinnati Directory* (Cincinnati: The Williams Directory Co., 1933), 667; Barbara Glycine Grier, November 4, 1933, State of Ohio, Office of Vital Statistics, Certification of Birth #193308067; Detroit City directories, 1931/32, 1937, 1940; "Michigan Board," *The Druggist Circular* (September 1924), 371. Barbara was born at Doctor's Hospital, Cincinnati.

4. Barbaretta Niven immigrated to the United States in 1866 and reportedly married John Brown. See Barbara [*sic*] Niven, listed in the William Niven household, 1870 federal population census, Erwin, Steuben County, New York; and Retta Brown, listed in the 1892 New York State population census, Hornellsville, New York, Ward 3.

5. Mabel Nivens [*sic*], Della Niven, Internet Broadway Database (www.ibdb.com), accessed September 20, 2013; William Niven household, 1900 federal population census, Manhattan, New York, 1900. According to the 1900 federal population census for Louisville, Kentucky, the traveling troupe was residing with Elijah Davis. Barbara Grier claimed the actor David Niven as a distant relative, but it could not be verified.

6. Retta [*sic*] Brown, 1920 federal population census, Detroit, Wayne County, Michigan, Ward 1.

7. While still in New York, Strang practiced law, preached in the Baptist church, and served as postmaster of Chautauqua County until 1843, when he lost his position. See James Jesse Strang, *The Diary of James Jesse Strang, Transcribed, Introduced, and Annotated* (East Lansing: Michigan State University Press, 1961); "Who was James Jesse Strang?" The Society for Strang Studies, http://www.strangstudies.org/James_Jesse_Strang/ (accessed July 9, 2013).

8. *Ibid.* The David and Clara Grier family is listed in the 1880 federal population census for Carmel, Eaton County, Michigan.

9. Philip Grier graduated from high school in 1918 and served briefly in World War I before enrolling at Ferris Institute (now Ferris State University). Philip and Iva Grier Divorce Record, Docket No. 187764, Michigan Department of Health. Filed October 1,

1930, granted April 2, 1931. Dorothy Grier told her daughters about helping Iva Grier and her sons.

10. Mrs. Doris Lyles [Pseud.], "My Daughter is a Lesbian," 5.

11. Barbara Grier was named for her paternal grandmother, Glycine Tower Grier and her maternal great-grandmother, Barbaretta Niven Brown.

12. Barbara Grier to Jane Rule, March 26, 1967, Jane Rule fonds, Box 29.

13. Grier to Rule, October 20, 1966, Jane Rule fonds, Box 29; Manuela Soares interview with Barbara Grier, November 1987, Lesbian Herstory Archives-Daughters of Bilitis Video Project.

14. Diane Grier, interview with author, May 5, 2012; Manuela Soares interview with Barbara Grier.

15. Boucher, *Heartwomen*, 222.

16. Grier to Rule, July 27, 1967, Jane Rule fonds, Box 29. The author was not able to locate documentation of Dorothy Grier's first marriage to or divorce from Philip Grier.

17. Grier to Anyda Marchant and Muriel Crawford, October 15, 1975, Grier-Naiad Press Collection, GLC 30, Box 1, Anyda Marchant folder, San Francisco Public Library; "I Can't See Myself Being Anywhere But in This Relationship," [interview with Barbara Grier and Donna McBride], *Partners: The Newsletter for Gay and Lesbian Couples* (October 1989), shared with the author by Donna McBride.

18. Barbara Grier, "The Garden Variety Lesbian," in *The Coming Out Stories*, edited by Julia Penelope Stanley and Susan J. Wolfe (Watertown, Mass.: Persephone Press, 1980), 236.

19. Barbara Grier to Lee Lynch, December 13, 1970, Lee Lynch Papers, Box 18.

20. Gene Damon, "When it Changed, or, Growing up Gay in America with the Help of Literature," Barbara Grier-Naiad Press Collection, GLC 30, Box 1, Beth Hodges folder.

21. Grier to Rule, May 20, 1967, Jane Rule fonds, Box 29.

22. Grier to Rule, May 20, 1967, Jane Rule fonds, Box 29.

23. Boucher, *Heartwomen*, 215; Grier to Rule, December 23, 1966, July 27, 1967, Jane Rule fonds, Box 29; Manuela Soares interview with Barbara Grier, November 1987, Lesbian Herstory Archives-Daughters of Bilitis Video Project.

24. For more information, see Donna Penn, "The Meanings of Lesbianism in Post-War America," *Gender & History* 3 (August 1991): 190-203; Craig M. Loftin, "Unacceptable Mannerisms: Gender Anxieties, Homosexual Activism, and Swish in the United

States, 1945-1965," *Journal of Social History* 40 (Spring 2007), 577-596; and Randolph W. Baxter, "Homo-Hunting in the Early Cold War: Senator Kenneth Wherry and the Homophobic Side of McCarthyism," *Nebraska History* 84 (September 2003): 118-132. Findings about male homosexuality are from Alfred. Kinsey, et al., *Sexual Behavior in the Human Male* (Philadelphia: W. B. Saunders, 1948), p. 651.

25. Grier, "The Garden Variety Lesbian," *The Coming Out Stories*, 238.

26. Grier to Lyndal Cowan, March 25, 1976, Eric Garber Papers, Box 6.

27. Grier recounts the theft of *The Well of Loneliness* in Grier to Tee Corinne, January 3, 1986, Grier-Naiad Press Collection, GLC 30, ADD Box 16. Her lifelong fascination with Gale Wilhelm is recounted in Grier, "What Happened to Gale Wilhelm?" Phyllis Lyon-Del Martin Papers, Box 12. For more on her early love of books, see Gene Damon, "When It All Hanged," Grier-Naiad Press Collection, GLC 30, Box 1, Beth Hodges folder, and transcript of Maida Tilchen interview with Barbara Grier, [June 1977], in the author's possession.

28. Grier to Lee Lynch, July 15, 1970, Lee Lynch Papers, Box 18.

29. Ray Lewis White, *Gore Vidal* (New York: Twayne Publishers, 1968), 49-50; Isabel Bolton, *The Christmas Tree* (New York: Charles Scribner's Sons, 1949), 211. Taber divorced her husband in 1946 and moved to Southbury, Connecticut, where she shared a house with Eleanor Sanford Mayer, a childhood friend who often was mistakenly identified as her sister.

30. Meaker's pen names included Ann Aldrich, M.E. Kerr, Mary James, Vin Packer and Laura Winston. Yvonne Keller, "Was it Right to Love Her Brother's Wife So Passionately? Lesbian Pulp Novels and U.S. Lesbian Identity, 1950-1965," *American Quarterly* 57.2 (2005): 385-410. *Women's Barracks* sold 4 million copies in the United States. See "Tereska Torrès," *The Daily Telegraph*, September 26, 2012.

31. Grier to Rule, September 27, 1966, Jane Rule fonds, Box 29.

32. Grier to Rule, October 23, 1964. Jane Rule fonds, Box 29; Donna McBride, email to the author, December 20, 2012.

33. Grier, "The Garden Variety Lesbian," p. 238; Penni Grier Martin, email to the author, May 10, 2012.

34. Grier to Rule, June 30, 1967, Jane Rule fonds, Box 29.

35. Karin Kallmaker and M.J. Lowe, interview with Barbara Grier and Donna McBride, December 11-12, 2006. A transcript is in the

author's possession. See also Boucher, *Heartwomen*, 229; Grier to Rule, May 20, 1967, Jane Rule fonds, Box 29.

CHAPTER TWO

1. Barbara Grier to Del Martin, February 22, 1962, Phyllis Lyon-Del Martin Papers, Box 11.
2. Manuela Soares interview with Barbara Grier, November 1987, Lesbian Herstory Archives-Daughters of Bilitis Video Project.
3. Helen was born in Iowa to Charles and Frances Burkhart on July 30, 1917. She is enumerated with her parents in the 1930 federal population census in Zearing, Story County, Iowa. In 1940, she is listed as a lodger in Washita Township, Custer County, Oklahoma. Grier discussed Harold Burkhart's sexuality in Grier to Jane Rule, December 1, 1965 and September 15, 1966, Jane Rule fonds, Box 29.
4. Grier to Rule, November 5, 1966, Jane Rule fonds, Box 29; Grier, "The Garden Variety Lesbian," *The Coming Out Stories*, 237.
5. Grier, who liked to observe anniversaries, noted that the affair began on February 22, 1952, in Grier to Del Martin, February 22, 196[2], Phyllis Lyon-Del Martin Papers, Box 11. For the account of being caught by Shorty Bennett, see Manuela Soares interview with Barbara Grier, November 1987, Lesbian Herstory Archives-Daughters of Bilitis Video Project.
6. Boucher, *Heartwomen*, 216-17.
7. Grier to Rule, June 16, 1965, Jane Rule fonds, Box 29; Manuela Soares interview with Barbara Grier, November 1987, Lesbian Herstory Archives-Daughters of Bilitis Video Project; "Harold Burkhardt," *Jefferson City Post Tribune*, October 15, 1952, p. 2.
8. Grier to Rule, July 6, 1965, Jane Rule fonds, Box 29.
9. Mary Sundblom to Daughters of Bilitis, September 26, 1964, Phyllis Lyon-Del Martin Papers, Box 3.
10. Penni Grier Martin, email to the author, July 3, 2013; Diane Grier, phone interview with the author, May 5, 2012.
11. Boucher, *Heartwomen*, 219.
12. Penni Grier Martin, email to the author, May 28, 2012.
13. Barbara Grier to Del Martin, March 22, 1962, Phyllis Lyon-Del Martin, Box 11.
14. Grier worked for such companies as Pyramid Life Insurance, Macy's Department Store, the Singer Sewing Machine Company,

Dictaphone, Consumer Credit Counseling, Draughon's Business College and several banks. The WATS line gave companies discounted rates for long-distance calls.

15. Grier to Rule, November 16, 1964, Jane Rule fonds, Box 29.

16. Grier to Del Martin, February 22, 1962, Phyllis Lyon-Del Martin Papers, Box 11; Book Collection Card Files, Barbara Grier-Naiad Press Collection, GLC 30, Box 37.

17. Grier to Rule, October 9, 1966, Jane Rule fonds, Box 29; [letter to the editor from G.D., Kansas City], *The Ladder* 1 (August 1957): 24-25. Grier used review copies to expand her private library of gay and lesbian literature.

18. Grier to Lee Lynch, December 2, 1970, Lee Lynch Papers, Box 18.

19. Joanne Passet, *Sex Variant Woman: The Life of Jeannette Howard Foster* (New York: Da Capo Press, 2008), 172.

20. Grier, email to the author, October 21, 2006.

21. "Women Sex Deviates in Books," *Kansas City Star*, March 2, 1957; Foster's book, in the author's possession, was inscribed on February 15, 1957. Reprinted in 1976, and again in 1985, it became a foundational text for lesbian book collectors and students of lesbian literature and history.

22. Gene Damon, *Lesbiana* (Reno, Nevada: Naiad Press, 1976), 51; Grier, email message to the author, December 29, 2006; Grier to Lynch, December 2, 1970, Lee Lynch Papers, Box 18.

23. Grier to Rule, January 4, 1967, Jane Rule fonds, Box 29.

24. Grier to Jeannette Howard Foster, September 19, 1977, Grier-Naiad Press Collection, GLC 30, Box 33; Grier, email message to the author, May 17, 2005.

25. Karin Kallmaker and M.J. Lowe interview with Barbara Grier and Donna McBride, December 11-12, 2006.

26. Grier to Rule, November 28, 1970, Jane Rule fonds, Box 29. Newman's bookshop was at 326 West 15th St., New York, New York.

27. Grier to Rule, August 24, 1966, and December 7, 1970, Jane Rule fonds, Box 29.

28. Grier to Del Martin, July 31, 1958, Phyllis Lyon-Del Martin Papers, Box 11; Marcia Gallo interview with Barbara Grier, December 30, 2003, shared with the author by Gallo.

29. In 1947, a Los Angeles woman writing under the pen name "Lisa Ben" (an anagram for lesbian), courageously hand-circulated the first issue of a ten-page typed publication entitled *Vice Versa*. Lasting just nine months, it marked the beginning of the gay and lesbian

press. Three years later, Harry Hay, who had honed his activism in the Communist party, held a meeting in his Los Angeles home to discuss strategies for mobilizing homosexuals to act. This group, which met in secret and named itself the Mattachine Society, grew slowly. In January 1953 a subset of that group formed ONE, Inc., and began publishing *ONE*, a monthly magazine distributed through the US mail. *ONE*'s debut coincided with federal efforts to crack down on the distribution of obscene materials through the mail. Citing the threat they posed to the nation's moral fiber, and the fact that homosexuality was illegal in most states, post office officials monitored homosexual publications to determine if they were in violation of federal obscenity law. Its first year, *ONE* published no images and no racy stories, but its bold and defiant editorials on civil rights, police harassment and politics attracted the FBI's attention. Los Angeles postal authorities inspected each issue to determine if it violated anti-obscenity laws. It held the August 1953 issue for three weeks before granting permission for it to be mailed. Slightly more than a year later, postal officials cited the Comstock Act of 1873 when they seized the October 1954 issue featuring a lesbian short story entitled "Sappho Remembered" and an ad for men's intimate wear. ONE, Inc. sued, losing the initial case and the appeal heard by the Ninth Circuit Court of Appeals. Ultimately, however, the United States Supreme Court reversed the decision, giving renewed momentum to publishers and organizations who wished to distribute materials with gay and lesbian content. For more on lesbian life in the post-World War II era, see Lillian Faderman, *Odd Girls and Twilight Lovers: A History of Lesbian Life in Twentieth-Century America* (New York: Columbia University Press, 1991), especially Chapters 5-7; and Elizabeth Lapovsky Kennedy and Madeline D. Davis, *Boots of Leather, Slippers of Gold: The History of a Lesbian Community* (New York: Routledge, 1993).

30. For the history of the founding of the Daughters of Bilitis, see Marcia Gallo, *Different Daughters: A History of the Daughters of Bilitis and the Rise of the Lesbian Rights Movement* (New York: Carroll & Graf, 2006), especially Chapter 1. For a discussion of DOB meetings, see Nan A. Boyd interview with Del Martin and Phyllis Lyon, December 2, 1992, accessed September 25, 2013 at http://www.glbthistory.org/research/oh/MartinDel_LyonPhyllis_1992-12-2_web.pdf. The reference to "haven of sanity" is from Priscilla Royal, email to the author, May 6, 2013.

31. Del Martin and Phyllis Lyon, "Daughters of Bilitis and the Ladder that Teetered," *Everyday Mutinies: Funding Lesbian Activism*, edited by Esther D. Rothblum and Nanette Gartrell (Binghamton, New York: Harrington Park Press, 2001), 116. The Daughters of Bilitis incorporated in 1959 in California.

32. Anne W. Merigold to *The Ladder*, June 1, 1957, Phyllis Lyon-Del Martin Papers, Box 11.

33. Boucher, *Heartwomen*, 217; G.D. [Gene Damon], [letter to the editor], *The Ladder* 1 (August 1957): 24-5.

34. Vern Niven [pseudonym for Barbara Grier] to Del Martin, n.d. See also Grier to Martin, September 25, 1958, Phyllis Lyon-Del Martin Papers, Box 11.

35. Gene Damon to Del Martin, June 21, 1958, Phyllis Lyon-Del Martin Papers, Box 11. Grier's brown notebooks are on loan to the author from Donna McBride.

36. Grier to Martin, August 8, 1958, Phyllis Lyon-Del Martin Papers, Box 11; Grier to Lyndall Cowan, March 25, 1976, Eric Garber Papers, Box 6.

37. Gene Damon, "Readers Respond," *The Ladder* (September 1961): 26. For an acknowledgement of one of Grier's monetary gifts to *The Ladder*, see Ev Howe to Grier, September 27, 1961, Phyllis Lyon-Del Martin Papers, Box 6.

38. Grier to Del Martin, July 31, 1958, Phyllis Lyon-Del Martin Papers, Box 11.

39. Gene Damon, "Chance," *The Ladder* 2 (November 1957), 8-10; "Girls Across the Hall," *The Ladder* 2 (January 1958), 9-11; "Mrs. Morrison's Casserole," *The Ladder* 3 (January 1959), 4-6; Vern Niven, "Perfect Control," *The Ladder* 3 (November 1958), 9-12, "Will Call," *The Ladder* 3 (May 1959), 17-20; Vern Niven, "When I Was 17," *The Ladder* 2 (April 1958): 12-13.

40. B.G., "Essay on a Lesbian," *The Ladder* 2 (November 1957): 20.

41. Gene Damon, "Lesbian Marriage," *The Ladder* 2 (August 1958): 12-13.

42. B.G., Kansas City, "Readers Respond," *The Ladder* 3 (February 1959): 22-23; C. H., Pasadena, *The Ladder* 2 (March 1958): 20-21. Barbara sometimes used the terms "homosexual" and "lesbian" interchangeably, but she typically used "homosexual" when referring to gay men.

43. Grier to Lynch, October 12, 1970, Lee Lynch Papers, Box 18.

44. Much of Barbara Grier's biographical research was collected and anthologized in *Lesbian Lives: Biographies of Women from The Ladder*,

edited by Barbara Grier and Coletta Reid (Oakland, Calif.: Diana Press, 1976).

45. Beginning with entry #47 in February 1958, and continuing through #346, in October 1966, Barbara wrote virtually every entry. She recorded each of her entries published in brown notebooks lent to the author by Donna McBride.

46. Damon, *Lesbiana*, 9.

47. *Ibid.*, 121, 160, 292.

48. Marion Zimmer Bradley, "Readers Respond," *The Ladder* 2 (January 1958), 28.

49. Bradley, *Astra's Tower, Special Leaflet #2* (Rochester, Texas: The Author, 1958). The pamphlet may have been entitled #2 because Bradley and Royal Drummond had published a leaflet entitled "Fairy Tales" circa 1952. It reviewed "some of the better-known literature of homosexuality for the uninitiated."

50. Bradley, *Astra's Tower, Special Leaflet #3*, (Rochester, TX: The Author, 1959); Bradley, *Checklist: A Complete, Cumulative Checklist of Lesbian, Variant and Homosexual Fiction in English* (Rochester, Texas: The Author, 1960), n.p. Barbara Grier's annotated copies are on loan to the author from Donna McBride. Grier described the process of compiling the checklist in Grier to Rule, August 17, 1967, Jane Rule fonds, Box 29.

51. Bradley, "Editorial Remarks," *Checklist Supplement 1961*, ed. by Bradley and Damon (Rochester, Texas: Bradley, 1961), 3.

52. Grier to Del Martin, February 22, 196[2], Phyllis Lyon-Del Papers, Box 11; Gene Damon to Bradley, May 6, 1964, Barbara Gittings and Kay Tobin Lahusen Gay History Papers, Box 57.

CHAPTER THREE

1. Barbara Grier to Barbara Gittings, January 12, 1964, Barbara Gittings and Kay Tobin Lahusen Gay History Papers, Box 57.

2. Grier to Del Martin, December 17, 1961, and January 1962, Phyllis Lyon-Del Martin Papers, Box 11.

3. For insight into Barbara Grier's relationship with Helen Bennett, and for their handling of incoming and outgoing mail, see Grier to Rule, June 11, 1965, Jane Rule fonds, Box 29.

4. Grier to Gittings and Kay Tobin, March 11, 1964, and Gittings to Grier, [after March 11, 1964], Barbara Gittings and Kay Tobin Lahusen Gay History Papers, Box 57; and Grier to Gittings, September 25, 1963, Box 55.

5. "1958: Barbara Gittings," in Jonathan Katz, *Gay American History: Lesbians and Gay Men in the U.S.A.* (New York: Thomas Y. Crowell Company, 1976), 422-4.

6. *Ibid.*, 424, 428-30.

7. Gittings to Martin, August 9, 1959, Phyllis Lyon-Del Martin Papers, Box 1.

8. Gittings to Jaye Bell, September 9, 1961, Phyllis Lyon-Del Martin Papers, Box 6.

9. Gittings to Bell, October 6, 1961, Phyllis Lyon-Del Martin Papers, Box 11.

10. "Paul Coates Interview," *The Ladder* 6 (July 1962): 15. Jean Nathan was president of the Los Angeles Chapter in 1962, and "Terry" was a pseudonym used by the president-elect. For more information on the Los Angeles Chapter, see Phyllis Lyon-Del Martin Papers, Box 6, Folder 20, and Daughters of Bilitis Records, 1955-86, Box 9, Folder 9, Special Collections Department, University of California, Los Angeles.

11. Other causes had begun to compete for some members' time and energy. In the early 1960s, two of the original founders, Del Martin and Phyllis Lyon, became interested in the Prosperos Society and in the teachings of its spiritual leader, Thane Walker, who had been influenced by the philosophy of Russian mystic G. I. Gurdjieff. Los Angeles members of the DOB convention's planning committee grew resentful when Martin invited Walker to keynote the convention without consulting them. Walker's address, tinged with a combination of mysticism, psychology, and astrology struck a chord with some because of his openness to homosexuality, bisexuality and androgyny. A number of California DOB members, among them Billye Talmadge, Stella Rush and Helen Sandoz, joined Martin and Lyon in Prosperos. Many lesbian writers also joined Gurdjieff's group, known as "The Rope," including Solita Solano, Kathryn Hulme, Margaret Anderson, Jane Heap and Georgette Leblanc. See William Patrick Patterson and Barbara C. Allen, *Ladies of the Rope: Gurdjieff's Special Left Bank Women's Group* (Fairfax, California: Arete Publications, November 1998). For more information about The Prosperos and DOB, see Thane Walker Collection on The Prosperos, ONE National Gay and Lesbian Archives, Los Angeles; *Bodies of Evidence: The Practice of Queer Oral History*, edited by Nan A. Boyd and Horacio N. Roque Ramirez (New York: Oxford University Press, 2012), 216; and Marcia M. Gallo, *Different Daughters*, 78-9. Oral Interview with

Del Martin, May 12, 1987, Lesbian Herstory Archives-Daughters of Bilitis Video Project.

12. Del Martin to the DOB Governing Board, October 26, 1960, Phyllis Lyon-Del Martin Papers, Box 6; and Kay Lahusen to Florence Jaffy, January 2, 1965, Florence "Conrad" Jaffy papers, GLC 33, Box 1, for a discussion of attracting thinking people to the DOB.

13. Del Martin to the DOB Governing Board, October 26, 1962.

14. Gene Damon, "Review of Philip Jose Farmer, *Fire and the Night*," *Mattachine Review* (July 1962), Gene Damon, "Review of William P. McGivern, *A Pride of Place*," *Mattachine Review* (December 1962). The column began in April 1963 and continued into early 1965. The column and most of her reviews appeared under the pseudonym "Gene Damon," but occasionally she also wrote as "Larry Marvin." For a complete listing of Grier's reviews, articles and columns in *Mattachine Review*, see her brown notebooks, on loan to the author from Donna McBride. For more on the publication history of *Mattachine Review*, see Martin Meeker, *Contacts Desired: Gay and Lesbian Communications and Community, 1940s-1970s* (Chicago: University of Chicago Press, 2006). In 1952, Harold Call was arrested while working for *The Kansas City Star* and charged with "lewd conduct." Resigning his position, Call moved to San Francisco, where he became involved with the Mattachine Society. He also founded the Dorian Book Service, which Barbara used to search for gay and lesbian books. See James T. Sears, "Hall Call (1917-2000): Mr. Mattachine," in Vern Bullough, ed., *Before Stonewall: Activists for Gay and Lesbian Rights in Historical Context* (New York: Harrington Park Press, 2002), 151-9.

15. Del Martin to Barbara Gittings, December 6, 1962, and Grier to Gittings, January 4, 1963, both in Barbara Gittings and Kay Tobin Lahusen Gay History Papers, Box 55. Grier discussed her view of Gittings's plans in Grier to Florence Jaffy, April 11, 1963, Florence "Conrad" Jaffy Papers, GLC 33, Box 1.

16. For a discussion about the return of manuscripts, see Gittings to Grier, June 13, 1963, Barbara Gittings and Kay Tobin Lahusen Gay History Papers, Box 55. The quotes are from Gittings to Del Martin, December 10, 1963, Phyllis Lyon-Del Martin Papers, Box 12.

17. For the "30 kittens" reference, see Grier to Gittings, September 25, 1963, and for the cricket references, see Grier to Gittings, December 3, 1963, both in Barbara Gittings and Kay Tobin Lahusen Gay History Papers, Box 55.

18. Grier to Gittings, November 22, 1963, Barbara Gittings and Kay Tobin Lahusen Gay History Papers, Box 55.

19. For proposed communication plan, see Gittings to Del Martin, December 10, 1963, Phyllis Lyon-Del Martin Papers, Box 12. For Bell's frustration, see Jaye Bell to Barbara Gittings, June 19, 1963, Phyllis Lyon-Del Martin Papers, Box 11. For Grier's assessment of Cleo Glenn, see Grier to Gittings, January 4, 1964, Barbara Gittings and Kay Tobin Lahusen Gay History Papers, Box 55.

20. R. L, New York, and M.G., California, letters to "Readers Respond," *The Ladder* 8 (May 1964): 22-23.

21. Gene Damon, "Readers Respond," *The Ladder* 7 (August 1963): 25; Grier to Gittings, December 12, 1963, Barbara Gittings and Kay Tobin Lahusen Gay History Papers, Box 55.

22. Gittings to Grier, January 6, 1964, Barbara Gittings and Kay Tobin Lahusen Gay History Papers, Box 57.

23. "Beginning DOB Book Service," *The Ladder* 4 (May 1960): 9. Its first offerings included Jeannette Howard Foster's *Sex Variant Woman in Literature*, Reverend Robert W. Wood's *Christ and the Homosexual*, and two paperback novels, *Odd Girl* and *The Third Sex* by Artemis Smith (a pen name for poet and writer Annselm Morpurgo).

24. Gittings to Grier, May 8, 1964, Barbara Gittings and Kay Tobin Lahusen Gay History Papers, Box 57; Jess Stearn, *The Grapevine* (Garden City, N.Y.: Doubleday & Co., 1964). For more insight into the homophobia of this era, see Robert J. Corber, *Cold War Femme: Lesbianism, National Identity, and Hollywood Cinema* (Durham, North Carolina: Duke University Press, 2011), 3.

25. Gene Damon, "Lesbian Literature in '64," *The Ladder* 9 (February-March 1965): 22; Grier to Gittings, January 8, 1964 and January 12, 1964, Barbara Gittings and Kay Tobin Lahusen Gay History Papers, Box 57.

26. Gittings to Grier, n.d. [January 1964] and Grier to Gittings, January 20, 1964, both in Barbara Gittings and Kay Tobin Lahusen Gay History Papers, Box 57.

27. Grier to Gittings, January 25, 1964, Barbara Gittings and Kay Tobin Lahusen Gay History Papers, Box 57; Gittings to Florence Jaffy, July 17, 1964, Florence "Conrad" Jaffy papers, GLC 33, Box 1.

28. Grier to Gittings and Lahusen, January 28, 1964, Barbara Gittings and Kay Tobin Lahusen Gay History Papers, Box 57.

29. Gittings to Florence Jaffy, February 15, 1964, Florence "Conrad" Jaffy Papers, GLC 33, Box 1; Gittings to Grier, January 31, 1964,

Grier to Gittings, March 10, 1964, and Grier to Dear Friends, March 4, 1964, all in Barbara Gittings and Kay Tobin Lahusen Gay History Papers, Box 57.

30. Grier to Gittings, March 23, 1964, Barbara Gittings and Kay Tobin Lahusen Gay History Papers, Box 57. In the March 1964 issue of *The Ladder*, Grier's six-item "Lesbiana" column was labeled "Lesbian Literature in '63: A Comprehensive List by Gene Damon."

31. For the reference to working in a vacuum, see Gittings to Cleo Glenn, April 7, 1964, Phyllis Lyon-Del Martin Papers, Box 12. For the reference to being "under fire," see Gittings to Grier, May 24, 1964, Barbara Gittings and Kay Tobin Lahusen Gay History Papers, Box 57.

32. Grier shared Foster's impressions of the meeting in Grier to Gittings, June 30, 1964, Barbara Gittings and Kay Tobin Lahusen Gay History Papers, Box 57.

33. Gittings to Grier, July 3, 1967, Barbara Gittings and Kay Tobin Lahusen Gay History Papers, Box 57. The "bar-fly" quote is from Gittings to Jaffy, July 17, 1964, Florence "Conrad" Jaffy Papers, GLC 33, Box 1.

34. Grier to Gittings and Lahusen, July 7, 1964, Barbara Gittings and Kay Tobin Lahusen Gay History Papers, Box 57.

35. See Gittings to Grier, February 25, 1965 (for criticism of DOB leaders), Barbara Gittings and Kay Tobin Lahusen Gay History Papers, Box 59; and Cleo Glenn, Del Martin, and Phyllis Lyon to Gittings, July 7, 1965, Phyllis Lyon-Del Martin Papers, Box 12.

36. Grier to Gittings, February 3, 1966, Barbara Gittings and Kay Tobin Lahusen Gay History Papers, Box 60; For discussion of gay men writing to Grier's home address, see Richard A. Inman to Barbara Grier, February 4, 1966 in Barbara Gittings and Kay Tobin Lahusen Gay History Papers, Box 75, NACHO General folder. For Grier's plans for and perceptions of the meeting and its goals, see Grier to Gittings, February 3, 1966, and February 15, 1966, Barbara Gittings and Kay Tobin Lahusen Gay History Papers, Box 60, and Grier to Jane Rule, February 22, 1966, Jane Rule fonds, Box 29. Del Martin discusses meeting Grier in her May 12, 1987 Lesbian Herstory Archives-Daughters of Bilitis Video Project interview.

37. Grier to Frank Kameny, February 25, 1966, Kameny Papers, Library of Congress, Manuscripts Division, Box 4, Folder 7. For further insights into Grier's views about picketing, see Grier to Rule, March 22, 1968, Jane Rule fonds, Box 29.

38. Grier to Gittings, August 24, 1965 and October 30, 1965. Gittings discussed picketing the White House in Gittings to Grier, October 27, 1965, Barbara Gittings and Kay Tobin Lahusen Gay History Papers, Box 59.

39. NACHO Minutes, Barbara Gittings and Kay Tobin Lahusen Gay History Papers, Box 75; for the "amalgamated and absorbed" quote, see Grier to Barbara Gittings, December 14, 1965, Barbara Gittings and Kay Tobin Lahusen Gay History Papers, Box 59.

40. Shirley Willer, "What Concrete Steps Can Be Taken to Further the Homophile Movement?" *The Ladder* 11 (November 1967): 17-18; Gittings to Grier, December 12, 1966, Barbara Gittings and Kay Tobin Lahusen Gay History Papers, Box 60.

41. Grier to Esme Langley, January 29, 1964, and Grier to Langley, March 9, 1964, Barbara Gittings and Kay Tobin Lahusen Gay History Papers, Box 57. Clark Polak asked Grier to write for *Drum*. See Grier to Gittings, August 27, 1966, Barbara Gittings and Kay Tobin Lahusen Gay History Papers, Box 60.

42. Gittings to Cleo Glenn, January 22, 1964, Phyllis Lyon-Del Martin Papers, Box 12.

43. Gittings to Grier, March 16, 1964, and Grier to Langley, May 12, 1964, Barbara Gittings and Kay Tobin Lahusen Gay History Papers, Box 57. Grier assured Langley that she was "WHOLLY uninterested in her [Barringer] as an individual."

44. C.B., c/o A3, to Miss Grier, mailed May 22, 1964, and Grier to Esme Langley and Clare B., May 26, 1964, Barbara Gittings and Kay Tobin Lahusen Gay History Papers, Box 57. For examples of Gene Damon's reviews in *Arena Three*, see volume 1 (June 1964), 8; (September 1964), 5. Her review as Vern Niven appeared in volume 3 (January 1966). As I[rene] F[iske], she also wrote "The Strange Case of Dr. James Barry: Britain's First Woman M.D.," *Arena Three* 3/3 (March 1966): 3-8

CHAPTER FOUR

1. Barbara Grier to Anyda Marchant and Muriel Crawford, August 19, 1977, Grier-Naiad Press Collection, Box 1.

2. All quoted material in this paragraph is from Grier to Jane Rule, June 16, 1965, Jane Rule fonds, Box 29.

3. *Ibid.*

4. Gene Damon, "Readers Respond," *The Ladder* 9 (December 1964): 25-26.

5. Grier to Beverly Lynch, March 27, 1971, Lee Lynch Papers, Box 18; Grier to Barbara Gittings, October 16, 1964, Barbara Gittings and Kay Tobin Lahusen Gay History Papers, Box 57.

6. E.M. [Evelyn Mancini], Florida, "Readers Respond," *The Ladder* 5 (August 1961): 25; Del Martin to Barbara Grier, December 17, 1961, Phyllis Lyon-Del Martin Papers, Box 11.

7. Grier to Martin, January 12, 1962, Phyllis Lyon-Del Martin Papers, Box 11.

8. E. Mancini, "A Sunday Kind of Love," *The Ladder* 7 (May 1963): 20.

9. B.G., Missouri, *The Ladder* 6 (December 1961): 25; Grier to Martin, February 22, 196[2], Phyllis Lyon-Del Martin Papers, Box 11.

10. Grier to Jane Rule, July 7, 1966, Jane Rule fonds, Box 29. It has not been possible to verify the publication of Mancini's book.

11. The reference to "a true blue queer" is from Grier to Barbara Gittings, May 2, 1964, Barbara Gittings and Kay Tobin Lahusen Papers, Box 57; the reference to "serious fictional study" is from Grier to Rule, May 25, 1964, Jane Rule fonds, Box 29.

12. Rule to Grier, June 14, 1964, shared with the author by Donna McBride.

13. Rule to Grier, June 2, 1994, shared with the author by Donna McBride.

14. Rule to Grier, May 29, 1964, shared with the author by Donna McBride; Grier to Rule, June 17, 1964, Jane Rule fonds, Box 29.

15. Roz Warren, "Rough Draft of a Career," *The Gay & Lesbian Review Worldwide* 19.3 (2012): 43. See also Jane Rule, *Taking My Life* (Vancouver, British Columbia: Talon Books, 2011).

16. Grier to Rule, August 24, 1964, Jane Rule fonds, Box 29; Rule to Grier, September 5, 1964, shared with the author by Donna McBride.

17. The "I am not superior" quote is from Rule to Grier, October 10, 1964, shared with the author by Donna McBride, and the reference to following rules is from Grier to Rule, October 13, 1964, Jane Rule fonds, Box 29.

18. Grier sent her first letter to Barringer in care of Esme Langley. See Grier to Esme Langley, May 12, 1964; Barringer to Grier, May 22, 1964, Barbara Gittings and Kay Tobin Lahusen Gay History Papers, Box 57; and Pamela Rust to the author, March 10, 2014.

19. Grier discusses her correspondence with Barringer in Grier to Gittings, August 19, 1964, Barbara Gittings and Kay Tobin Lahusen Gay History Papers, Box 57. The "low ebb" quote is from Pamela Rust to the author, June 21, 2012. Grier explains how she

terminated the correspondence with Pamela in Grier to Rule, December 17, 1964, Jane Rule fonds, Box 29.

20. Grier to Rule, December 8, 1964, Jane Rule fonds, Box 29.

21. Rule to Grier, December 10, 1964, shared with the author by Donna McBride.

22. *Ibid.*

23. For the "colossal ass" quote, see Grier to Rule, December 17, 1964, Jane Rule fonds, Box 29. For the "smug, misguided" quote, see Rule to Grier, January 9, 1965, shared with the author by Donna McBride.

24. Grier to Rule, April 14, 1965, Jane Rule fonds, Box 29.

25. Grier to Rule, June 11, 1965, Jane Rule fonds, Box 29.

26. Pamela Rust described Rule's visit in a letter to the author, August 7, 2012. For the "I could forgive" quote, see Grier to Rule, June 2, 1965, Jane Rule fonds, Box 29.

27. Rule to Grier, June 5, 1965, shared with the author by Donna McBride.

28. *Ibid.*

29. For Rule's comments on a relationship built on freedom, see Rule to Grier, June 14, 1965, shared with the author by Donna McBride, and for Grier's response, see Grier to Rule, June 16, 1965, Jane Rule fonds, Box 29.

30. Grier to Rule, June 29, 1965, July 10, 1966, and September 15, 1966, Jane Rule fonds, Box 29.

31. Grier to Sarton, July 8, 1965, Grier-Naiad Press Collection, Box 33.

32. Sarton to Grier, July 10, 1965, Grier-Naiad Press Collection, Box 33. Sarton's published work in the 1930s included a volume of poems, *Encounters in April* (1937), and a novel, *The Single Hound* (1938).

33. Sarton to Grier, July 24, 1965, Grier-Naiad Press Collection, GLC 30, Box 33.

34. The quotes are from Grier to Barbara Gittings, August 4, 1965, Barbara Gittings and Kay Tobin Lahusen Gay History Papers, Box 59.

35. Gittings to Grier, July 19, 1965, Barbara Gittings and Kay Tobin Lahusen Gay History Papers, Box 59.

36. Grier to Gittings, July 20, 1965, Gittings to Grier, July 22, 1965, Barbara Gittings and Kay Tobin Lahusen Gay History Papers, Box 59. Barbara Grier's essay on Sarton's work appeared in *Tangents* 1 (January 1966): 22-24.

37. Foster had moved to St. Charles with her partner, Hazel Toliver, in 1960. For discussion of the poems, see Foster to Grier, November 21, 1965, Grier-Naiad Press Collection, Box 33. For more on Sarton's life, see Margot Peters, *May Sarton: Biography* (New York: Ballantine Books, 1998).

38. May Sarton to Grier, February 3, 1966, and Sarton to Grier, November 5, 1965, Grier-Naiad Press Collection, Box 33.

39. Sarton to Grier, January 15, 1966, Grier-Naiad Press Collection, Box 33.

40. Sarton to Grier, January 27, 1966, and February 8, 1966, Grier-Naiad Press Collection, Box 33.

41. Sarton's friend was librarian and editor Dorothy Nyren, who wrote under the name Dorothy Nyren Curley. See Sarton to Grier, March 3, 1966 and March 11, 1966, Grier-Naiad Press Collection, Box 33.

42. Grier to Duffy March, 11, 1966, April 15, 1966, and Duffy to Grier, March 18, 1966, Grier-Naiad Press Collection, Box 33. Born in England in 1933, Duffy edited a poetry magazine in the early 1960s before dedicating herself to writing. Her first novel, *That's How It Was*, received critical acclaim when it appeared in 1962. She set *The Microcosm* in a nightclub known as the House of Shades and based on it famous lesbian Gateway's Club in London.

43. Grier explains the book in Grier to Gittings, July 22, 1966, Barbara Gittings and Kay Tobin Lahusen Gay History Papers, Box 60. Her review of *The Microcosm* appeared in Gene Damon, "Reader at Large," *Tangents* 1 (Aug. 1966): 24.

44. Grier to Duffy, April 15, 1966, Grier-Naiad Press Collection, Box 33. For Barbara's comments on butch and femme, see Manuela Soares interview with Barbara Grier, November 1987, Lesbian Herstory Archives-Daughters of Bilitis Video Project.

45. Gittings to Grier, May 20, 1966, Grier to Gittings, May 23, 1966, Barbara Gittings and Kay Tobin Lahusen Gay History Papers, Box 60.

46. Grier to Gittings, September 19, 1966, Grier to Gittings, July 12, 1966, Barbara Gittings and Kay Tobin Lahusen Gay History Papers, Box 60.

47. For Barbara Grier and Jane Rule's discussion of Barbara Gittings, see Grier to Rule, May 31, 1966, Jane Rule fonds, Box 29, and Rule to Grier, June 18, 1966 and June 28, 1966, shared with the author by Donna McBride. For Barbara's comments about her relationship with Helen, see Grier to Gittings, October 3, 1966,

Barbara Gittings and Kay Tobin Lahusen Gay History Papers, Box 60.

48. Grier to Rule, July 7, 1966, Jane Rule fonds, Box 29.
49. Gittings to Grier, August 27, 1966, Barbara Gittings and Kay Tobin Lahusen Gay History Papers, Box 60.
50. Gittings to Grier, July 11, 1966, Grier to Gittings, September 16, 1966, Barbara Gittings and Kay Tobin Lahusen Gay History Papers, Box 60.
51. Shotwell was born circa 1917. See James Barr Fugate to Jody Shotwell, October 23, 1954, J. B. Fugate Folder III, One Subject files, cited in *Unmasked Voices*, and Stein, *City of Sisterly & Brotherly Loves* (Chicago: University of Chicago Press, 2000), p. 191. Shotwell defended bisexuality in *The Ladder* 4 (August 1960): 17-18.
52. Grier discusses her fan letter to Shotwell in Grier to Gittings, April 23, 1965, Barbara Gittings and Kay Tobin Lahusen Gay History Papers, Box 59. Shotwell aspired to be a novelist, and in the summer of 1965 began an unsuccessful quest to find a publisher. Barbara read Shotwell's story and serialized it in *The Ladder* during her term as editor. Information about Shotwell is from Florence Logee to Del Martin and Phyllis Lyon, July 27, 1960, and first day of Autumn, 1960, Phyllis Lyon-Del Martin Papers, Box 11.
53. Grier to Gittings, October 30, 1965, Barbara Gittings and Kay Tobin Lahusen Gay History Papers, Box 59.
54. The "be a good butch" quote is from Grier to Gittings, September 27, 1966, Barbara Gittings and Kay Tobin Lahusen Gay History Papers, Box 60. The reference to "completely blank" is from Grier to Rule, September 29, 1967, Jane Rule fonds, Box 29. Years later, Grier speculated that none of Shotwell's papers would have survived because "she had too much to hide, and despite her behavior, she was shrewd." Grier, email to the author, October 23, 2006.

CHAPTER FIVE

1. Grier to Rule, December 1, 1965, Jane Rule fonds, Box 29.
2. Theodore, "The Life and Death of a Lesbian Novel," *The Ladder* 5 (December 1960): 16-17. Barbara's private notebook of her work included this essay.
3. David Smith, "Lesbian Novel Was Danger to Nation," *The Observer*, January 1, 2005, accessed online at http://www.theguardian.com/uk/2005/jan/02/books.gayrights (February 18, 2014); Sherri

Liberman, "Banned Books Week: *The Well of Loneliness* by Radclyffe Hall," New York Public Library, accessed online at http://www. nypl.org/blog/2013/09/26/banned-books-week-well-loneliness (February 18, 2014).

4. Margalit Fox, "Tereska Torrès, 92, Writer of Lesbian Fiction, Dies," *New York Times*, September 24, 2012.

5. Donna Allegra, "Between the Sheets: My Sex Life in Literature," in Karla Jay, ed., *Lesbian Erotics* (New York University, 1995), 71-72.

6. Katherine V. Forrest, ed., *Lesbian Pulp Fiction: The Sexually Intrepid World of Lesbian Paperback Novels, 1950-1965* (New York: Cleis Press, 2005), xviii. For more on the history of pulp fiction, see Susan Stryker, *Queer Pulp: Perverted Passions from the Golden Age of the Paperback* (San Francisco: Chronicle Books, 2001).

7. Grier to Barbara Gittings and Kay Lahusen, January 20, 1964, Barbara Gittings and Kay Tobin Lahausen Gay History Papers, Box 57.

8. *The Evil Friendship* was based on the Parker-Hulme murder case in New Zealand. Meaker also writes highly successful young adult novels as M. E. Kerr.

9. Ann Bannon, *Odd Girl Out* (Greenwich, Conn.: Fawcett Publications, 1957), 191; Ann Bannon, email to the author, October 11, 2013; "Lesbian Culture, Past and Present," undated panel presentation with Ann Bannon, Valerie Taylor and Barbara Grier, [videorecording], Grier-Naiad Press Collection, Box 41. For more on Bannon's *Beebo Brinker* and on lesbian pulps, see Stephanie Foote, "Deviant Classics: Pulps and the Making of Lesbian Print Culture," *Signs: Journal of Women in Culture and Society* 31/1 (2005): 169-190.

10. Grier to Gittings, February 19, 1965, Barbara Gittings and Kay Tobin Lahausen Gay History Papers, Box 59.

11. For the review of *I Am a Woman*, see Lennox Strang, "The Lesbian in Contemporary Literature," *The Ladder* 3 (February 1959): 18. For the discussion of Valerie Taylor's work, see Gene Damon, "Lesbiana," *The Ladder* 5 (April 1960): 17.

12. Ann Aldrich, *We Walk Alone* (Greenwich, Conn.: Fawcett Publications, 1955), 5; Del Martin, "Open Letter to Ann Aldrich," *The Ladder* 2 (April 1958): 4-6.

13. Gene Damon, "An Evening's Reading," *The Ladder* 4 (August 1960): 6-7; Del Martin, "We're Flattered, Miss Aldrich!" *The Ladder* 4 (August 1960): 9-10; Jeannette Howard Foster, "Ann of 10,000 Words Plus," *The Ladder* 4 (August 1960): 7-9.

14. Grier described her admiration for writers in Manuela Soares interview with Barbara Grier, November 1987, Lesbian Herstory Archives-Daughters of Bilitis Video Project.

15. Grier to Rule, April 5, 1966, Jane Rule fonds, Box 29. For examples of Grier's stories, all dating from 1958 and 1959, see "Unusable Materials Folder," Barbara Gittings and Kay Tobin Lahusen Gay History Papers, Box 63.

16. Several of Grier's pseudonyms originated in her family tree. They included Marilyn Barrow, Gladys Casey, Malvina Creet, Gene Damon, Irene Fiske, Dorothy Lyle (sometimes Lyles), Vern Niven, Lennox Strang and Lennox Strong. Grier published most of her fiction as Gene Damon and Vern Niven.

17. Rule to Grier, May 6, 1966, shared with the author by Donna McBride; Grier to Rule, May 10, 1966, Jane Rule fonds, Box 29. According to historian of pulp fiction Gary Lovisi, email to the author, June 5, 2013, Grier's claims about writing for the pulp market appear credible, based on information she gave about payment, lack of copyright and speed of writing the novels. Grier said she had "managed to work myself up to $1000 for a book," in Grier to Rule, April 7, 1967, Jane Rule fonds, Box 29.

18. In Grier to Barbara Gittings, October 30, 1965, Grier mentioned receiving an advance for a "kitty book for children," and she promised to send a complimentary copy of it in Grier to Gittings, April 26, 1966, Barbara Gittings and Kay Tobin Lahusen Gay History Papers, Box 59. For more on the children's book market, see Rachel DeAngelo, "Children's Book Publishing," *Library Trends* 7 (Summer 1958): 220-33.

19. Elaine Williams, U.S. Social Security Death Index, accessed June 10, 2013, at http://familysearch.org/pal:MM9.1.1/JKGM-3ZV. According to the Social Security Death Index, Elaine Williams was born Dec. 28, 1932, and died in December 1963. Barbara Grier to Barbara Gittings, April 28, 1964, Barbara Gittings and Kay Tobin Lahusen Gay History Papers, Box 57.

20. Gene Damon, "Lesbiana [review of *First Person, 3rd Sex*]," *The Ladder* 4 (April 1960): 18; Gene Damon, "Lesbiana [review of *Meet Marilyn*]," *The Ladder* 5 (Feb. 1960): 22; Grier to Gittings and Lahusen, [early May 1964], Barbara Gittings and Kay Tobin Lahusen Gay History Papers, Box 57.

21. Grier to Rule, May 10, 1966, Jane Rule fonds, Box 29.

22. For information on Adela Maritano, see Bryce Maritano to Katherine V. Forrest, November 5, 2010, shared with the author via email, June 3, 2013.

23. Rule to Grier, May 21, 1966, shared with the author by Donna McBride; Grier to Rule, November 18, 1965, Jane Rule fonds, Box 29; Diane Grier, phone interview with the author, May 5, 2012; Penni Grier, email message to the author, May 25, 2012.

24. Grier to Jane Rule, May 10, 1966, Jane Rule fonds, Box 29. Grier discusses Violet Soup in Grier to Jane Rule, May 25, 1966, Jane Rule fonds, Box 29.

25. Rule to Grier, May 21, 1966, shared with the author by Donna McBride.

26. Grier to Rule, May 25, 1966, Jane Rule fonds, Box 29.

27. Rule to Grier, July 6, 1966, shared with the author by Donna McBride. The hand-corrected manuscript contains many penciled corrections and marginal comments and is in the Grier-Naiad Press Collection, Box 39.

28. For Grier's response to Rule's critique, see Grier to Rule, July 7, 1966. For Rule's comments on "Temple of Athene," see Rule to Grier, August 19, 1968, shared with the author by Donna McBride.

29. Maida Tilchen, transcript of interview with Barbara Grier, Bates City, Missouri, June 1977, shared with the author by Tilchen, pp. 43-45; Manuela Soares interview with Barbara Grier, November 1987, Lesbian Herstory Archives-Daughters of Bilitis Video Project. Grier also was reported as writing paperback novels in Arthur S. Brisbane, "Granny's Lesbian Legacy," *The Kansas City Times*, February 15, 1980. Eric Garber quizzed Grier about her writing of pulp fiction in Garber to Grier, March 28, 1983, Eric Garber Papers, Box 5.

30. "For Adults Only" appeared on the cover until the July 1967 issue. Gittings to Grier, November 22, 1964, Barbara Gittings and Kay Tobin Lahusen Gay History Papers, Box 57.

31. Gittings expressed her anger with Gene Damon in Gittings to Florence Jaffy, July 17, 1964, Florence "Conrad" Jaffy Papers, Box 1. It is also discussed in Gittings to Grier, September 13, 1964, Barbara Gittings and Kay Tobin Lahusen Gay History Papers, Box 57. Her opinions of the DOB Book Service are expressed in Gittings to Cleo [Glenn], August 9, 1964, Phyllis Lyon-Del Martin Papers, Box 12.

32. The Langley inquiry is discussed in Gittings to Jaffy, July 17, 1964, Florence "Conrad" Jaffy Papers, Box 1.

33. Gene Damon, "Lesbian Literature in '63: A Comprehensive List," *The Ladder* 8 (February 1964): 12-19.

34. Gittings to Grier, September 13, 1964, Barbara Gittings and Kay Tobin Lahusen Gay History Papers, Box 57; Gittings to Yvonne

MacManus, September 20, 1964, and Paula Christian to Gittings, September 23, 1964, both in Barbara Gittings and Kay Tobin Lahusen Gay History Papers, Box 56.

35. Gittings to Grier, November 13, 1965, Barbara Gittings and Kay Tobin Lahusen Gay History Papers, Box 59; Grier to Gittings, July 19, 1965, Barbara Gittings and Kay Tobin Lahusen Gay History Papers, Box 59, and Grier to Gittings, September 16, 1964 and September 28, 1964, Barbara Gittings and Kay Tobin Lahusen Gay History Papers, Box 57. Barbara made similar statements in Gene Damon, "Reader at Large," *Tangents* 4 (April 1966): 24-27.

36. Grier to Gittings, November 9, 1965, Barbara Gittings and Kay Tobin Lahusen Gay History Papers, Box 59.

37. Slater discussed his actions in Slater to Gittings, April 19, 1965 and September 28, 1965, Barbara Gittings and Kay Tobin Lahusen Gay History Papers, Box 59. Joseph Hansen, who would later receive recognition for his crime novels featuring gay insurance investigator Dave Brandstetter, was at the time publishing such pulp novels as *Strange Marriage* (1965) and *Known Homosexual* (1968) under the pen name James Colton. Grier to Gittings, November 24, 1965, Barbara Gittings and Kay Tobin Lahusen Gay History Papers, Box 59. *Tangents* published until the October/December 1969 issue. A prolific reviewer, Barbara published book notes in the British lesbian magazine, *Arena Three*, beginning in January 1966.

38. Grier to Yvonne MacManus, December 3, 1966, Barbara Gittings and Kay Tobin Lahusen Gay History Papers, Box 60.

39. Yvonne Keller, "'Was It Right to Covet Her Brother's Wife So Passionately?': Lesbian Pulp Novels and U.S. Lesbian Identity, 1950-65," *American Quarterly* 57 no. 2 (June 2005): 387.

40. Grier to Gittings, December 3, 1966, on the copy of a letter from Yvonne MacManus dated November 1, 1966, Barbara Gittings and Kay Tobin Lahusen Gay History Papers, Box 60.

CHAPTER SIX

1. Barbara Grier to Jane Rule, July 5, 1968, Jane Rule fonds, Box 29.
2. Grier to Rule, August 17, 1966, Jane Rule fonds, Box 29.
3. Judith M. Saunders, "Stella Rush a.k.a. Sten Russell (1925-)," in Vern Bullough, ed., *Before Stonewall: Activists for Gay and Lesbian Rights in Historical Context* (New York: Harrington Park Press, 2002),135-44. See also Stella Rush, "Helen Sandoz a.k.a. Helen Sanders a.k.a. Ben Cat (1920-1987), in *Before Stonewall*, 145-7.

Sandoz used the pseudonym Sanders because she thought her homosexuality would damage the reputation of a distant cousin, the novelist Mari Sandoz.

4. Helen Sandoz and Sten Russell, interviewed by Sara Yager, May 15, 1987, Lesbian Herstory Archives-Daughters of Bilitis Video Project; Helen Sandoz to Del Martin, October 20, 1966, Phyllis Lyon-Del Martin Collection, Box 11. For information about the DOB's use of a commercial distributor, see Gittings to Grier, December 12, 1966, Barbara Gittings and Kay Tobin Lahusen Gay History Papers, Box 60.

5. "Your Name Is Safe!" *The Ladder* 1 (November 1956): 10-11. Information about national distribution is from Grier to Barbara Gittings, December 25, 1966. For Barbara Gittings's discussion of editing the mailing list, see Gittings to Grier, December 3, 1966, both in Barbara Gittings and Kay Tobin Lahusen Gay History Papers, Box 60.

6. Grier to Rule, September 15, 1966, and November 23, 1966, Jane Rule fonds, Box 29.

7. Grier to Rule, November 23, 1966, Jane Rule fonds, Box 29.

8. Rule to Grier, December 4, 1966, Jane Rule fonds, Box 29.

9. Grier to Rule, December 23, 1966, Jane Rule fonds, Box 29; Rule to Grier, December 28, 1966, shared with the author by Donna McBride.

10. Grier to Rule, April 7, 1967, Jane Rule fonds, Box 29.

11. For a discussion of Willer and Glass's efforts to organize local chapters, see Gallo, *Different Daughters*, 129-30.

12. For discussion of the anonymous donor, see Shirley Willer, DOB Oral History Project, July 11, 1987, Lesbian Herstory Archives; and Gallo, *Different Daughters*, p. 141.

13. Grier to Rule, February 25, 1967, Jane Rule fonds, Box 29. On several occasions, Barbara referred to the mystery donor as a female New York State legislator.

14. Grier to Jane Rule, July 28, 1967, Jane Rule fonds, Box 29.

15. Rule to Grier, August 14, 1967 and August 23, 1967, shared with the author by Donna McBride; Grier to Rule, August 17, 1967, Jane Rule fonds, Box 29.

16. Grier to Rule, August 26, 1967, Jane Rule fonds, Box 29.

17. Grier to Rule, September 29, 1967, Jane Rule fonds, Box 29.

18. Valerie Taylor to the Editor, "Readers Respond," *The Ladder* 11 (June 1967): 21-22; Jane Rule to the Editor, "Readers Respond," *The Ladder* 12 (December 1967): 30-31.

19. Gene Damon to the Editor, "Readers' Respond," *The Ladder* 12 (Jan. 1968): 29-30.

20. Lori [Whitehead], "Unhappening," *The Ladder* 11 (June 1967): 32. The reference to dishonesty is from Rule to Grier, November 6, 1967, Jane Rule fonds, Box 29; and the reference to "reputable big magazines" is from Rule to Grier, November 10, 1967, shared with the author by Donna McBride. The "common thief" reference is from Grier to Rule, November 9, 1967, Jane Rule fonds, Box 29.

21. Rule to Grier, November 20, 1967, shared with the author by Donna McBride.

22. Grier to Rule, November 24, 1967, Jane Rule fonds, Box 29.

23. Rule to Grier, February 17, 1968, shared with the author by Donna McBride.

24. For the discussion of Helene Rosenthal's poetry, see Rule to Grier, January 6, [1968], shared with the author by Donna McBride; for the reference to "the way to my heart," see Grier to Rule, January 11, 1968, Jane Rule fonds, Box 29. Rosenthal's poems appeared as "Selection of Poems," *The Ladder* 12 (February/March 1968): 2-7.

25. The "growl" quote is from a postscript on Grier to Rule, January 20, 1968, Jane Rule fonds, Box 29; the "dump" quote is from Rule to Grier, May 14, 1968, shared with the author by Donna McBride.

26. Rule to Grier, January 23, 1968, shared with the author by Donna McBride.

27. Rule to Grier, January 29, 1968, shared with the author by Donna McBride: Grier to Rule, February 2, 1968, Jane Rule fonds, Box 29; Jane Rule, "Three Letters to a Poet," *The Ladder* 12 (May-June 1968): 5-7.

28. Rule to Grier, January 29, 1968. The letters, attributed to P.S. from North Carolina, B.L.H. and G.B. of Arkansas, "Readers Respond," appeared in *The Ladder* 12 (Jan 1968): 28-29. Kogan, whose covers appeared on the August and November 1967 issues, studied art at Columbia University, gained recognition for her paintings of Amazons.

29. The "express it when I vote" quote is from Grier to Rule, March 7, 1968, the reference to the campaign for fair housing referendum is in Grier to Rule, March 22, 1968, and the "Black Power" quote is in Grier to Rule, April 10, 1968, all in Jane Rule fonds, Box 29.

30. Grier to Rule, May 29, 1968, Jane Rule fonds, Box 29.

31. Jane Rule, "My Country Wrong," *The Ladder* 12 (August 1968): 8-18; Rule to Grier, June 1, 1968, Jane Rule fonds, Box 29; Grier to Rule, June 13, 1968, shared with the author by Donna McBride.

32. "Important Letter from National [DOB] President," June 1968, Vertical File [DOB], The Kinsey Institute for Research in Sex, Gender, and Reproduction, Bloomington, Indiana; "Bi-ennial Assembly and Convention," *The Ladder* 12 (July 1968): 30. Denver meeting attendance suffered from lack of a host chapter, inadequate publicity and no theme or featured speaker.

33. Information about Rita Laporte is found in Julie Smith, "Choosing the Gay Way of Life," *San Francisco Chronicle*, June 30, 1969, and "Death Leap of Woman Foiled on Gate Bridge," *San Francisco Chronicle*, May 5, 1953. For more discussion of the DOB dress code, see Gallo, *Different Daughters*, 24.

34. Grier to Rule, August 12, 1968, Jane Rule fonds, Box 29.

35. The reference to "internal bickering" is from Grier to Rule, July 5, 1968; "hoopla" is from Grier to Rule, July 13, 1968, Jane Rule fonds, Box 29; the "amounts to a damn" quote is from Grier to Rule, February 2, 1968, Jane Rule fonds, Box 29.

36. Grier to Rule, July 5, 1968, Jane Rule fonds, Box 29.

37. Grier to Rule, August 12, 1968, Jane Rule fonds, Box 29; Priscilla Royal, email to the author, May 6, 2013. Royal recalls Barbara's broken tooth and Helen Bennett's painful shyness. She found Grier "a bit ruthless" but "admired her singlemindedness about preserving a literature that was endangered." Karen Wilson used the pseudonym Karen Wells in *The Ladder*.

38. Grier to Rule, August 28, 1968, Jane Rule fonds, Box 29. For more on the "United Daughters of Bilitis, Inc." proposal, see Gallo, *Different Daughters*, 141-2.

39. For Grier's assessment of the circulation volunteers, see Grier to Rule, August 28, 1968, Jane Rule fonds, Box 29, and for samples of Rita Laporte's essays, see "The Bosom Theory: Masculinity-Femininity in Lesbianism," *The Ladder* (April 1968): 16-18, and "Living Propaganda," *The Ladder* (June 1966): 21-22. The information about distrust of Laporte is from Priscilla Royal, email to the author, May 6, 2013.

40. Grier to Rule, August 12, 1968, Jane Rule fonds, Box 29.

41. Grier to Rule, July 5, 1968, Jane Rule fonds, Box 29.

CHAPTER SEVEN

1. "Gene Damon Is My Editor," Lee Lynch papers, Box 18, University of Oregon.

2. Barbara Grier to Florence "Conrad" Jaffy, September 6, 1968, Jaffy Papers, Box 1.
3. Grier to Rule, July 5, 1968, Jane Rule fonds, Box 29.
4. Grier to Rule, August 28, 1968, Jane Rule fonds, Box 29.
5. Helen Sanders to DOB Governing Board, September 5, 1968, Phyllis Lyon-Del Martin Papers, Box 6.
6. Rita Laporte to Helen Sanders and Members of the DOB Governing Board, August 31, 1968, Phyllis Lyon-Del Martin Papers, Box 6.
7. Grier to Rule, August 28, 1968, Jane Rule fonds, Box 29.
8. Sanders to Governing Board, September 6, 1968, Phyllis Lyon-Del Martin Papers, Box 6. Sanders was describing the airmail envelopes Grier used.
9. Grier to Rule, October 2, 1968, Jane Rule fonds, Box 29.
10. Ilonka's *Sex Cage* was advertised in *The Ladder* 14 (October/November 1969): 46.
11. Grier to Rule, October 16, 1968 and November 13, 1968, Jane Rule fonds, Box 29.
12. Grier to Florence Jaffy, October 19, 1968, Florence "Conrad" Jaffy Papers, Box 1.
13. Alice Lawrence, "Sex Roles: A Glance at Four Cultures," *The Ladder* 13 (February/March 1969): 4-6; Val Vanderwood, "The Homophile and Income Tax Inequities," *The Ladder* 13 (February/March 1969): 7-10.
14. Rule to Grier, January 27, 1968, Jane Rule fonds, Box 29. Wood was an ordained minister in the United Church of Christ who wrote and played a major role in opening dialogue between organized religion and the gay and lesbian community. Hansen worked with Don Slater at *Tangents* magazine and got his start as a writer in the original paperback novel market before going on to become a bestselling author of crime fiction.
15. Grier to Rule, August 28, 1968 and October 9, 1968, Jane Rule fonds, Box 29; Jane Rule, "House Guest," *The Ladder* 13 (December 1968-January 1969): 23-29, the quote is from page 28.
16. Rule to Grier, September 4, 1968, September 17, 1968, and May 23, 1968, shared with the author by Donna McBride. The poems ("One August Morning," "in the place where" and "The Centipede's Poem") appeared in *The Ladder* 13 (December-January 1968-69): 40, 42-44.
17. Rule to Grier, November 25, 1970 and May 22, 1970, shared with the author by Donna McBride; Grier to Rule, November 28, 1970, Jane Rule fonds, Box 29.

18. Grier to Gittings, January 25, 1966, Barbara Gittings and Kay Tobin Lahusen Gay History Papers, Box 60.

19. The reference to "brooding women" is from Grier to Rule, March 1, 1971, Jane Rule fonds, Box 29. The quotes from "upper middle class" through "pickled okra" are from Grier to Rule, April 19, 1971, and the "fantasy school teacher" quote is from Grier to Rule, March 1, 1971, Jane Rule fonds, Box 29; for the reference to copies of *The Ladder* sent to Canada, see Rule to Grier, October 6, 1970, shared with the author by Donna McBride. For more about the Kansas City Women's Liberation Union, see *Kansas City Women's Liberation Union Newsletter* 1 #8 (May 1971).

20. Martha Shelley, phone interview with the author, January 29, 2013. Born Martha Altman, Shelley renamed herself after her favorite poet, Percy Bysshe Shelley. For more on Shelley, see Paul D. Cain, "Martha Shelley," *Encyclopedia of Lesbian, Gay, Bisexual, and Transgender History in America*, edited by Marc Stein (Detroit: Charles Scribner's Sons, 2004), accessed via *Biography in Context*. Web. June 20, 2013.

21. The reference to "super paranoid society" is from Grier to Lee Lynch, June 13, 1970, Lee Lynch Papers, Box 18. The "Fay Wray" quote is from Grier to Rule, January 22, 1971, and she elaborated on her comments on the incident in Grier to Rule, January 31, 1971, Jane Rule fonds, Box 29. For more on Johnston's coming out as a lesbian in *Village Voice*, see Jill Johnston, "Dance Journal," *Village Voice* XVI (January 14, 1971), accessed online at http://blogs.villagevoice.com/runninscared/2010/11/jill_johnston_1.php 6/28/2013, and Sara Warner, *Acts of Gaiety: LGBT Performance and the Politics of Pleasure* (Ann Arbor: University of Michigan Press, 2012), 118.

22. Grier to Rule, September 13, 1968, Jane Rule fonds, Box 29. Martha Shelley also wrote under the name Alice Kobayashi.

23. Robin Morgan to Gene Damon, April 23, 1969, Grier-Naiad Press Collection, Box 33; Gene Damon, "The Least of These: the Minority Whose Screams Haven't Yet Been Heard," in *Sisterhood Is Powerful!*, ed. Robin Morgan (New York: Random House, 1970): 297-306. Grier discussed the essay in Grier to Rule, April 28, 1969, Jane Rule fonds, Box 29.

24. Grier to Rule, May 12, 1969, Jane Rule fonds, Box 29.

25. Grier discusses the impact of Helen Sanders's departure from *The Ladder*'s production staff in Grier to Rule, January 15, 1970, Jane Rule fonds, Box 29.

26. Grier to Rule, June 5, 1969, Jane Rule fonds, Box 29.

27. Rita Laporte, "An Open Letter to Mary Daly," *The Ladder* 13 (October/November 1968): 24; Rita Laporte to "*Playboy* Forum," *Playboy* (June 1969): 69; Rita Laporte, "What Is D.O.B.?" *New York DOB Newsletter* (June 1970): 3; and "Editorial," *New York DOB Newsletter* (June 1970): 3.

28. "ECHO De-structured," *Newsletter* (NYDOB), April 1970, n.p.; Grier to Lee Lynch, May 14, 1970, Lee Lynch Papers, Box 18. Jane and Barbara also discussed the editor's plan in Grier to Rule, May 27, 1970, Jane Rule fonds, Box 29, and Rule to Grier, June 3, 1970, shared with the author by Donna McBride.

29. Florence Jaffy to Kay Lahusen, January 26, 1965, Jaffy Papers, Box 1. For insight into Gittings's ideas about *The Ladder* as an independent publication, see in Kay Lahusen to Grier, [after March 11, 1964], Barbara Gittings and Kay Tobin Lahusen Gay History Collection, Box 57.

30. Grier to Rule, June 6, 1970, Jane Rule fonds, Box 29.

31. Rita Laporte, "To New York Chapter DOB, June 16, 1970," *Newsletter* [New York DOB] (July 1970).

32. Grier to Rule, February 28, 1970 and June 28, 1970, Jane Rule fonds, Box 29.

33. "A Letter from Roz to Gene Damon," *Newsletter* [New York DOB] (July 1970): 3.

34. "Report of General Assembly's Actions," *Newsletter* [New York DOB] (August 1970): 1.

35. *Ibid.*

36. Helen Sanders, "Letter to the Delegates," 1970, Phyllis Lyon-Del Martin Papers, Box 7.

37. Karen, "A Selfish Plea from a Weary Co-Editor," *SISTERS* 13 (January 1971): 2.

38. Grier to Lee Lynch, October 31, 1970, Lee Lynch Papers, Box 18.

39. The mailing to 7,000 women is described in Grier to Rule, August 30, 1970, and the reference to *Writer's Digest* is from Grier to Rule, April 6, 1971, Jane Rule fonds, Box 29.

40. Jeanne Córdova, interview with the author, November 23, 2010.

41. *Ibid.*

42. Robin Morgan to Grier, September 23, 1970, Grier-Naiad Press Collection, Box 33.

43. For insight into Laporte's feminism, see Rita Laporte to Del Martin, October 1, 1970, Phyllis Lyon-Del Martin Papers, Box 28.

44. Grier to Lee Lynch, January 19, 1970, October 15, 1970, November 27, 1970, Lee Lynch Papers, Box 18.

45. Rita Laporte, "Can Women Unite?" *The Ladder* 14 (August/September 1970): 5.

46. "Cross Currents," *The Ladder* 13 (August/September 1969): 44-5. Wilda Chase, "Lesbianism and Feminism," *The Ladder* 14 (December 1969/January 1970): 14, 16.

47. Rita Mae Brown, "The Woman-Identified Woman," *The Ladder*14 (August/September 1970): 6-8; "Correction," *The Ladder*14 (October/November 1970): 46; Grier to Rule, October 17, 1970; Grier to Lee Lynch, October 27, 1970, Lee Lynch Papers, University of Oregon, Box 18.

48. The "historical leap" quote is from Rule to Grier, August 12, 1970. For more about recruiting Millett to write for *The Ladder*, see Rule to Grier, August 25, 1970, shared with the author by Donna McBride.

49. For "light years away," see Rule to Grier, October 31, 1970; for "penis hatred" and Paul Mariah's work, see Rule to Grier, October 13, 1970; for "won't do at all," see Rule to Grier, October 6, 1970. All of Rule's letters were shared with the author by Donna McBride.

50. Morgan to Grier, September 23, 1970, and Grier to Morgan, September 25, 1970, Grier-Naiad Press Collection, Box 33; Pauline Oliveros, "Women Composers," *The Ladder* 15 (June/July 1971): 37-39. Morgan promised to put an ad for *The Ladder* in *RAT*.

51. "Journeys in Art" first appeared in the February/March 1971 issue. For a description of Whitworth, who initially wrote as "Jean Louise," see Grier to Rule, January 22, 1971, Jane Rule fonds, Box 29.

52. Anita Cornwell, "Open Letter to a Black Sister: Women's Liberation Is Our Thing Too," *The Ladder* 16 (October/November 1971): 33-6; "Letter to a Friend," *The Ladder* 16 (December/January 1972): 42-5; and "From a Soul Sister's Notebook: The Lesser of the Worst," *The Ladder* 16 (June/July 1972): 43-4.

53. Rule to Grier, April 14, 1972, shared with the author by Donna McBride.

CHAPTER EIGHT

1. Barbara Grier to Anyda Marchant, September 18, 1974, Grier-Naiad Press Collection, Box 1.

2. Barbara Grier and Donna McBride Interview with Karin Kallmaker and M.J. Lowe, December 11, 2006; "I Can't See Myself Being

Anywhere But in This Relationship," *Partners: The Newsletter for Gay & Lesbian Couples*, in Katherine V. Forrest Papers, San Francisco Public Library, Box 9.

3. Barbara Grier and Donna McBride to Gloria Greenfield, August 20, 1981, Grier-McBride Collection, Box 2.

4. Donna McBride, email to the author, January 3, 2013.

5. "I Can't See Myself Being Anywhere But in This Relationship," McBride, email to the author, March 23, 2012.

6. Donna McBride, personal interview with the author, February 22, 2012.

7. "I Can't See Myself Being Anywhere But in This Relationship" and Donna McBride personal interview with the author, February 22, 2012.

8. Donna McBride, email to the author, July 22, 2013.

9. "I Can't See Myself Being Anywhere But in This Relationship."

10. Grier to Jane Rule, December 19, 1970, January 2, 1971, and May 6, 1971, all in Jane Rule fonds, Box 29.

11. Grier to Lee Lynch, March 1, 1971, Lee Lynch Papers, Box 18; Donna McBride, email to the author, July 15, 2013.

12. Grier to Lynch, March 10, 1971 and March 1, 1971, Lee Lynch Papers, Box 18.

13. Grier to Rule, June 16, 1971, Jane Rule fonds, Box 29. Martha Shelley described Barbara's correspondence during this period in Shelley, interview with the author, January 29, 2013.

14. For the reference to "Helen's Rules of Order," see Grier (Phragility Phristle) to Gittings and Kay, April 28, 1964, Barbara Gittings and Kay Tobin Lahusen Gay History Papers, Box 57.

15. Donna McBride, email to the author, June 13, 2013.

16. Rule to Grier, June 21, 1971, shared with the author by Donna McBride.

17. Donna McBride, personal interview with the author, February 22, 2012.

18. Jane Rule responded to news of the move in Rule to Grier, September 14, 1971, and to Barbara's illness, September 20, 1971, Jane Rule fonds, Box 29.

19. Grier to Lyndall Cowan, March 25, 1976, Eric Garber Papers, Box 6.

20. For "helpless dependency," see Rule to Grier, January 13, 1972; for "not loving," see Rule to Grier, November 22, 1971; for "hand and toe holds," see Rule to Grier, December 30, 1971, shared with the author by Donna McBride.

21. Grier to Janet Soule, March 18, 1981, Grier-Naiad Press Collection, Box 33; "I Can't See Myself Being Anywhere But in This Relationship."

22. Grier cites the figure of 12,000 books in Grier to Lynch, February 2, 1970, Lee Lynch Papers, Box 18.

23. Grier to Barbara Gittings, February 4, 1972, Barbara Gittings and Kay Tobin Lahusen Gay History Papers, Box 54.

24. Grier to Marchant, November 25, 1974, Grier-Naiad Press Collection, Box 1; Hope Thompson, "Book Review," *The Ladder* 16 (Aug./Sept. 1972): 40-2. Barbara may have chosen to leave Rita Laporte's pseudonym intact so it would appear that *The Ladder*'s staff was stable, and she could have published items Laporte submitted before their disagreement. Paula Buckingham to Barbara Grier, November 23, [1976], Grier-Naiad Press Collection, Box 33.

25. Donna McBride, personal interview with the author, February 22, 2012.

26. Donna McBride, personal interview with the author, February 24, 2012.

27. "I Can't See Myself Being Anywhere But in This Relationship;" McBride, email to the author, March 23, 2012; Donna McBride, email to the author, January 9, 2013.

28. Grier to Robin Morgan, February 1, 1972, Grier-Naiad Press Collection, Box 33.

29. Barbara Grier and Donna McBride to Dear Friends, December 11, 1973, shared with the author by Donna McBride; Barbara discusses the naming of 20 Rue Jacob Acres in Grier to Lyndall Cowan, April 1976, Eric Garber Papers, Box 6. Martha Shelley, who visited during her drive across country, captured the moment in a poem that began "Barbara, at forty/newly turned Missouri farmer." See Shelley, *Crossing the DMZ* (Women's Press Collective, 1974).

30. Grier to Lyndall Cowan, April 1976, Eric Garber Papers, Box 6; Grier to Dear Friends, June 6, 1976, shared with the author by Donna McBride.

31. Manuela Soares interview with Barbara Grier, November 1987, Lesbian Herstory Archives-Daughters of Bilitis Video Project. Honey Lee Cottrell commented on Barbara and Donna's relationship in Cottrell, phone interview with the author, September 2, 2012.

32. Maida Tilchen, oral interview with Barbara Grier, [1978], transcript shared with the author by Tilchen.

CHAPTER NINE

1. Anyda Marchant to Barbara Grier, March 20, 1974, Grier-Naiad Press Collection, GLC 30, Box 1.

2. "The Furies," The Rainbow History Project, http://www.rainbowhistory.org/html/furies.html (accessed July 8, 2013) first appeared in January 1972. Members included Ginny Berson, Joan E. Biren, Rita Mae Brown, Charlotte Bunch, Sharon Deevey, Helaine Harris, Susan Hathaway, Nancy Myron, Tasha Peterson, Coletta Reid, Lee Schwing, and Jennifer Woodul. Reid and Myron became involved with Diana Press, Harris began Women in Distribution with Cynthia Gair, Biren (JEB) is a well-known photographer, Brown became a successful novelist, Berson founded Olivia Records, and Bunch began *Quest*.

3. Committed to the production of affordable books, the multi-class and multi-racial collective bought the cheapest paper it could find, even if it had holes or came in different colors. For more, see "Women's Press Collective," *Sinister Wisdom* 1 no. 2 (1976): 121; Julie R. Enszer, "The Whole Naked Truth of Our Lives: Lesbian Feminist Print Culture from 1969 through 1989," Ph.D. diss. (University of Maryland, 2013), Chapter One; and Martha Shelley, transcript of interview by Kelly Anderson, October 12, 2003, Voices of Feminism Oral History Project, Sophia Smith Collection, accessed at http://www.smith.edu/libraries/libs/ssc/vof/vof-intro.html (December 26, 2013), 53.

4. Daughters' greatest monetary achievement occurred in 1977 when Bantam Books paid $250,000 for the paperback rights to Brown's novel, *Rubyfruit Jungle*. See Judy Klemesrud, "Rita Mae Brown Suddenly a Writing Star of the Gay Women's Movement," *Lakeland Ledger*, October 16, 1977. Commercial success led such feminists as Bertha Harris to question Bowman and Arnold's business practices, for instance, making editorial decisions and selling rights without consulting the authors. Daughters, Inc. ceased in 1978 after publishing twenty-three books by eighteen women, among them Arnold, Brown, Harris, Elana Nachman (Dykewomon), and Joanna Russ. Bowman and Arnold removed themselves from the public eye and ongoing feminist critique when they relocated to Arnold's hometown of Houston, Texas. Despite the criticism their business model had generated, Daughters, Inc. had published transformative literature and fed a growing audience's hunger for lesbian fiction.

5. Coletta Reid and Nancy Myron, of Diana Press, and Rita Mae Brown all formerly belonged to The Furies, and shared a strong commitment to feminist business principles, for example, making fair payment to producers a priority over profit. The women of Diana Press published six books plus calendars and a day book in their first two years of business. In 1977, Diana moved to Oakland, where the collective and press succumbed two years later to financial troubles, vandalism and internal disagreements. For more on Diana Press, see Enszer, "The Whole Naked Truth," Chapter One.

6. Grier to Coletta Reid, February 22, 1974, and Reid to Grier, May 15, 1974, Grier-Naiad Press Collection, Box 33. Prior to the Copyright Act of 1976, books were copyrighted for twenty-eight years, with the option for a twenty-eight-year renewal. Diana never published the books that Grier recommended.

7. The "broken shoe string" reference is from Jeannette Howard Foster to Grier, November 7, 1975, and the "PERFECT job" quote is from Foster to Coletta Reid, May 21, 1976, both are in the Grier-Naiad Press Collection, Box 33. For insight into Elsa Gidlow's interactions with Diana Press, see Grier to Elsa Gidlow, November 26, 1977, Gidlow to Grier, February 22, 1978, and March 7, 1978, Grier-Naiad Press Collection, Box 33. For press coverage of the Diana Press vandalism, see Shirl Buss, "Diana Press Ransacked," *Lesbian Tide* 7 (January/February 1978): 18; "Diana Press Vandalized," *Big Mama Rag* 5 no. 9 (November-December 1977); and "More Problems for Diana Press," *Lesbian Tide* 8 (September/October 1978): 16. For information on royalties, see Jeanne Córdova, "Rita Mae Sues Diana," *Lesbian Tide* 8 (March/April 1979): 16; Coletta Reid and Kathy Tomyris, "Diana Suspends Publishing, Apologizes," *Lesbian Tide* 8 (May 1979): 14, and "Diana Press," *Big Mama Rag* 7 (June 1979): 25. There were many rumors about the vandalism that destroyed books and printing equipment. Some attributed it to feminists who were against the Feminist Economic Network (FEN) of which Diana was a part, while others raised the possibility of self-sabotage. Grier fell in the latter camp, speculating that the act had been calculated to gain sympathy, time and donations. After Rita Mae Brown filed a lawsuit for breach of contract in 1978, Grier joined the cacophony, demanding royalties for Foster's book and the three *Ladder* anthologies.

8. Grier provided a detailed biography of Anyda Marchant in Grier to Suzanne Hyers, August 26, 1988, Grier-Naiad Press Collection, Box 1.

9. Marchant wrote about her personal history in Marchant to Grier, November 18, 1971, Grier-Naiad Press Collection, Box 1.

10. Anyda Marchant, Personal Journal, Entry for November 4, 1978, shared with the author by Fay Jacobs.

11. Marchant to Grier, September 14, 1972, Grier-Naiad Press Collection, Box 1.

12. The "no barriers" quote is from Grier to Marchant, January 28, 1972, the "between-the-lines" reference is from Marchant to Grier, September 25, 1972, and the "plot enormously" quote is from Grier to Marchant, February 19, 1972, Grier-Naiad Press Collection, Box 1.

13. Grier to Marchant, March 12, 1973, Grier-Naiad Press Collection, Box 1.

14. The references to "confronting the real issues" and "social and economic class" are from Marchant to Grier, May 28, 1974, and the reference to "tracts" is from Marchant to Grier, March 20, 1974, Grier-Naiad Press Collection, Box 1.

15. For more information on self-publishing, see the "Hogarth Press," The Modernism Lab at Yale University, http://modernism.research.yale.edu/wiki/index.php/Hogarth_Press (accessed July 8, 2013), and "Lesbian and Gay Voices: A Tribute to Isabel Miller" (recorded presentation from the 1994 Michigan Writers Symposium), Vincent Voice Library, Michigan State University, East Lansing, Michigan.

16. Marchant to Grier, May 8, 1974, and Grier to Marchant, June 28, 1974, Grier-Naiad Press Collection, Box 1.

17. For a discussion of the naming of Naiad Press, see Marchant to Grier, March 29, 1974, and Grier to Marchant, April 2, 1974. Donna McBride confirmed information about naming the press in an email to the author, August 9, 2013. The reference to "Great Works" is from Marchant to Grier, June 10, 1974, and to "certain type of lesbian novel" is from Marchant to Grier, August 18, 1975. The Grier-Marchant correspondence is all from the Grier-Naiad Press Collection, Box 1.

18. Marchant to Grier, April 8, 1974, Grier-Naiad Press Collection, Box 1.

19. Donna McBride, email to the author, April 15, 2013.

20. Grier to Marchant, April 2, 1974. According to Marchant to Grier, April 27, 1977, it took nearly three years for the book to sell 1,400 copies. Both letters are in Grier-Naiad Press Collection, Box 1. Grier discussed plans for publicity in Grier to Marchant, September 16, 1974, Grier-Naiad Press Collection, GLC 30, Box

1. For more discussion of Grier's efforts to promote *The Latecomer*, see Grier to Marchant, November 8, 1974, Grier to Book People, September 18, 1974, and Grier to Helaine Harris, November 5, 1974, Grier-Naiad Press Collection, Box 1.

21. Sherry Thomas, phone interview with the author, March 12, 2012. The advent of *The Women's Review of Books* in 1983 brought much-deserved national and international attention to literary writers, but many others remained beyond its scope.

22. Grier to Marchant, November 8, 1974, Grier-Naiad Press Collection, Box 1.

23. See Marchant to Grier, May 28, 1974, August 13, 1974, and September 23, 1974, Grier-Naiad Press Collection, Box 1.

24. Grier to Ambitious Amazons, April 11, 1975, Grier-Naiad Press Collection, Box 1.

25. The *off our backs* reference is from Grier to Marchant, May 29, 1974, the "out of my tree" reference is from Grier to Marchant, November 11, 1974, and the "stop rankling" reference is from Grier to Marchant, November 8, 1974, Grier-Naiad Press Collection, Box 1.

26. Susie, It's About Time Women's Bookstore, Seattle, to Naiad Press c/o *The Ladder* [mid-July 1975], Grier-Naiad Press Collection, Box 1.

27. Grier to Marchant, October 8, 1974, Grier-Naiad Press Collection, Box 1.

28. For more on the publication of the Index, see Grier to Marchant, July 22, 1974, Grier-Naiad Press Collection, Box 1, and Grier to Kathryn Davis, October 2, 1974, Grier-Naiad Press Collection, Box 33.

29. Gene Damon, Jan Watson, and Robin Jordan. *The Lesbian in Literature: A Bibliography*, 2nd ed., Reno, Nev.: The Ladder, 1975. The reference to "'loose' collective" is from Grier to Kirsten Grimstad and Susan Rennie, November 26, 1974, Grier-Naiad Press Collection, Box 1. For a review, see Norman Lederer, "[Review of] *The Lesbian in Literature*," *ARBA* 76: (1976), 721.

30. For examples of Barbara's fretting, see Grier to Marchant, October 8, 1974 and January 6, 1975, for Jean Wallen's low bid, see Wallen to Grier, January 31, 1975, and for cost savings on typing see Kathy Mengle to Grier, February 14, 1975, Grier-Naiad Press Collection, Box 1. When Barbara learned that it would cost approximately $2,400 to print two thousand copies of the book, she informed Marchant that she had approximately one thousand advance orders, and requested a loan of $1,000, to be paid from the book's income.

31. The call for "Barbara Bread" is mentioned in Grier to Marchant, September 20, 1974, Grier-Naiad Press Collection, Box 1; Martha and Lucy, Porpoise, to Barbara Grier, July 3, 1976, Grier-Naiad Press Collection, Box 33.

32. Bertha Harris to Grier, February 25, 1975, Grier-Naiad Press Collection, Box 33. Other correspondents included Karla Jay, Gayle Rubin, Beth Hodges and Joanna Russ.

33. Grier to Grimstad, December 16, 1974, Grier-Naiad Press Collection, Box 1. For an example of Grier saying *The Ladder* would resume publishing, see Grier to Dolores Klaich, November 27, 1974, Grier-Naiad Press Collection, Box 33.

34. M.J. Kuda to Barbara Grier, May 5, 1975; Grier to Kuda, June 3, 1975, Grier-Naiad Press Collection, Box 1.

35. Grier to M.J. Kuda, September 30, 1974 and October 2, 1974, and Kuda to Grier, September 26, 1975, Grier-Naiad Press Collection, Box 1. For more on the Lesbian Writers Conferences, see Jorjet Harper, "Lesbian Writers Conferences: Sharing Words," in *Out and Proud in Chicago: An Overview of the City's Gay Community*, ed. Tracy Baim (Chicago: Surrey Books, 2008), p. 123; and "Some Notes on the Writer's Conference," *Lavender Woman* (December 1975): 14. Grier, "The Possibilities Are Staggering," September 19, 1975, reprinted in Robert B. Marks Ridinger, ed., *Speaking for Our Lives: Historic Speeches and Rhetoric for Gay and Lesbian Rights, 1892-2000* (New York: Harrington Park Press, 2004): 247-52.

36. E. [no last name given] to M.J. Kuda, October 1, 1976, shared with the author by M.J. Kuda.

37. For examples of Grier's correspondence with lesbian feminists, see Grier to Beth Hodges, February 6, 1975, Grier-Naiad Press Collection, Box 1; Karla Jay to Grier, February 22, 1975, Karla Jay Papers, Box 3; and Joanna Russ to Barbara Grier, April 22, 1975, Grier-Naiad Press Collection, Box 33.

38. Gayle Rubin to Barbara Grier, January 5, 1975; and Program, Kansas State University Educators Conference, October 1975, Grier-Naiad Press Collection, Box 1. For more information on queering the curriculum, see Susan Freeman, "Building Lesbian Studies in the 1970s and 1980s," in *Breaking the Wave: Women, Their Organizations, and Feminism, 1945-1985* (New York: Routledge, 2010): 232.

39. Bertha Harris to Barbara and Donna, November 16, 1975, Grier-Naiad Press Collection, Box 33; Grier to Marchant, October 7, 1975, Grier-Naiad Press Collection, Box 1.

40. For Barbara's impressions, see Grier to Marchant, December 2, 1975 and December 16, 1975, Grier-Naiad Press Collection, Box 1.

41. Barbara believed that the twenty-nine authors whose work had been selected would not mind her splitting the royalties with Reid because most of them had written for the magazine "out of love and caring." See Coletta Reid to Grier, Received February 21, 1974, Grier to Reid, February 22, 1974 and October 23, 1974, Grier-Naiad Press Collection, Box 33.

42. The reference to "selling power" is from Reid to Grier, April 1975, and to "PROUD of being a Lesbian" is from Grier to Reid, May 2, 1975, Grier-Naiad Press Collection, Box 33.

43. Grier to Dears [Anyda Marchant & Muriel Crawford], June 15, 1975; Marchant to Grier, July 22, 1975, Grier-Naiad Press Collection, Box 1. *Tottie* was published by Naiad Press and distributed by *The Ladder*.

44. The reference to "What flavor of tale" is from Grier to Marchant, after Aug. 5, 1975 (Post-it note); for Marchant's response, see Marchant to Grier, August 18, 1975, Grier-Naiad Press Collection, Box 1.

45. Grier to M.J. Kuda, October 2, 1975, Grier-Naiad Press Collection, Box 1.

46. Maida Tilchen, "Review of *Lesbiana*," *Body Politic* (Issue 31), (March 1977): 3. Publication information for Naiad's 1976 publication can be found in *Catalog of Copyright Entries; Third Series, Volume 30, Pt. 1, No. 2, Section 2, Books and Pamphlets, July–December 1976, 1738A759488*. Washington, D.C.: Library of Congress Copyright Office, 1977. Thrilled with the publicity, Barbara was not upset by the negative review of Jordan's book in *Big Mama Rag* 4 (December 1976): 12, and she was equally delighted when the American Library Association's *Booklist* mentioned Naiad's publication of *A Woman Appeared to Me* in its March 1, 1977 issue.

47. Marchant to Grier, June 3, 1976, Grier-Naiad Press Collection, Box 1. Marchant incorporated the Naiad Press as an S corporation, with the shares divided 30-30-30-10. She later reallocated shares, giving each director 25 percent.

CHAPTER TEN

1. Grier to Anyda Marchant, May 12, 1977, Grier-Naiad Press Collection, Box 1.

2. For more on the history of the WIP movement, see Trysh Travis, "The Women in Print Movement: History and Implications," *Book History* 11 (2008): 275-300; Sonja L. Jones, ed., *Gay and Lesbian Literature Since World War II: History and Memory* (New York: Routledge, 1998), 124-8; Kay Ann Cassell, "Women in Print, an Update," *Library Journal* 102 (June 15, 1977), 1352-5; Charlotte Bunch, "Women in Print Movement," *Sinister Wisdom* 13 (1980): 71-7.

3. Grier to Lyndall Cowan, April 7, 1976, Eric Garber Papers, Box 6.

4. Grier to Vicki P. McConnell, August 1, 1977, Grier-Naiad Press Collection, Box 12.

5. Manuela Soares interview with Barbara Grier, November 1987, Lesbian Herstory Archives-Daughters of Bilitis Video Project.

6. Grier-McBride interview with Karin Kallmaker and M.J. Lowe, December 11-15, 2006.

7. *Ibid.*

8. Ruth Mountaingrove, phone interview with the author, January 17, 2013; Carol Seajay, phone interview with the author, January 8, 2012.

9. Marie J. Kuda, "*Feminist Bookstore News* Closes," *Windy City Times*, 7/26/2000. Accessed online at http://www.windycitymediagroup. com/lgbt/Feminist-Bookstore-News-closes/28678.html (January 4, 2014).

10. Dedication, *Sinister Wisdom* 1 (Fall 1976), inside front cover.

11. Paula Buckingham to Grier, November 23, [1976], Grier-McBride Collection, Box 33; Grier to Dear Friends, December 16, 1976, shared with the author by Donna McBride.

12. Grier to Tea Corrine, December 24, 1976, Grier-Naiad Press Collection, Box 1.

13. For more on the founding of women's bookstores, see Junko Onosaka, *Feminist Revolution in Literacy: Women's Bookstores in the United States* (New York: Routledge, 2006) and Kristen Amber Hogan, "Reading at Feminist Bookstores: Women's Literature, Women's Studies, and the Feminist Bookstore Network," Ph.D. diss., University of Texas, 2006.

14. "A Personal History of Charis with Linda Bryant," http://charis. indiebound.com/personal-history-charis-linda-bryant (accessed July 22, 2013).

15. Linda Bryant, phone interview with the author, March 13, 2013; Barbara Grier-Donna McBride interview with Karin Kallmaker and M.J. Lowe, December 11-15, 2006.

16. Lyndall Cowan to Grier, February 10, 1977, with postscript from Grier added, Eric Garber Papers, Box 6; Grier to Julia P. Stanley, April 5, 1977, Grier-Naiad Press Collection, Box 33; Grier to Dear Friends, March 20, 1977, shared with the author by Donna McBride. The visit with Gidlow is described in Grier to Dear Friends, March 5, 1977, shared with the author by Donna McBride.

17. The "Old Dykes" quote is from Nikki & Johnie to Grier, July 4, 1977, Grier-Naiad Press Collection, Box 1. The incident at the San Jose Women's Week is described in Grier-McBride interview with Karin Kallmaker and M.J. Lowe, December 11-15, 2006.

18. The "Professor of Lesbian Studies" quote is from Gayle Rubin to Grier, February 16, 1977, Grier-Naiad Press Collection, Box 1; Rubin, interview with the author, June 10, 2012. The invitation to speak is in Rubin to Barbara and Donna, April 6, 1977, Box 1. Barbara described the visit with her half-brothers and paternal grandmother, Glycine, in Barbara Grier and Donna McBride to Dear Friends, April 28, 1977, shared with the author by Donna McBride.

19. Barbara discussed her dismissal from Macy's in Grier to Lyndall Cowan, April 4, 1977, Eric Garber Papers, Box 6; Kathy Mengle to Barbara and Donna and Anyda and Muriel, n.d. [April 1977], and Marchant to Grier, April 16, 1977, Grier-Naiad Press Collection, Box 1.

20. The "What we envision now" quote is from Grier to Sandia Belgrade, April 15, 1977. For a discussion of Grier's plans for the transition, see Grier to Kathy and Marc, April 12, 1977, Grier-Naiad Press Collection, Box 1.

21. Grier to Marchant, May 18, 1977, Grier-Naiad Press Collection, GLC 30, Box 1.

22. Grier and McBride to Dear Friends, June 24, 1977, shared with the author by Donna McBride; Grier to Marchant, May 4, 1977; News Release, June 28, 1977, Grier-Naiad Press Collection, Box 1.

23. The "without my keeper" reference is from Grier to Marchant, July 19, 1977; Sandia Belgrade to Grier, July 17, 1977, Grier-Naiad Press Collection, Box 1. The reference to "old days" is from Grier to Vicki McConnell, August 1, 1977, Grier-Naiad Press Collection, Box 12.

24. Donna McBride, email to the author, August 9, 2013; Grier to Marchant, May 2, 1977, Grier-Naiad Press Collection, Box 1.

25. Grier to Anyda and Muriel, November 2, 1977, Grier-Naiad Press Collection, Box 1.

26. Donna McBride, email to the author, March 29, 2013.

27. The reference to "last forever" is from Grier to Marchant, October 13, 1977, Grier-Naiad Press Collection, Box 1; the story of contacting Helen Bennett is from Donna McBride, email to the author, August 9, 2013. Jane Rule responded to Barbara's confidences about the relationship in Rule to Grier, October 25, 1977, shared with the author by Donna McBride.

28. Grier to Marchant and Crawford, November 2, 1977, Grier-Naiad Press Collection, Box 1.

29. Grier to Marchant, November 2, 1977; Grier-Naiad Press Collection, Box 1; Donna McBride, email to the author, March 29, 2013; Grier and McBride to Dear Friends, November 24, 1977, shared with the author by Donna McBride.

30. Holly Dorna, "An Interview with Barbara Grier," *Dinah* (May/June 1979), 4.

31. Cindy K. Erbes to Grier, March 22, 1979; Annis Wolley to Grier, March 22, 1979, both in Grier-Naiad Press Collection, Box 33.

32. First NWSA Convention Program, Box 1, NWSA Archives, University of Maryland Archives; Grier to Marchant, September 2, 1977; Sharon DeLano, "An Interview with Barbara Grier (Gene Damon)," *Christopher Street* 1 (October 1976), 41-49.

33. Harriet Desmoines and Catherine Nicholson, *Sinister Wisdom* 1, no. 2 (Fall 1976), 127-8.

34. *Ibid.*, 129.

35. The reference to "political possibilities" is from Julie R. Enszer, "'The Whole Naked Truth of Our Lives': Lesbian-Feminist Print Culture in the United States from 1969-1989," Ph.D. diss., University of Maryland, 2013, read in draft, p. 87. Marchant's discussion of feminism is from Marchant to Grier, April 29, 1977, Grier-Naiad Press Collection, Box 1. She considered Vicki P. McConnell's novel *Berrigan* (1978) "as near to that sort of thing" as she wanted to be. For a discussion of what Naiad would not publish, see "The Naiad Press," *Sinister Wisdom* 1.2 (1976): 117.

36. Grier to Elsa Gidlow, November 26, 1977, Grier-Naiad Press Collection, Box 33. Despite a promising beginning, Diana's involvement with the Feminist Economic Network (FEN) contributed to its downfall. At a conference held in Detroit in 1975, representatives from the Feminist Federal Credit Union of Detroit and the Oakland Feminist Credit Union proposed the formation of a feminist holding company. Advocates argued that it could achieve greater economic viability than any single

feminist business, but in the end, Diana Press was one of only five organizations supporting the creation of FEN. When FEN collapsed the following September, Coletta Reid and her partner, Casey Czarnak, suffered a financial setback because they had to pay $5,000 to extricate the press from the FEN holding network.

37. Marchant to Grier, February 26, 1978 and May 9, 1977, Grier-Naiad Press Collection, Box 1.

38. Grier to Tee Corinne, April 15, 1977; Marchant to Grier, March 25, 1977, both in Grier-Naiad Press Collection, Box 1. Since Marchant wrote her book in longhand, Naiad had the additional cost of hiring a typist to prepare the rough draft that Anyda edited.

39. Marchant to Grier, January 24, 1977, Grier-Naiad Press Collection, Box 1.

40. McConnell to Grier, December 14, 1977; Marchant to Gingerlox, December 1977, Grier-Naiad Press Collection, Box 12; McConnell, email to the author, April 16, 2013 and November 16, 2013. Elsa Gidlow discusses the Diana contract in Gidlow to Grier, February 22, 1978, Grier-Naiad Press Collection, Box 1. McConnell's four books include *Berrigan*, *Mrs. Porter's Letter*, *The Burnton Widows*, and *Double Daughter*.

41. Marchant to Grier, February 10, 1979, Grier-Naiad Press Collection, Box 1.

42. Marchant to Grier, June 14, 1977; Grier to Margy Lesher, *Lesbian Connection*, June 24, 1977, both from Grier-Naiad Press Collection, Box 1; Grier to Dear Friends, June 24, 1977, shared with the author by Donna McBride. For discussion of begging, see Grier to Catherine and Harriet, July 7, 1977, Grier to *off our backs*, July 7, 1977, Grier to Marchant and Mengle, July 7, 1977, Grier-Naiad Press Collection, Box 1.

43. Shebar Windstone to Grier, December 8, 1975 and August 14, 1979, Grier-Naiad Press Collection, Box 33; Lyndall Cowan to Grier, April 13, 1976, Grier-Naiad Press Collection, Box 1.

44. Janis Kelly to Grier, September 16, 1977; Grier discusses payment to Corinne in Grier to Marchant and Crawford, May 31, 1978, the reference to "bloodsucker" is from Grier to Marchant, August 19, 1977, all in Grier-Naiad Press Collection, Box 1.

45. Grier to Margy Lesher, *Lesbian Connection* June 24, 1977, Grier-Naiad Press Collection, Box 1.

46. Grier to Vicki P. McConnell, May 9, 1977, and McConnell, email to the Author, April 16, 2013; the reference to "donkey work" is from Marchant to Grier, June 3, 1978, and to "little viper" is

from Marchant to Grier, January 21, 1979, Grier-Naiad Press Collection, Box 1.

47. Margy Lesher, Lesbian Connection, to Grier, [before 12/11/1975], Grier-Naiad Press Collection, Box 1.

48. Lyndall Cowan to Barbara Grier, September 3, 1976, Grier-Naiad Press Collection, Box 1.

49. Marchant to Grier, February 17, 1977, Grier-Naiad Press Collection, Box 1.

50. Grier to Marchant, May 10, 1977, Grier-Naiad Press Collection, Box 1. In contrast with Marchant's old-fashioned prose, Mengle's coming-of-age story touched a chord with younger women and, unlike Marchant's novels, nearly recovered its publication costs of $2,100 within a year of publication.

51. Grier to Marchant and Crawford, August 21, 1977, and August 31, 1977, Grier-Naiad Press Collection, Box 1.

52. Grier to Marchant and Crawford, August 31, 1977. For more on Dorothy M. Broderick, see her obituary, published in *VOYA*, December 19, 2011, accessed online at http://www.voyamagazine.com/2011/12/19/dorothy-m-broderick-1929-2011/ (August 1, 2013). Broderick reviewed Barbara's anthologies, *Lavender Herring* and *Lesbiana*, in the *Emergency Librarian*. Her effort to become a petition candidate for president of the ALA was not successful.

53. Grier to Marchant and Crawford, August 31, 1977, Grier-Naiad Press Collection, Box 1.

54. Grier to Elise Collins, September 21, 1982, Grier-Naiad Press Collection, Box 1; Grier to Dear Friends, May 2, 1979, shared with the author by Donna McBride.

55. For the goal of "PUBLISH BOOKS," see Grier to Laura Kaye, August 29, 1977; Ferol to Grier, August 1, 1979, both in Grier-Naiad Press Collection, Box 1. First-wave feminism, with its emphasis on suffrage and legal obstacles to gender equality, spanned from the mid-nineteenth to the early twentyieth century. Second-wave feminism originated in the 1960s and addressed such issues as domestic violence, reproductive rights, sexuality, and workplace equality.

56. Jones, *Gay and Lesbian Literature Since World War II*, pp. 128, 132; Helaine Harris, email to the author, March 24, 2014.

57. For Barbara's view of WIND's failure, see Grier to Dear Friends, July 1, 1979, shared with the author by Donna McBride; for her solutions, see Grier to Marchant, June 28, 1979, and the reference to "uphill battle" is from Grier to Iowa City Women, June 28, 1979, Grier-Naiad Press Collection, Box 1.

58. The reference to "sobersides" is from Marchant to Grier, August 27, 1979, and to "heckling bookstores" is from Marchant to Grier, September 7, 1979, Grier-Naiad Press Collection, Box 1.
59. Grier to Dear Friends, October 13, 1979, shared with the author by Donna McBride.

CHAPTER ELEVEN

1. Grier to Donna McBride, n.d. [June 1980], shared with the author by Donna McBride.
2. Donna McBride, email to the author, July 24, 2013 and August 30, 2013. Barbara discussed the impact of Donna's absences in Grier to Vicki McConnell, July 26, 1980, Grier-Naiad Press Collection, Box 1. Barbara announced Donna's new position in Grier and McBride to Dear Friends, May 29, 1980, shared with the author by Donna McBride.
3. Grier and McBride to Dear Friends, May 29, 1980, shared with the author by Donna McBride.
4. Grier to McBride, June 17, 1980, and June 27, 1980, shared with the author by Donna McBride.
5. The quoted material is from Grier to McBride, July 8, 1980, July 28, 1980, and July 31, 1980. See also Grier to McBride, July 12, 1980, shared with the author by Donna McBride.
6. Grier to McBride, June 27, 1980, shared with the author by Donna McBride.
7. Grier to Rule, July 24, 1980, Jane Rule fonds, Box 30.
8. Grier to Dear Friends, November 22, 1980, shared with the author by Donna McBride; Grier to Rule, October 15, 1980, Jane Rule fonds, Box 30; Grier to Dear Friends, December 1980, shared with the author by Donna McBride.
9. Grier to Anyda Marchant, June 28, 1979, Grier-Naiad Press Collection, Box 1.
10. Grier to Elsa Gidlow, November 26, 1977, Grier-Naiad Press Collection, Box 33.
11. Grier to Marchant, March 12, 1980, and Marchant to Grier, March 10, 1980, Grier-Naiad Press Collection, Box 1. Ultimately, the first printing was 5,000 copies.
12. Pat Califia to Grier, August 17, 1979, Grier-Naiad Press Collection, Box 4.

13. Rubin discusses meeting Califia in Gayle Rubin to Grier, February 25, 1978, and her research on leather bars in Rubin to Barbara & Donna, August 16, 1978, both in Grier-Naiad Press Collection, Box 1. The reference to "known forever" is from Califia to Grier, April 21, 1979, Grier-Naiad Press Collection, Box 4.

14. Rubin to Grier, [N.D., 1979], Grier-Naiad Press Collection, Box 1. For more on the founding of Samois, see Gayle S. Rubin, *Deviations: A Gayle Rubin Reader* (Duke University Press, 2001), Chapter 4. Rubin, Califia, and 16 others formed Samois, a lesbian BDSM organization in San Francisco.

15. Grier to Rule, October 14, 1981, Jane Rule fonds, Box 30.

16. For Barbara's initial response to the *Sapphistry* manuscript, and her suggestion of an additional chapter, see Grier to Califia, November 6, 1979 and December 6, 1979, Grier-Naiad Press Collection, Box 4.

17. Califia to Grier, November 11, 1979, Grier-Naiad Press Collection, Box 4.

18. For Califia's account of Grier's phone call, see Pat Califia, "The Culture of Radical Sex," *Public Sex: The Culture of Radical Sex*, second ed. (New York: Cleis Press, 2000).

19. Califia to Grier, January 7, 1980, and May 2, 1980, Grier-Naiad Press Collection, Box 4. For examples of Califia's essays, see "Feminism vs. Sex," *The Advocate*, February 21, 1980, and "The Great Kiddy Porn Scare of '77 and Its Aftermath," *The Advocate*, April 17, 1980.

20. Harriet [Desmoines] and Catherine [Nicholson] to Grier, February 15, 1980, Grier-Naiad Press Collection, Box 4. In the early 1980s, when Desmoines and Nicholson decided that they had too much work, Barbara hired Sandi Stancil, who went on to typeset four hundred thirty books for Naiad Press.

21. Grier to Vicki P. McConnell, July 26, 1980, Grier-Naiad Press Collection, Box 1.

22. Ferol to Grier, August 1, 1979, Grier-Naiad Press Collection, Box 1.

23. For a sample of Barbara's persuasiveness, see Grier to Vicki P. McConnell, August 14, 1980, and for the Douglas quote, see Grier to Carol Anne Douglas, August 13, 1980, both in Grier-Naiad Press Collection, Box 1. McConnell's review, entitled "*Sapphistry: Striking Out at Feminism 'Til It Hurts*," appeared in *Big Mama Rag*.

24. Califia to Grier, April 6, 1981, Grier-Naiad Press Collection, Box 4; Christine Jenkins to Naiad Press women, May 3, 1981, Tee A.

Corinne Papers, Coll. 263, Special Collections and University Archives, University of Oregon.

25. Reina Lewis, "Sadomasochism," in *Lesbian Histories and Cultures: An Encyclopedia*, ed. Bonnie Zimmerman (New York: Garland Publishing, Inc., 2000): 659-61.

26. Donna McBride, email to the author, February 23, 2014; Grier to Rule, November 23, 1980, Jane Rule fonds, Box 30.

27. Grier to Rule, December 2, 1980. With the business expanding so rapidly in the early 1980s, it soon outgrew this storage unit and they rented a warehouse in Tallahassee.

28. Barb, Iowa City Women's Press, to Grier, November 7, 1980, Grier-Naiad Press Collection, Box 1; Grier to Rule, December 22, 1980, Jane Rule fonds, Box 30. The reference to "unethical" is from Iowa City Women's Press to Grier and McBride, December 12, 1980, and to the "Naiad Press factory" is from Grier to Marchant, April 8, 1981, Grier-Naiad Press Collection, Box 1.

29. The reference to getting Naiad "large enough" is from Grier to Rule, July 24, 1980, Jane Rule fonds, Box 30; to "making time move" and the fiftieth birthday is from Grier to Rule, July 12, 1980, Jane Rule fonds, Box 30.

30. For examples of Grier's promotion of *Outlander*, see Grier to Rule, March 1, 1981, March 16, 1981, and May 7, 1981; for discussion of the Robin Morgan review, see Grier to Rule, June 19, 1981, and for the publication date of August 1982, see Grier to Rule, September 4, 1981, all from Jane Rule fonds, Box 30. For Grier's efforts to obtain the HBJ rights, see Irene Skolnick to Grier, April 14, 1981, Grier-Naiad Press Collection, Box 14.

31. Grier and McBride to Gloria Greenfield, August 20, 1981, Grier-Naiad Press Collection, Box 2.

32. Greenfield to Grier, August 18, 1981, Grier-Naiad Press Collection, Box 2, also in Persephone Press Records, 1974-83, Carton 3, Schlesinger Library, Boston, Massachusetts.

33. Grier and McBride to Greenfield, August 20, 1981, Grier-Naiad Press collection.

34. Pat Hansen, "Persephone Press and the Politics of Publishing," Pat Hansen, *Washington Blade*, March 6, 1981, p. B-3.

35. Julie R. Enszer, "'The Whole Naked Truth of Our Lives': Lesbian-Feminist Print Culture in the United States from 1969-1989," Ph.D. diss., University of Maryland, 2013, read in draft, p. 172.

36. Grier's response to Women in Print coordinators questionnaire, July 1, 1981, Grier-Naiad Press Collection, Box 1. For more on

the WIP meeting, see Fran Moira, "Women in Print: Overview," *off our backs* 11 (December 31, 1981): 2.

37. Anyda Marchant, Personal Journal, Entry for October 8, 1981, shared with the author by Fay Jacobs.

38. Sherry Thomas, interview with the author, March 12, 2012.

39. Barbara discusses bindings and covers in Grier to Dear Friends, July 30, 1982 and Grier to Barb of Iowa City Women's Press, December 30, 1981, Grier-Naiad Press Collection, Box 1. Karla Jay recounted a conversation with Donna McBride about bindings in Karla Jay to Barbara Deming, November 7, 1982, Barbara Deming Papers, MC 408, Schlesinger Library, Radcliffe Institute. Barbara's request related to *Prism* is from Grier to Iowa City Women's Press, February 15, 1982, and her reference to "Any threat" is from Grier to Joy Fergoda, August 24, 1982, all from Grier-Naiad Press Collection, Box 1. In the end, women's printing operations produced approximately 110,000 volumes for Naiad Press.

40. Grier to Jane Rule, November 19, 1981, Jane Rule fonds, Box 30.

41. Sheila Ortiz Taylor, interview with the author, January 25, 2013.

42. Grier to Rule, June 19, 1981, Jane Rule fonds, Box 30; Grier to Marion Zimmer Bradley, December 28, 1981, Grier-Naiad Press Collection, Box 33; Rule to Grier, December 4, 1981, shared with the author by Donna McBride.

43. Sheila Ortiz Taylor, interview with the author, January 25, 2013. Barbara described their first trip to the American Booksellers Association in Grier to Dear Friends, June 9, 1995, shared with the author by Donna McBride.

44. Barbara discusses the sale of international rights for *Faultline* in Grier to Dear Friends, February 1982. The reference to the International Feminist Bookfair is from Barbara Grier and Donna McBride to Dear Friends, July 11, 1988. The summary of Barbara's promotional efforts on behalf of *Faultline* is from Grier to Rule, March 16, 1982, Jane Rule fonds, Box 30, Grier to Rita Mae Brown, March 31, 1982, and Grier to Lily Tomlin, May 22, 1982, both from Grier-Naiad Press Collection, Box 1.

45. Barbara, a shell collector, wanted to name the line "Top Shell," but cover designer Tee Corinne objected, "You're not going to name this line top anything." Manuela Soares interview with Barbara Grier, November 1987, Lesbian Herstory Archives-Daughters of Bilitis Video Project. Volute Books titles appeared in 1982 and 1983, but the imprint was short-lived because that format cost nearly as much to produce as a trade paperback.

46. Anne Borchardt to Grier, February 18, 1983, David Robinson, Talon Books, to Grier, April 10, 1984, and Grier to Robinson, April 18, 1984, all from Grier-Naiad Press collection, Box 14.

47. Ann Bannon as quoted in Tricia Lootens, "Ann Bannon: A Writer of Lost Lesbian Fiction Finds Herself and Her Public," *off our backs* 13/11 (December 1983): 12; and Ann Bannon, email to the author, March 28, 2013. Bannon's five Beebo Brinker novels included *Odd Girl Out, I Am Woman, Women in the Shadows, Journey to a Woman,* and *Beebo Brinker.*

48. Bannon, email to the author, March 28, 2013. Barbara discussed her plans to announce Bannon at Ortiz Taylor's reading in Grier to Eric Garber, April 24, 1982, Eric Garber Papers, Box 12.

49. Grier and McBride to Dear Friends, July 24, 1983, shared with the author by Donna McBride; Bannon, emails to the author, March 28, 2013 and February 21, 2014.

50. Katherine V. Forrest, "Memories of Barbara Grier," written for the Golden Crown Literary Society annual meeting, 2012. Shared with the author by Forrest.

51. Manuela Soares interview with Barbara Grier, November 1987, Lesbian Herstory Archives-Daughters of Bilitis Video Project.

52. The account of selling the cat book is included in Barbara Grier and Donna McBride to Dear Friends, October 1, 1987, shared with the author by Donna McBride. The Baltimore incident is described in Katherine V. Forrest, "Memories of Barbara Grier."

53. Grier to Rule, August 26, 1983, Jane Rule fonds, Box 30; Katherine V. Forrest to Lee Lynch, March 30, 1990, Katherine V. Forrest Papers, Box 8, San Francisco Public Library; Forrest, interview with the author, March 7-8, 2013.

54. Claire Morgan [Patricia Highsmith], "Afterword," *The Price of Salt* (Tallahassee: Naiad Press, 1984), [277-78].

55. Jacqueline Lapidus to Grier, November 9, 1982, Grier-Naiad Press Collection, Box 4; Grier to Highsmith, November 28, 1982, Grier-Naiad Press Collection, Box 13.

56. Highsmith to Grier, February 6, 1983, Grier to Highsmith, February 11, 1983, and March 4, 1983, Grier-Naiad Press Collection, Box 13.

57. Gene Damon, "Iniquity," *The Ladder* 4 (May 1960): 12. For discussion of Grier's research on Wilhelm, see Grier to Jeanne Shebley, September 12, 1984, Katherine V. Forrest Papers, Box 6, and Grier to Katherine V. Forrest, September 12, 1984, Katherine V. Forrest Papers, Box 3.

58. A friend to Naiad Press, April 19, 1985; Kathleen Huebner to Barbara and Donna, June 1, 1985; Wilhelm to Grier, September 10, 1985; July 22, 1985, August 8, 1985, and September 20, 1985, and Huebner to Barbara and Donna, September 20, 1985, all in Grier-Naiad Press Collection, Box 18. Grier recounted the visit to Eric Garber in Grier to Garber, August 4, 1985, Eric Garber Papers, Box 12. Marie J. Kuda questioned Grier's intentions in Kuda, "[Review of] *Torchlight to Valhalla*," newspaper clipping [1985], Anyda Marchant Papers, Box 12, Lesbian Herstory Archives.

59. Nancy Bereano, interview with the author, January 23, 2012.

60. *Ibid.*

61. Sherry Thomas, interview with the author, March 12, 2012.

62. Joan Denman, interview with the author, October 23, 2013. Denman owned Rubyfruit Books from 1982-1996.

63. The store's name came from Amy Lowell's "Books are either dreams or swords." For information on its establishment, see "Interview with Harriet Clare," by Rose Norman, 17 August 2001. http://www.uah.edu/english/wip/interview_dreams_swords.htm <accessed 8/3/2011>; Kathy Whyde Jesse, "Feminist Businesswoman Devoted to Family, Store," *Indianapolis Star*, January 14, 1990, p. H2; May Sarton, *After the Stroke: A Journal* (New York: 1988), 171. For insight from regular customers, see Judy Richter and Gloria Barnes, telephone interview with the author, August 7, 2011.

64. Dawn Oftedahl, interview with the author, April 3, 2013; Carol Seajay, phone interview with the author, January 8, 2012.

65. Rule to Grier, October 16, 1984, Jane Rule fonds, Box 30.

66. "Bookstores," in *Encyclopedia of Lesbian, Gay, Bisexual, and Transgender History in America*, ed. Marc Stein (New York: Charles Scribner's Sons, 2004), 149. The Labonté quote is from Bonnie Ruth Beebe, "Happy Birthday, Naiad!," *Lambda Book Report* 6.7 (February 1998): 23.

67. Grier to Rule, January 24, 1984, Jane Rule fonds, Box 30.

CHAPTER TWELVE

1. Barbara Grier and Donna McBride interview with Karin Kallmaker and M.J. Lowe, December 11-15, 2006.

2. Rosemary Curb, interview with the author, Albuquerque, New Mexico, November 22, 2008.

3. Ruth Baetz, taped communication to the author, August 2011. Anthologies included Ginny Vida, *Our Right to Love: A Lesbian*

Resource Book (1978), Margaret Cruikshank, *The Lesbian Path* (1980), Ruth Baetz, *Lesbian Crossroads* (1980), Julia Penelope Stanley and Susan J. Wolfe, *The Coming Out Stories* (1980), Cherríe Moraga and Gloria Anzaldúa, *This Bridge Called My Back: Writings by Radical Women of Color* (1981), and Evelyn Torton Beck, *Nice Jewish Girls: A Lesbian Anthology* (1982).

4. Carol Seajay, phone interview with the author, January 8, 2012; Seajay, quoted in Tricia Lootens, "Third Women in Print Conference," *off our backs* 15.8 (September 1985): 8. The tragic death of singing nun Jeanine Deckers in a double suicide occurred on March 29, 1985, nearly converging with the release of *Lesbian Nuns: Breaking Silence.*

5. Rosemary Curb to Barbara Grier, October 26, 1980, and December 7, 1980, Grier-Naiad Press Collection, Box 1; Nancy Manahan and Rosemary Curb, interview with the author, November 22, 2008.

6. *Ibid.* Announcements about the project appeared in *Telewoman: A Women's Newsletter* [California] (February 1982), [Modern Languages Association Gay Caucus] *Gay Studies Newsletter* 9 (March 1982), *Lesbian Connection* 5/4 (May 1982), and publications issued by Dignity and the Conference for Catholic Lesbians.

7. The opening and closing quotes are from Curb and Manahan interview with the author, "Lesbian Former Nuns: Our Spirituality Now," Michigan Womyn's Musical Festival flyer, August 14, 1981, in Nancy Manahan Papers, Tretter Collection, University of Minneapolis; Nancy Manahan described the Michigan gathering in "A Lesbian Ex-Nun Meets Her Sisters," *Common Lives/Lesbian Lives* 8 (Summer 1983), 90.

8. Grier to Curb and Manahan, July 31, 1983, Grier-Naiad Press Collection, Box 5; "Memorandum of Agreement," Contracts Folder, Nancy Manahan Papers, Tretter Collection, University of Minnesota, Box 2: Curb and Manahan interview with the author, November 22, 2008. Clause 2 of the 1983 contract granted the publisher "full, exclusive and sole right" to make arrangements for serial publication, public readings, radio, television, and motion picture rights.

9. Folder entitled "The Closet in the Cloister," Grier-Naiad Press Collection, Box 5; Grier to Nancy Manahan, March 9, 1983, in Rosemary Keefe Personal papers, accessed during a 2008 visit to her home in Albuquerque, New Mexico.

10. "Sister Ann Campbell" to Rosemary Curb, July 22, 1985, Rosemary Curb papers; Helen Fairfield Dickey to Manahan, August 7, 1985,

"Contributors' Correspondence," Manahan Collection, Box 2; Eileen Brady, email message to the author, January 23, 2011.

11. Grier to Dear Friends, July 24, 1983, shared with the author by Donna McBride.

12. Rosemary Curb discussed the book's structure in Curb, interview with the author, November 22, 2008; Manahan to Grier and McBride, May 9, 1984, Grier-Naiad Press Collection, Box 17; for the jacket copy, see the book's back cover.

13. Curb to Grier, October 1, 1984, Grier-Naiad Press Collection, Box 4.

14. Margaret Cruikshank, conversation with the author, June 10, 2011.

15. NWSA Conference Program, June 24-28, 1984, NWSA Archives (ACC 2006-105), University of Maryland, Box 1.

16. Curb discussed Barbara's initial reference to *Donahue* in Rosemary Curb, "Press Release to *off our backs, Gay Community News, Womanews, Plexus,* and other alternative women's publications," June 12, 1985, Rosemary Curb Personal Papers. Barbara shared her intention to get Curb and Manahan on *Donahue* in Grier to Eric Garber, October 20, 1983, Eric Garber Papers, Box 12.

17. Manuela Soares interview with Barbara Grier, November 1987, Lesbian Herstory Archives-Daughters of Bilitis Video Project.

18. Grier to Dear Friends, January 27, 1985, shared with the author by Donna McBride; Grier to Rosemary Curb and Nancy Manahan, January 31, 1985, Grier-Naiad Press Collection, Box 6.

19. Patricia McMillen, *Donahue,* to Grier, December 28, 1984, and Grier to B. Dalton, January 25, 1985, to Waldenbooks, January 28, 1985, and Grier to Dear Friends, February 2, 1985. For correspondence with book clubs, see Grier to Susan Weinberg, Quality Paperback Book Club, January 29, 1985, Grier to Olga Vezeris, Literary Guild, February 2, 1985, all in Grier-Naiad Press Collection, Box 6. *Lesbian Nuns: Breaking Silence* became the main selection for the Century Book Club in April 1985.

20. For a record of serial rights, see Grier-Naiad Press Collection, Box 5. The Warner Books payment was disbursed as $32,500 upon signing and an additional $32,500 on first publication. For full details, see Dennis Dalrymple, Director of Contracts and Copyrights, Warner Books, to Barbara Grier, March 26, 1985, Grier-Naiad Press Collection, Box 5. The ABC-TV film never materialized. See "Naiad Hopes to Out Lesbian Nuns," *Publishers Weekly,* February 15, 1985, p. 58. The "main chance" quote is from Grier to Curb and Manahan, January 31, 1985, Grier-Naiad Press Collection, Box 6.

21. Manuela Soares interview with Barbara Grier, November 1987, Lesbian Herstory Archives-Daughters of Bilitis Video Project.

22. For examples, see "Hate Mail," Grier-Naiad Press Collection, Box 5.

23. Accounts of the book's launch are contained in Nancy Manahan's book tour journal, March 29, April 2, April 8, May 8, and May 9, 1985, shared with the author by Manahan, and in Rosemary Curb's Book Tour Journal, April 8, 1985, shared with the author by Curb. Tapes of *Donahue*, which aired on April 8, 1985, the Monday after Easter, are in the Grier-Naiad Press Collection, Box 41.

24. Helga Dietzel to Rosemary Curb, July 21, 1985, Rosemary Curb papers, Albuquerque, New Mexico; Helga Dietzel, phone interview with the author, July 25, 2011; Mary Mendola, email message to the author, August 3, 2011.

25. For examples of contributor concerns, see "Sister Ann Campbell" to Rosemary Curb, July 22, 1985, Rosemary Curb papers, and Mab Maher, quoted in Tricia Lootens, "Women in Print Conference," *off our backs* 15.8 (September 1985): 8. Quotes are from Diana Di Prima to Rosemary Curb, July 8, 1985, and Wendy Sequoia to Curb, May 25, 1985, Rosemary Curb papers.

26. Rosemary Curb Book Tour Journal, March 13, 1985.

27. Information about numbers of reviews is from Grier to Jane Rule, February 14, 1986, Jane Rule fonds, Box 30. The "gate crasher" quote is from Patricia Gozemba, interview with the author, July 12, 2011.

28. Kay Longcope, "Nuns Speak Out on Love, Sex in Forthcoming Book," *Boston Sunday Globe*, March 17, 1985.

29. Rev. Conley was quoted in Jeannine Gramick, "Lesbian Nuns' Book: Ignored, Raped, Sexploited," *National Catholic Reporter* (September 6, 1985), clipping from Grier-Naiad Press Collection, Box 5. The "People Are Talking" appearance was scheduled for May 9. See also Dudley Clendinen, "Book on Lesbian Nuns Upsets Boston, Delighting Publisher," *New York Times*, April 12, 1985, A12.

30. See Whitney Strub, "Lavender, Menaced: Lesbianism, Obscenity Law, and the Feminist Anti-pornography Movement," *Journal of Women's History* 22.2 (2010): 83-107; Carolyn Bronstein, *Battling Pornography: The American Feminist Anti-Pornography Movement, 1976-1986* (New York: Cambridge University Press, 2011), 281; and Mary Gabriel, letter to the editor, *Feminist Bookstore News* 8 (June 1985): 6.

31. See Gayle S. Rubin, *Deviations*, Chapter 5. The chapter originally was presented at the Scholar and Feminist 9 Conference, April 24, 1982, Barnard College, New York City, and published in Carol S. Vance, *Pleasure and Danger: Exploring Female Sexuality* (Boston: Routledge and Kegan Paul, 1984), 267-319.

32. For an in-depth look at ethical issues raised by the sale of excerpts to *Forum*, see Susanna J.Sturgis in *Feminist Bookstore News* 7/6 (Spring 1985): 14. In the 1980s, Penthouse, Ltd. published a number of titles, including *Omni*, a popular science and science fiction magazine. For information about feminist campaigns against *Penthouse*, see Melissa Farley, "Fighting Femicide in the United States: The Rampage Against Penthouse," in Jill Radford and Dianna E. H. Russell, eds., *Femicide: The Politics of Woman Killing* (New York: Twayne Publishers, 1992), 341.

33. "Nuns' Stories Sold to Penthouse's *Forum*," *Gay Community News* 12/40 (April 27, 1985): 1; Cheryl Moch, "Lesbian Nuns [letter to the editor]," *WomanNews* (NYC), June 1985; Sister Mary Joan to the editor, *Gay Community News* 12/43 (May 18, 1985): 5; Carol D. Mortimer and Judith E. Kottke, "How Could You Do It?" *Gay Community News* 12/44 (May 25, 1985): 4, Grier-Naiad Press Collection, Box 6.

34. Rosemary Curb press release, August 27, 1985, Rosemary Curb Book Tour Journal, March 13, 1985, "Lesbian Nuns Controversy: Rosemary Curb Responds," *off our backs* 15 (October 31, 1985): 27.

35. Grier to Curb and Manahan, January 31, 1985, Grier-Naiad Press Collection, Box 6, San Francisco Public Library. Information about feminist publishing and bookstores is from the author's phone interviews with Carol Seajay, January 8, 2012, and Sherry Thomas, March 12, 2012.

36. Rosemary Curb Book Tour Journal, May 15, 1985; "Lesbian Nuns Controversy: Rosemary Curb Responds," *off our backs*, 15 (October 31, 1985), 27. The Naiad contract was between the publisher and co-editors, not with individual contributors, who had signed releases.

37. Helga Dietzel, phone interview with the author, July 25, 2011.

38. The meeting is recounted in Lootens, "Women in Print Conference," p. 8. See also Pam Mitchell, "Controversy and Dialogue at Women in Print," *Gay Community News*, n.d, clipping from Grier-Naiad Press Collection, Box 6. For another account, see the Jean Swallow papers, GLC 50.

39. Lootens, "Women in Print Conference," *off our backs* 15.8 (September 1985): 8. For Barbara's comments on censorship, see Wendy Patterson, "Lesbian Nuns: News and Reviews," *WomaNews* (June 1985): 5. For an in-depth look at ethical issues raised by the sale of excerpts to *Forum*, see Susanna J. Sturgis, "Breaking Silence, Breaking Faith: The Promotion of Lesbian Nuns," *Lesbian Ethics* 1 #3 (Fall 1985), available at http://www.susannajsturgis.com/article.php?id=28 (accessed October 6, 2012).

40. Barbara's comments are from "Women in Print Conference," *off our backs* (August/September 1985): 25-26.

41. *Ibid.*; Jean Swallow Notes [1985], Jean Swallow Papers GLC 50.

42. "1985 WIP Publishers Accords," *The Feminist Bookstore News* 8 (September 1985): 19, 21. See Sherry Thomas to Denise Kulp, *off our backs*, July 9, 1985, in "Women's Magazine Publishing Ethics, 1985" folder, *off our backs*, Box 21, University of Maryland Archives; "Controversy & Dialogue at Women in Print," *Gay Community News*, June 22, 1985, 1; and Ann Forfreedom, "Women in Print Conference," *The Wise Woman*, 12, Grier-Naiad Press Collection, Box 6.

43. "Mary Brady" to the editor, "Margaret" to the editor, *off our backs* 15 (July 1985); Jan Raymond and Pat Hynes to the editor, *off our backs* (June 1985): 30.

44. Elizabeth Kerwin, "The Flowering of Feminist Publishing: Women in Print," *Au Courant* 3 (July 15, 1985): n.p.; Mary Gabriel to *Feminist Book Review*, *Feminist Bookstore News* 8 No. 2/3 (September 1985): 6, all in Grier-Naiad Press Collection, Box 5.

45. Helaine Harris to *Feminist Bookstore News* 8 (September 1985): 7.

46. "Mary Brady," Grier-Naiad Press Collection, Box 4; and "Margaret," email communication with the author, January 14, 2011, and February 24, 2011.

47. Sherry Thomas, interview with the author, March 12, 2012. Nancy Manahan's record of income from sale of serial and subsidiary rights can be found in the Nancy Manahan Papers, Box 2.

48. [Letter to the editor], *off our backs* 15 (December 1985): 25; *Feminist Bookstore News* No. 2/3 (September 1985): 51.

49. Julie Enszer, conversation with the author, March 7, 2013.

50. Jeanne Córdova, interview with the author, November 23, 2010; Mary Gay Hutcherson, email to the author, November 20, 2008; Kelli Dunham, interview with the author, August 14, 2011.

51. Jane Rule to Grier, July 24, 1985, shared with the author by Donna McBride.

CHAPTER THIRTEEN

1. Barbara Grier to Jane Rule to Grier, November 15, 1985, Jane Rule fonds, Box 30.
2. Grier and McBride to Dear Friends, [February 1], 1986, shared with the author by Donna McBride.
3. Katherine V. Forrest, interview with the author, March 7-8, 2013.
4. Maggie Malley, NWSA Exhibit Coordinator, to Grier, April 25, 1986, NWSA Archives, National Women's Studies Association Archives, Box 14, Special Collections Department, University of Maryland.
5. Barbara Grier lecture at the University of Wisconsin, Stevens Point, 1983, Grier-Naiad Press Collection, Box 41.
6. Katherine V. Forrest, "Memories of Barbara Grier," Golden Crown Literary Society, 2012.
7. Forrest, interview with the author, March 7-8, 2013.
8. In 1987, a time when Naiad had more than one thousand bookstores on its mailing list, thirty-three of them did between $3,000 and $16,000 in direct business. Another seventy four stores placed $500 or more in direct orders.
9. Both Silver Moon and Gays the Word (a gay and lesbian bookshop in the Bloomsbury district of London) encountered problems when they imported gay and lesbian books from the United States. A case charging Gays the Word with importing obscene material through Her Majesty's Post Office was thrown out of court, while Silver Moon endured a period "when parcels from Giovanni's Room kept arriving beaten up, kicked around, and their contents damaged." The co-owners of the shop demanded a meeting with the head of the office where their parcels were delivered, and were assured that "there was 'no policy' of damaging our parcels and that this must have been done by a 'rogue' member of staff." After the meeting, however, the damage ceased. See Jane Cholmeley, email to the author, January 17, 2014 and February 27, 2014.
10. *Ibid.*
11. Jane Cholmeley, email to the author, January 17, 2014.
12. Barbara Grier to Dear Bookseller, December 20, 1991, shared with the author by Donna McBride.
13. Richard Labonté, email to the author, March 9, 2013.
14. Linda Bryant, interview with the author, March 13, 2013; Richard Labonté, email to the author, March 9 and 16, 2013; Grier to Dear

Bookstore, September 17, 1991, shared with the author by Donna McBride.

15. Linda Bryant, interview with the author, March 13, 2012; Dawn Oftedahl, interview with the author, April 3, 2013; Linda Bubon, interview with the author, June 23, 2013.

16. Richard Labonté, email to the author, March 9 and 16, 2013.

17. Alex Jaeger, interview with the author, March 25, 2013; Grier-McBride interview with Karin Kallmaker and M.J. Lowe, December 11-15, 2006.

18. Jane Troxell, email to the author, November 12, 2013. Troxell also shared a copy of Grier to Troxell, March 6, 1989 with the author.

19. Amanda Kyle Williams, interview with the author, October 28, 2013; Darlene Vendenga, email to the author, October 13, 2013. While attending the National Women's Music Festival in the early 1990s, Vendenga volunteered to serve as a first reader after hearing Barbara speak about the process of lesbian publishing.

20. Marianne K. Martin, email to the author, January 31, 2014.

21. Linda Hill, "By, For, and About Lesbians," AWP Conference, Boston, March 7, 2013; "Barbara Grier as Remembered by Claire McNab," shared with the author via email on March 19, 2014

22. Diane Salvatore, email to the author, January 11, 2014.

23. Katherine V. Forrest, interview with the author, March 7-8, 2013; Jackie Calhoun, email to the author, October 16, 2013.

24. Grier to Dear Author, December 26, 1990, shared with the author by Donna McBride, Sheila Ortiz Taylor, interview with the author, January 25, 2013, Jackie Cochran, email with the author, October 14, 2013. For another example of Barbara instructing an author to shorten a book, see Grier to Lynn Lonidier, February 12, 1983, Lynn Londier Papers, GLC 1, Box 6, San Francisco Public Library.

25. Katherine V. Forrest, interview with the author, March 7-8, 2013.

26. Elisabeth Nonas, interview with the author, October 25, 2013.

27. Brandon Judell, undated interview with Barbara Grier for the Gay Cable Network, Box 41; Forrest, interview with the author, March 7-8, 2013.

28. Others included Amanda Kyle Williams' lesbian CIA operative, Madison McGuire, and Lauren Wright Douglas' lesbian Canadian private investigator Caitlin Reece. Jaye Maiman's character was Robin Miller, Penny Micklebury created Gianna Maglione, a Washington, D.C. police lieutenant, and Pat Welch featured Helen Black, an ex-cop who became a private investigator in San Francisco.

29. Sherry Thomas, interview with the author, March 12, 2012.

30. Maida Tilchen, email to the author, November 10, 2013. Anderson, with Jane Heap, edited *The Little Review*, and was a part of the literary scene in Chicago, New York, and Paris, where she moved in the 1920s.

31. Cherry Bennett to Barbara Grier, August 31, 2000, shared with the author by Donna McBride.

32. Judell, interview with Barbara Grier for the Gay Cable Network; Katherine V. Forrest, interview with the author, March 7-8, 2013.

33. Lee Lynch, email to the author, November 9, 2013.

34. *Ibid.*

35. Jackie Cochran, email to the author, October 14, 2013; Amanda Kyle Williams, interview with the author, October 28, 2013.

36. Jane Rule to Katherine V. Forrest, January 20, 1987, Katherine V. Forrest Papers, Box 3; Ann Bannon, email to the author, March 22, 2013; Lee Lynch, email to the author, November 9, 2013.

37. Ethan Ellenberg, "All About Royalties," New York: The Ethan Ellenberg Literary Agency, paper delivered to the Romance Writers of America, 1999, accessed November 8, 2013 at http://ethanellenberg.com/all-about-royalties/. For a ten dollar book, ten percent royalties would earn one dollar per book while the publisher would pay expenses from the remaining nine. According to Ellenberg, publishers margins (profit after expenses have been deducted) have historically been as low as ten percent.

38. Vicki P. McConnell, email to the author, April 16, 2013; Katherine V. Forrest, interview with the author, March 7-8, 2013.

39. Amanda Kyle Williams, interview with the author, October 28, 2013.

40. Lee Lynch, email to the author, November 9, 2013; Sarah Schulman, interview with the author, November 13, 2013.

41. Ann Bannon, email to that author, March 22, 2013, March 28, 2013.

42. Roberta Rostorfer-Stocker, email to the author, January 13, 2013.

43. Rickilie Stone, Interview with Barbara Grier and Donna McBride for *Southern Circuit*, Fall 1985 [recording], Grier-Naiad Press Collection, Box 41.

44. Marianne K. Martin, email to the author, January 31, 2014.

45. Donna McBride to the author, November 3, 2013, Marjorie Menzel, "Softball, I Know You Know" *Lesbian Views and News* (June 1985), 23-24.

46. Sue Gambill to the author, January 24, 2013; Roberta Rostorfer-Stocker, interview with the author, January 13, 2013. Gambill also appreciated the opportunities she had to correspond with authors Gale Wilhelm and Jane Rule.

47. Rita Mae Reese, "By, For and About Lesbians: The Life of Barbara Grier,"http://ritamae-reese.blogspot.com/2011/12/by-for-and-about-lesbians-life-of.html, December 1, 2011; phone interview with Candis Creekmore, January 20, 2013.

48. Alex Jaeger, interview with the author; Sherry Thomas, interview with the author, March 25, 2013; Nancy Bereano, interview with the author, January 23, 2012.

49. Reese, "By, For and About Lesbians."

50. Roberta Rostorfer-Stocker, interview with the author, January 13, 2013. Rostorfer-Stocker remained on the job until an allergy to red ants forced her to move away from Tallahassee.

51. Rouse comments for AWP Conference, March 2013, emailed to the author, March 19, 2013; Sue Gambill, email to the author, January 21, 2013; Candis Creekmore, phone interview with the author, January 28, 2013.

52. Alex Jaegar, interview with the author, March 25, 2013.

53. Sue Gambill, "Firebrand Books: Making Available the Quality Work of Lesbian and Feminist Writers," *Hotwire* (July 1986): 21; Gambill, "Naiad Press: The World's Oldest and Largest Lesbian-Feminist Publishing House," *Hotwire* (March 1987): 18-20.

54. Alex Jaeger Interview with the author, March 25, 2013; the "hard shell, soft spot" quote is from Roberta Rostorfer-Stocker; Donna McBride, email to the author, October 6, 2013.

55. Alex Jaeger, interview with the author, March 25, 2013.

56. Alex Jaeger, interview with the author; Kristen Rouse, email to the author, March 19, 2013.

57. Sue Gambill, email to the author, January 15, 2013.

58. Roberta Rosterfer-Stocker, interview with the author, January 13, 2013; Sherry Thomas, interview with the author, March 12, 2012; Alex Jaeger, interview with the author, March 25, 2013; Rouse comments for AWP Conference, March 2013, emailed to the author, March 19, 2013.

59. Sue Gambill, email to the author, January 15, 2013; Rita Mae Reese, email to the author, January 3, 2013.

60. Deacon Maccubbin, email to the author, December 5, 2013.

61. Roberta Rostorfer-Stocker shared her perception of Barbara's intended audience in an interview with the author, January 13,

2013; Lee Lynch, "Crying for Barbara Grier," email to the author, November 9, 2013.

CHAPTER FOURTEEN

1. Barbara Grier to Dear Friends, August 1, 1993, shared with the author by Donna McBride.
2. Elizabeth Sims, email to the author, October 8, 2012. When Elisabeth Sims went to work at a suburban Detroit bookstore in the late 1980s, she was pleased and surprised to find that it featured a forty-eight shelf section of gay and lesbian books.
3. Barbara Grier and Donna McBride to Dear Friends, November 7, 1991, and to Dear Authors, February 2, 1992, shared with the author by Donna McBride.
4. Marchant to Marie Kuda, [July 6, 1998], The Marie J. Juda Collection, Kinsey Institute. Anyda Marchant, Personal journal entry for December 3, 1992, shared with the author by Fay Jacobs. Marchant stipulated that her shares would go first to Crawford, then to Grier, and then to McBride, while Crawford's shares went to Marchant, then McBride. Fay Jacobs, phone interview with the author, April 4, 2012, confirmed that Crawford was afraid of being rejected by her church if people knew she and Marchant were partners. An article appearing on the front page of the *Wilmington (Del.) Journal* in June 1994 left Crawford horrified, but when they attended church the following Sunday, the entire church applauded. The couple celebrated their fiftieth anniversary in 1998.
5. Edwin McDowell, "North Point to Stop Publishing Books," *New York Times*, November 30, 1990. North Point closed in 1991. According to McDowell, the press was not able "to move it up the notches that were necessary to survive." The dribble" quote is from Barbara Grier and Donna McBride to Dear Authors, February 2, 1992, shared with the author by Donna McBride.
6. Barbara Grier and Donna McBride to Dear Friends, July 18, 1992. See also Grier and McBride to Dear Friends, May 5, 1992, shared with the author by Donna McBride.
7. The quote is from Barbara Grier and Donna McBride to Dear Friends, March 5, 1993. The anthologies were: *The Erotic Naiad* (1992), *The Romantic Naiad* (1993), *The Mysterious Naiad* (1994), *The First Time Ever* (1995), *Dancing in the Dark* (1996), *Lady Be Good* (1997), *The Touch of Your Hand* (1998), and *The Very Thought of You* (1999).

8. Barbara discussed good news in Barbara Grier and Donna McBride to Dear Friends, June 6, 1992. The Lambda Literary Award winners included Katherine V. Forrest for *The Beverly Malibu* in 1990, Lauren Wright Douglas, co-recipient for *The Ninth Life* in 1991, Katherine V. Forrest in 1992 for *Murder by Tradition*, and Jaye Maiman, co-recipient in 1993 for *Crazy for Loving.* Diane Salvatore's *Love, Zena Beth* became Naiad's third book in hardcover. For a review of *Love, Zena Beth*, see *Publishers Weekly*, June 29, 1992 (http://www.publishersweekly.com/978-1-56280-015-4) accessed December 19, 2013.

9. Barbara Grier to Dear Friends, November 23, 1993, shared with the author by Donna McBride.

10. Grier-McBride interview with Karin Kallmaker and M. J. Lowe, December 11-15, 2006. Barbara described the Founders Day dinner in Barbara Grier and Donna McBride to Dear Friends, November 23, 1993. Information about the sale of Barbara and Donna's papers to the Library Foundation, the Foundation's donation of the collection to the San Francisco Public Library, and the dinner came from Tim Wilson, email to the author, October 15, 2013, and February 21, 2015.

11. The Women of Naiad Press to Dear Friends, February 6, 1993, shared with the author by Donna McBride.

12. Jane Troxell, email to the author, January 3, 2014; Barbara Grier and Donna McBride to Dear Friends, May 5, 1993, shared with the author by Donna McBride.

13. Grier to Dear Authors, January 13, 1994, shared with the author by Donna McBride. The decision affected twenty-three authors, among them Sheila Ortiz Taylor, Lee Lynch, and Sarah Aldridge. See Marchant to Marie J. Kuda, March 9, 1998, and July 6, 1998, Anyda Marchant Papers, Box 12, Folder 3, Lesbian Herstory Archives, Brooklyn. Barbara discussed Marchant's assessment of herself as a writer in Grier-McBride interview with Karin J. Kallmaker and M.J. Lowe, December 11-15, 2006.

14. Marchant discusses Barbara's ambition in Marchant to Valerie Taylor, April 8, 1996, The Marie J. Kuda Collection, Kinsey Institute. Marchant informs her partners of the decision to dissolve the press in Marchant to Barbara and Donna, April 25, 1994, Grier-Naiad Press Collection, Add. Box 4.

15. Hurley, Morgan, & Potts to Michael Gruver, April 27, 1994, Grier-Naiad Press Collection, Add. Box 4.

16. Michael Gruver to Barbara O'Leary [Anyda and Muriel's attorney], April 27, 1994. Grier-Naiad Press Collection, Add. Box 4.

17. Anyda Marchant to Grier, April 29, 1994, Grier-Naiad Press Collection, Add. Box 4. The Lighthouse Point house had been purchased for $113,000, and since 1989 Barbara and Donna had paid the taxes, insurance, pest control, and maintenance of the property.

18. After noting that Naiad Press had been incorporated as an S Corporation in 1976 and converted to a C Corporation in 1982 (with each of the four directors holding 25 percent of the company), the firm of Sheldrick, McGehee & Kohler based its estimate of the company's value on net assets, earning and dividend-paying capacity, market price for comparable companies, and "recent sales of equity interests in the subject company." According to the Internal Revenue Service, a C corporation is taxed separately from its owners, and shareholders then pay taxes on dividends. See www.irs.gov/Businesses/Small-Businesses-&-Self-Employed/Corporations.

19. Anyda Marchant's books, written as Sarah Aldridge and published by Naiad Press, include *The Latecomer* (1974), *Tottie* (1975), *Cytherea's Breath* (1976), *All True Lovers* (1978), *The Nesting Place* (1982), *Madame Aurora* (1983), *Misfortune's Friend* (1985), *Magdalena* (1987), *Keep to Me, Stranger* (1989), *A Flight of Angels* (1992), and *Michaela* (1994).

20. Grier to Marchant and Crawford, January 3, 1995, GLC 30, Add Box 4; Michael Gruver to Carolyn Olive, January 31, 1995, Grier-Naiad Press Collection, Add Box 4. The transaction was completed on February 22, 1995.

21. Barbara Grier and Donna McBride, "Dear Friends," February 15, 1995, shared with the author by Donna McBride; Anyda Marchant to Marie J. Kuda, March 9, 1998, The Marie J. Kuda Collection; Yvonne Shinhoster Lamb, "Anyda Marchant, Author, Publisher," *The Washington Post*, February 7, 2006.

22. This list of bestselling Naiad titles covered the period from October 1, 1993 through December 31, 1995.

23. Forrest, Personal Interview with the Author, March 7-8, 2013.

24. *Ibid.* Forrest grew convinced that when she did edit a gem like Teresa Stores' *Getting to the Point*, the Lambda Literary Award committee failed to take it seriously because of Naiad's reputation.

25. Grier to Dear Author, January 31, 1995. For Grier's public announcement of Forrest's departure, see "Check it Out," *Lambda Book Report* 4 (March/April 1995): 39. The article noted that Forrest left after 12 years and 12 books, three of which she co-edited with Grier.

26. Katherine V. Forrest, phone conversation with the author, July 22, 2011, and email to the author, November 4, 2013.

27. Christi Cassidy, phone interview with the author, October 5, 2013.

28. Barbara Grier to Jane Rule, April 20, 1986, Jane Rule fonds, Box 30. Barbara's expectations for lesbian film were in part grounded in the optioning of *Lesbian Nuns: Breaking Silence* to ABC-TV and the sale of movie rights for Ann Bannon's Beebo Brinker series in the spring of 1986. Neither film materialized in Barbara's lifetime.

29. Katherine V. Forrest, email to the author, March 5, 2014.

30. Nicole Conn, email to the author, January 9, 2014; Grier to Leoni, Samuel Goldwyn Publicity Department, January 10, 1986, Jane Rule fonds, Box 30; the "Rent those buses" quote is from Barbara Grier and Donna McBride to [Dear Friends], May 5, 1993; Donna McBride, email to the author, October 13, 2013.

31. Grier discussed the potential film adaptation of *Murder at the Nightwood Bar* in Grier to Jane Rule, July 15, 1991. Kaplan's *Devotion* was made into a feature-length film in 1995.

32. Betsy Schmidt discussed Marchant's objections to video distribution in Schmidt, phone interview with the author, April 7, 2012. Other details are from Barbara Grier and Donna McBride to Dear Friends, July 14, 1993. For the list of best sellers, see Grier to Dear Authors, January 5, [1996], both shared with the author by Donna McBride. "Claire of the Moon" was in first place, followed by the film, "Salmonberries," in second.

33. Barbara and Donna discussed "spectacular growth" in an interview with Karin Kallmaker, 2006. For more on bookstores in the 1990s, see "Gay/Lesbian Bookstores Victims of Acceptance," *219 Magazine* (July 15, 2009), Accessed December 2, 2013, at http://www.219mag.com/2009/07/15/gay-bookstores-victims-of-wider-acceptance/. Grier to Dear Authors, February 2, 1992, shared with the author by Donna McBride.

34. Carol Seajay, email to the author, October 31, 2013. At the peak, Seajay estimates, there were approximately 110 women-owned/run/oriented bookstores in the United States and Canada, plus an additional thirty alternative and gay bookstores with a strong commitment to selling lesbian books. By 2013 the number had declined to a handful. Randie Farmelant, "End of an Era: Will the Feminist Bookstore Soon be a Thing of the Past?" *off our backs* (May-June 2003): 20. For more on feminist bookstores at the turn of the twenty-first century, see Kathy McGrath, "Pushed to the Margins: The Slow Death and Possible Rebirth of the Feminist

Bookstore," *Feminist Collections* 25 no. 3 (Spring 2004): 4-9 (for statistics about numbers of stores in 1997 and 2004). "The State of Emergency in Feminist Publishing," *off our backs* 30 (August/September 2000): 5. Ellen Degeneres appeared on the cover of *Time* in 1997 with the caption, "Yep, I'm gay."

35. Information about Labonte is from Charlotte Abbott, "Battening Down the Niche," *Publishers Weekly* 248 (Apr. 23, 2001): http://www.publishersweekly.com/pw/print/20010423/30019-battening-down-the-niche.html (accessed 10/14/2013). See Rose Norman interview with Harriet Clare, August 17, 2001, http://www.uah.edu/english/wip/interview_dreams_swords.htm (accessed 8/3/2011). Simone Wallace, interview with the author, December 4, 2013. For more on bookstore responses to changing economic trends, see Junko Onosaka, *Feminist Revolution in Literacy*, page 98.

36. Jane Troxell, email to the author, January 3, 2014.

37. Linda Bubon, interview with the author, June 23, 2013. The Women's Voices Fund was established in November 2005. For more, see the Women and Children First website at http://www.womenandchildrenfirst.com/womens-voices-fund (accessed December 9, 2013).

38. Jane Cholmeley, email to the author, February 9, 2014.

39. Barbara discussed the offer from Kensington in Grier-McBride interview with Karin Kallmaker and M.J. Lowe, December 11-15, 2006. According to Donna McBride, email to the author, October 17, 2013, someone at Alyson Press also expressed interest in acquiring Naiad; however, at the time it was impossible because the press was having problems of its own.

40. Jane Chomeley, email to the author, February 9, 2014.

41. Kelly Smith is quoted from Kathleen DeBold, "Bellas Lettres: Naiad Midwives a New Lesbian Press," *Lambda Book Report* 9.2 (September 2000): 11; Grier to Dear Friends, January 18, 2002, shared with the author by Donna McBride.

42. Amanda Kyle Williams, interview with the author; Jackie Calhoun to the author, October 28, 2013; Darlene Vendegna, email to the author, October 13, 2013. Vendegna worked as a "first reader" for Naiad Press and Bella Books."

43. Grier to Dear Friends, June 13, 2000, and November 7, 2000, shared with the author by Donna McBride.

44. Information on Firebrand Books and Rising Tide Press is from Kevin Howell, "Changes Hit Gay/Lesbian Businesses," *Publishers Weekly* 247 #30 (July 24, 2000), 12. For additional discussion of

publishing trends, see Claire Kirch, "Bookseller of No Returns," *Publishers Weekly* (January 31, 2005): 26; Judith Niemi, "Publishing for the Love of It," *Women's Review of Books* 22 n3 (December 1, 2004): 20. "Joan Drury on the State of Lesbian Publishing," *Lambda Book Report* 9.2 (September 2000): 13.

45. Kelly Smith, email to the author, October 16, 2013. The six authors Bella published in 2000 included Peggy J. Herring, Therese Szymanski, Lyn Denison, Saxon Bennett, Jackie Calhoun, and Diana Braund.

46. Smith, email to the author, October 17, 2013; Grier-McBride interview with Karin Kallmaker and M. J. Lowe, December 11-15, 2006, Becky Arbogast, email to the author, October 28, 2013. For more on the LPC bankruptcy, see Calvin Reid and Steven Zeitchik, "LPC Group Files for Chapter 11 Bankruptcy," *Publishers Weekly* 249/14 (April 8, 2002).

47. Linda Hill, interview with the author, October 21, 2013.

48. Smith, email to the author, October 16, 2013 and October 17, 2013; Grier-McBride interview with Karin Kallmaker and M. J. Lowe, December 11-15, 2006; and Linda Hill, interview with the author, October 21, 2013. The author was unable to interview Terese Orban.

49. McBride to the author, October 15, 2013; Linda Hill, interview with the author, October 21, 2013; "Bella Reborn," *Publishers Weekly* (August 25, 2003): 32; "Bella Books," *Books to Watch Out For* 1 n.4 (February 2004) online, accessed October 21, 2013 at http://btwof-blog.com/enews_extras/Images4LES/4LES_HTML.html. Hill, a savvy businesswoman ramped up publication of lesbian romances and mysteries to two per month plus reprints, introduced the edgier "Bella After Dark" line, acquired the back stock of the defunct Rising Tide Press, and added the distribution rights for New Victoria Press. Today, the company is flourishing as a publisher and distributor of print and e-books.

50. Barbara Grier and Donna McBride to Dear Friends, January 18, 2002, shared with the author by McBride; Donna McBride in Grier-McBride interview with Karin Kallmaker and M.J. Lowe, December 11-15, 2006; Naiad Press website, http://www.naiadpress.com/ (accessed February 28, 2014); "Naiad Pulls Back, Bella Bursts Forth," *Feminist Bookstore News* 22/6 (2000).

51. Linda Hill, "By, For, and About Lesbians," AWP Conference, Boston, March 7, 2013.

52. Karin Kallmaker, "Romance and Chocolate Blog: Writing, Reading, and Lesbians," November 10, 2011, accessed at http://

blog.kallmaker.com/2011/11/barbara-grier-reflections.html, January 5, 2011; "Marginalia," *Echo Magazine*, July 3, 2003, p. 65.

CHAPTER FIFTEEN

1. Donna McBride, email to the author, March 9, 2014.
2. Grier-McBride interview with Karin Kallmaker and M.J. Lowe, December 11, 2006; Therese Syzmanski, "Legendary Lesbian Publisher Writes Her Own Happily Ever After," *Lambda Book Report*, May 2002, 11. Diane Salvatore described the "cozy, charming" home in email to the author, January 11, 2014.
3. Grier discussed oversight of the construction in email to the author, May 25, 2005; and Donna discussed harassment in the Grier-McBride Interview with Karin Kallmaker and M.J. Lowe, December 11-15, 2006.
4. Grier-McBride interview with Karin Kallmaker and M.J. Lowe; Grier, email to the author, May 28, 2005; Manuela Soares interview with Barbara Grier, November 1987, Lesbian Herstory Archives-Daughters of Bilitis Video Project.
5. Grier, email to the author, March 30, 2006; "Barbara Grier, 1933-2011," *Tallahassee Democrat*, November 13, 2011.
6. Donna McBride, email to the author, March 9, 2014.
7. Grier, email to the author, March 26, 2007.
8. Sheila Jefferson, "Sheila Jefferson's Memories of Barbara Grier," shared with the author, March 16, 2014; Helaine Harris, email to the author, March 25, 2014.
9. "Barbara Grier as Remembered by Claire McNab," shared with the author, March 19, 2014.
10. Donna McBride, interview with the author, February 24, 2012.
11. Vicki P. McConnell, email to the author, November 16, 2013; Diane Salvatore, email to the author, January 11, 2014; Nicole Conn, email to the author, January 9, 2014; Therese Szymansiki and Katherine V. Forrest are both quoted in Victoria Brownsworth, "In Rememberance: Barbara Grier," *Lambda Literary Review*, November 11, 2011, accessed at http://www.lambdaliterary.org/features/rem/11/11/in-remembrance-barbara-grier/.
12. The quotes are from Elaine Woo, "Barbara Grier Dies at 78," *Los Angeles Times*, November 13, 2011; Victoria Brownsworth, "Obituary: Barbara Grier, Publisher, Activist," *Philadelphia Gay News*, November 17, 2011, "Op-ed: Barbara Grier, Lesbian Icon, Dies,"

The Advocate, November 11, 2011, http://www.advocate.com/politics/commentary/2011/11/11/oped-barbara-grier-lesbian-icon-dies (accessed March 4, 2014); and "Naiad Press Co-founder Barbara Grier Dies," *Windy City Times*, November 10, 2011, and updated November 16, 2011, http://www.windycitymediagroup.com/gay/lesbian/news/ARTICLE.php?AID=34723 (accessed December 3, 2012). For other examples, see Paul Vitello, "Barbara Grier, Publisher of Lesbian Books, Dies at 78," *New York Times*, November 13, 2011, Martin Childs, "Barbara Grier: Publisher Who Championed Lesbian Literature," *The Independent*, November 25, 2011, Alison Bechdel, "Barbara Grier," November 11, 2011, http://dykestowatchoutfor.com/barbara-grier (accessed March 4, 2014); and Bett Norris, "Loss, Literary Icons, and Me," November 11, 2011, http://bettnorris.wordpress.com/2011/11/11/loss-literary-icons-and-me/ (accessed March 4, 2014).

13. Grier to Lee Lynch, January 22, 1971, Lee Lynch Papers, Box 18.

SELECTED BIBLIOGRAPHY

Archival Sources and Collections

Gay, Lesbian, Bisexual, Transgender Historical Society, San Francisco, CA
    Elsa Gidlow Papers
    Eric Garber Papers
    Phyllis Lyon-Del Martin Papers
June L. Mazer Lesbian Archives, West Hollywood, CA
    Diana Press Collection
Kinsey Institute for Research in Sex, Gender, and Reproduction, Bloomington, IN
    Marie J. Kuda Papers
Lesbian Herstory Archives, Brooklyn, NY
    Anyda Marchant Papers
    Daughters of Bilitis Video Project
    Daughters of Bilitis Organizational Files
Library of Congress, Washington, DC
    Franklin Kameny Papers,
New York Public Library, New York, NY
    Barbara Gittings and Kay Tobin Lahusen Gay History Papers and Photographs
    Jonathan N. Katz Papers
    Karla Jay Papers
    May Sarton Papers
ONE Institute and Archives, University of Southern California, Los Angeles, CA
    Correspondence
San Francisco Public Library, San Francisco, CA
    Barbara Grier-Naiad Press Collection
    Florence "Conrad" Jaffy Papers

Jean Swallow Papers
Katherine V. Forrest Papers
Lynn Londier Papers
Schlesinger Library, Radcliffe Institute, Cambridge, Massachusetts
Barbara Deming Papers
Persephone Press Records
University of British Columbia, Vancouver, Canada
Jane Rule fond
University of Maryland, College Park, MD
National Women's Studies Association Archives
University of Minnesota Libraries, The Jean-Nickolaus Tretter
Collection, Minneapolis, MN
Nancy Manahan Papers
University of Oregon
Lee Lynch Papers
Ruth Mountaingrove Photograph Collection
Tee A. Corinne Papers

Private Collections

Barbara Grier and Donna McBride Papers and Library, Carabelle, FL
Gayle Rubin Papers and Library, San Francisco, CA
Rosemary Curb papers, Albuquerque, NM (used in 2008)

Newspapers and Periodicals Consulted

Advocate
Arena Three
Big Mama Rag
Christopher Street
Feminist Bookstore News
Gay Community News
Journal of Lesbian Studies
Kansas City Women's Liberation Union Newsletter
Lambda Book Report
Lesbian Connection
Lesbian Tide
Mattachine Review
off our backs
On Our Backs

ONE
One Confidential
The Body Politic
The Ladder
The Lesbian Letter (New York DOB Newsletter)
The Lesbian Tide
The New York Times
The Women's Review of Books
Signs
Sinister Wisdom
Sisters
Washington Blade

Oral Interviews

The author conducted numerous telephone, email, and in-person interviews while doing research for this book. Interviewees are noted in the acknowledgements. Of the many interviews recorded with Barbara Grier, the following were the most useful:

Barbara Grier, interview with Maida Tilchen, June 1977, shared with the author by Tilchen.

Barbara Grier, interview with Manuela Soares, November 1987, Lesbian Herstory Archives-Daughters of Bilitis Video Project.

Barbara Grier and Donna McBride, interview with Karin Kallmaker and M.J. Lowe, December 2006.

Barbara Grier and Donna McBride, interview with Joanne Passet, December 2006.

Works by Barbara Grier (excluding book reviews), in chronological order by pseudonym

Damon, Gene. "Chance." *The Ladder* 2 (November 1957): 8-10.

G., B. "Essay on a Lesbian." *The Ladder* 2 (November 1957): 20.

Damon, Gene. "Girls Across the Hall." *The Ladder* 2 (January 1958): 9-11.

Niven, Vern. When I Was 17." *The Ladder* 2 (April 1958): 12-13.

Damon, Gene. "Lesbian Marriage." *The Ladder* 2 (August 1958): 12-13.

Niven, Vern. "Perfect Control." *The Ladder* 3 (November 1958): 9-12.

Damon, Gene and Lee Stuart. "The Repressed Lesbian." *The Ladder* 3 (November 1958): 18-20.

Damon, Gene. "Radclyffe Hall." *The Ladder* 3 (December 1958): 8-9.

Damon, Gene. "Mrs. Morrison's Casserole." *The Ladder* 3 (January 1959): 4-6.

Damon, Gene and Lee Stuart. "Transvestism in Women. *The Ladder* 3 (February 1959): 11-13.

Damon, Gene and Lee Stuart. "Renée Vivien, Forgotten Lesbian Poet." *The Ladder* 3 (May 1959): 12-13.

Niven, Vern. "Will Call." *The Ladder* 3 (May 1959): 17-20.

Strong, Lennox. "Exception to the Rule." *The Ladder* 3 (August 1959): 10-11.

Damon, Gene. "Iniquity." *The Ladder* 4 (May 1960): 12.

Damon, Gene. "Village Tale." *The Ladder* 4 (June 1960): 16-19.

Damon, Gene and Lee Stuart. "On Censorship." *The Ladder* 5 (November 1960): 18-19.

Strong, Lennox. "Violet Florence Martin." *The Ladder* 5 (November 1960): 24-25.

Strong, Lennox. "The Royal Triangle." *The Ladder* 5 (January 1961): 23-24.

Damon, Gene and Lee Stuart. "Rosa Bonheur." *The Ladder* 6 (November 1961): 9-10.

Niven, Vern. "No Hamburgers." *The Ladder* 6 (March 1962): 22-24.

Damon, Gene. "The Gay Short Story." *Mattachine Review* 9/3 (March 1963): 21.

Strang, Lennox and Terri Cook. "Variant Poetry." *The Ladder* 7 (April 1963): 8-10.

Damon, Gene and Lee Stuart. "Queen Christina." *The Ladder* 7 (June 1963): 6-8.

Strang, Lennox. "To Be a Man." *The Ladder* 8 (October 1963): 7-10.

Barrow, Marilyn. "Living Propaganda." *The Ladder* 8 (November 1963): 4-6.

Niven, Vern. "Noblesse." *The Ladder* 8 (January 1964): 9.

Fiske, Irene. "Say! Who Were You Named After." *The Ladder* 8 (February 1964): 4-5.

Barrow, Marilyn. "Living Propaganda." *The Ladder* 8 (February 1964): 21-22.

Niven, Vern. "The First Woman Doctor in Britain: Dr. James Barry." *The Ladder* 8 (March 1964): 4-6.

Barrow, Marilyn. "The Very Vast Wasteland: the Celibate, the Passer and the Nun." *The Ladder* 8 (April 1964): 9-10.

Damon, Gene. "Encounters." *Arena Three* 1 (June 1964): 8.

Niven, Vern. "Marie Corelli." *The Ladder* 8 (July 1964): 17.

Damon, Gene. "To Tell or Not to Tell." *The Ladder* 9 (February/March 1965): 24-25.

Strang, Lennox. "Lady Hester Lucy Stanhope." *Arena Three* 2 (March 1965): 5-6.

Damon, Gene and Lee Stuart. "Of Woman Unto Woman." *The Ladder* 9 (April 1965): 6-8.

Strong, Lennox. "The Marble Statue." *Arena Three* 2 (July 1965): 5-6.

Barrow, Marilyn. "Good Night and Merry Christmas." *Tangents* 1 (December 1965): 19-21.

Niven, Vern. "The Romantic Stuarts." *Arena Three* 3 (January 1966): 16-18.

Fiske, Irene. "The Young Lesbian." *The Ladder* 10 (February 1966): 21-23.

Damon, Gene. "Together—Toward a Common Goal." *Tangents* 1 (March 1966): 31.

Fiske, Irene. "The Strange Case of Dr. James Barry: Britain's First Woman M.D." *Arena Three* 3/3 (March 1966): 38.

Damon, Gene. "The Lesbian Paperback." *Tangents* 1 (June 1966): 4-7.

Damon, Gene. "The Lesbian Paperback II." *Tangents* 1 (July 1966)): 13-15.

Niven, Vern. "The Life of Lady Hester Stanhope." *The Ladder* 10 (September 1966): 18-21.

Strong, Lennox and Terri Cook. "Poetry of Lesbiana." *The Ladder* 11 (November 1966): 20-28.

Damon, Gene and Lee Stuart. *The Lesbian in Literature: A Bibliography.* San Francisco: Daughters of Bilitis, 1967.

Niven, Vern. "Artistic Paths that Crossed." *The Ladder* 11 (January 1967): 13-16.

Niven, Vern. "Climbing the Family Tree." *The Ladder* 11 (April 1967): 5-7.

Strong, Lennox. "Suspended Ride." *The Ladder* 11 (May 1967): 18-20.

Niven, Vern. "Llangollen on the Left Bank." *The Ladder* 11 (June 1967): 8-9

Strong, Lennox. "The Formidable Blue Stocking—Vernon Lee." *The Ladder* 11 (June 1967): 2-5.

Barrow, Marilyn. "The Responsibility of Cain." *The Ladder* 11 (August 1967): 11-12.

Strong, Lennox. "American Women." *The Ladder* 12 (December 1967): 17-18.

Strong, Lennox. "American Women." *The Ladder* 12 (January 1968): 15-18.

Strong, Lennox. "Carey Thomas." *The Ladder* 12 (February/March 1968): 9-15.

Strong, Lennox. "In the Spotlight." *The Ladder* 12 (April 1968): 14-15.

Strong, Lennox. "American Women." *The Ladder* 12 (May-June 1968): 18-21.

Barrow, Marilyn. "Caroline from First to Last—the Life of Mazo de la Roche." *The Ladder* 12 (July 1968): 4-5.

Damon, Gene. "Rung by Rung." *The Ladder* 12 (August 1968): 4-6.

Barrow, Marilyn. "The Least of These." *The Ladder* 13 (October/ November 1968): 30-33.

Niven, Vern. "Sister of Sappho: Marie Laurencin." *The Ladder* 13 (June/July 1969): 46-47.

Damon, Gene. "Three Ways to Serve." *The Ladder* 14 (October/ November 1969): 4.

Strong, Lennox. "Ladies, Cowardice Does Not Become You." *The Ladder* 14 (June/July 1970): 27-28.

Niven, Vern. "My God It Happened to Me Too!" *The Ladder* 14 (August/September 1970): 22-23.

Damon, Gene. "Women's Liberation Catches up to *The Ladder*." *The Ladder* 14 (August/September 1970): 4.

Damon, Gene. "The Least of These." In *Sisterhood is Powerful*, edited by Robin Morgan. New York: Random House, 1970.

Strong, Lennox. "The Threat of Women." *The Ladder* 15 (August/ September 1971): 14-15.

Damon, Gene, Jan Watson, and Robin Jordan. *The Lesbian in Literature.* 2d edition. Reno, Nevada: The Ladder, 1975.

Grier, Barbara, and Coletta Reid, eds. *The Lavender Herring: Lesbian Essays from The Ladder.* Baltimore, MD: Diana Press, 1976.

Grier, Barbara and Coletta Reid, eds. *Lesbian Lives: Biographies of Women from The Ladder.* Oakland, CA: Diana Press, 1976.

Grier, Barbara. *Lesbiana: Book Reviews from the Ladder, 1966-1972.* Reno, Nevada: Naiad Press, 1976.

Grier, Barbara, and Coletta Reid, eds. *The Lesbians Home Journal: Stories from The Ladder.* Oakland, CA: Diana Press, 1976.

Grier, Barbara. *The Lesbian in Literature.* 3rd ed. Tallahassee, Fla.: Naiad Press, 1981.

Grier, Barbara. "The Possibilities are Staggering." In *Speaking for Our Lives: Historic Speeches and Rhetoric for Gay and Lesbian Rights (1892-2000),* edited by Robert B. Ridinger. New York: The Haworth Press, Inc., 2004, pp. 247-252.

Grier, Barbara and Rhonda J. Factor. "A Burning Love for Lesbian Literature." In *Everyday Mutinies: Funding Lesbian Activism*, edited by Nanette K. Gartrell and Esther D. Rothblum. New York: The Haworth Press, Inc., 2001, pp. 87-94.

Grier, Barbara, with Coletta Reid, eds. *The Lavender Herring: Lesbian Essays from the Ladder*. Baltimore: Diana Press, 1976.

Grier, Barbara, with Coletta Reid, eds. *Lesbian Lives: Biographies of Women from the Ladder*. Baltimore: Diana Press, 1976.

Grier, Barbara, with Coletta Reid, eds. *The Lesbian's Home Journal: Stories from the Ladder*. Baltimore, Diana Press, 1976.

Books and Articles

Adams, Kate. "Built Out of Books: Lesbian Energy and Feminist Ideology in Alternative Publishing." *Journal of Homosexuality* 34 n3/4 (1998).

Agee, Christopher Lowen. *The Streets of San Francisco: Policing and the Creation of a Cosmopolitan Liberal Politics, 1950-1972*. University of Chicago Press, 2014.

Aldrich, Ann. *Carol in a Thousand* Cities. New York: Fawcett/Gold Medal, 1960.

Aldridge, Sarah. *The Latecomer*. N.P.: Naiad Press, Reno, Nev.: Distributed by the Ladder, 1974.

Armstrong, Elizabeth A. *Forging Gay Identities: Organizing Sexuality in San Francisco, 1950-1994*. Chicago: University of Chicago Press, 2002.

Baetz, Ruth. *Lesbian Crossroads: Personal Stories of Lesbian Struggles and Triumphs*. New York: Morrow, 1980.

Baim, Tracy, ed. *Out and Proud in Chicago: An Overview of the City's Gay Community*, Chicago: Surrey Books, 2008.

Baxter, Randolph W. "Homo-Hunting in the Early Cold War: Senator Kenneth Wherry and the Homophobic Side of McCarthyism." *Nebraska History* 84 (September 2003): 118-132.

Beck, Evelyn Torton. *Nice Jewish Girls: A Lesbian Anthology*. Watertown, MA: Persephone Press, 1982.

Bérubé, Allan. *Coming Out Under Fire: The History of Gay Men and Women in World War II*. Chapel Hill: University of North Carolina Press, 2010.

Boucher, Sandy. *Heartwoman: an Urban Feminist's Odyssey Home*. San Francisco, CA: Harper & Row, 1982.

Boyd, Nan A. and Horacio N. Roque Ramirez, eds. *Bodies of Evidence: The Practice of Queer Oral History*. New York: Oxford University Press, 2012.

Bradley, Marion Zimmer. *Astra's Tower, Special Leaflet #2*. Rochester, Texas: The Author, 1958.

Bradley, Marion Zimmer. *Astra's Tower, Special Leaflet #3*. Rochester, TX: The Author, 1959.

Bradley, Marion Zimmer. *Checklist: A Complete, Cumulative Checklist of Lesbian, Variant and Homosexual Fiction in English*. Rochester, Texas: The Author, 1960.

Bradley, Marion Zimmer and Gene Damon. *Checklist Supplement 1961*. Rochester, TX: 1961.

Bronstein, Carolyn. *Battling Pornography: The American Feminist Anti-Pornography Movement, 1976-1986*. New York: Cambridge University Press, 2011.

Bullough, Vern L. *Before Stonewall: Activists for Gay and Lesbian Rights in Historical* Context. New York: Haworth Press, 2002.

Cain, Paul D. *Leading the Parade: Conversations with America's Most Influential Lesbians and Gays*. Lanham, MD: Scarecrow Press, 2002.

Califia, Pat. "The Culture of Radical Sex." *Public Sex: The Culture of Radical Sex*. Second ed. New York: Cleis Press, 2000.

Califia, Pat. *Sapphistry: The Book of Lesbian Sexuality*. Tallahassee, FL: Naiad Press, 1980.

Capsuto, Steven. *Alternate Channels: The Uncensored Story of Gay and Lesbian Images on Radio and Television: 1930s to the Present*. New York: Ballantine Books, 2000.

Corber, Robert J. *Cold War Femme: Lesbianism, National Identity, and Hollywood Cinema*. Durham, NC: Duke University Press, 2011.

Córdova, Jeanne. *Kicking the Habit: A Lesbian Nun Story*. Los Angeles: Multiple Dimensions, 1990.

_____. *When We Were Outlaws: A Memoir of Love & Revolution*. Midway, FL: Spinsters Ink, 2011.

Cornwell, Anita. *Black Lesbian in White America*. Tallahassee, FL: Naiad Press, 1983.

Cruikshank, Margaret, ed. *The Lesbian Path*. Tallahasse, FL: Naiad Press, 1980.

Curb, Rosemary and Nancy Manahan, eds. *Lesbian Nuns: Breaking Silence*. Tallahassee, FL: Naiad Press, 1985.

D'Emilio, John. *Sexual Politics, Sexual Communities: The Making of a Homosexual Minority in the United States, 1940-1970*. Chicago: University of Chicago Press, 1983.

_____. *The World Turned: Essays on Gay History, Politics, and Culture.* Durham: Duke University Press, 2002.

Doan, Laura. *Fashioniing Sapphism: The Origins of a Modern English Lesbian Culture.* New York: Columbia University Press, 2001.

Doughty, Frances. "Lesbian Biography, Biography of Lesbians," *Frontiers* 4 (Autumn 1979): 76-79.

Duberman, Martin, Martha Vicinus, and George Chauncey Jr., eds. *Hidden from History: Reclaiming the Gay and Lesbian Past.* New York: Penguin Books, 1989.

Duggan, Lisa. *Sapphic Slashers: Sex, Violence and American Modernity.* Durham: Duke University Press, 2000.

Echols, Alice. *Daring to Be Bad: Radical Feminism in America, 1967-1975.* Minneapolis: University of Minnesota Press, 1989.

Enszer, Julie R. "The Whole Naked Truth of Our Lives: Lesbian Feminist Print Culture from 1969 through 1989," Ph.D. diss. University of Maryland, 2013.

Evans, Sara. *Personal Politics: The Roots of Women's Liberation in the Civil Rights Movement and the Left.* New York: Penguin, 1979.

_____. *Tidal Wave: How Women Changed America at Century's End.* New York: The Free Press, 2004.

Faderman, Lillian. *Odd Girls and Twilight Lovers, A History of Lesbian Life in Twentieth Century America.* New York: Columbia University Press, 1991.

_____. *Surpassing the Love of Men.* New York: William Morrow and Co., Inc., 1991.

_____. *To Believe in Women: What Lesbians Have Done for America—A History.* Boston: Houghton Mifflin Company, 1999.

Faderman, Lillian and Stuart Timmons. *Gay L.A.: A History of Sexual Outlaws, Power Politics, and Lipstick Lesbians.* New York: Basic Books, 2006.

Foote, Stephanie. "Deviant Classics: Pulps and the Making of Lesbian Print Culture." *Signs: Journal of Women in Culture and Society* 31/1 (2005): 169-190.

Forrest, Katherine V., ed. *Lesbian Pulp Fiction: The Sexually Intrepid World of Lesbian Paperback Novels, 1950-1965.* San Francisco: Cleis Press, 2005.

Freeman, Susan. "Building Lesbian Studies in the 1970s and 1980s." In *Breaking the Wave: Women, Their Organizations, and Feminism, 1945-1985.* Kathleen A. Laughlin and Jacqueline Castledine, eds. New York: Routledge, 2010.

Gallo, Marcia M. *Different Daughters: A History of the Daughters of Bilitis and the Rise of the Lesbian Rights Movement.* New York: Carroll and Graf, 2006.

Gilmore, Stephanie, ed. *Feminist Coalitions: Historical Perspectives on Second-Wave Feminism in the United States*. Urbana: University of Illinois Press, 2008.

Grahn, Judy. *A Simple Revolution: The Making of an Activist Poet*. San Francisco, CA: Aunt Lute Books, 2012.

Hogan, Kristen Amber. "Reading at Feminist Bookstores: Women's Literature, Women's Studies, and the Feminist Bookstore Network." Ph.D. diss. University of Texas, 2006.

Hogan, Steve, and Lee Hudson, eds. *Completely Queer: The Gay and Lesbian Encyclopedia*. New York: Henry Holt and Company, 1998.

Jay, Karla. *Tales of the Lavender Menace: A Memoir of Liberation*. New York: Basic Books, 1991.

_____ and Allen Young, eds. *Lavender Culture*. New York: New York University Press, 1978, 1994.

Johnson, David K. *The Lavender Scare: The Cold War Persecution of Gays and Lesbians in the Federal Government*. University of Chicago Press, 2006.

Jones, Sonya L., ed. *Gay and Lesbian Literature Since World War II*. Binghamton, NY: Harrington Park Press, 1998

Katz, Jonathan Ned. *Gay American History: Lesbians & Gay Men in the U.S.A.* New York: Penguin Books, 1976, 1992.

Keller, Yvonne. "Was it Right to Love Her Brother's Wife So Passionately? Lesbian Pulp Novels and U.S. Lesbian Identity, 1950-1965." *American Quarterly* 57.2 (2005): 385-410.

Kennedy, Elizabeth Lapovsky and Madeline D. Davis. *Boots of Leather, Slippers of Gold: The History of a Lesbian Community*. New York: Penguin Books, 1994.

Martin, Del and Phyllis Lyon. *Lesbian Woman*. New York: Bantam Books, 1972.

Moraga, Cherrie and Gloria Anzaldua. *This Bridge Called My Back: Writings of Radical Women of Color*. Watertown, MA: Persephone Press, 1981.

Loftin, Craig M. "Unacceptable Mannerisms: Gender Anxieties, Homosexual Activism, and Swish in the United States, 1945-1965." *Journal of Social History* 40 (Spring 2007): 577- 596.

Meaker, Marijane. *Highsmith: A Romance of the 1950s*. New York: Cleis, 2003.

Meeker, Martin Dennis, Jr. *Contacts Desired: Gay and Lesbian Communications and Community, 1940s-1970s*. Chicago: University of Chicago Press, 2006.

Morgan, Robin, ed. *Sisterhood is Powerful!* New York: Random House, 1970.

Myers, JoAnne. *Historical Dictionary of the Lesbian and Gay Liberation Movements*. Lanham: Scarecrow Press, Inc., 2013.

Onosaka, Junko. *Feminist Revolution in Literacy: Women's Bookstores in the United States*. New York: Routledge, 2006.

Passet, Joanne. *Sex Variant Woman: The Life of Jeannette Howard Foster*. New York: Da Capo Press, 2008.

Penn, Donna. "The Meanings of Lesbianism in Post-War America." *Gender & History* 3 (August 1991): 190-203.

Peters, Margot. *May Sarton: Biography*. New York: Ballantine Books, 1998.

Ridinger, Robert B. Marks, ed. *Speaking for Our Lives: Historic Speeches and Rhetoric for Gay and Lesbian Rights, 1892-2000*. New York: Harrington Park Press, 2004.

Rothblum, Esther D. and Nanette Gartrell, eds. *Everyday Mutinies: Funding Lesbian Activism*. Binghamton, NY: Harrington Park Press, 2001.

Rubin, Gayle S. *Deviations: A Gayle Rubin Reader*. Duke University Press, 2001.

Rule, Jane. *Taking My Life*. Vancouver, British Columbia: Talon Books, 2011.

Shelley, Martha. *Crossing the DMZ*. Oakland, CA: Women's Press Collective, 1974.

Sibley, Agnes. *May Sarton*. New York: Twayne Publishers, 1972.

Stanley, Julia Penelope and Susan J. Wolfe, eds. *The Coming Out Stories*. Watertown, Mass.: Persephone Press, 1980.

Stearn, Jess. *The Grapevine*. New York: Doubleday & Co., 1964.

Stein, Arlene. *Sex and Sensibility: Stories of a Lesbian Generation*. Berkeley: University of California Press, 1997.

Stein, Marc. *City of Sisterly & Brotherly Loves*. Chicago: University of Chicago Press, 2000.

_____, ed. *Encyclopedia of Lesbian, Gay, Bisexual and Transgendered History in America*. Detroit: Charles Scribner's Sons, 2004

_____. *Rethinking the Gay and Lesbian Movement*. New York: Routledge, 2012.

Strang, James Jesse. *The Diary of James Jesse Strang, Transcribed, Introduced, and Annotated*. East Lansing: Michigan University Press, 1961.

Streitmatter, Rodger. *Unspeakable: The Rise of the Gay and Lesbian Press in America*. Boston: Faber and Faber, 1995.

Stryker, Susan. *Queer Pulp: Perverted Passions from the Golden Age of the Paperback*. San Francisco: Chronicle Books, 2001.

Strub, Whitney. "Lavender, Menaced: Lesbianism, Obscenity Law, and the Feminist Anti- Pornography Movement," *Journal of Women's History* 22.2 (2010): 83-107.

Trysh Travis, (2000). "The Women in Print Movement: History and Implications." *Book History* 11 (2008): 275-300.

Uhlan, Edward. *The Rogue of Publishers' Row*. New York: Exposition Press, 1956.

Zimmerman, Bonnie. *Lesbian Histories and Cultures: An Encyclopedia*. New York: Garland Pub., 2000.

Index

Bella Books, Inc.

Women. Books. Even Better Together.

P.O. Box 10543
Tallahassee, FL 32302

Phone: 800-729-4992
www.bellabooks.com